FRENCH REENTRY COURTS AND REHABILITATION

5-7, rue de l'École polytechnique, 75005 Paris

http://www.harmattan.fr
diffusion.harmattan@wanadoo.fr
harmattan1@wanadoo.fr

ISBN : 978-2-343-02461-5
EAN : 9782343024615

Martine HERZOG-EVANS

FRENCH REENTRY COURTS AND REHABILITATION

Mister Jourdain of Desistance

L'Harmattan

Criminology Collection
Edited by Robert Cario

Criminology is a multi and trans-disciplinary field, which pertains to knowledge, investigation, expertise and treatment. Unfortunately, it is rather contentious in France. However, it is essential to crime prevention and, when this fails, to penal treatment. Moreover it also contributes to the psychological and social restoration of those who are concerned by offences, be they offenders or victims.

In a lot of jurisdictions, criminology is taught at university, and produces studies and evidence-based practices. In a number of them, there are criminologists who work alongside or within the criminal justice, health, social and medical systems.

This collection endeavours to collect evidence-based scientific and empirical studies or essays produced in light of the established theories in the various sub-fields of criminology. Its public is large: students, teachers, researchers, judges, practitioners who are confronted to crime and citizens who are interested in the criminal justice system.

P.V. Tournier (Dir.), *Enfermements*
S. Abdellaoui (Dir.), *L'expertise psycholégale*
C. Rossi, *Homicide : les proches des victimes*
M. Herzog-Evans, *Le JAP : monsieur Jourdain de la désistance*
C. Condominas, *Sentiment amoureux et conjugalité violente*
P.V. Tournier (Dir.), *Une certaine idée de la criminologie*

Prison Field (Champ pénitentiaire) Collection
Edited by Paul Mbanzoulou

The Prison Field collection contributes to the circulation of knowledge about diverse and complex prison issues. The individual or collective books which are written by researchers or practitioners have one thing in common: they endeavour to improve the understanding of institutional dynamics, of the elaboration of professional practices, of offenders' supervision and care policies and of deprivation or restriction of liberty.

G. de Coninck, G. Lemire, *Etre directeur de prison*
P. Mbanzoulou, M. Herzog-Evans, S. Courtine (Dir.), *Insertion et désistance des personnes placées sous main de justice*
P. Mbanzoulou, F. Dieu (Dir.), *Administration pénitentiaire et justice*

To « therapeutic » practitioners

Main abbreviations

Cass. ...... Court of cassation

Crim. ...... Criminal Chamber of the Court of cassation

C.A.P. ..... Commission de l'application des peines (sentences' implementation commission)

C.P.A.L. ... Comité de probation et d'assistance aux libérés (probation and assistance to released offenders committee)

C.P.I.P. ... Conseiller pénitentiaire d'insertion et de probation (probation officer)

D.A.P. ..... Direction de l'administration pénitentiaire (Direction of the prison services)

D.P.I.P. ... Directeur pénitentiaire d'insertion et de probation (probation service middle manager)

D.S.P.I.P. .. Directeur de service pénitentiaire d'insertion et de probation (probation chief of service)

H.D.C. ...... Hors débat contradictoire (Judicial decision making without any hearing)

E.M. .... Electronic monitoring

E.N.A.P. ... Ecole nationale de l'administration pénitentiaire (Prison services national school)

J.A. .... Jours-amende (day-fine)

J.A.P. ...... Juge de l'application des peines (French reentry judge: Sentences' implementation Judge)

J.A.P.A.T. . Juge de l'application des peines antiterroriste (Antiterrorist JAP)

P.O.P. ...... Pemanence d'orientation pénale (Victims' Bureau)

P.P.C. ...... Penal Procedure Code

P.S.C. ...... Problem-Solving Court

P.S.E.S. .... Placement sous surveillance électronique statique (Electronic Monitoring measure)

S.A.P. ...... Service de l'application des peines (Service of Sentences' implementation)

S.P.I.P. ..... Service pénitentiaire d'insertion et de probation (Probation service)

S.S.J. .... Suivi socio-judiciaire (Social-judicial supervision)

S.T.I.G. .... Sursis avec mise à l'épreuve accompagné de l'obligation d'accomplir un travail d'intérêt général (suspended imprisonment plus probation plus community work)

T.A.P. ...... Tribunal de l'application des peines (sentences' implementation tribunal)

1

Introduction- Presentation of the Research

Origins of the research

This book [1] reflects on a two and a half year research project launched in September 2010. The main goal was to explore the professional culture of the *Juge de l'application des peines* (Sentences' Implementation Judge – hereafter JAP). The term JAP denotes a release, reentry and community sentences' supervision judge; a position created by France in 1945. This same year also saw the creation of Juvenile Judges, the probation service and a suspended sentence with probation. In 1958, the JAP experiment went to scale and was put into mainstream use across the entire judicial system (Faugeron, 1999; Perried, 2013). Further law reforms (mainly in 2000 and 2004) increased JAPs' powers (Herzog-Evans, 2009 and 2012-2013: Chap. 04). Today, JAPs are in charge of controlling and mapping the supervision of offenders who serve community sentences or are released back into the community. The probation service is responsible for the daily supervision of offenders, whereas JAPs are permitted to intervene should an incident occur, such as a violation of the obligations or a new offence. JAPs may also step in if it appears that the obligations require modification in order to better fit the offenders' circumstances. A JAP can sanction and recall the offender to prison. A three JAP tribunal (the *tribunal de l'application des peines* – Sen-

1. Its title was inspired by the interviews of several JAPs, such as JAP 40 who told the author: 'Oh I am a little bit like Mr Jourdain: I do prose without being aware of it.' The core idea here is that JAPs have a good knowledge of the desistance process, despite never having learnt the exact nature of desistance, nor having ever read desistance literature. Indeed, Mr Jourdain is the main character of Molière's famous theatre play (*Le Bourgeois Gentilhomme*) which tells the story of a bourgeois trying to behave like an aristocrat who realises with delight that by simply talking he is 'doing prose'.

tences' implementation tribunal – hereafter TAP) is in charge of the parole or humanitarian release of those who serve long sentences (ten years or more). The TAP is also competent when it comes to making sensitive decisions such as reducing a tariff, granting exceptional remission to offenders who provide information regarding forthcoming or on-going serious crimes, or placing sex or violent offenders who have served their entire sentence under mandatory supervision. The JAP also grants furlough, the exceptional temporary leave under escort of offenders whose family members are dying or deceased, and ordinary forms of remission. The JAP can even transform a custody sentence of up to two years into a community sentence or measure (art. 723-15 s. of the Penal Procedure Code – Hereafter PPC). Indeed, the latter power represents a very important part of a JAP's activity. A good proportion of his/her decisions do abide by due process rules: an adversarial [2] hearing takes place, whilst the person is present and can be assisted by an attorney [3] who has access to the file, and can appeal the decision. However, due process is somewhat of a recent development, and has resulted from two fundamental law reforms: the 'presumption of innocence' law of June 15, 2000 (n° 2000-516 – see Couvrat, 2001) and the law of March 9, 2004 also known as the 'Perben 2' law (Couvrat, 2004). Indeed, both of these laws judicialised sentences' implementation, i.e. acknowledged that JAPs were courts of law and as such the full consequences of due process should be complied with from now on. It was only following this realisation that the JAP became a real judge (Herzog-Evans, 1999a), although this came at a price. Whereas before this era JAPs and probation services would work in unison from the same building at the tribunal, the JAP occupying the role of chief of service, in 1999 probation services obtained their full autonomy (Couvrat, 2004; Perrier, 2013). From then on, they gradually left tribunals before being placed under the wing of the prison services and their newly appointed local chiefs. Indeed, this meant the end of the daily communication and partnership between the JAPs and the probation services (Herzog-Evans, forthcoming a and e).

Over the last decade, repeated upheavals have changed the landscape of offender supervision (Herzog-Evans, 2012-2013: Chap. 04). Politicians, and particularly during Nicolas Sarkozy's ten years in power, first as a very pre-

---

2. The French word for this is '*contradictoire*', which is more balanced, and less pugnacious than 'adversarial'. It implies that both parties have their say, but not necessarily that they are opponents.

3. For the present book, I shall use the American word 'attorney' rather than the more confusing U.K. terms of 'solicitor' and 'barrister'. This is due to the fact that, in France, similar to the U.S.A. there is only one profession (: '*avocat*'); a position which brings with it full advisory and assistance competence, including in courts.

sent minister of Interior (2002-2007), then as president (2007-2012), suddenly realised that they could also appear tough on crime in the field of sentences' implementation. Prior to this, any matters related to prisons or sentences' implementation were deemed to be taboo: politicians feared they would appear to be wasting time thinking about already sentenced offenders rather than taking care of law-abiding, early-rising workers (Herzog-Evans, 2009). From 2005 on, France was hit by a frenzied wave of legal reform. All of these laws – at least a major reform each year followed by its usual host of decrees and sub-decrees – created a 'bifurcation' effect (Pratt, 2002), whereby JAPs and TAPs were suddenly perceived by a puffed up Napoleonic executive as being a nuisance. On the one hand, they were accused of being too soft on serious offenders and serious offences, whilst reforms put then on a tight leash; on the other hand, they were considered to be too demanding with offenders who had committed less serious crimes or who were serving shorter or mid-range sentences. The prison service became very powerful, particularly given their recent conquering of probation. They were thus put in charge of drafting all the law reforms pertaining to prison and probations: they ensured that release measures' unique goal would be to free overcrowded prison cells. As a result, the executive (in this case the prison and probation services) or prosecutors who, in France, are not independent of the executive, were assigned the task of overtaking JAPs so as to automatically release offenders who had four months left to serve under electronic monitoring (hereafter EM).

Against this backdrop, in June 2010, I organised a conference at the ENAP, the Prison School of Agen, in order to discuss issues pertaining to desistance and the French concept of reinsertion. The final stages of this two day conference saw a visit from Paris by one of the right arms of the prison services Director. Indeed, after being absent for the majority of the conference he began to tell an astonished crowd that the probation service's unique task was not reinsertion, but the prevention of reoffending, thereby implying that one could be completely severed from the other. He added that JAPs had absolutely no idea as to the nature of reinsertion and that they 'operated without any compass' or guidelines of any sort; in brief, that they were capricious and erratic judges who had no idea what they were doing. This diatribe literally stunned the audience. As for myself, I had been working in this field for over twenty years and had seen numerous JAPs whose culture had thus appeared to me to be fully reinsertion oriented and who were definitely for the most part 'therapeutic" (Herzog-Evans, forthcoming g) in the 'therapeutic jurisprudence' sense (Winick & Wexler, 2003; Berman & Feinblatt, 2005). After all, these judges had been labelled – and this was meant to be deprecatory – 'super social assistants' or 'Santa Claus'. Moreover, as a specialist of sentences' implementation law, I was also aware that accusing JAPs of having no guidelines or compass was ill-suited. In France, judicial discretion is strictly bound by a written law legal system comprising thickly layered codes and thousands upon thousands of articles. In particular, article 707 of the PPC, a general guideline laying down the principles which should guide sentences' implementation courts, probation and prison staff, leaves little room for manoeuvre. It states: 'Sentences' implementation favours the reintegration of convicted persons as well as the prevention of reoffending, whilst respecting the interests of society and the rights of victims'. Section 2 adds that a prisoner should never serve his full sentence and should be released, as long as possible, beforehand, and then be supervised in the community.

In spite of all this I wondered whether the upheavals and reforms of the last ten years might have changed the role of JAPs without my knowing. After all, legal research is not empirical research and despite my frequent presence in the field, it was possible that I had a false perspective on things. A month before the Agen conference, I had travelled to Barcelona to participate in a workshop organised by the Community Sanction and Measure subgroup of the European Society of Criminology (ESC), of which I am a member. There, I gave a presentation to my colleagues from various European countries on JAPs, including who they were and what their missions were. Some of my colleagues lived in jurisdictions where there was no or virtually no judicial intervention in probation or release. They asked many questions and wondered what could possibly be the added bonus of such a system. Fergus McNeill, of the University of Glasgow bluntly told me: 'your system sounds great on paper, but it can only work if the judges are good people who believe in rehabilitation. In my country, it would not work as judges are usually punitive.' In September of the very same year, I participated in another subgroup of the ESC (: 'sentencing'). It was there that a young doctorate student, Veerle Scheirs who was embarking on a thesis pertaining to the recently created Belgian JAP, presented her very first findings. In Belgium, the reform which created the position of JAP in 2006 has only partly been implemented. Only three judges – one JAP and two assessors –court, called, like its French counterpart, the TAP, has been created thus far; it could release prisoners sentenced to three years or more. People sentenced to less than three years were still released by prison governors (Snacken et al., 2010). At the time I had just completed a two year research about probation officers' professional culture, and particularly their understanding of the desistance process (Herzog-Evans, 2011 b and c). Combined, this research and the Agen, Barcelona and Liege conferences convinced me that it was time to conduct an in depth research project on JAPs. Its aim would be to assess whether they had kept their proverbial humanistic culture whilst also retaining a reinsertion or desistance 'compass' in their head in the new punitive, managerial, 'prison thinking' and prison services superpower context. Inevitably I discovered that the tectonic plaques shifts of the last ten years had indeed had an important impact on their missions. However, for the most part, the desistance compass remained intact.

The literature

In the realm of sentences' implementation, as in those of sentencing and prison studies, France long abstained from field work. Lawyers would arrive late to legal studies because 'sentences' implementation' (*droit de l'exécution des peines*) and prison law only became separate fields in the early 2000s. Two colleagues of mine and I were actually at the forefront of the construction of these new legal fields in the early 1990s (Céré, 1994; Péchillon, 1999; Herzog-Evans, 1994), which had until then only been partially explored (Bouloc, 1991; Staechele, 1995). It was during the same decade that the first empirical sociological studies were conducted, initially only in prison settings (Chauvenet et al., 1994; Combessie, 1996). With regard to 'sentences' implementation', the French label for probation which I shall use in the present book, no field research was carried out until very recently. For my part, I first spent two decades fighting for this legal discipline's recognition – along with prison law – and laying down its 'legal bricks'. During all these years, sentences' implementation thus remained the domain of legal scholars who either published treaties (see the four successive editions of Herzog-Evans *Droit de l'exécution des peines:* 2002, 2005, 2007 and 2012-13), or manuals (Bouloc, 1991, 1998, 2005, then 2011, Poncela, 1996, and then 2001; and the newcomers: Garçon & Peltier, 2010) or practitioner's guides (Lavielle et al., 2012-2013; Duflo & Martin, 2011). The first empirical studies were only published at the very end of the 2000s, and actually ignored the JAP concept, preferring instead to concentrate on probation services. Such was the case of the pioneering piece of work by the psycho-sociologist Dominique Lhuilier (2007) who studied the professional identity of probation officers after the aforementioned judicialisation of 2000-2004. She found that the aforementioned tectonic shifts, along with the increasing recruitment of lawyers amongst their ranks, was indeed causing rapid identity changes. She also found that JAP and probation officers got along very well. However, Dominique Lhuilier had conducted her study before a very important 2008 internal circular of the prison services (Circ. AP, 19 mars 2008, NOR: JUSK084001C) resulted in two hugely important changes to the probation service. Firstly, it suddenly announced to all probation officers that, despite their lack of training in this field, they were 'clinical criminologists'. Secondly, it placed the prevention of reoffending at the forefront of probation service missions. Their staff would have to concentrate on supervision and control whilst gradually abandoning social work, which was an on-going process already initiated several years ago, as demonstrated by my Master Plus student Nelly Rintaud (2008). In the context of this new landscape, a young sociologist, Xavier de Larminat recently defended his PhD thesis. He had focussed on the new goals of French probation (Larminat, 2012). Indeed, he did confirm, whilst also updating them, some of the earlier findings of Lhuilier. However, he too set the JAP concept aside, despite their crucial role in supervision. In addition, and like Lhuilier, he had not read any international probation literature, which also limited the significance and impact of his study. A year earlier, Sarah Dindo, a lobbyist with vast experience in probation and prison practice and a sociologist herself, conducted a study for the Ministry of Justice, on the French equivalent of probation orders. Whilst unfortunately setting the JAP concept aside, she, contrary to previous authors, made abundant reference to the international literature, which gave a so far unseen structure to her report (Dindo, 2011). She also went way beyond probation orders and actually studied French probation officers' practices. In particular, she pointed to their lack of evidence-based support and extreme variability. At the same time, I had conducted a multi-layered series of research on probation officers, which pertained to their professional identity in the year 2010 and to their understanding and practice of desistance support (Herzog-Evans, 2011a, 2011c, 2012a and forthcoming a)). In 2012, another research, funded by the Mission Law and Justice (Mission Droit et Justice) endeavoured to describe the state of the relationship between prison – including probation – services and the judiciary. However, the authors failed to make their methodology clear, particularly in terms of the exact number and conditions of the interviews which they said they had conducted, and about the conditions of the observations they had made. In particular, it was apparent that they had not systematically studied the work and activities of the practitioners they had interviewed. More importantly, it was clear from the very first lines of their report, that they had a strong prison services bias. The entire research consisted of justifying their hypothesis which was that thanks to centralisation and the hierarchical structure of prison services, French probation services now had uniform practices, whereas the judiciary acted like a club of unpredictable divas (Mouhanna, 2011). The first statement completely contradicted Lhuilier, Dindo and our own findings. The second statement is, for the most part, contradicted by the present research.

Methodology

In order to develop a better understanding of who JAPs were, but also in order to keep my own pro-JAP bias at bay, I decided to use a host of methodological approaches and, in particular, to **mix qualitative and quantitative work**. I wanted to analyse what the JAPs had to say about themselves, but I also wanted to confront them over their actual practices, specifically whether or not they were interacting with offenders or victims or whether they wrote their rulings. I also wanted to confront their discourse as to what their professional partners thought about them.

JAP discourse was first studied through a traditional qualitative approach. My students (see below) and I interviewed seventy-five JAPs, based in all French regions, including overseas territories: forty-two females and thirty-three males. A questionnaire formed the basis for in depth semi-structured interviews which lasted between forty-five minutes to two and a half hours. Details pertaining to JAPs were found via various sources: an add was placed in the Bulletin of the National Association of JAP; a message sent on the JAP's listserv 'Justpeines' (which can either mean Justice and sentences or fair sentences); I was referred – sometimes renounced – to other JAPs by attorneys; I attended conferences and workshops in order to obtain more names, and so forth. JAPs are extremely busy judges who have very little time. The judiciary is traditionally very discreet and tends to be suspicious of outsiders since it has access to exceptionally confidential data. It certainly helped that I was one of the founders of these practitioners' legal field and that many of them had my treaty (Herzog-Evans, 2012-2013) in their office. It also helped that I had prepared a four page description of the study's goals and methodology, in which I detailed how their anonymity would be guaranteed. Additional details were provided by email or phone if required. During the second year, more contacts were made possible thanks to Ms Fitte-Vallée, a trainer at the Judge School of Bordeaux, the ENM (*Ecole Nationale de la Magistrature*) in charge of training newly appointed JAPs, and someone whom I want to profusely thank here. The total account of seventy-five JAPs interviewed represented at the time of our study 20.71% of the entire profession. Adding to these formal interviews were hundreds of other contacts or exchanges via phone or email, during meals, coffee breaks or meetings, as well as discussions before and/or after hearings and prison commissions, during conferences and so on.

The second part of the research focussed on **'JAP in action'**. It consisted of two sections. The first section, more qualitative in nature, consisted of attending hearings, obligations' notifications, preparatory meetings with offenders prior to the procedure of article 723-15 of the PPC [4] and sentences' implementation commissions (*commissions de l'application des peines* – hereafter CAP) [5]. With the exception of one, all the JAPs whose hearings the

4. A procedure which allows JAPs to transform, before they are actually implemented, custody sentences of up to two years into community sentences (up to one year if the offender is a recidivist) (Herzog-Evans, 2012-2013: Title 31).

5. CAP are held within prison settings and comprise the JAP, the prosecutor, the governor and, usually, several guards and probation officers. During CAP, JAPs may grant furlough and remission without a hearing (art. 712-5 of the PPC).

team observed were interviewed. During these hearings or meetings, we took ample and detailed notes about what was taking place, about the socio-demographic details of the offenders and the purpose of the case (gender, age, offence, nature of the application of object of the hearing, and so on), and about the proceedings. We also took notes about the setting, tone of voice, body language, silences, where everyone was sitting, whether the judge, prosecutor or attorney were wearing their robe, and so on and so forth. All of these details were coded by the author. In total we attended forty-six hearings, CAP and equivalent situations, which dealt with 530 probationers.

The second section of the 'Jap in action' part of the research focussed on their rulings. I collected all the rulings during the first year and coded them during the second. Most of them were collected amongst JAPs and attorneys. This enabled me to go beyond the seventy-five JAPs who were interviewed. I felt that there might have been a bias due to the voluntary nature of the interviews and thought it was also necessary to look into what those who had not wanted to talk did. I also hoped to reduce my personal bias in favour of JAPs. I even collected some Court of Appeal rulings on the official website legifrance.gouv.fr, but eventually decided not to use them, as I knew Courts of Appeal judges were bound to have a different professional culture and should be subjected to a different study. In all, I gathered and coded 1,300 written rulings.

Lastly, the research comprised a third part, whereby I confronted JAPs' interviews, hearings and rulings to **their partners' perception**. This consisted of semi-structured interviews with practitioners from virtually all French regions. These interviews lasted from fifty minutes to over three hours. Again, I obtained these practitioners' details through a number of sources. The team of students and I interviewed comprised thirty eight probation officers; eight middle probation managers (chief of service or DPIP); eight probation service chiefs (DSPIP); five probation officer trainees; thirteen prosecutors operating in a sentences' implementation office of their respective tribunals; and thirty-two criminal lawyers. Due to the extreme difficulty faced when obtaining authorisation to access prison staff, we only managed to interview five prison governors and three prison clerks, from which no significant findings could be drawn. We only interviewed three JAP clerks (courts' paralegals), due to my decision to conduct a separate research study focussing on their profession. Despite these limitations, no less than one hundred and fifteen professional partners of the JAP were interviewed.

Naturally, all of the interviews were anonymous and all practitioners were guaranteed total anonymity. They were given a code name – which they were not aware of – such as JAP 1, JAP 2, prosecutor 1, Attorney 5, PO

10. They were also promised that their names would never appear in forthcoming publications. I have obviously respected this promise.

As if often the case in France, this research was not funded. Indeed, this proved both an inconvenience and an advantage, with the inconveniences far more obvious than the advantages. The main limitation concerned the places where we could go. However, this was counterbalanced by the fact that the team of students came from the three different universities where I teach: Reims, in the North-East, Nantes, on the West Coast, and Agen, in the South West. Some of our students had family in other areas which could thus be covered as well [6]; I interviewed most JAPs myself and conducted many of the interviews by phone, along with a significant number of other practitioners' interviews. Whenever possible I used Skype. I typed – which I do extremely fast – all interviews virtually verbatim. Students, on the other hand, were asked to do live interviews and to record them. I could thus guide them with their interviewing technique. All recorded interviews were transcribed verbatim. I then coded all interviews. The lack of funding nonetheless had several advantages. First and foremost, it allowed us to remain free from any pressure or interfering with our methodology and findings. As foreign examples have shown, state funding, and particularly Ministries of Justice funding comes with a high risk of affecting researchers' independence (Pawson & Tilley, 1997: 14s.). In France, the most serious risk is interference of prison services and pure and simple refusal to access material, which the author has unfortunately come across with other research. Second, the lack of resources allowed us to remain free of our decisions and adaptable. We could organise our time and work in the way which most suited us and our interviewees.

Working with students in the course of a university year requires a very strict timing, and as such I had to create detailed and immediately operational protocols. Working with students, and law students at that, means being constantly and instantly reactive – via emails or phone. Indeed, it is important to supervise and monitor them very strictly – they would probably say irritatingly –, to organise numerous meetings and write numerous instruction manuals, to control each and every recording and transcription, and so on. From their feedback I know that they all suffered a great deal, but that they also all appreciated this unique experience. I wish to pay homage to all of them: Clémentine Danet, Brice Peigné, Marceline Bobinet, Marlène Brouca, Lucie Benoist, Cécile Bigayon, Aurélie Bruyant, Jeremy Chené et Habib Benmed Jamed (the latter two being probation officers). Their collab-

---

6. Each student collected some of the material and wrote his or her own Master II thesis based on a limited amount of data, although students were also encouraged to support each other and exchange interviews.

oration made this research possible. It also allowed me to reduce even further my own aforementioned bias.

In spite of its importance, this research has several obvious limitations. Firstly, we were unable to interview enough prison staff, and chose early on not to pursue this line of investigation because obtaining the authorisation from the national headquarters of the prison services would have been hazardous and would have taken the best part of the first year of research. Indeed, there was a high risk that the authorisation would never have been granted, potentially leaving several students stranded and without any material for their Master's thesis. Students only have ten months to conduct their research and write their thesis. Indeed, during the second year of the present research, this actually happened with another original research on prison guards' professional values, thus leaving eight of my students without any material for their work. I could simply not expose more of them to such a risk.

A second similar patent limitation of this study was the lack of offenders' interviews. Again, this choice was made because of the high difficulty experienced when attempting to access a sufficient number of probationers from a variety of regions. Probation services typically refuse to help, as they fear violating professional secrecy (Article 226-13 of the Penal Code) or offending their privacy. The same goes, due to identical reasons, for prison staff and attorneys. Prison and probation services also typically refer such requests to their national headquarters and this leads us back to our previous paragraph. Moreover, in recent years, the national headquarters have become increasingly weary of my research and even small scale local studies must now be referred to Paris. It now seems unlikely that I could repeat the one off study I conducted on desisters (Herzog-Evans, 2011 c). For these reasons it seemed prudent not to attempt it again. However, as I am writing this, I have begun a small research study with four students, which will complete the present study. We have started interviewing formerly supervised offenders. Their details have been provided to us by some JAPs who do not need to abide by the prison services' orders. If we manage to collect enough material, further publication will make our findings public.

In spite of these serious limitations, the present research is the first ever empirical study to address the nearly seven decades old concept of JAPs. It is *a fortiori* and the first comprise a mix of qualitative and quantitative methodology. Indeed, the first study is particularly effective, as it looks into their rulings and analyses them not from the expected legal viewpoint but from an empirical viewpoint – although, as we shall see *infra* this analysis would not have been possible without in depth legal knowledge of how judges' rulings are drafted.

The research has answered the main question pertaining to JAPs and desistance. It has also raised a host of additional issues such as: the relations between JAP and probation officers and their chiefs; fair trial in offender supervision; the role of attorneys; JAP, public safety and the media; how they deal with offenders denying they committed the offence; JAPs' innovative traits or how they draft their rulings. The research showed that JAPs are humane judges (Chapter 1) and that, even though their training does not refer to the concept of desistance, they are indeed 'Monsieur Jourdain of desistance' (Chapter 2). Alas, they encounter a great number of obstacles with those of most importance including their complex relationship with probation services, their enormous workload and the appalling poverty of French tribunals (Chapter 3). It is thus difficult for them to remain faithful to due process principles, particularly in big urban jurisdictions (Chapter 4). A statistical and analytical study of their rulings reveals that JAPs nonetheless manage to adapt their reasoning and decision-making to their diverse public and their complex circumstances and offences along with the various natures of the sentences and measures at stake (Chapter 5).

1

The 'chicken or the egg'? The origins of a 'therapeutic' judge

The main goal of the research was to determine whether JAPs are good judges ('*Good Courts*': Berman & Feinblatt, 2005), i.e. are 'therapeutic' judges (Wexler, 1995; Winnick & Wexler, 2003 and, in French: Herzog-Evans, 2011d). According to the 'therapeutic jurisprudence' literature a 'therapeutic judge' is a judge who focusses on the consequences which both the law and the justice system can have on people and their circumstances. Such a judge is driven by both material and ethical forces. Therapeutic literature was also one of the transverse grounds of my research. A second ground was the legitimacy of justice literature (Tyler, 2006 and 2012), which has showed that citizens feel they must obey the law and court decisions if justice is seen as 'legitimate'. Legitimacy of justice comprises a set of components: on the one hand, respect and good reception and respect for people attending trial and, on the other hand, fair procedural rules such as those which apply in Europe. With regards the present research I spent quite a lot of time on these principles, which are dealt with in Chapter 4. Chapter 1 will thus pertain to a first main question: are JAP courts 'good courts'?

The research did indeed confirm that, for the most part they are good judges (§-1). How strong these qualities are depends, however, on their personal and professional background. In light of this observation a question arose: *are* JAPs good judges because they bring to this position a host of personal and professional skills or do they *become* good judges because they experiment '*Japperie*', the nickname for their activity? The research showed that the truth lay in a combination of both (§2).

§ 1. The egg: Who are the JAPs?

In the following chapters we will delve deeper into JAPs' knowledge of the desistance process as well as their actions thereof and on their practice of fair trial. In order to ascertain whether JAPs are good judges, the research first focussed on the reasons why they turned to '*Japperie*'.

'We must implement the 2H rule; humanity and humility.' (JAP 61)

A. How do they become JAPs?

The research endeavoured to explore into the reasons why JAPs had wanted to become JAPs in the first place. One must bear in mind that in France, judges seldom had a prior career – although this type of recruitment is currently increasing – but are essentially the best of our law faculty students along with a few political science students. They are young when they start their career, and are rarely older than twenty-five when they leave the Judge School of Bordeaux (the ENM: *Ecole Nationale de la Magistrature*) [7]. At the ENM, they only receive short and general training about '*Japperie*', which, as we uncovered, is not what leads them to opt for this position. It is usually in the course of an internship with a JAP that they develop an interest for '*Japperie*'. When they decide to choose a JAP position, they then return to Bordeaux for a more intense and specialised two weeks training (known as 'pre-allocation training'). The same applies to judges who have held other positions and then decide to become JAPs.

When I started specialising in this field more than twenty years ago, those wanting to become JAPs included only the judge students at the ENM who fared the worst at the final exam, along with a small handful of passionate people. This job was frowned upon because it was deemed not lawyerly enough and too social. From the legal viewpoint, the JAP was not considered as being a court of law until in the introduction of two important laws in 2000 and 2004. JAP 2, a former social worker herself, remembered in the course of her interview that when she first became a JAP in 1991, nobody wanted that position. After the law of 2000, she decided to become a JAP again, because, in the meantime, this profession had become more respected. Indeed, the reforms of 2000 and 2004 gave JAPs the status they had thus far lacked. Moreover, the numerous reforms which followed at an increasing

---

7. Once they are recruited via an exceptionally selective national exam, these young judges –called 'justice auditors' whilst they are at the ENM – have to spend two years in the Bordeaux school, during which they receive a highly practical training which alternates between numerous internships with the police, juvenile services, prisons, probation services and so on.

pace, transformed the autonomous legal field of sentences' implementation into an exceptionally complex and technical one. Not only are JAPs now considered as 'real' judges, but they are also perceived by their peers as being very good lawyers. It is indeed impossible to operate in this field without being an excellent legal technician. Therefore, JAPs no longer have anything in common with the social workers which they were formerly accused of being. Meanwhile, they also had to embrace due process rules in their daily activities. In spite of this, their work is also a form of social work. The research showed that the reforms of 2000-2004 did not dry out the recruitment of a distinct type of people who are looking for the same things their eldest of twenty years back did: the social culture of '*Japperie*' remains very much present. However, thanks to these reforms they are now also adorned with the procedural fineries of legitimacy of justice as defined by Tyler.

The questions pertaining to the reasons why these judges had chosen to become JAPs yielded remarkably similar responses. This is very telling given the fact that this was an open question, thus meaning that all the answers were spontaneous. The reasons which our interviewees listed uncover fascinating traits.

A high number of JAPs (55.3%) told us that they became JAPs in order **to have a close relationship with '*justiciables*'** – '*justiciables*' being a neutral word which refers to any person who has to be in contact with a court of law, be it an offender, a victim, a member of a family, a divorcee, a contract or tort opponent, and so forth [8]. Equally, they referred to the human relationship and the human interaction they had with '*justiciables*' or other similar phrasing.

'Amongst criminal justice position, ours is the only one that is oriented towards the future and this in a positive way' (JAP 65).

Having a close relationship with '*justiciables*' – and in their case essentially with offenders and victims – relates to an informal one-to-one meeting in their office and in a prison setting. JAP hearings are conducive of intimate communication. JAPs, as we shall see, do not usually wear their robes (Herzog-Evans, forthcoming d) and no not operate in courtrooms but in uncluttered settings, with no elevated bench: the judge faces the probationer; most of the time only his desk separates them. Numerous times we were the witnesses of highly spontaneous discussions which such settings authorise. Probationers spoke their mind without hesitation and were extremely candid. Although they would reveal personal traumas or problems, and also cry, they

8. Interestingly, JAPs never use the word 'offender': they either refer to '*justiciables*' or to legally descriptive terms such as 'the sentenced' (i.e. 'the sentenced person') or the 'probationer' (Herzog-Evans, forthcoming c).

would often leave the room with renewed hope, their backs straightened and with a handful of practical advice. JAPs manage to mix this intimacy and proximity whilst seemingly remaining dispassionate, whilst at times we ourselves could hardly contain our emotions. Such was, for instance, the case with a particular thirty year old man, who had recently been released from prison, after an umpteenth incarceration caused by his drug abuse and his social instability. He had just discovered that his ex-partner had dropped their five year old son on his doorstep and had disappeared. There is no doubt that their status as judges and the modest setting helps the JAP. In this particular case, the JAP managed to remain encouraging and empathic, whilst giving highly useful and practical advice which the offender could apply there and then. The '*justiciable*', whose face was ravaged and who had extremely sad eyes, ended up smiling and even laughing at one of the JAPs' gentle jokes. He left with the same minimal smile on his face. In this case, lack of empathy would have been just as inappropriate as excessive emotional involvement. This JAP was exactly in the middle. He conducted his hearings with all the skills and qualities which specialists of 'core correctional practices' such as Chris Trotter (Trotter, 2006) advocate. However, hearings and other meetings with *justiciables* are often laden with emotion:

'We see people at a point in their lives when there is a lot of emotion. We see scared people and then they let go. Sometimes they confide in us and sometimes we have to push a button that actually hurts, in order to solve that particular issue and then to support them and listen to them. Working with this suffering humanity is really interesting' (JAP 46).

JAPs are acutely aware that they have to **find the right distance**. Still, they are often more involved than they think they are. For instance, JAP 2, who denied being too close to 'her' '*justiciables*' nonetheless answered that the best moments in her job were:

'When we receive a "thank you" letter with the photos of a first baby!'

Other JAPs spontaneously mentioned the thank you letters or visits they received:

'We live really intense moments at times. For instance, when you tell someone it is too early to release him as it is not the right time for him and he actually thanks you for saying this. There are really intense moments. They also come back and visit. It is the same when you are a Youth judge: they call you "My Judge"' (JAP 16).

Others insisted that offenders have a 'right to be forgotten' (Herzog-Evans, 2011 a) and that JAPs should not expect to have any news from their probationers:

'I think that it is a good thing that they forget about criminal justice altogether. If they have been truly rehabilitated I don't expect them to be thankful. On the rare occasions where I do get a thank you, I have to admit that I found it pleasant and gratifying. But I try not to put too much emotion into what I do; I am just doing my job. However, sometimes, they give us a "thank you" when we parole them. I always tell them that they do not have to say thank you; that they built up a release plan; that they proved they could obtain it; and that the law states that there comes a time when they should have another chance and that's it. So I do not expect them to thank me' (JAP 40).

A significant proportion of JAPs (48%) also quoted a second reason for opting for this position: 'the need to do something useful' or to '**help people with their reinsertion**' or 'to **individualise sentences'** or other similar variants. A few (N5) even referred to a quasi-parental role. In other words, JAPs want to help offenders desist. The questionnaire contained an open question relating to the best moments in their job, and what made them happy. Most answered with a surprised laughter. Whilst some answered 'when I have dealt with all my files', something we shall come back to, most mentioned moments where *'justiciables'* had considerably progressed during their supervision, or when drug addicts or alcoholics had returned to their office and having turned their lives around, their demeanour and appearance drastically different. However, the JAPs were modest about the role they play in such transformations. They were proud and above all happy to have played a role, but their usual response when asked about such instances was 'we're not alone. It's the whole system, the probation service, the clerks, the third sector, etc.'.

'Thinking that we may have played a small part in this Uturn in their lives, even though maybe I did not play that small part at all but at least I have been a witness of it and this feels great' (JAP 9).

'Yes sincerely I do think we can make a difference, but I do not do it alone. It is the work I do with the prison services because I am very lucky to have such a dynamic team here' (JAP 63).

Their satisfaction was nonetheless obvious as the following quotes reveal:

'We have the feeling – and I don't want to sound pretentious here– that we've put in one's two cents in a person's future' (JAP 2).

'With the Youth judge we are probably the only judges for whom the future counts' (JAP 3).

'Like Penelope the JAP patiently undoes what other judges have done. For public opinion, this is unacceptable, but in terms of desistance, it's fantastic!' (JAP 19).

'With homeless people it's great: one can see them changing physically!' (JAP 23).

In fact, they illustrated this with vivid examples which they recounted with a patent emotion in their voice:

'The successes, the files which turn out well, where you see '*justiciables*' two years down the line when they have only a few weeks left on their probation order and their circumstances have stabilised both from the professional and the personal viewpoint and they have found housing, have just started settling down with a partner and have a child. They have a job; there has been no reoffending as they have all the cards in their hands to make sure it does not happen again' (JAP 9).

'When you see them several months later and after treatment, they are already totally different physically; they are now capable of giving a narrative explaining what they have gone through and we think that perhaps we have been useful. Still, it is also there that we have the biggest disappointments' (JAP 28).

Emotion was just as palpable when they discussed putting a lot of energy into a given case and thinking the offender had turned his/her life around, only for them to relapse. Such was the case with JAP 46 who, whilst I was sat in his office, received a phone call from the prosecutor's office telling him that a young addict to whom he had dedicated a lot of time, attention and even emotion, had committed yet another offence and was currently in police detention.

As the JAP told us repeatedly, they are not alone, but part of a chain. Even if, as we shall elaborate *infra*, the obstacles to collaborative work are numerous, nonetheless, a significant number of JAPs (24.3%) answered our open question by stating that they chose to become JAPs in order to **'work in partnership' or in 'collaboration'** with other agencies or people (see *infra* and Herzog-Evans, 2013 a). Partnership interests them not only in order to communicate and work in close collaboration with local authorities and charities, as mentioned by JAP 32, but also in order to create grass root programmes which might have a significant impact on offenders:

'What I'd really love to do would be to create new 'placements in the community' programmes [9], to find third sector agencies for homeless people in order to avoid incarcerating them, to increase the number of release measures, to target people with difficult social circumstances, to create structures which would be able to deal with addict *'justiciables'*. So that's it really: trying to have a concrete impact on people's lives as opposed to incarcerating them, then releasing them, then re-incarcerating them, then releasing them, which does not work at all' (JAP 33).

They were also aware that partnership is the only way, as we shall see later, – and the literature confirms this – to make a real difference:

'If the entire criminal justice system really commits with all its might and I don't mean just through incarceration and sentences. If we, that is the judges and the prosecutors, did work in a coordinated fashion on long term offenders for instance by merging their different sentences together and that's really important for instance; if everybody worked in the same direction, with the prison and probation services and the outside world, then we would have the means to really do something of significance' (JAP 73).

Indeed, JAPs are good judges who focus on the future. At the same time, the reforms of 2000 and 2004 allowed them to keep their judge's culture intact, whereas beforehand, this culture had been under threat as they were not clearly distinguished from educators or social workers. The following two reasons which they gave us for having chosen this position – contrary to the three aforementioned ones– clearly refer to their legal and judicial culture. Amongst these, the fourth reason revealed a great interest, sometimes even a fascination, with the legal field of sentences' implementation. 21.3% of them referred, with pride and enchantment, to the **extreme technicality and the exceptional legal complexity of this field**. It was plain to see that they have an intellectual curiosity along with a desire to learn and enhance their technical skills. There is no doubt that this is also a matter of status: being a JAP and managing means that one must also be a particularly competent lawyer and this, amongst their peers, is highly respected.

Linked to this, the fifth reason, mentioned by 17.3% of the JAPs, is an **intellectual curiosity about what goes on after the sentence is passed**. These judges generally have a criminal lawyer identity and would like to or have tried every single position which criminal justice offers: correctional tribunal, prosecution, investigation and… JAP.

---

9. 'Placement in the community' refers to a release measure or sentence whereby the offender is really supported via housing, employment or training, treatment and care (Herzog-Evans, 2012 d).

It is important to mention at this point that reasons four and five were not exclusive of reasons one to three; most JAPs who mentioned legal reasons for choosing that position, also quoted social or human reasons. However, four judges referred only to either reason four or five. Still, only one of these four actually belonged to the 'Bad JAP' category which we shall present *infra*.

- Beyond these five reasons, which accounted for most of the JAPs, **other reasons** were occasionally mentioned. Some referred once more to the need to do a social or human job as the following list shows:

- Creating new programmes (such as 'placement in the community') was mentioned by 7/75 JAPs;

- Supervising offenders in the long run rather than taking a one minute decision as is the case in penal courts where magistrates have no idea what happens to those they sentence, was mentioned by 3/75;

- Repairing the damage caused by an unfair criminal justice system was mentioned by 1/75 JAP.

Other JAPs referred to the pleasure they got from this atypical profession:

- 6/75 JAPs mentioned the lack of routine;

- 2/75 referred to the fact that '*Japperie*' was a hands-on and practical position where they really had to get their hands dirty;

- 3/75 mentioned the fact that '*Japperie*' was a 'specialised' rather than a generalist position.

It does not come as a surprise that some JAPs referred to the practical dimension of their job. Indeed, during the course of the research, we saw that they could move mountains in order to solve problems or obstacles. For instance, I saw JAP 13 spending several hours trying to find the right phone number and the right interlocutor in order to organise an urgent furlough under escort for a young man whose father had been hospitalised with a life threatening illness. In the same vein, this other one told us the following:

'The huge problem that we face is that an increasing number of people have psychiatric issues and our biggest problem is what do we do with these people? Clearly they are not taken care of adequately. Several times I had to appraise the local public security prefect given the seriousness of the problem. I remember that lady who was totally delirious and who had been violent to her child. She obsessed about one thing: abducting her child as she said he was possessed. She did try and abduct him several times. The psychiatric expert confirmed she was seriously sick. I was told: "why don't you incarcerate her?" "Duh, because I don't incarcerate mentally ill people!" was my answer. Eventually, being on everyone's case I managed to get her committed. But I learnt that the prefect had called the prosecutor to confirm I was legit! This woman then was incarcerated for a long time. It's so incredibly tiring to have to constantly fight against the entire world! And in this particular case we were lucky that she did go see the psychiatrist. But if she hadn't!' (JAP 67).

9.3% of the JAPs spontaneously referred to another reason why they chose to become JAPs: the desire to contribute to **'giving meaning to the sentence'**. To this small percentage, however, one must add the great number of JAPs – and virtually all prosecutors – who, in the course of their interviews, referred to the French concept of 'the meaning of the sentence'. Lastly, as we shall see in Chapter 5, a great number of court rulings refer to 'the meaning of the sentence' or lack thereof. This French concept is not easy to explain in an international context. It is not mentioned in legal rules – with the exception of the Prison Law n° 2009-1436 of November 24, 2009, which alludes to it. It is, however, often referred to by politicians. For instance, former Prime Minister Lionel Jospin put this concept at the forefront of the list of objectives around which a future prison law was to revolve – this law was never eventually voted on (Mansuy, 2005). Academics, be them sociologists (Chauvenet and Orlic, 2002) Medical doctors (Planiol, 2002) or lawyers (for instance, Kerchove, 2008; Salas, 2005) have also referred to this notion. Despite being rather fuzzy, this concept meets general approval. It refers to a host of principles and ideas and mainly to the desire to be efficient in sentencing and sentences' implementation along with the desire to obtain a positive outcome. Those who use it hope that the sentence and its implementation will have a big picture impact, whereby the person subjected to it will adhere to its meaning and purpose and will seize the opportunities which will be laid in front of him. It also refers to a general end result, namely offenders' reinsertion and desistance.

'I find that giving meaning to the sentence is something that does not exist in the first phases of the penal process and in particular in the course of the sentencing phase; but it has everything to do with sentences' implementation' (JAP 42).

Conversely they are extremely frustrated when the decision has no meaning at all:

'This just happened on Friday: I was on call for a violation of SSJ [10] and indeed there were plenty of violations. And there I faced someone who was completely passive, who was not doing anything so I sent him back to prison for a bit. The police took him there and I wondered what the meaning of this

10. SSJ, i.e. socio-judicial supervision is a sentence which allows imposing mandatory supervision to sexual or violent offenders either as a sole sentence or as a measure following release from prison.

could possibly be. On the other hand, I could not do nothing. This man was a young traveller who had been sentenced for a gang rape in really disturbing circumstances and had been sentenced to five years. Then he had this SSJ to serve. When he was released, he rapidly fell into his big baby status within his family and so on. This decision did not feel right. What would have been useful would have been to cut him out of his family environment coupled with supervision by a really dynamic person. But I don't live in dreamland. After that I had to call the supervising medical doctor who had alerted me – I really work well with her. We did this because we have no other option, but we don't kid ourselves that it will lead to anything much. There were times where I had to recall a person under probation and it felt like I was stopping a downward spiral. That had meaning. Whereas in this case!' (JAP 67).

Most of the JAPs we interviewed hoped that in the course of their work they would discover or realise at least part of the goals and aspirations which they listed. **Those who had become JAPs by pure accident were** clearly **a minority**. Only 12% said they had opted for this position for geographical reasons, although only two JAPs said that this was the only reason. It is interesting to note that neither of these two JAPs belonged to the 'bad JAP' (see *infra*) category which we had such a hard time finding. This is one of the first signs of a fascinating phenomenon, on which we shall elaborate later, i.e. that '*Japperie*' transform human beings.

A few JAPs mentioned a rather legitimate desire to get promoted. For instance, JAP 19 wanted to become a 'VP', i.e. a vice-president of a tribunal, a title which comes with a higher wage and pension. The only available position as a 'VP' was that of a JAP position. In a similar vein, JAP 43 who was formerly a high ranking civil servant became a judge later in his career and the only position he was offered was that of a JAP. Still, when I observed him *in situ*, he was one of the most holistic and therapeutic JAPs of all. JAP 62 had followed a similar path: he became a judge after having been an attorney for several years. He said he was positively enchanted with his new position. Lastly, we shall return to JAP 24, an antiterrorist JAP who had initially been chosen because he was known as a punitive judge, but who confessed to having become, with time, a more human and open-minded judge.

Many JAPs told us they discovered this position during **an internship** whilst they were training at the ENM, with a 'great JAP' who strongly impressed them. They then decided to become JAPs well. For instance, JAP 13 had initially made up her mind to become a prosecutor, but was strongly impressed by her internship master, 'a fantastic guy and a great teacher', and thus decided to become a JAP. Other judges, however, wanted to be a JAP from the start:

'I got my ranking at the last exam. I could choose between being a judge or a prosecutor. I chose to be a judge because I wanted to be a JAP. That was my first choice' (JAP 54).

To sum up, we did uncover a strong uniformity in terms of JAPs' aspirations and main goals in addition to, as we shall see *infra*, some of their decisions, such as with sanctions. With this said however, they do have different personalities.

B. Different JAP

JAPs certainly do have different personalities. It would be absurd to imagine that they render justice in a strictly identical fashion, even though, as we shall see later, such can be the unrealistic desire of some of their partners. In particular, they have different backgrounds: some had former careers outside of the justice system; others had prior positions as judges. This inevitably leads to different professional cultures.

We saw that JAPs aspire to have regular and close contact with *justiciables*. Such contacts also exist in other judges' positions such as **Family judge** (JAF: *juge aux affaires familiales*), **Youth judge or '*juge d'Instance*'** – a local judge who deals with small disputes. A youth judge is very similar to a JAP, as it also deals with offenders and, since 2004, they have taken over the supervision and release of minors. Beforehand, JAPs were also responsible for minors (Herzog-Evans, 2012-2013 : Chap 131). 12% of all the JAPs we interviewed had formerly been Youth judges; 10.6% had been *Juges d'instance* and one had been a JAF [11]. Importantly, many of the JAPs told us that in the future, when they would have to change jobs [12], they would want to choose either one of these three similar positions. Other judges had formerly held jobs which seemed to destine them to become JAPs later in their life. Such was the case of four former **probation officers**, educators or probation **social workers.** Such was also the case of two former human resources directors who on top of having been exposed to years of close human contact and management also had an excellent knowledge of community networks pertaining to housing, employment and benefits. JAP 29 explained that she had been strongly influenced by her childhood in a social service environment and culture as her mother was the president of a reentry charity and she had been a volunteer herself. The total number of JAPs with a professional or third sector background which would have ex-

11. However, three JAP were part time JAP and part time JAF.

12. Judges recruited after 2001 are not allowed to remain more than ten years in a given position.

posed them to being aware of and sensitive to human and social issues was 30.6%. This partly validates the 'egg before the chicken' hypothesis.

However, other judges were, on paper, ill equipped to become good JAPs. This was particularly the case with those who had prior 'law and order' types of positions: **prosecutors, investigating judges, or prison governors**. Their total percentage was 18.6% of the interviewed JAPs (with only one former governor). These jobs, and particularly the first two, tend to focus on public security and can imprint in practitioners a strong defiance towards offenders, which is miles apart from JAPs' culture. What our research showed was that reality was far more complex than this, particularly with regard to prosecutors. Firstly, JAPs themselves are also in charge of public security and the prevention of reoffending. In fact, this is the duty assigned to them by article 707 of the PPC. Secondly, some of the former prosecutors we interviewed who had become JAPs, actually worked in sentences' implementation prosecutor's offices rather than in court or investigation. No empirical research has thus far studied the professional culture of the prosecutors who work in these offices [13]. However, our own observations and the analysis of their closing speeches – systematically mentioned in JAPs' rulings – revealed that their professional culture is not as punitive, by far, as that of other prosecutors. The role and the missions of these prosecutors have become considerably diversified over the last few years (Milburn et al., 2010); a notion particularly true in the field of sentences' implementation. which they are now in charge of: the control of the legality of the nature and length of sentences, the execution of sentences; writing and presenting closing arguments in sentences' implementations procedures; appraising the JAP of cases – in particular breach cases and *ab initio* transformation of sentences cases [14]; and, lastly since the aforementioned prison law of 2009, contributing to the rapid release of certain offenders (Herzog-Evans, 2012-2013: chapters 111 et 112). Following the 2000 Law, many prosecutors did not approve the advent of fair trial and the right to appeal JAPs' decisions. A decade later, things have obviously drastically changed. We observed prosecutors during the hearings we attended and analysed their closing arguments. Indeed, in the 1.300 rulings we coded, it was discovered that prosecutors

---

13. Our former Master Plus student Clémentine Danet, has just started her PhD on this subject.

14. According to articles 723-15 s. of the PPC, people sentenced to imprisonment sentences of up to two years (one if the person is a recidivist) are not executed – unless the tribunal decides to immediately send the offender to prison – and are instead referred by the prosecutor to the JAP who can then transform these custodial sentences into community sentences or measures. This has helped to limit the extent of prison overcrowding. However, the current Minister of Justice, Christiane Taubira has announced that she wants to reduce article 723-15 quanta down to one year for first-time offenders and six months for recidivists.

often do not oppose released decisions or other decisions favourable to offenders. They now understand that their duty to protect public security lies in the nature of the release measure and of the obligations attached to it. This has undoubtedly prepared prosecutors who work in sentences' implementation offices to then embrace a JAP position. Not only do they at least partly share a common culture with them, but they also know them well as they have worked in close interaction with them whilst they are in such offices. Five of the JAPs we interviewed had formerly worked in a sentences' implementation prosecutor's office. JAP 38 had in fact initially wanted to become a JAP but had to fall back on a prosecutor position. She then obtained a transfer as a JAP and told us that she thought that going from one to the other was very consistent. Still, she displayed a mixed identity. On the one hand, she shared a number of traits with other JAPs. For instance, and *inter alia*, she embraced the desire to avoid incarceration; she shared their lenient sanction practice; she was very happy when offenders turned their lives around. On the other hand, she still shared some of the prosecutors' characteristics. For example, she thought that probation officers should not behave as social workers, that there was a limit to how much one could use the aforementioned *ab initio* procedure of article 723-15 and so on. It is important to note, however, that she was still a 'rookie JAP' at the time we interviewed her as she had only been a JAP for six months. JAP 41 had a similar profile and JAP 68 also clearly had a mixed culture:

'There were times where I had to recall someone to prison and I was actually happy to do so because they were really going down a very dangerous route and it felt good to avoid high risks. It is sometimes a very violent thing to incarcerate a person. It is never a good thing to send someone to prison, but in these cases, there is no way it can be avoided'.

JAP 72 conceded he had a hard time shedding all signs of his prosecutor's identity, but when we asked him how long it took for him to actually do so he laughed: 'in three months tops that was it!' he said before explaining:

'This position does that. Here we see the total sum of offenders. So I see an enormous amount of people and I was thrown into the deep waters of offenders' lives from the very start. This, plus the intimate meetings with '*justiciables*' is what does the trick: aside from formal hearings, the one-to-one meetings I have with people. The rapport is very different than in a prosecutor's office where one sees people straight out of the police cells. Also, we don't wear our robes and this allows us to get deeper into people's lives, into very practical issues relative to these people. It's way more social and personal and more intimate. We have no choice but to get involved in people's lives'.

As we shall see with the example of the 'rookie JAP', JAP positions progressively acculturate judges. Thus, even former prosecutors who never worked in a sentences' implementation prosecutor's office and former investigation judges had indeed been contaminated by the '*Japperie*' bug. For instance, JAP 42, a former prosecutor, who had been a JAP for two and a half years at the time of his interview, had totally embraced '*Japperie*' culture. Whilst she may have referred more often than other JAPs to legal rules and appeared less empathic towards offenders, at the same time, like all her colleagues, she totally embraced the ethos of sentences' management [15]. Such was also the case with JAP 33, a former investigation judge. In short, only one prosecutor still had such a strong prosecutor's culture at the time of his interview that he had never truly embraced '*Japperie*''s culture This JAP, JAP 45, could not be labelled as a 'rookie JAP' for at the time of his interview he had been a JAP for a year and eight months. Clearly this had had no acculturation impact on him and he candidly admitted as much:

'I became a JAP later in life and I do not have a JAP culture. I have a culture of implementing sentences, not of managing them'.

This JAP admitted to having been greatly disappointed by the position, to which he had initially been drawn out of pure intellectual curiosity: he wanted to know what happened after a sentence was passed. He added that he would not choose to be a JAP again. He did not once mention that he liked or wanted to be in close contact with '*justiciables*' or to contribute to rehabilitation or the individualisation of sentences. He was one of the rare JAPs whose answers to our questions regarding desistance factors and process were mostly wrong, even though he told us he had attended general criminology classes when he was at university. During his interview he sounded blasé. Having been a prosecutor for more than twenty years and a president of a correctional tribunal at other times, he had met thousands of offenders who had told him every single lie under the sun and, as a result, it would have been impossible for him to ever trust them. He was also the only JAP amongst the 75 we interviewed who said he was totally indifferent to the possible disappearance of JAPs in the near future and to the transfer of all his competence to the prison services.

A second category of judges, namely ***'juges placés'*** seemed ill prepared to be good JAPs. '*Juges placés*' are substitute judges who seldom stay in the same place or position for more than a few months. The system of '*juges placés*' is probably very rational in that headcount management makes immediate adaptation to urgent local needs possible. It is thus financially ap-

15. The French concept of 'sentence management' is rather difficult to translate. It refers to the adaptation of a sentence to the changing circumstances of an offender; it also refers to the principles laid down in article 707 of the PPC according to which a custody sentence should never end brutally but should end with a release measure and supervision.

pealing. Conversely, it was highly criticised by the other judges we interviewed who said it did not allow substitutes to truly settle in a court or a jurisdiction, nor to fully understand the characteristics of its *'justiciables'* and the local environment. In their opinion, it did not allow a judge to fully embrace the *'Japperie'* culture. In short, their professional identity is that of a *'juge placé'* rather than that of a JAP or of any other position for that matter. Whilst we only interviewed four *'juges placés'*-JAPs, all but one seemed to have adapted well to their function, and none deserved to be assigned the label of 'bad JAP'. Still, our 'sample' – if we can even use that term – was too small to prove anything and we would tend, for that reason, to put more faith in other judges' opinion. Still, the research did yield some interesting details. The first three *'juges placés'* seemed to exercise their mission adequately and did not fit the description that other judges had given of substitute judges. For instance, JAP 34 was strictly identical to other JAPs. JAP 14 had been a JAP for fifteen months in a row in the Paris region. This is a rather long period of time for a *'juges placé'*; long enough to become acculturated. Although he had not initially chosen this position he had become fond of it: he told us he intended to stop being a *'juges placé'* and to become a full time JAP. He explained that he loved this position but also found it rather frustrating to put programmes and good practices into place and then have to leave. JAP 34 also told us she wanted to become a JAP, which is not really surprising as she had formerly been a JAF and a Youth judge, which are, as we have seen, positions which have a lot in common with *'Japperie'* and a particularly close interaction with *'justiciables'*. This is precisely the reason she gave us for opting for a JAP position. Lastly, JAP 64 had managed to string together several positions as a JAP during his time as a *'juges placés'* which totalled three and a half years. Indeed this was because it was one of his favourite jobs.

In contrast with these *'juges placés'*, who had become JAPs without difficulty, JAP 36, who, it must be said, had only been a JAP once for four months and then a second time in another region for six months, had already left at the time he was interviewed. He had clearly not been given much choice and was not very happy to be appointed as a substitute JAP. Still, this must also be interpreted in light of a general unhappiness about being a judge in the first place. 'My job was never a passion' he commented. He added that people and situations he had to deal with were rather gloomy. He also said that a good day was a day when he was on holiday. His identity was strongly that of a *'juge placé'*; not that of a JAP or any other type of judge. Albeit being an unhappy JAP he did not qualify as a 'bad JAP' as he ticked all the other boxes of a good JAP: he gave me the right answers to the questions pertaining to desistance and the role of a JAP; his practice of sanctions was identical to that of his colleagues; he gave humane as well as empathic answers and points of views about offenders, sentences' implementation, and so on.

The cumulative examples of prosecutors and '*juges placés*', seem to validate the chicken before the egg hypothesis, i.e. the idea that judges are acculturated by their position as JAPs. Indeed, it proved extremely difficult to find a 'bad JAP'.

C. The vain search for 'bad JAP'

A rather odd and even amusing aspect of the research was that my team and I had to exert tremendous energy over the long run in order to try and find a 'bad JAP'. I wanted to make sure that our sample was not flawed. I assumed that the JAPs who had agreed to take part in this research may not be representative and would be the most enthusiastic and open-minded ones. Given my own initial bias it seemed even more imperative to succeed in finding a sufficient number of counter-examples. Indeed, my own bias was partly amended by the interviews of other practitioners and the rulings' coding. Still, it did not appear to be sufficient.

In order to merit the label of 'bad JAP' a judge had to meet some or all of the following criteria:

- He/she would not give correct answers to our questions regarding desistance factors;

- He/she would use a tone or vocabulary which was harsh, and/or distrustful or even disrespectful to '*justiciables*';

- During the hearings, he/she would not really listen to '*justiciables*' or would not let them fully have their say;

- He/she would mostly express punitive views;

- He/she would not refer to the principles of reinsertion or resocialisation – the French operative and legal words for desistance which, as mentioned above, are referred to in the law – but would for instance have a purely legalistic view of sentences' implementation and be disconnected from its human dimension;

- He/she might not like being a JAP or would not embrace its ethics and professional ethos.

With this said however, I decided not to include in this list the fact that a JAP would not release 'enough' offenders. Indeed, this was because it would have been impossible to determine a pertinent criterion for all the JAPs, given the extreme diversity of local situations, of the populations they are in charge of and of the settings in which they operate: some operate in high security prisons, others in remand prisons, others in the community, and others still in a variety of settings. On the other hand, because I would have had to build statistics for each and every JAP office, the means and time at my disposal were not sufficient. A research must be as rigorous as possible; it must also be realistic (Pawson & Tilley, 1997) even if it must also embrace the extreme complexity of human activities (Pawson, 2013).

Still, because I attempted to find these 'bad JAPs' via attorneys, I inevitably cut into this criterion, since attorneys are inevitably subjective due to the fact that they are focussed on their current cases and thus tend to think a bad JAP is a JAP who does not render the decision their clients expect. Conversely, I did not include probation officers' definition of 'bad JAP' as I expected their own criteria would have been even less pertinent, given the subject of this research. When defining what a 'bad JAP' was, many of them answered for instance: 'a JAP who asks us to write too many reports' or 'a JAP who listens to offenders more than us' or 'a JAP who does not keep his place'.

In spite of two consistent years of effort, I was only given the name of three JAPs who really fitted the label of 'bad JAP'. A fourth seemed *prima facie* to tick the boxes but was in fact more cynical than bad. Two attorneys gave us the name of a fifth so-called bad JAP, although he turned out to be no different than the other JAPs.

The three 'bad JAPs' did tick enough of the aforementioned boxes. Such was the case with JAP 4, who considered a good day to be one where sentences were 'really executed' and a bad day to be where they were only virtual, thereby reflecting an overall punitive attitude which was rather atypical. His frustration with the virtual execution of sentences may be shared by other JAPs. However, what other JAPs usually mean by this is that it removes all educational virtue from sentencing and they will illustrate with instances such as probation orders which are only implemented months, and sometimes years after the offence has been committed or the sentence has been passed – a common situation in big jurisdictions as we shall see later. Conversely, JAP 4 felt that the lack of swift sentences' implementation was a problem for *him* along with a matter of principle. Moreover, he answered all of our questions from a purely legalistic viewpoint: according to him, a good decision was a decision which fitted the offender's personality, which would have been an interesting reply had he not referred exclusively to legal obligations as laid out, *inter alia*, in article 707 of the PPC. Furthermore, he said he preferred the new generation probation officers because, according to him they focussed more on control and inspection rather than on what he called bleeding heart assistance. Listening to his discourse and vocabulary made plain that he had no sympathy for *'justiciables'*. He confided in me that before he would rule, he would mainly read the sentence decision and sentencing file to determine the nature and number of the offences and sentences; not once did he mention a single social factor or refer to a single human or social element. Lastly, he did insist that he thought that the criminal justice system could force a justiciable to comply with decisions by resorting to threats – despite the fact that the literature has shown that it does not work, and actually favours reoffending (Trotter, 2006: 53).

My second 'bad JAP', JAP 57, had, 'after twenty-five years as a judge' and by his own admission, 'no response' to the question regarding what led people to desist. Several attorneys and probation officers had mentioned his name: practitioners seemed to unanimously testify against him. The attorneys portrayed a JAP who spoke harshly to probationers, did not listen to them, and nor for that matter to their counsel. In the course of his interviews, he told me, as JAP 4 had, that in order to force offenders to plea, he threatened to recall them to prison. One must be absolutely clear here: other JAPs did have to inform probationers, in the course of the '*recadrage*' procedures which we shall describe later, that unless they now complied with their obligations, they were running the risk of returning to prison. In such instances however, it was not a threat but rather a warning about what their behaviour might expose them to. A threat represents an entirely different frame of mind. This particular JAP had been an investigating judge for twelve years and had also worked as a prosecutor. He was not really ill intentioned and did release offenders, as the law actually requires. Nonetheless, he was not in the right place as a JAP. Just like JAP 45, JAP 57, the third 'bad JAP' whom we mentioned above and who had, of his own admission, spent too much time in a prosecutor's office and, for several other years as a sentencing judge, could not trust probationers and could not help but see them, first and foremost as offenders. These two judges were clearly resistant to the '*Japperie* bug'.

Prima facie, a fourth JAP, JAP 56, also seemed to fit the 'bad JAP' label. His answers to our questions were blasé and unconcerned. He seemed to have no illusion whatsoever as to what the criminal justice system could really achieve to help with the desistance process and with people's lives. Indeed, he added that when this nonetheless did happen, he did not feel anything whatsoever. Nonetheless, this very long interview with him also revealed that he was a very disillusioned person in general and had a very pessimistic personality spiced up with a very black sense of humour. Still, the interview also showed that he was very humane and, just like his colleagues, dealt with breach cases very leniently and had a very sharp understanding of the desistance process. Overall, he was a sombre person rather than a black sheep.

JAP 63 had been recommended by two attorneys who presented him as being a very 'bad JAP' because he had to their 'utter surprise' rejected their release applications for their clients and because he was reputed as having a very prudent jurisprudence when it came to releasing inmates. With this in mind, I was extremely eager to interview him. However, when I read some of his rulings, which I had gathered from various sources, he did not strike me as being particularly harsh, in light of the type of cases he was in charge of. His interviews allowed me to paint the picture of a JAP who was very similar to all the others. He had been a JAP for seven years and declared that he 'adored' this position as it was 'humanly exceptionally enriching'. Prior to this he had been a Youth judge and said he, like any other JAP, was interested in positions where he would have close and direct contact with '*justiciables*'. He had the same lenient practice of breach cases and his jurisprudence did not contrast with that of his colleagues. It is true that his knowledge of desistance factors was not great. However, this JAP had been operating all these years in a very specific context, which could have explained both his lack of knowledge regarding what happened after offenders were released –hence his lack of understanding of desistance factors – and why attorneys had an unfavourable opinion of him. Indeed, contrary to most JAPs, who will at one point in time work in prison settings and at the tribunal and thus deal with both inmates and people sentenced to community measures, he himself had only worked in a high security prison. Rather than yielding a solid experience with all sorts of offenders, situations and contexts, he was exclusively in charge of high risk offenders and never saw what became of them in the community. As a result, he was naturally more prudent than other JAPs when dealing with these inmates' applications for release, thus inevitably leading him to reject more applications than his colleagues; this, in turn irritated lawyers who had put in a lot of effort into supporting their client's plea.

To sum up, despite two years of constant effort, I only found three real 'bad JAPs' versus 75 good ones who were interviewed and others whose rulings I analysed. This is not a high proportion; however, a single 'bad JAP' can cause a great deal of human and institutional damage. As JAP 71, who had worked for several years at the Ministry of Justice, told me, probation services do not go out of their way to send letters, notes or reports to the Ministry of Justice, to praise the merits of good JAPs. The only messages which the Ministry of Justice will receive will thus be those where probation staff complain about the few bad apples. This leads to a distorted view of the Ministry of Justice – and in particular at the Directorate of Prison Services level to which probation services are attached – of what JAPs actually are. One vividly remembers the case of the JAPs of Lyon who were so punitive that they rallied everybody against them. The prison services Directorate (hereafter the DAP: *Direction de l'administration pénitentiaire*) received numerous messages and complaints. This led several policy makers and high rank managers to think that all the JAPs ware uncontrollable and dangerous, when in reality, most of them have nothing in common with these adjectives.

D. Enthusiastic Judges

A great number of JAPs were **extremely enthusiastic** about their profession. Some of them used very strong adjectives to describe their passion:

'It is extremely enriching and fascinating; this job is totally fascinating (JAP 6).

'This profession is pure bliss!' (JAP 3).

'This profession is a true gem.' (JAP 18).

'Yes you are meeting a happy JAP!' (JAP 2).

'This is an extremely lively profession which keeps changing all the time and this I have always loved... Enthusiasm is when you have a new project for the service such as placement in the community' (JAP 35).

'Yes this is a profession for which I have had a real passion as it has been profoundly transformed with all these law reforms since 2000; that way I have never grown tired of it nor did I have to continue doing things the same way as I did before' (JAP 51, who had been a JAP for twenty-two years at the time he was interviewed).

'I discovered this position at the ENM and it has truly fascinated me and I absolutely wanted to become a JAP when I left the school' (JAP 71).

'It is a humane, social and dynamic position. This is why I have such fondness for it' (JAP 33).

A judge's dignity is not compatible with jumping in one's seat with excitement, nor with using superlatives. This sample of responses is thus even more striking. Most JAPs, however, answered with a more moderate tone and vocabulary that they really loved being a JAP, and that this position was very satisfying. With most JAPs, the interviews, hearings and other informal meetings such as the meals which we shared, showed that their interest for this job went way beyond the polite and controlled presentation they gave us. Two of the JAPs I interviewed had managed to remain JAPs for twenty-two years; another had been a JAP for thirteen years. Thus, JAP 27 described his job with obvious pleasure, a permanent smile on his face and cheerfulness in his voice. If the judges who have been recruited after 2001 now have to change position every ten years at least, those who were recruited before are not bound by the new rule; these three judges had taken advantage of this loophole. On the other hand, we saw several JAPs who had to abandon – and no this word is not too strong – their position as JAPs after the very maximum of ten years, leaving like a cow on its way to the abattoir. Every single one of them wanted to get back to '*Japperie*' as soon as possible. In fact, 20% of the JAPs we interviewed had previously held the position of JAP.

Amongst the other JAPs, 17.3% told us spontaneously – there was no question on this subject – that they would become JAPs at a later stage.

Conversely, and just as interestingly, **only two JAPs** of the seventy-five we interviewed told us that they **wanted to leave** '*Japperie*' altogether. JAP 7 said he could not tolerate the sheer poverty of the criminal justice system. He would indeed be confronted with this poverty in other positions; however, it is inarguable that JAP services are exceptionally under-equipped and overloaded. JAP 21 told me that she was sick and tired with the feud orchestrated by the prison services against the JAPs and that the recent decrees and sub-decrees which they had single-handedly written and which attacked the prerogatives of the JAP [16] had been the final blow and that, despite six years as a JAP and being someone who had loved this job, she simply could not take it any longer.

Although he did not say he actually wanted to leave this position now, JAP 45 admitted that he would not always remain a JAP. We have already mentioned this particular judge, who had the culture of a prosecutor rather than that of a JAP, owing to his disappointment regarding what he had discovered with '*Japperie*': a legal system which was far too complex and totally schizophrenic; indeed, on the one hand, people serving long sentences were not to be released and, on the other hand, those serving short sentences were to be released whatever the cost. 'I prefer when short sentences are really executed' he said. This judge, as seen previously, had not been acculturated to '*Japperie*' in the least.

Yet being a JAP is not easy: these judges have an extremely heavy caseload; they take on particularly taxing responsibilities and the risk of being blamed for an incident or a crime is constant: they are permanently confronted by economic and human misery, by dramatic situations, by illness and mental illness and addictions; they have derisory material resources, bordering on the scandalous. Surprisingly though, we have not found, save a few exceptions, any signs of professional stress or burnout amongst them. Even those who had to endure particularly abominable working conditions, such as JAP 13 still held on because of the sheer human and intellectual interest which came with this position. Still, an increasingly abundant literature shows that people, and particularly those who work in the criminal justice field can be hit by a form of stress called 'vicarious', or trauma by proxy as a

16. Décret n° 2011-1876 du 14 décembre 2011 relative aux attributions respectives du juge de l'application des peines, des autres magistrats mandants et du service pénitentiaire d'insertion et de probation et à leurs relations et circulaire Garde des sceaux du 16 décembre 2011 relative aux attributions respectives du juge de l'application des peines, des autres magistrats mandants et du service pénitentiaire d'insertion et de probation, NOR :JUSK1140065C.

result of being repeatedly confronted by other people's unhappiness and difficult circumstances (Silver et al., 2004; Izzo & Carpel, 2011; Vrklevski & Franklin, 2008). Progressively, this may leave an imprint in practitioners' brain if they do not learn to protect themselves against it. Other research has pointed out the difficulty of endorsing extremely heavy responsibilities, particularly with high risk offenders (Severson & Pettus-Davis, 2013). If French JAPs appeared to be protected against this risk, it may be because they are able to make decisions. Agencies do help them deal with stress.

§ 2. The chicken: becoming a better judge by being a JAP

As we have seen, with time many JAPs become acculturated to '*Japperie*'. Indeed, a particularly striking case related to former prosecutors and '*juges placés*' who had stayed long enough in a JAP office. I wanted to measure this impact by focussing part of the research on newly appointed JAPs, whom I called 'rookie JAPs'. I hoped to uncover the first signs of the aforementioned acculturation through their interviews and actions. On top of this particular section of the research I was extremely lucky to interview an antiterrorist JAP (JAPAT) whose outstanding path had already drawn my attention when as a lawyer I was analysing antiterrorist jurisdictions' rulings from a legal viewpoint. The sample, so to speak, is on both accounts not large. However, when added to the above-studied prosecutors and the '*juges placés*', with whom a similar effect was observed, we have sufficient grounds to say that there is indeed an acculturation effect; a 'zombie effect' which occurs in the course of exercising JAPs functions.

A. 'Rookie JAP': the 'zombie effect'

During my two years of research I hoped to interview all of the newbies leaving the ENM, although I was not able to obtain permission. I had to contend myself with the random referencing of **'rookie JAP'**; still, I eventually managed to interview **nine of them**. Included in this category were all of the judges, whether freshly emerging from the ENM and taking up an initial position as a JAP, or more experienced judges who had just become JAPs after having held other positions previously. None of them had to have been a JAP for more than a year.

On these grounds, and like most prosecutors and '*juges placés*', newbies did exhibit a **'zombie effect'**: they were undergoing the process of acquiring a JAP identity and did display some of the signs; yet, they still revealed some of the marks of their former identity (other position or young student). Thus, JAP 18, a young man who had only been a judge for three years exhibited a contrasted image: on the one hand he was very humane and acutely aware of the desistance process and factors; on the other hand, he was very lawyerly and his discourse and thoughts were somewhat superficial. At the time of his interview, JAP 22 had only been a JAP for the last six months. Indeed he was one of the rare JAPs in our sample who only had a vague idea of what it took for a person to desist, although his criminological ignorance was counter-balanced by his knowledge of the PPC provisions, which, after all, insist judges should focus on social and family circumstances. At the same time he was indeed a 'hybrid'. This was particularly so with regard to his jurisprudence pertaining to breach cases, as he was on exactly the same page as all the other JAPs. JAP 26 had formerly been a prosecutor and also had a PhD in legal history. She had decided to become a JAP *inter alia* to contribute to rehabilitation and to the individualisation of sentences and aspired to have direct contact with *'justiciables'*. She also mentioned that she enjoyed working in a team, to accomplish humane laden tasks and so on. From this viewpoint, she was very similar to the other JAPs. However, her actual practice revealed traits of her prosecutor background. For instance, she referred to the necessity to prevent reoffending and to balance offenders' rights to rehabilitation and victims' rights. She also stated that she would not mind whether the position of JAP was stripped of all its competence accept for the competence to deal with breach cases, as some probation practitioners and the national headquarters of the prison service would want. She was very lawyerly, punitive and did not display any concern or even interest in the uncertain future of JAPs. JAP 38 was rather similar to JAP 26.

Other 'rookie JAPs' were presumably **predisposed to practicing this job** rather well **because of** the **former positions** they had held or because of their personality. In the first category, JAP 19 was not a 'rookie judge' as he had been a Youth judge for twenty-five years. Indeed, he was instead a 'rookie JAP' as he had only been in this position for five months at the time of his interview. Theoretically speaking, transferring from a Youth judge office to a JAP office is not a quantum leap. Indeed, as we mentioned previously, Youth judges were created during the pioneering post WWII era, in 1945, and share with JAPs a similar care for *'justiciables'* best interest, interact with them on a daily basis and must, whether by necessity or choice, concern themselves with environmental and human crime factors. The skills which these two types of judges must possess are quite similar. However, minors are not adults and are not treated in the same fashion by the criminal justice system. In particular, it is extremely difficult for a Youth judge to send a minor to prison. When he or she eventually does, it is because he/she will have exhausted every possible other avenue. For this very reason, when he eventually throws in the towel and does so, even though he has no illusion about the outcome, it is next to impossible for him to then send a contradictory message to the juvenile and tell him 'I just incarcerated you, yet I am now going to parole you'. For the same reason when offenders are then paroled or otherwise early released he/she will tend to a sanction breach more harshly than a JAP would do with an adult. This is exactly what JAP 19 told me. By his own admission, during the first few months of being a JAP he was 'a reactionary'. He explained that he eventually adapted his jurisprudence to his new clientele and context and, particularly with breach cases, he did now take into account offenders' circumstances and personalities. Another former Youth judge, JAP 25, had already fully caught the '*Japperie*' bug after only five months of practice. He was virtually identical to all the other JAPs, in terms of his aspirations, his satisfaction with the job, his knowledge of the desistance process and his breach jurisprudence. He had clearly been well prepared for his new functions by his former position. This was also the case for JAP 41, despite the fact he had only been a JAP for four months at the time of his interview. However, he was a former probation officer, meaning that from the very start he had an excellent knowledge of the people with whom and the context in which he would be working. Interestingly he had lost his probation officer identity, and totally identified with the role of JAP. For instance he complained when they did not respect the judicial mandate.

'They have to work within the boundaries of a judicial mandate. So I am an authority and they are accountable to me, naturally under the auspices of their own hierarchy and chiefs. But the judicial authority is right here in this seat'.

Other 'rookie JAPs' were probably **predisposed** for this job and consequently their acculturation was just as fast, **because of** their **personal traits and skills**. Such was the case of two of the 'rookie JAPs' we interviewed. First, and even though she had only been a JAP for three months at the time, JAP 35 had exactly the same aspirations as all the other JAPs. She told us that she had wanted to become a JAP, on the one hand out of intellectual curiosity and, on the other hand, because, having been a judge for twenty-three years and having practiced virtually all the other judicial positions under the sun she wanted to try the only one she had not yet experienced and, on the other hand, she also wanted a position where she would have close interaction with '*justiciables*'. Moreover, and importantly, her personality did prepare her perfectly for her new position: she really did care for her '*justiciables*'; she was never as happy as when her offenders seemed to be turning their lives around, and never as frustrated as when she could not help them; she was enthusiastically planning projects which would help to support offenders and addicts, and so on. Despite having no comparable experience, another JAP did have a perfect personality for such a position. JAP 46 was a very young judge, freshly out of the ENM and JAP was his first position. Despite his lack of experience, he was perfect for this position. During his hearings, he displayed a perfect balance of humanity and empathy and the right distance with offenders. He managed to calmly but firmly set the necessary boundaries, whilst also being totally committed to his social and educational role. He did care, help and support whilst not being submersed with emotions when dealing with the difficult psycho-social or economic circumstances of his probationers. Indeed he told me:

'I never think about work when I go home. Mind, nor do think about home when I am at work. This is probably due to my personality, I guess'.

JAP 46 really listened to the offenders, but guided them gently and firmly towards his goals: i.e. compliance and desistance. His constant calm and natural communication skills had an immediate effect on probationers. I saw many a time *'justiciables'* entering his office either stressed out or pacified and reassured, yet clearly aware that they would have to comply with the requirements and achieve.

If many young JAPs rapidly got used to their position because of their prior experience and personal skills, one must also stress that in recent years, the ENM has drastically changed its teaching methods and curriculum content [17]. ENM is now, as its motto states, not only training judges in knowing 'how to do' (*savoir faire*) but also in 'how to be' and how to be/behave' (*savoir être*). Clearly those who had been trained at the ENM after this reform were better prepared. This is how JAP 70 described it:

'We first do the internship during our general training. Then [once we know what place we shall be appointed to] we do the pre-allocation training period at the ENM for six weeks after which we have two months and a half internship in a tribunal and we do nothing but *'Japperie'*. So what I found was that our training had really prepared me very well and when I arrived in my court, of course I was a little anxious, but I realised that I was rather operational' (JAP 70).

To sum up, 'rookie JAPs' are transformed by their position or are, by nature, adapted to it thanks to prior experience or their personality. The antiterrorist JAP who I was extremely lucky to meet belonged to the first category.

17. This happened in the aftermath of a highly publicised 'Outreau case' where several fathers and mothers were wrongly incarcerated and accused of having participated in a paedophile ring whose victims included their children. They spent up to four years in prison; one of them committed suicide; most of them were ruined and lost their positions; all of them had a very hard time getting back custody of their children upon their release despite being declared innocent. One of the criticisms which was then made against the judiciary was that the ENM focussed on training excellent lawyers rather than good human beings.

B. The antiterrorist JAP: a metamorphosis

In France, all terrorist criminal cases have long been dealt with by a Parisian investigation judge and criminal Courts. This system, called the 'centralisation of terrorism cases' was later extended to sentences' implementation courts by law n° 2006-64 of January 23, 2006. Only the Parisian antiterrorist JAP (the JAPAT) and the antiterrorist three JAP tribunal (the TAPAT) [18] would deal with the release and supervision of terrorists (Bianchi, 2006; Herzog-Evans, 2012-2013, n° 131.51s.). There is not a shadow of a doubt that this 'centralisation' is mainly aimed at being more punitive with terrorists *inter alia* by putting more pressure on the judges, as the main executive decision bodies are located in Paris (Bianchi, 2006). In order to make this happen, the executive ensured that the judges who would be appointed were sufficiently punitive and precautious. The same objective applied to JAPs, although, and this is telling, not a single JAP wanted to hold this newly created position, precisely in view of the reformers' punitive agenda. They were not wrong in their analysis of reformers' intent as it was patent that the latter had not imagined for one minute that former terrorists would also desist, even if their own desistance path was unquestionably different (LaFree & Miller, 2008; Wheatley & McCauley, 2008). In particular, they may embrace legitimate political action avenues. Such was the case with Jean-Marc Rouillan, a former Action Directe [19] member, who, when he was released, joined the far left, but legit, political party of Mr Besancenot [20] who himself was a candidate at the former presidential elections. Such was also the case with this former Basque terrorist who then went on to simply participate in pacifistic demonstrations [21].

When I met and interviewed JAP 24, he had fully become a JAP, identical to all the others, even though he only had terrorism cases. He confessed that he had been recruited precisely because he was well known for having publicly expressed punitive views about delinquency. It was thus assumed that he would be punitive with terrorists. Indeed, he conceded that at first he did not have an ounce of sympathy for that particular type of offender and was ill prepared to be a soft JAP who would release them easily. Yet, at the time of his interview, he had been a JAP for five years and his discourse and

---

18. With serious cases such as the reduction of a tariff or paroling a person serving a long sentence, only this JAP court, the *tribunal de l'application des peines* (TAP), is competent.

19. Action Directe was the French equivalent of the German Rote Armee Fraktion, and the Italian Brigate Rosse.

20. Court of Appeal of Paris, Antiterrorist Chamber, dec. 4, 2008, *D.*, 2009, n° 20, pp. 1388-1393.

21. V. Court of cassation, Criminal Chamber, 30 mars 2011, pourvoi n° 10-86.999, *Ajpénal* 2011: 477-478, obs. M. Herzog-Evans.

practice – which I had observed throughout the years by reading and commenting on his most famous rulings – was clearly that of any other JAP. He candidly admitted that the position had rubbed off on him. Being close to offenders, seeing them, talking to them, he explained, made all the difference. Interestingly he explained how this change occurred. At first, he followed the guidelines of article D 49-80 of the PPC, which stated that he should be holding his hearings in Paris and conducting proceedings via videoconferencing. This practice aims to compensate for the geographical distance between Paris and the various regions where terrorists were bound to be incarcerated. As long as he abided by this rule, he had a hard time paroling these offenders because, as he explained, he was not 'exposed to their humanity'. One day, however, he decided to go all the way down to Marseille and to hold his hearing 'live'. There, he revealed he was moved by the human being who faced him and realised that he would not be able to rule in the same distant manner ever again. He decided that from then on he would only use videoconferencing for unimportant issues or when there was an emergency; with all his cases he would take a TGV and go there in person. From then on, he said he learnt to know 'his' '*justiciables*', and to see the human beings behind the terrorists. He also learnt a great deal about the different types of terrorisms, what drew these people to such shocking behaviour, but also about their specific desistance path. He recounted with erudite details the different types of terrorisms which are present on French soil: Al Qaida, Basques, '*Action Directe*' and Corsican '*Independentistes*'. During his five years in office, he had undeniably acquired a considerable amount of information and knowledge. Naturally he did remain prudent towards this particular type of offender, but no longer hesitated to give them a chance when the time and the circumstances were right. In short, as he concluded:

'To sum up, I do think that centralisation in Paris was a good idea after all. Offenders are now released, whereas before, they never were. I remember this file – the famous file X. At the time, the local JAP said that they would systematically deny all X's parole applications. When I became competent for these cases, as a JAPAT, I, by law, had to ask for this local JAP's opinion. This time, she ruled in favour of release! Specialisation does give me a clear vision of terrorism issues. Besides, when a terrorist is transferred to another prison, I am still the one in charge. The very fact that they have the same JAP all along is a good thing in terms of supervision' (JAP 24).

Academics and practitioners had initially reacted in a very negative way to the law of 2006; which centralised sentences' implementation in Paris. At the time, nobody foresaw that it would also lead to a better knowledge and understanding regarding the desistance process of this very specific type of offender. Commentators were not aware of the powerful acculturation nature of '*Japperie*', which can, as we have seen, transform even the more reluctant judge. For they are, despite their lack of adequate training, authentic 'Mister Jourdain of desistance'.

2

JAP and desistance

The research did show that JAPs have an overall good understanding of both desistance factors and the desistance process and act accordingly. It showed that JAPs are overall rather holistic judges, whose aim is for offenders to take 'the hand that tries to help them' through supervision. Despite a difficult legal and media context, JAPs do persist in releasing prisoners. However, in order to shield themselves from these difficulties, they have had to improve their rulings and to be even more attentive to every detail of each case. Some of them even go as far as to create experimental schemes which are very close to evidence-based foreign programmes. Unfortunately, a minority tend to wrongly focus on offenders' various forms of denial of the offence or personal responsibility. Moreover, their relationships with their partners, and particularly probation services, have become extremely complex over the last few years.

§ 1. What JAPs say and do

A. An overall good knowledge of the desistance process

We saw that JAPs aspire to work closely with *'justiciables'* and to participate in reinsertion, i.e. the legal and operational French term for desistance (Herzog-Evans, 2012 a). However, most of them cannot possibly base their understanding on an academic or theoretical knowledge of the desistance process taught either at university or at the ENM. When asked whether or not they ever attended criminology classes, 36.5% stated that they did attend general criminology classes at university, but none of these classes ever mentioned desistance. 19.4% of the JAPs had attended various criminology long-life training sessions, which had not mentioned desistance either. Overall, only 44.4% had never attended any criminology training whatsoever. However, most of them said that if these classes had been intellectually stimulating, none had provided them with any useful information or tools which they could apply in their job. This undeniably relates to the extreme and chronic difficulty with developing criminology as an autonomous field in French universities (Cario et al., 2012; Herzog-Evans, 2012 b) and even more so as an applied science [22].

Nonetheless, the most interesting result was that 55.5% of all the interviewed JAPs were interested in improving their knowledge of the causes and the treatment of crime. Many of them said they would want to attend applied criminology classes which would provide them with information and tools which would improve their competence in helping with the desistance process.

'Yes that's missing. We would need more information on reoffending factors and on what we can expect in terms of treatment' (JAP 75).

'We're told probation officers are supposed to be criminologists, but we would need that knowledge as well' (JAP 21).

'It would be useful to develop this at the ENM' (JAP 51).

JAPs' **point of view with regards the training they received at the ENM** was rather **contrasted**:

- 37.1% said it was satisfying;

- 14.2% said it was rather satisfying whilst also stating they would have needed more criminology or sentences' implementation law classes;

- 27.1% said it was not satisfying;

Those amongst the JAPs who said they were not satisfied with the training they received expressly pointed to a lack of knowledge in both criminology and in sentences' implementation law. Indeed, as mentioned above, this legal field has become, as a direct result of constant law reform, so complex that the French Constitutional Council has recently deplored it in one of its rulings (Cons. constit. 4 August 2011, décis. n° 2011-635 DC ; Herzog-Evans, 2012-2013 : Chap. 04). It is plain to see that JAPs would have benefitted from more in depth and complete classes in this legal field. However, three generations of JAPs should, in this respect, be distinguished. Firstly, those who were trained in '*Japperie*' before 2000 – whether they had been JAPs for a very long time when they were interviewed or whether they had

22. Conversely, see the Community Justice Social Work curriculum, which will be taught at the University of Reims, starting in the term 2013-2014, in partnership with several European universities and criminal justice, prison and probation institutions : http://www.cjsw.eu – also see the presentation of the curriculum on the author's website homepage : http://herzog-evans.com.

been JAPs prior to this before the year 2000 – i.e. before the judicialisation reform. At the time, sentences' implementation law was much simpler than today. These JAPs felt they had been taught all they needed at the time and only had to update their knowledge as time passed. Secondly, the judges who were trained in the years which followed the judicialisation, but before the ENM drastically changed its training methods following the high profile Outreau case had much more reserved feelings with regard to the quality of their training. In the course of the Outreau case, a young inexperienced investigation judge had sent innocents accused of paedophile sexual offences to prison for four years. The scandal was enormous and this judge became the scapegoat of a whole judicial system which had clearly failed. At the time, it was pointed out that rather than training judges to know it all, the ENM should train them to be decent people. Following this line of criticism, the ENM did undergo a large-scale reform which pertained both to the teaching programmes and the teaching methods. As previously mentioned, the new school's byword became 'know how to do and know how to be' in order to emphasise that the school also intended to focus on the human dimension of being a judge. The research showed that those who had been trained after the Outreau induced reform were much more satisfied with their training. In concrete terms, the newly recruited judges must first take a short general class in sentences' implementation during their original general training at the ENM. This, they said, is not very useful and is never enough to generate vocations. Such vocations are created during one of the mandatory internships that they have to go through whilst at the ENM. Following this, those who chose to become JAPs when they leave the ENM along with those who were already judges and chose to become JAPs during their career must all return to the ENM for a specialised class.

'Well there was the internship which gave me a good idea of what this job entailed. Then on top of this there is the "pre-allocation" training at the school during six weeks where we do nothing but, followed by two months and a half in a court where we do nothing but. So I thought that my training had prepared me really well for this job' (JAP 70).

Whilst most JAPs who were trained after Outreau are satisfied with their pre-allocation training, some insist that their pre-allocation training internship was more interesting than their added weeks at the ENM:

'The original training only lasted a few days so we did not fully study JAPs' functions. For the pre-allocation, I did not think it added much to what the JAP who had trained me during my internship had told me which was really extensive' (JAP 74).

In practice, some judges cannot take the pre-allocation classes, particularly when they have to take up their post urgently. Such was the case with JAP

73 who thus had to self-train and explained how difficult this rough adaptation had been for him.

Most JAPs also cited their listserv '*Justpeines*' as being their main reliable source of information and lifelong training. For some of them it is the only lifelong form of training they have as their tribunals have no subscriptions to the major criminal law journals. A research study conducted ten years ago following the first judicialisation law had reached the same conclusion (Herzog-Evans & Péchillon, 2003). Only JAP 51, who had been a JAP for nine years, mitigated that if this was indeed a useful source of information for the newbies, each generation of JAP tended to ask the same questions over and again, which became boring at times. He also questioned some of the advice given and added that new generations of JAP would be better inspired to read the ENM Manual of sentences' implementation, which was regularly updated.

None of the various forms of training received by JAPs had exposed them to desistance literature. We asked them if they have ever heard of this concept. 61.4% of them replied they had never heard of it; 38.5% that they had heard of it but added that they did not know much about it. Amongst this smaller proportion of JAPs, most mentioned the special issue of the law journal, *Actualité Juridique Pénal*, which I had chaired in September 2010, following a conference I co-organised at the Prison Academy (the ENAP) in June 2010. During this conference I translated into French great names of desistance such as Shadd Maruna, Fergus McNeill, Gwen Robinson and Chris Trotter (v. Mbanzoulou et al., 2012). At the beginning of the year 2012, I also presented with my doctorate student Clémentine Danet, during the Annual Congress of the JAP's association (the ANJAP) the first findings of the research (see audio file on http://herzog-evans.com/activites-activities/conferences/). Later, in 2012, a French researcher popularised desistance literature by translating other famous names (Marwan, 2012). As a result, whilst when the research started few JAPs had ever heard of desistance, by the end of the second year a greater proportion had an overall idea of what it was. Many of them had read the special issue of *Actualité Juridique Pénal* and all of those who had heard of desistance expressed real interest and the desire to learn more. One of the JAPs who had attended the ENAP conference went as far as to test Shadd Maruna's statement at the conference regarding the mean age for desisting from crime:

'After the Agen conference last year, I tried to categorise my probationers by age group and see what came out of it. For instance, in 2010 I was in charge of 1,338 probationers and 968 of them were aged between 18 and 26; and, 107 between 27 and 37. So two thirds were less than 36 and the oldest were either mentally ill or alcoholics. I have had some offenders who were older than 60… I do mention people's age in my rulings' (JAP 17).

Some JAPs went on to make deprecatory comments about France:

'I found that it was all so ahead of us. We are still in the age of slogans and political stances!' (JAP 17).

Conversely, a very small minority of JAPs displayed a culturally entrenched suspicion towards science applied to individuals:

'The problem with all these theories is that they are theories which can add food for thought and even be fascinating intellectually but cannot apply in real life' (JAP 3).

We also wanted to know whether JAPs had, aside from desistance literature, **any understanding of the desistance process**. This was an open question, which asked them to list desistance factors, or rather, as we put it more simply: 'what makes people stop offending'. Following this, we informally discussed these factors and whether they thought offenders' motivation was more important than external factors or vice versa. Most JAPs were perfectly aware of the major desistance factors (work or qualifications, housing, family, health, and personal agency). Most JAPs were able to understand how personal factors and motivation interacted with offenders' external circumstances. Most understood that this was a process, which could be long and complex and could include relapse, particularly if the probationers were also addicted to drugs or alcohol – and this was a domain where they did not have unrealistic expectations. On this basis the research showed that:

- 83.8% of the JAPs had a fairly good understanding of the desistance process;
- 11.7% had an imperfect knowledge of this process;
- 2.9% clearly had no idea about what this process entailed.

It is possible that JAPs' understanding of the desistance process is influenced by the law itself. After all, most legal provisions pertaining to sentences' implementation refer directly or indirectly to work, training, education, treatment, housing, family ties, and so on (Herzog-Evans, 2012-2012). However, JAPs did refer spontaneously to other factors, such as agency, social capital or the environment.

A former research study showed that French probation officers did not understand the importance of peers, particularly with regard to relapse – and conversely how crucial leaving peers behind could be in the desistance process (Herzog-Evans, 2011c; 2012a). JAPs were no different: only 10.2% spontaneously mentioned peers. Just like probation officers, most of them ignored how important it could be to learn to balance a budget and survive on less money than what one had earned whilst committing offences.

It is interesting to note JAP 49's point of view. After having worked with people serving long sentences, he had a rather clear view of how for this particular type of offender, who belonged to organised crime networks, peers could interfere with the desistance process:

'Especially for those who are involved in serious organised criminality, and there are a lot in X [23], their reinsertion potential is rather limited. Still how they go through their incarceration can tell us a lot. The inmate who, at one point in time decides to isolate himself completely from his group and especially from its internal trafficking, would be an interesting case. The one who can verbalise that he will not sort his life out if he stays with the same people he grew up with and has been with all his life. It is extremely difficult in prison to decide to service one's sentence all by oneself. It's a really difficult thing to do and it's precisely why it's so telling'.

Interestingly, most JAPs also knew their environment very well and liked to talk about it in great detail. They enjoyed describing the specificities of Oversees territories and their local culture as well as the difficulties associated with rural areas, or, conversely, with densely populated regions. They described with precision the exact nature of the local delinquency and the local economic or social issues which distinguish it from other regions. For instance, JAP 13 was loquacious when she talked about the Parisian suburb where she worked, its population, the specificities of the serious drug trafficking which abounded, the obstacles encountered by foreigners when applying for a residence permit, and so on. A strikingly different context was described by JAP 18 who worked in the North of France:

'There is such social poverty in X! On the other side of the jurisdiction, you have the prosperous city of Y and other small little seaside towns. So it's a rather difficult area. We also have serious drug addiction problems. I am in charge of about 1,000 people and more than half have a drug addiction. If one adds alcohol, it's virtually all my probationers who have an addiction'.

JAPs are also very knowledgeable about the third sector network which they can rely on along with other institutional partners such as the security prefect, the city council, hospitals, psychiatrists, asylums, dangerous mentally ill offenders' units, and so on. As a result, they are usually realistic about what they can expect and what can be done. JAPs working in rural areas generally adapt to the transportation obstacles which prevail. Some however, are in striking contrast. Such was the case with a particular JAP we did not interview, but who was mentioned by PO 36, who required ideal housing conditions – e.g. a retirement house in the nearby city – for the sexual offenders she released into this deserted rural area. This was clearly an unreal-

23. In order to preserve the anonymity of all the practitioners who were interviewed, I shall use the letter X – and at times Y or Z – to refer indifferently to all the jurisdictions which they referred to. It will not therefore represent a single or identical place.

istic demand since there were precisely many applicants for such retirement houses as the prison to which she was assigned housed a lot of older sex offenders who would also be released shortly.

Most JAPs were aware of the very difficult economic situation and the fact that probationers were ill equipped, with their host of behavioural problems, their addictions and lack of qualifications, to find their place in society. During the hearings and in their rulings, it clearly appeared that they contended themselves with sometimes very little: vocational training with rather uncertain outcomes; a few hours of part time employment from time to time; irregular temporary jobs; and so on. They often ruled without much illusion as to society's capacity to welcome back these offenders, although this still did not discourage them from trying:

'The guy who really works hard on his community sentence job and who goes as far as to do overtime without even telling the probation service or the JAP, because he dreams about hypothetically being hired at the end of it! When one sees people who haven't worked in a number of years, who have had to do training after training else their employment benefits would be withdrawn… There's this person in particular, a great guy who was a huge alcoholic, and who does not drink any alcohol at all now and really puts a lot into it. But I wonder what is going to happen after his community work. We won't be able to ask him to do anything anymore. He's forty-seven and still lives with his mother. His mother is getting very old now and she could pass away. If he's on his own, things could really get worse. And then we would not be able to do anything. I think that if only this chap could find a job. But he has no qualifications. In this area the unemployment rate is astronomical and without any qualifications and at forty-seven! Right now, the impact of the sentence is hugely positive. He used to spend his time drinking in front of the telly. Now he works and gets treatment and his mind is elsewhere. But long term, I don't know' (JAP 51).

A similar feeling of frustration – mixed with the desire to solve problems, and in this respect JAPs can spend an incredible amount of energy – is perceived as mental illness. There is a serious dearth of institutions.

Despite of this, **JAPs think that** the penal system and in particular **sentences' implementation can play a role in the desistance process**. However, they may not have grandiose illusions in this matter and do agree that motivation, agency, and circumstances are the most important factors. Still, they think that the very reason for release measures and community sentences is to help offenders desist for a series of reasons. Firstly, because the offender will be supervised:

'Society is more protected by such a measure than without it' (JAP 11).

Secondly, because the person must prepare a project in view of his parole application or other release or bifurcation measures (Herzog-Evans, 2012-2013: Title 31). In other words, as many of the JAPs put it: '*justiciables*' have to put a lot of themselves into their release plan or project.

Thirdly, many people will, at least in theory, thus help the offender: the probation service, third sector volunteers, medical doctors and other therapists, local institutions or administrations and of course, the JAP. All will contribute to helping and supervising the person.

Fourthly, in terms of inmates, this generates a form of 'reentry' period (Travis & Visher, 2005), i.e. a form of decompression chamber between prison and the outside world, where the person will not be left on his own to face problems.

JAP hearings are particularly interesting as they relate to the criteria of 'legitimate' justice as is described by Tyler and other authors (Tyler, 2007 and 2012; Liebling, 2007; Robinson & McNeill, 2008). These authors demonstrated the importance of due process rules and respect and care for offenders in terms of compliance with judicial decisions. In fact we observed that most JAPs really listen to probationers; are usually human and problem-solving and spend a lot of time on each case, despite the current managerial context (see *infra*). They do abide by due process rules because the law requires them to, but they also understand why they are important in terms of legitimacy of justice and of their impact on probationers.

As this research has shown (Herzog-Evans, 2012 c; and forthcoming e and f and *infra*), JAPs hardly ever recall offenders on community sentences or release measures in the course of the first breach hearing. We found that they uniformly do what they call a '*recadrage*', i.e. solemnly remind the person of the law and their obligations before attempting to address the reasons behind their non-compliance. It is only if this '*recadrage*' does not work, and the offender still does not comply, that JAPs then sanction the offender – yet still not systematically (see *infra* Chap. 5). Moreover, JAPs do not only use recall; they also use other types of sanctions.

This is undoubtedly a difficult balancing act, yet some JAPs are very adept at it as demonstrated by the following illustration, based on one of JAP 46's hearings. The '*justiciable*' was a female, born in 1969, who entered this young JAP's office sulking. She did not have an attorney. She was convoked by the JAP for a '*recadrage*' as she had violated three of her obligations: she had missed several appointments with her probation officer (hereafter PO); the probation service report stated that she was not looking for a job, and she was not paying the damages that she owed. The JAP started with the classic '*recadrage*', and sternly reminded her what the sentence entailed and what her obligations were. However, he then allowed the probationer to explain why, in her view, the girl had not fully complied with her order and what her circumstances were; he dealt with each and every single one of these in a very pragmatic way. He thus learnt that she lived in a remote hamlet on the rural side of his jurisdiction and that she had chosen this location because rent was not expensive, but that there was also virtually no public transport. Literature has indeed shown that distance is a cause of supervision attrition (Lockwood, 2012). This probationer had to walk 2.5 miles to reach the nearest bus stop and there was only one bus a day which could take her into town, where the SPIP was. The JAP knew that the probation service had had a permanency closer to this woman's residence in the past, but that it had to be closed as it cost too much in terms of human resources and because there simply were not enough service cars available. Unfortunately this probationer did not have enough money to have a car of her own. The JAP logged onto his computer to check the bus schedules and what the best options were for her to go to the probation service. He told her that he understood her problems but that she did not have a choice but to go to the service and attend the meetings. The '*justiciable'* then told him that she had to be at home for the lunch break as her children would be home to eat and she could not afford the canteen which cost ten euros a meal for the both of them. This was also why she was unable to find a regular job. Nonetheless, she added proudly, she had found a few hours of housework and the JAP congratulated her for this. The judge and the probationer then discussed how her supervision could go on. She explained: 'my probation officer treats me like I am a criminal. She talks down on me. She talks to me scornfully and makes me feel like I am nothing'. Such a situation is extremely difficult for a JAP. On the one hand, the probation officer is not present to defend him/herself and it is plain that many offenders lie about this sort of thing. On the other hand, there may be instances where the offender is indeed right or where the probation officer and the offender do not get along. In this particular case, though, the JAP answered that he knew the probation officer, Ms Y, very well and that he would be extremely surprised to learn that she harboured such negative feelings towards her probationers. He added that this particular probation officer had much more serious cases than her and still treated them politely and respectfully. He then gently said that perhaps the '*justiciable*' herself had projected her own feelings onto her probation officer. He added with a bit of humour that she herself had conceded during the discussion that she had a strong personality and that this very strong personality was possibly the reason why her probation officer talked to her a little coldly. He added that it was indispensable that she herself sat on her pride and tried a little harder and better; that she '*was'* not a criminal (which he repeated twice), but that she '*had'* committed an offence. He added that everybody around her was doing his/her best to understand and support her, but that she had no other choice but to comply with the sentence and her obligations. During this dialogue, the probationer went from a sulking and provocative look and bent poise, looking at her shoes, to a straight in her chair poise where she looked the JAP in the eyes and had a much happier and at times smiling face. She progressively started to actively take part in the discussion and in solving her problems and the issues at stake. The JAP thus managed to convey his message, to set the boundaries clearly and firmly, whilst having a productive and constructive exchange with the '*justiciable*'.

This type of exchange and relationship was described by another JAP as being what researchers, drawing on psychological language, have called a **therapeutic alliance**. We now know that such an alliance is essential in supervision (Raynor et al., 2010):

'We might call this a "reminding of the law" [or *recadrage*] but I am never in an oppositional position. I try and understand why things are going wrong in order to create a therapeutic alliance and to gain the person's adhesion to the measure. One can indeed half-heartedly go along, but I tell them: 'If you commit yourself to this measure you will benefit from it' (JAP 71).

JAP's rulings' coding yielded a fascinating discovery: **spontaneously they refer to recent criminological literature findings**. We found in particular abundance references to the desistance process – which was usually called 'reinsertion', its equivalent French legal term. JAPs systematically pointed towards concrete signs of reinsertion efforts made by the offenders; they underlined them and grand, as the law requires in the Criminal Procedure Code, released measures whose purposes are to strengthen offenders' still weak motivation and to encourage it. Thus, JAP 3 noted in a ruling of February 11, 2011 whereby he granted a '*conversion-STIG*' – that is transformed a custody sentence into a suspended sentence with community work and probation – that such a decision was necessary 'in order to preserve, in the long run, the insertion factors – albeit embryonic – such as the fact that the offender had begun treatment'.

Even more favourable measures, such as the '*conversion-jours-amende*' whereby the JAP can transform a custodial sentence into a day-fine, are usually granted during the second or further stages of the desistance process. For instance, JAP 28, in a December 14, 2010 ruling, explained that this conversion to day-fine was justified by the fact that the offender had now really started his insertion process, and as such could justify a host of insertion factors as he had a job, a young child he took care of, an important motivation and a clear discourse about his own responsibility in the offence he had committed.

We even found references to what Maruna termed 'Making Good' (Maruna, 2001). For instance, JAP 1 explained in his ruling of January 20, 2011 that he granted a 'conversion-STIG' because the person 'expressed his desire to work and that he thought he could be useful to the community'. Here, the person adhered to the community work in light of making good.

Our research even showed that in many cases JAPs took into account offenders' self-narratives.

B. JAP and probationers' self-narrative

Shadd Maruna showed (particularly in Maruna, 2011) that the desistance process was accompanied, but also nurtured, by the changes which occurred in the person's own description of his/her delinquent past, which Maruna called 'self-narrative'. Regardless, and as we have seen, JAPs are usually unaware of the desistance literature, although most have a clear understanding of the complexity of the desistance process and of the different desistance pathways which offenders may choose.

'A good JAP or TAP is one that can understand that the reinsertion pathway is an extremely hard one' (Attorney 10).

JAPs were asked what signs they detected in their probationers which allowed them to think that they were on the right path. Several of them spontaneously referred to offenders' self-narrative, i.e. how they explained their past:

'For those who are desocialised and socially excluded, I would say that I perceive that something is changing in their discourse and how they talk about what they did, who they are and also how they respect their commitment' (JAP 23).

'I first note how they re-examine their life course' (JAP 15).

It seems that even though they are a minority, the attorneys whom we shall *infra* call 'holistic attorneys' equally acquire, especially compared to more classic attorneys, a good understanding of the desistance process thanks to their closer ties with their clients:

'The individual capacity of each individual to question oneself, to reassess each one of his/her priorities in one's existence, and on top of this, a desire to live differently, to accept, without rejecting everything that one was, yet moving on and changing, making progress and raising one's self-confidence and eventually, accessing self-esteem' (Attorney 10).

Substantive compliance is probably more conducive to such progress.

C. JAP expect substantive, not instrumental compliance

The literature has studied various forms of compliance with community sentences and measures (Bottoms, 2001; Robinson & McNeill 2008 and 2010; Ugwudike & Raynor, 2013). These authors put forth various typologies of compliance, although they all adhered to the idea that one should distinguish, on the one hand 'instrumental' compliance and 'substantial' compliance. Instrumental compliance refers to an offender who does comply with the obligations and regulations which are attached to the measure but does not adhere to it; they present a superficially obedient front. Substantial compliance, on the other hand, refers to an offender who understands and accepts the measure, and can even adhere to it as he or she perceives that it also implies help and support. In the French language, which JAPs indeed use, one can thus distinguish between **submission and adhesion**.

Interviews, hearings and rulings converged in this respect: JAPs were never fully satisfied with submission. Their goal was substantial compliance or adhesion. They hoped that the person, thanks to the supervision which accompanied the measure, would walk his first steps into the desistance pathway. As an example, during a JAP 8 hearing we heard the following dialogue:

'Jap 8: 'Only one meeting? Seeing a shrink every three months that's useless! It sounds like you don't want to go. You like treatment? You want to go?'.

Probationer: 'Uh, I go because I have to'.

JAP 8: 'Well that's actually the problem: you go because you have to!'.

Linked to this, in their interviews, JAPs frequently referred to the **'meaning of the sentence'** or **'the meaning of the release measure'** and to whether the offender does understand this 'meaning'. 61.3% of their rulings which pertain to sanctions expressly mentioned the lack of meaning of the measure. For these judges, an offender understands the meaning of a sentence or measure when he/she understands the reasons behind it, when he/she understands why these past actions were not good for him/her and, conversely, understands that the sentence or measure can help him/her. None of the JAPs interviewed ever used the work punishment. Au contraire, JAPs felt that release measures belong to the offender, and that he/she must want it and hope for it, and must build a project – with the help of other people or services – and that this reveals his/her agency. Such a philosophy is deeply rooted in JAPs' professional culture: what they hope is for offenders to take back control of their lives. Such a philosophy is also deeply rooted in the French legal system, and is visible, *inter alia*, in the guiding principles laid out in article 707 Sections 2 and 3 of the Penal Procedure Code (Herzog-Evans, 2012-2013 : 01.131 s.). It is also rooted in the choice which was made long ago – although for now this is under imminent threat given the current Ministry of Justice's announced future law reform [24] – to opt for a discretionary release system rather than an automatic release system (Herzog-Evans, 2011c).

The question of the 'meaning of the sentence' is also at the heart of JAPs' resistance to the 'dejudicialised' release of inmates procedures, from which JAPs are either marginalised (PPC, art. 723-19 s. allows for probation services to prepare a release measure which the JAP is expected to sign) or eliminated altogether (PPC, art. 723-28 allows for probation services, under the control of prosecutors to release offenders who have four months left to serve on electronic monitoring) and which the Prison Law of 2009 created (Herzog-Evans, Ibid) [25]. In these particular instances, the traditional reinsertion goal of a release measure is totally absent: there is no supervision, virtually no release plan, no formal application or even desire from the offender to be released who is in practice asked by a probation officer if he might be interested, no thinking forward by the offender; in other words, there is no real transition to the free world [26]. Conversely, traditional release procedures are a collaborative exercise which federate several parties: the offender and his attorney, the prosecutor, but also the probation and prison services and the judge him/herself.

'Our job is to customise, to perceive the exact time when a person is on the doorstep of change, is about to stop offending and to lead, as they often say, a normal life' (JAP 35).

These dejudicialised procedures also focus excessively on electronic monitoring, thus adhering to a regrettable one-size-fits-all policy (Herzog-Evans, 2012 d).

JAPs insist with reason that **instrumental compliance** is pointless as it **does not guarantee that the end-result**, i.e. desistance, will be achieved:

'Experience shows that it is often the very people who conform the most with judicial decisions who in fact, deep inside, do not conform to it at all and have no intention to resocialise… Some people are extremely polite, extremely cautious about respecting their obligations, but really, they are totally impervious to judicial injunctions… and also, the 'clever' offenders

---

24. See: http://herzog-evans.com/commentaire-du-projet-sur-la-peine-de-contrainte-penale-french-probation-order-bill-a-comment/.

25 The same will probably apply to all offenders serving a sentence of up to five year if the aforementioned Ministry of Justice Bill is voted by Parliament.

26 See: http://herzog-evans.com/commentaire-du-projet-sur-la-peine-de-contrainte-penale-french-probation-order-bill-a-comment/.

who are either swindlers or big drug traffickers only appear to confirm to their obligations' (JAP 40).

JAPs' involvement leads some of them to feel very hurt by some probationers' reoffending, return to prison, their inevitable recall or their drug or alcohol abuse relapse even though they are fully aware of the zigzag dimension of the desistance process (Maruna, 2001; Burnet, 2004).

'We are frustrated for the person. We have put a maximum in place in order to help that person get better and resocialise and he does not. He falls back into delinquency and we are powerless. We catch ourselves trying to convince them whereas really there are moments where…' [laughter] (JAP 68).

'When I realise that this person will never change I do not fell successful' (JAP 73).

Conversely, many JAPs answer our question of 'what is a good day' with something akin to this:

'When we had a hearing or a meeting and we feel we have managed to convey our message and to make the offender think about his life course' (JAP 75).

There is no doubt that it is their understanding of the desistance process which allows JAP to release offenders despite the political and media climate.

D. The courage to release prisoners in spite of the media

Just like in England and Wales, with the headline-making Sonnex case (Cluley, 2010; Fitzgibbon, 2011), a few French cases have recently drawn attention to the probation services who, up until then, had been ignored by the media. A case of particular note here is **'the Pornic case'**. This was a denomination based on the name of the place where an abduction followed by rape and murder was committed at the very beginning of 2011, also known as **'the Meilhon case'**, i.e. the name of the culprit. Indeed, this case generated immense criticism against JAPs and the probation service. This offender had been released in the Nantes region, and due to a terrible caseload for both the probation service – up to 200 cases per probation officer – had not been supervised at all. The total inexistence of valid risk assessment tools was also criticised (Herzog-Evans, 2012 f) along with the lack of coordination between services (Herzog-Evans, 2013 a). Indeed, Mr Meilhon had not been supervised because he was not considered dangerous due to the fact he had not been sentenced for a serious offence. It was only on this basis that his reoffending risk was assessed. Nobody paid any attention to the vast number of priors he had, nor to the fact that, during a former incarceration he had attempted to rape his co-inmate (Inspection des services pénitentiaires and Inspection judiciaire, 2011). Shortly after his release, he committed a horrendous crime which was headline news for a long period of time. The main 'result' of the media attention was that the probation chief was dismissed, when in fact responsibilities mainly lay with policy makers and agencies as a whole. The second consequence was a new policy which abandoned the dismissal of non-serious cases. However, this was replaced by an 'administrative supervision', unlikely to prevent any new Pornic case, since it was reduced to a mere formal verification of obligations' compliance. It was decided that prison guards could take over this task. None of the real issues with French probation were addressed. The Pornic case took place four months after we had commenced our research and at a time when we were just about to start our interviews.

Many of the JAPs spontaneously mentioned this case in their interviews. The questionnaire contained a question which pertained to **'the fear of the eight-O'Clock news'**, i.e. the fear that, following a negligence in a case followed by a serious crime, a JAP would find his/her name in the newspapers and television news. This question yielded very diverse responses. 36.5% of the JAPs told us they were not afraid and that this had no impact on their decisions; 50% told us they were afraid (sometimes or often); 13.4% answered that it was complicated.

Amongst the minority of judges who were not afraid, there was clear **bravado**:

'No not at all. I mean *really* not in the least!' (Jap 17).

'What public opinion could think about me, I could not give a damn, I really mean really not a dingle dime! I hope none of my colleagues will be telling you otherwise!' (Jap 1).

'By definition we take risks; that's at the very heart of our job' (JAP 41).

'No, else you're better off leaving' (JAP 9).

'I think about it but I'll take responsibility to the end!' (JAP 30).

'No I can take care of my own defence. My decisions are strong and solidly based on the law and on facts. But perhaps I am being stupidly optimistic' (Jap 8).

Others seemed to resort to **wishful thinking**:

'I recently released three inmates who went together to an unsupervised shelter and they went on to assault another one with an axe. They are now at large and I do hope they will behave' (JAP 11).

'We pray for it never to happen. But it does not influence the decisions we make' (JAP 14).

Several JAPs told us of **near miss situations** where they had come very close to a catastrophe:

'There was this person, a young man who had been sentenced as a minor to two months probation for having assaulted a police officer and I have this file because he had turned 18. And he was not complying with my convocations. We sort of knew he was, but one day he was here, another there, and we could not nail him down. So I launched an investigation. I thought: 'I'm not going to launch an arrest warrant for this!' Besides, the expert's testimony was telling me that he was not dangerous. And then this youngster was stopped by the police over the weekend and the prosecutor let him go. But right after this this youngster mugged a couple of tourists and the man he'd violently hit on the head fell into a coma. Here it did not draw much media attention, but the prosecutor completely panicked. The Ministry of Justice also panicked and everybody came to check what I had done. Everything was scrutinised. I was not blamed for anything, but I did feel the waves of utter panic. I felt that Justice could completely lose it and look for a scapegoat. It really got to me. After this, the prosecutor told me that in the future I should systematically launch an arrest warrant in order to protect us all. I felt that there was such utter violence in this scapegoat slippery slope! A huge violence that I could become a victim of one of these days, and I have to confess that it really affected me' (JAP 52).

Other JAPs mentioned cases where they were saved from media exposure because at the time another story was making the headlines:

'A friend of mine who's a probation chief got a case similar to the Pornic case; a sexual reoffending case. But then the next day we had the DSK [Dominique Strauss Khan] case and this saved her from the media' (JAP 14).

JAP 28 told us that one of his high profile delinquents had reoffended and that she really thought 'that the phone would ring the very next Monday' but nothing happened'.

In other words, as several interviewees told us, the '8 O'clock news risk' is rather contingent and public opinion is highly versatile.

'No because public opinion just like the law right now, is extremely versatile and depends on the media: one day it trashes the nasty judge who leaves a poor innocent chap in prison, and the next, the very same judge is accused of being too lenient because he released the offender' (JAP 36, and in very similar terms: JAP 57, JAP 58).

A few JAPs wanted to discuss this issue further and dwelled on the **causes of media attention**. Some of them pointed in the direction of the lack of communication between agencies (JAP service and probation service; JAP and prosecutors' offices; prison services and the Judiciary; police and the Judiciary, and so on). Undoubtedly France does have a partnership problem (Herzog-Evans, 2013 a) and *infra*), much more so than in other jurisdictions which, at the very least, are conscious of the importance of interagency collaboration (Pycroft & Gough, 2010).

'The 8 O'clock news syndrome is actually a network failure' (JAP 19).

A great number of JAPs referred to terrible workloads in their own services as well as in the probation service. Thus JAP 41 told us that there was a pile of unattended files in his office, which included a murder. This file had not made the headlines but it could just as well have been the case.

Naturally, JAPs' responses to this media exposure question varied considerably depending on the type of probationers they were in charge of. Those who were not in charge of dangerous offenders or only had a handful of them to supervise were much more at ease:

'I don't feel any burden; probably because I don't have scary people with my local prison and my community sentences' (JAP 62).

However, it only takes one troubling case for a JAP to change his/her perspective. Thus, JAP 39 told us she had never been scared until one day when she found herself in charge of a dangerous offender who had been transferred from another region.

Precisely, those who have **dangerous profiles** to supervise **tend to be more scared**:

'I feel that I am playing Russian roulette. In X, Pornic created total havoc. They were all petrified. In any case it makes one think: "tomorrow it's us"' (JAP 27).

In this respect, JAP 71 sounded particularly worried:

'When I started as a JAP, when the phone rang on a Sunday evening, for six months I was afraid that it was someone notifying me of an incident. After that, it petered out. Once my president [of the tribunal] called me at my parents' house whilst I was on holiday and I immediately thought about that'.

At the same time, one may become used to risk. Such is clearly the case when it comes to those who are in charge of many high risk cases. It can help them distance themselves from the current climate and do their job. In addition, article 707 of the PPC provides them with legal support inasmuch as it states, as a general principle, that sentences should not be fully executed and that their natural end must take the shape of a release measure, so as to prevent reoffending and to facilitate reinsertion.

'And I mean otherwise we would do nothing. One has to take some measure of risk. If I listened to my prosecutor I would not do this job. And we would not make much headway. Clearly I have had a few scares. I have had people not coming back from furlough and this with people who were really worrying cases. I sweated for several nights until they were caught up. In X it's really very complex. For most of them the end of their sentence is very far ahead. Are we supposed to wait until the last minute to release them? The first year I was really fearful. Even if one tells us that it's crazy to go ahead, after all we have legal prescriptions and we have to go ahead' (JAP 49).

Three JAPs suggested a dichotomy between two types of fear. On the one hand, the fear of one of their dangerous probationers reoffending, for which they might be criticised as the result of a professional mistake. This fear they rejected in the sense that it should not interfere with their job. On the other hand, there is the fear of the moral weight of their decisions which, conversely, was permanently present. As JAP 5 stated, not only would this mean another offence had been committed, but also that other people's lives would be destroyed.

Those who confessed they were frightened regretted the climate which placed them in such a position:

'I would lie to you if I told you that I don't give a damn. It would not be true. I noticed that two or three times I thought: "I really don't want to make the headlines!" And once you're thinking that sort of thing then it's really disturbing'.

This JAP would illustrate his point as follows;

'For instance, yesterday, for the very first time I placed somebody under GPS-EM even though, fundamentally, philosophically, I do not agree with this measure. But I thought there is danger here and I am not taking any risk when four or five years ago I might have' (JAP 2).

What makes things worse is that **JAPs** themselves **feel insecure**. They are very worried about their dependency on agencies when it comes to the supervision of offenders and obtaining information in order to make decisions, since they will be held responsible if something goes wrong. They particularly referred to the probation services on which they depend to a great extent and worried in particular about the quality of supervision – as well as its intensity – and about probation officers' reports. In this respect, the aforementioned Decree of December 14, 2011, which eliminated bi-annual reports from the JAP for each case, is a serious source of concern. Contrary to what some probation officers think, they did read them:

'We are often put in an awkward position. I think about it increasingly and in X we have a probation service which is seriously understaffed and we could have been in the same position as the judge in the Pornic case' (JAP 74).

'Also, we walk on eggshells because we have a huge number of cases. Our clerks' services are understaffed and we are concerned they might miss something out. And often, we get after the facts fears with files for which we realise we should have done something' (JAP 71).

A number of JAPs told us about situations where they had been particularly worried as a result of the lack of information they found in the file or a report, or because another agency, particularly the probation service or the clerks' service (*greffe*), had made a mistake:

'A few days ago, a probationer placed under socio-judicial supervision [27] was released and this person stays in a hotel so he has no fixed abode. The probation service has not given him another appointment despite knowing that it had no address he could send the convocation to. I found this really out of order! The person in charge told me that he had told them he would get a PO box later and they just took it on face value! On top of that, in this sex offence case, the Court of appeal had decided that the socio-judicial supervision comprised of mandatory treatment. I had convoked him in order to notify him of his mandatory treatment. What happened was that he did not go see the medical doctor and the probation service now cannot contact him. Such lack of caution aggravates me' (JAP 67).

'Unfortunately some only do administrative supervision. Thankfully it's not all of them and not all the time, but it is really scary' (JAP 68).

The fact that the Decree of October 2011 does not allow them to give instructions in individual cases to the probation services has increased their feeling of dependency towards the probation service, as they also share the responsibility of the cases. For this reason, some JAPs continue to give individual instructions:

'I used to read all these reports and I wrote on APPI [28] that I disagreed. Indeed, the decree gives them the right to define [supervision] on their own. But my disagreement puts them in an uneasy spot because if I say I want

27. As seen *supra*, social-judicial supervision is a sentence which applies to sex of violent offenders and comprises of mandatory post release probation and treatment (Herzog-Evans, 2012-2013: 428).

28. APPI is the internet server shared by the probation service and JAPs. All files opened in APPI are fed by both the JAPs and the probation service and are, at least in theory, read by both parties.

reinforced supervision and they say 'no, normal supervision' and something happens, they'll be held responsible. So they tend to follow through with what I say. They are very aware of the Pornic case' (JAP 32).

As we shall see *infra*, JAPs', paralegal, probation or even the Court's mail services share a common poverty and overload which more often than not sheds responsibility onto the other. For instance, JAP 13 told us that her Court's mail service had refused to transfer the highly sensitive file of a multi-recidivist paedophile to the JAP who was now in charge of his supervision, with the excuse that said file was too heavy – and of course it was given the criminal past of this individual – and it was too expensive. She had to fight for weeks until she eventually decided to split the file into several smaller packages – obviously an illegal move – which won the mail service over. During these weeks, the offender could not be supervised by anybody.

'We don't have enough means to do our job. We have no experts for instance. In the jurisdiction where I was before we kept piling up delays because we had a lot of sexual offenders and we had to wait for months and months for experts to come. It is in times like this that we make the least satisfying decisions and reject applications, whereas on paper we should accept them' (JAP 64).

Here the question arises of, how do JAPs manage to protect themselves from the risk of being held accountable for incidents or serious mistakes? The research showed that they resort to several strategies. As we have seen, some have recourse to wishful thinking or choose not to think about the risk of media exposure. Naturally they do not all manage do to so. Others may draw upon their legal and judicial culture: they become more cautious and demanding of themselves and their partners. Those who tend to rapidly process cases without hearings (see *infra*) then go back to the reassurance of a formal hearing in order for them to see for themselves who the person they are making the decision about is. They assess the content of the file and the credibility of the documents with increased caution: is the employment a real job; has the employer the capacity to hire, and so on. As we shall see *infra*, this added caution irritates the probation service. Moreover, JAPs draw upon their natural culture of judicial documenting: they take notes of each one of their acts, upload onto APPI each and every one of their moves and information; they motivate their rulings as meticulously as possible. This polish is however counter-balanced by the huge number of rulings they are in charge of and even more so by the fact that they are also assigned other tasks in the tribunal. At minimum they must take part once a month in correctional tribunal (in charge of felonies) sessions and are regularly asked to take part in criminal tribunal (in charge of serious crimes) sessions. A maxima some of them have another part time activity as a family judge or another position. Our analysis of the 1,300 collected rulings clearly showed that the decisions pertaining to the more serious cases and the longer sentences were themselves much longer; they contained more pages, more details and information, as well as more references to other agencies or professionals' opinions, whilst also referring to more legal norms which were more meticulously explained.

'I haven't had lots of cases of this sort. But I have one where I had paroled this person who the very same week killed his girlfriend by stabbing her fifty times. I was saved by my perfectionism' (JAP 67).

'One says 'always surprised never fucked'. Risk taking requires planning. It has to be acceptable if we have done our job well' (JAP 73).

Still, most JAPs **cannot make their decisions solely based on the risk of media exposure** – even if attorneys sometimes say they do exactly that – or based on what public opinion of them would be.

'It's not the role of the judge to be the voice of public opinion' (JAP 4).

'No, decisions don't concern – that is so far – public opinion. On the other hand, what the victim might think does concern me' (JAP 61).

Another JAP had a more nuanced opinion:

'I do take into account what public opinion could think of a decision. A decision cannot be made by artificially shutting oneself from the environment' (JAP 59).

One must remember that JAPs are not the only magistrates who can be hit by the media naming and blaming judges syndrome. Two JAPs and a prosecutor thus recounted their recent trouble with the local press. For instance, JAP 46 told us that one of his inmates had started a hunger strike following the decision he made to deny him release, which was inevitable since he did not meet any of the legal requirements. The local press still took hold of this story. The JAP – whose exceptionally calm personality we commended *supra* – took this little run down with a lot of serenity and humour. Conversely, his prosecutor, whom we interviewed as well, was clearly much more exasperated. JAP 51 told us with equal irritation about his involuntary encounter with the local press, whilst pretending he was indifferent to it:

'Precisely there's just been a paper in the local press. I could not care less about it. I don't give a damn about the impact of the radio as long as I do my job. If one disagrees one should appeal'.

E. JAP as Mr Jourdain of evidence-based international practices

In France, it is a very difficult experiment because of the fundamental principle of legality, which also applies to sentences' implementation (Mansuy, 2005), since this legal field does belong to penal law. This principle means that penal courts of law must always refer to the law, are not allowed to create new sentences, release measures, or obligations and must always apply the law strictly as it is written (Herzog-Evans, 2012-2013: 00.14). This also explains numerous French penal transfers in the realm of sentences (: probation in 1958; community work in 1983; electronic monitoring in 1997...). Despite this, JAPs do manage to be creative. Some of their innovations echo foreign programmes, whilst some are very promising or evidence-based, despite the fact that French JAPs have never had access to the international literature. Indeed, whilst none of these innovations has thus far been evaluated, their creativity is nonetheless very interesting.

1. Intensive or perhaps normal probation

RNR (risk, needs, responsivity: Bonta & Andrews, 2010) literature has shown that one must adapt the intensity of supervision to the level of risk presented by the person at stake. Following this theory, numerous programmes have been developed. Here, the concept of risk refers to the risk of reoffending rather than to the loose concept of dangerousness.

For this reason, it seems logical to increase the intensity of the supervision of offenders who have numerous criminogenic needs. However, it is impossible to realise this with state probation, which has huge caseloads. This is why a public prosecutor, Mr Jean-Philippe Vicentini [29], decided to complement state probation in order to be able to address the needs of offenders. His project was first created in the Northern city of Cambrai where this prosecutor was concerned about the lack of qualitative supervision which the probation service was capable of offering to those offenders with the greatest tendency to reoffend. Clearly public services were unable to offer a good enough level of treatment and support in order to solve the psycho-social issues which were at the very root of these people's repeated offending. Mr Vicentini thus decided to work in partnership with community third sector agencies and to look for local or regional funding. He did in fact obtain, without any difficulty, significant funding from local councillors which included the wages of a 'coordinator' for the project who would meet offenders. The idea was to better address the social and psychological issues of offenders and to offer them more frequent interviews, including some

29. Mr Vicentini is also an associate professor at the law faculty of Reims.

meetings with JAPs – who became partners of the project – and the prosecutor whilst working with community agencies such as the MEDEF – businessmen's Union – in order to facilitate offender employment. Indeed, in France 'normal' probation usually takes the form of one meeting every two months with a probation officer and very loose support (Herzog-Evans, 2011 c et 2012 a); indeed, state reinforced probation, which usually applies to sex offenders or dangerous offenders – but not to multi-reoffenders – consists of one meeting a month, sometimes every fortnight. Cambrai and Beauvais' reinforced probation goes beyond that. It consists of multiagency partnership, something which is extremely rare in France, particularly in probation (Herzog-Evans, 2013 a). At first, it was difficult to secure the participation of the local probation service as they saw this initiative as an attack on their own prerogatives. However, this difficulty was gradually solved by making sure that reinforced probation would be a complement – not a competitor – of regular probation. In fact this programme has now been exported to Beauvais, where Mr Vicentini was later transferred.

This programme has yet to be evaluated. I have launched a three year research project in conjunction with other students so as to contribute to a better understanding of the outcome of reinforced probation. The first year has been completed and consisted of qualitative work. A study of the literature pertaining to 'intensive probation' was also necessary. I wanted to clarify the French concept of 'reinforced probation' in light of foreign experiences of 'intensive' probation (see Worrall, et al., forthcoming).

One must first not confuse, on the one hand, the intensity of probation and supervision and, on the other hand, the intensity of enforcement, i.e. an increased vigilance for non-compliance along with swift and strong reactions to it. The latter has been at the heart of some American and U.K. forms of intensive probation. It does not lead to a better outcome, is more expensive and overall counter-productive as it sends more – sometimes a lot more – people back to prison [30]. It should therefore not come as a surprise that when intensive probation takes the shape of more control and harsh reactions to obligations' violations, the outcome in terms of reoffending is not positive (Hearnden & Millie, 2003). Indeed, this in turn means that delinquents' behaviour is not significantly influenced by the level of intensity of supervision (*Ibidem*). Moreover, none of the first generations of American and British intensive probations had a positive outcome in terms of reoffending. Some even increased reoffending. All sent more people back to prison whilst costing more money (Petersilia, 1990; Moore et al., 2006; Mair et al., 1994).

30. Recall to prison went from 10 to 32% from 1994 to 2004. Home Office, « Offender management caseload statistics 2004 », *Home Office Statistical Bulletin* 17/05, London, Home Office, 2005.

Cambrai and Beauvais 'reinforced' probation is based on an entirely different philosophy. Rather than reinforcing control – even if the increased number of interviews might be perceived as such – or to react more rapidly or harshly to violations, it aims to put multi-recidivist offenders on a par in terms of opportunities, with less prolific offenders. In fact the sanction of the violation of probationers' obligations is a return to the much more meagre state probation – which in any case runs parallel to reinforced probation. As a matter of fact, as we shall see *infra*, French practice in terms of sanctions is particularly lenient, which could well be more efficient (Herzog-Evans, 2012 c and forthcoming c). However, third generations of England and Wales' intensive probation are more interesting and may be slightly closer to what has taken place in Cambrai and Beauvais. They were in sharp contrast with former generations of intensive probation in three different ways. Firstly, rather than solely selecting offenders based on the number of their offences, they also considered their criminogenic needs. Their psycho-social and cognitive needs were assessed with evidence-based tools and as a result it was more likely that the programmes would target the right people. Secondly, third generation projects not only intended to control or to support, but to do both. A third difference was that this was an interagency project which involved probation staff, doctors and other health practitioners, Job centre plus, benefit agencies and even police officers; this was of course contentious but is now considered as being particularly important (Mawby, 2011). In fact, much like in problem-solving courts, partnership is a core component of success (Herzog-Evans, 2013 a). Moreover, partners can be reached 24/7, which is another essential component of successful programmes such as circles of support and accountability (COSA).

The French experience only ticks the second box and only imperfectly the third; it does not tick the first which pertains to risk assessment with evidence-based tools.

However, if one superficially reads the research evaluations of the British third generation's intensive probation projects, one risks being disappointed. For indeed, when one only considers whether another offence registered in criminal records has been committed, one cannot see any improvement – with the exception of Newcastle-under-Lyme (Hope et al., 2001). However, researchers now know that it is not always pertinent to focus exclusively on reoffending rates. One must also take into consideration other outcomes such as: compliance with obligations; survival rates; and, lastly, the cost of crime. Precisely, England and Wales' programmes showed that there were less offences and less drug or alcohol relapse whilst people were on intensive probation (Worrall & Mawby, 2004 a and b; Farrall et al., 2009). One must also be realistic given the type of people these programmes apply to. These probationers have a host of social and psychological problems, addictions, and so on. It therefore makes little sense to expect these people never to commit another offence after their probation. What is reasonable, though, is to expect them to reduce the severity and the number of their offences and to see some of the criminogenic needs which contribute to their offending behaviour addressed. This might make the next supervision they will be submitted to more efficient. It is also noteworthy that England and Wales' intensive probation projects are seen very favourably by participants (Moore et al., 2006) who appreciate being kept busy, being coached and supported with their addiction and being helped with their housing, employment problems and with restoring their damaged ties with their families. A similar finding was made for the Cambrai and Beauvais French experience (Worrall et al., forthcoming).

To sum up, these programmes seem to have a positive impact on 'primary' desistance: offenders do seem to be able to stop or reduce their reoffending whilst they are being supervised. However, they do not have any visible impact on 'secondary desistance', that is, when an offender fully stops offending and turns his/her life around. This lack of longer term impact might be caused by the negative side-effects of the harsh reaction to non-compliance. One is aware that imprisonment does postpone secondary desistance (Farrall et al., 2009). Unnecessary harshness may negatively impact the relationship between offenders and probation practitioners and it has also recently been argued that early stages of desistance benefit greatly from the probation approach which develops motivation (King, 2013 a).

However these results do not necessarily transfer to the French context since French 'reinforced' probation is different in many ways from American and British intensive probation. It seems rather positive that the French touch with revocations and other sanctions for non-compliance with obligations is much more humane and soft. From a negative view point however, France is not well versed in multi-agency work or in any form of partnership for that matter: French practitioners and agencies work parallel with each other with virtually no contact and limited information circulation (Herzog-Evans, 2013 a). Moreover, French reinforced probation, in theory, lasts only six months whereas it lasts one year in England – which is often considered as being too short. It seems doubtful that offenders' multiple criminogenic needs will be addressed in such a short timeframe. However, in practice this official six months limit is not observed and reinforced probation lasts from one months to two years, depending on the person's needs. Lastly, French reinforced probation has not been created against the backdrop of any given theoretical framework or formerly assessed programme. It is the result of a purely rule of thumb appreciation by practitioners. This is troubling given that we know, for instance that for low risk offenders, it is better to opt for light or normal supervision (Barnes et al., 2001), and, more importantly, that submitting them to intensive supervision increases reoffending (Bonta et al., 2000). Moreover, the 'treatment' programmes mostly consist of cognitive-behavioural methods, which are at the heart of RNR theory (Andrews et Bonta, 2010). This simply does not exist in French reinforced probation. Another difference opposes intensive probation and reinforced probation. Whereas in England and Wales, normal probation consists of one meeting per week and intensive probation for four weeks – typically one with the probation officer and three with other practitioners – French reinforced probation consists of one meeting a month for minors and one every three months for adults. This indeed runs parallel to regular probation and whether there are other interventions in terms of housing, employment, etc. In other words, French reinforced probation would correspond to very light English probation. Simply put, none of the research findings for intensive probation can be transposed to French reinforced probation.

Nonetheless, Cambrai and Beauvais are very interesting experiments. They show that French practitioners are capable, despite their difficulties, of innovating and showing enthusiasm, which includes networking with community agencies and looking for local funding. Other experiments are isolated acts, although they can nonetheless also be fascinating.

2. A 'quasi COSA'

One of the interviewed JAPs, namely JAP 32, recalled an *ad hoc* experiment she conducted following a rather extraordinary set of circumstances where, just like with multi-reoffenders, French daily practices would not have been satisfying.

This judge was in charge of a sex offender who, in light of the seriousness and the number of his offences on his criminal record and his extremely volatile personality, was particularly dangerous. He accumulated mental impairment, mental illness and alcohol addiction. He had been released into the community and had found housing, food and employment with religious charity Emmaüs. Although she was not versed in the use of risk assessment tools such as ACUTE 2007 (Hanson et al., 2007) and had no specific training, her practice had taught her how to detect signs of imminent risks. Indeed, she was notified that the offender had started drinking heavily again; a well-known risk factor for sex offenders' relapse.

From the judicial viewpoint, there was not much she could do. Strictly speaking, in the French legal system, even significant alcohol intake does not constitute a violation. Indeed, articles 132-44 and 132-45 of the Penal Code, which list offenders' obligations, do not allow a court to impose abstinence or even to reduce one's alcohol intake. Contrary to drug intake – which is illegal per se and constitutes reoffending – alcohol intake is not illegal. Because of the aforementioned legality principle, the JAP could not impose a drinking ban on this offender, nor could she recall him. What she did was to create an *ad hoc* supervision which is fairly similar to a Canadian COSA. She did create a sort of circle around the probationer, which comprised volunteers from Emmaüs, herself, but also the hospital addiction specialist who had been treating him. Everybody reported to the JAP. One might wonder how it was legally possible for this JAP to rely on the community to help her out. As it was she could count on the provisions of article 740 of the PPC, which allow JAPs to 'entrust...any qualified person' with the execution of community sentences and measures' obligations. As it was, this little experiment proved rather fruitful: the probationer completely stopped drinking and a few months after her interview, JAP 32 told us that the offender had so far not reoffended, nor violated his obligations and that he himself said that he was happy to have been contained at a point in time where he could very well have got out of control.

This JAP did not have the necessary means, the structure, the organisation, or the training, and yet she did create a 'quasi COSA' experiment. In the Canadian experience, which is being exported in other jurisdictions, one of the main ingredients of their exceptional success with reoffending (Wilson & McWhinnie, 2008, 2010, and 2012 – also see for Europe: Höing, 2011) has been the collaboration of partners with different backgrounds and professional cultures (Wilson et al., 2007).

Fortunately, JAPs' daily practice is just as rich when it comes to the possibility of supporting desistance.

F. JAP judicial ritual as a desistance ritual

In his ground-breaking 2001 publication, Shadd Maruna (Maruna, 2001, also see Maruna 2011 a et b), one of the leaders of the desistance movement wrote that it would be highly pertinent to draw upon humans' natural tendency to ritualise each important passage or transformation in their life, in order to reinforce on-going desistance (also see Garapon's essay: Garapon, 2001 and Tait, 2002). In particular, Maruna suggested that such a transformation from one state (offender) to another (desister) should be solemnly acknowledged in a judicial hearing. It is precisely on judicial rituals that problem-solving courts rely. Judicial rituals, and particularly procedural guarantees are also at the heart of legitimacy of justice (Tyler & Huo, 2002; Tyler 2006, 2007 and 2013). Fair trial reinforces compliance with obligations, as does judges' respectful and caring attitude towards '*justiciables*'. It is precisely this type of behaviour which is generally displayed by JAPs during their hearings or meetings with offenders.

Interviews ended with two reflective questions. The first consisted of evoking Shadd Maruna's aforementioned ritual theory and asking the JAPs what they thought of it. 91.1% of them told us it would be an excellent idea to create a desistance ritual. They immediately saw what the advantage could be for probationers:

'Publicity and symbolism are indeed very important. I can guarantee you that for this high security prison's lodgers, decorum is essential. Some of them go as far as to criticise me for not wearing a tie' (JAP 73).

And for the whole community:

'It would be useful not only for the offender, but for the entire community which could thus realise how far the offender has gone. Some citizens have an exclusionary discourse, and at times an elimination discourse as a result of their lack of knowledge or out of fear. This could reduce their fear' (JAP 15).

Some JAPs nonetheless pointed to the difficulty for a Western world culture to import desistance rituals:

'I totally agree with this, but it seems to me that it's not in our Western world culture' (JAP 46).

'It would be transferrable to France, but applauding, that would not work here!' (JAP 23).

'I'll admit that in France we lack solemnity when comes the time to admit that a guy is making efforts' (JAP 56).

Conversely, many of the JAPs saw the link between Maruna's recommendations and French legal possibilities. As we have argued, French judicial rehabilitation allows for the ritual acknowledgment that desistance has been achieved (Herzog-Evans, 2011 a and 2012-2013: Chap. 1023). Some JAPs also mentioned 'early null and void' (*non-avenu anticipé*) procedures, whereby JAPs can put an early end to a probation order if the offender has fully complied with his order and turned his life around. '*Non-avenu anticipé* has a retroactive effect, thus meaning that the sentence is deleted from the National Criminal Records (Herzog-Evans, 2012-2013: 421.181 s). Those JAPs who have enough time to organise such hearings are very aware of the usefulness of this procedure:

'When I started I used to send a little letter. Now I convoke the person and the prosecutor and I tell the person he did well and we congratulate him. For a judge it also is a good moment' (JAP 21).

Unfortunately most of the JAPs in charge of community sentences deplore that they do not have enough time to use this procedure:

'I too believe quite a lot in rituals. It's interesting. But we are overloaded. It's hard' (JAP 19).

Indeed, JAPs' enormous caseload is a strong obstacle to desistance rituals. These judges have to endure an increasing managerial pressure from their chiefs of court who want them to reduce the number of hearings they hold. Moreover, JAPs do not receive enough reports from the probation service or, unfortunately too often, receive reports which are not sufficiently complete, thus meaning that they are not able to detect on time the cases where offenders are making significant progress. Lastly, probationers, who can theoretically file 'early null and void' applications hardly ever do so. Those who do, typically seek an immediate outcome, such as being allowed to apply for a given employment from which they were previously banned because of their criminal record.

In this respect some JAPs also mentioned a new procedure which was created by the Prison Act of November 24, 2009 and allows JAPs to delete entries on offenders' criminal records.

'[This] in a way is a form of rehabilitation that they can thus obtain' (JAP 42).

Beyond the legal possibilities, some JAPs mentioned other practices such as the progressive reduction of the level of supervision imposed on those offenders who fare well (Herzog-Evans, 2012 d). Others told us they had created their own end-of-measure hearings:

'I never release a person without a prison hearing. I congratulate them when it is relevant' (JAP 11).

'I would find it interesting if we generalised these rituals. I do this with serious cases, such as when I release long sentences. I congratulate them and I tell them that they have come a very long way' (JAP 16).

However, the most fascinating responses were those where JAPs told us that, after all, the very fact that the law had created the position of JAP in 1945, and then judicialised supervision in 2000-2004, was in itself a form of ritualisation of offender release and supervision. Such ritualisation had therefore actually increased because of judicialisation, since it had added the most important component, i.e. fair trial, the 'motivation' of rulings, namely the obligation for courts to explain in detail in their rulings why they made the decision, and appeal. When offenders see JAPs in a solemn – albeit not too solemn as we shall see below – but also a humane and caring context, their desistance motivation is probably reinforced.

'JAPs already do this; symbolically because they are judges and besides they tell '*justiciables*' that they did well when such is the case' (Jap 40).

'I know that they leave the room telling me I do them a lot of good. When they leave they are invigorated and have an added sense of dignity' (JAP 10).

With their indisputable human qualities and their implementation of 'therapeutic jurisprudence' principles (Winick & Wexler, 2003; Berman and Feinblatt, 2005; Herzog-Evans, 2011 d) JAPs are clearly the best possible judges for such rituals.

'I am the first person to criticise what I do in the course of my hearings and there was a point where I realised that I was often mentioning negative things during these hearings even when I released someone. But in fact I am a partisan of telling people when they are doing great. Clearly we spend less time talking about what is positive. This is something we have to work on. People fare better when they are supported. This is something I keep in mind. At the end of a ruling I try and write encouraging words even if I reject an application. Well, this is not necessarily going to be read... and hearings frustrate me because we are not ruling immediately and we cannot tell the person what we think before we have made the decision. We would like to say: 'You will get there, congratulations!' (JAP 49).

'In my job, I do this spontaneously. When I see somebody I tell him: 'let us consider your future. Let us set some goals, I trust you'. I let them foresee: 'your situation will improve' (JAP 52).

I told Shadd Maruna that JAPs considered that their daily practice was actually a form of reinforcement of the desistance process. He sent me the following mail (June 18, 2012): ''I was fascinated with the responses you got about rituals. I think the JAPs you interviewed were right, we shouldn't just think of rituals as one-off events that last an hour or whatever. Rituals can indeed be continuous or at least long-term... I also agree that this symbolic relationship is probably made more powerful by the symbol-heavy judiciary than the symbol-light social worker... I think at some level the message that the judiciary sends is that 'this is important stuff and it is being taken seriously'.

This research indeed became fascinating when it touched upon the issue of judges' robes. A former research study (Herzog-Evans & Péchillon, 2002) and the author's permanent immersion over the last two decades in the field of sentences' implementation had taught her that most JAPs had opted out of wearing their robe during their hearings. The present research confirmed this. As an exception, many of the JAPs wear their robes during the hearings of the three JAP courts, and the TAP; others wear it for sanctions hearings. We exceptionally saw that in Paris, sanctions hearings took place in the correctional tribunal rather than in the JAP's office and probably because of the more formal setting, the JAPs wore their robes. By contrast, in problem-solving courts judges usually wear their robe. If French JAPs do not, this is probably due, firstly, to the setting, and the fact that it does not seem compatible with formalism. They either rule within the prison, in a meeting or office room, or at the tribunal in their own office. In addition, JAPs are conscious that it is necessary to create a proximal and intimate environment with '*justiciables*'. The robe represents the nexus of what JAPs are. They have to find the right balance between, on the one hand, Justice's solemnity with its ritual and symbolism, which is necessary to reinforce the desistance process and whenever necessary to set the boundaries, and, on the other hand, a therapeutic relationship with '*justiciables*' (also see Herzog-Evans, forthcoming b). In this process, they might indeed lose a little solemnity and ritualisation [31]. This original balance can be explained by the history and culture of JAP. Most JAPs excel at this.

G. A fascination for problem-solving courts

Problem-solving courts (hereafter PSC) were created in the United-States in 1989, as the result of local judges' lack of satisfaction with their work. At the time, Miami was hit by the booming crack epidemic. At the core of their innovation were the following ingredients: Judicial intervention with 'therapeutic' and humane judges; offender accountability (the famous 'tough love' model); partnership work; one-stop-shop centralisation of all services on site; and, specialisation (drugs, domestic violence, mental illness, and so forth). These courts have spread around the world as a result of their spectacular outcome in terms of reoffending (Nolan, 2009 – for their impact for France Herzog-Evans, 2011 d). These results can be explained by the fact that they draw upon several success factors as listed in probation, and *inter alia*, therapeutic alliance, partnership, problem-solving and one-stop-shop which reduces offenders' demoralisation and attrition.

In other words, Americans reinvented the position of JAP. Simply put, French JAPs are Neanderthal PSC, whereas North-American and Australian PSC are Cro-Magnon. The metaphor seems to work rather well. Indeed, on the one hand, French JAPs, like Neanderthals, are more solid than PSC: unlike them, they have been mainstreamed and cover the entire territory; no offender is thus left out. Even though there are now many PSC, they nonetheless run parallel to the regular penal system. On the other hand, however, JAPs are less sophisticated than PSC: they do not display all the components which explain the success of PSC: if they do abide by fair trial principles and are therapeutic judges, they have a hard time working in partnership (Herzog-Evans, 2013 a) and *infra*). Moreover, their tribunals do not host all the agencies and services which can help offenders solve their problems. Before probation services – at the time called CPAL ('*comités de probation et*

31. At this point, it is important to remind the reader that hearings are not public (PPC, 712-6 – Herzog-Evans, 2012-2013: 01.251-01.255), contrary to problem-solving courts as we shall see *infra*.

d'assistance aux libérés': Probation and assistance to released prisoners' committees) – left tribunals in 1999, they did work in partnership with them and did host services and other one-stop shops. However, this is no longer the case. The sad result is that they are now not as much in a capacity to solve problems (Herzog-Evans, forthcoming d) as they were before.

Precisely, our last question to the interviewed JAP pertained to PSC. After explaining to them in detail what these courts were, we asked them whether they would like to work in such an environment. Most of them immediately saw how this related to their own practice, and to what they lacked. This question made them talk about the frustrations they had: how difficult it had become to work with the probation service; the distance with other partners and agencies and the consecutive dispersal of available services to *'justiciables'*; the lack of means and opportunities to solve probationers' problems. Unfortunately, when our students did their share of the interviewing, they did not explain the nature of PSC as clearly as we did. For this reason, their results were slightly different. Still, 80% of the JAPs interviewed by students said they would like to work in a PSC; 93.3% of those I interviewed did. In fact, most JAPs were extremely enthusiastic. To some, PSC reminded them of a lost paradise:

'This sounds like the former JAP system' (JAP 5).

'When the probation service was on site I thought that this was fantastic: people left my office and went straight to the probation service. Besides, if we had a problem, we could immediately go and see probation staff. I really think we have lost a lot' (JAP 20).

'I experienced the CPAL where everybody worked together. This proximity was great, even if it was not always easy to work together. But it facilitated a better understanding of each other, and the circulation of information. It was holistic care and that's always better. In 1990-92, when psychiatrists used to come to our CPAL meetings, the quality of the information exchange was exceptional. We have lost that. Now we cannot organise meetings with medical doctors. It's everyone to his own mess. Nobody knows how the other works, what he/she can provide or does' (JAP 27).

Other JAPs underlined the proximity of what they do on a daily basis and the PSC model:

'Why not?! But we already do this a little. Especially with Mr X, with reinforced probation' (JAP 47).

In direct line with our previous developments on substantial compliance, JAP need to feel secure in terms of the quality of supervision. It is therefore not surprising that they are specifically interested in what PSC can offer in terms of facilitating substantial compliance. They also perceived that, as a result, such a work environment would be much more satisfying professionally:

'We would not feel so doomed to fail' (JAP 39).

'People who work in this fashion have a better perception of their job; they see what works and what doesn't' (JAP 13).

Others referred to problems they had with working in partnership with probation services:

'I deplore that probation services are not in our premises any longer and that we do not communicate enough' (JAP 48).

'It could be interesting. We would not feel so powerless. In terms of means, on the other hand, the problem is that in our country we only think short term' (JAP 49).

Thus, some JAPs were immediately fascinated with the PSC model and said they would 'immediately sign':

'It would be fascinating to do this' (JAP 13).

'It's a dream!' (JAP 16).

'It's an ideal world!' (JAP 38).

However, a handful of JAPs, albeit interested in this model, doubted it could be imported in France because of the sheer poverty of its judicial system:

'Yes but this requires human and material means' (JAP 15).

Others manifested an interest in the added solemnity of PSC hearings and for their publicity:

'It is important for offenders to get positive validation. Hence the importance of applauds. Hearings' solemnity adds weight to what we say' (JAP 16).

Conversely, the few JAPs who said they would not work in a PSC expressed concern with what they saw as being too much proximity with '*justiciables*'.

'The problem I see is that proximity with offenders can be a bad thing. Our position as judges is rather good' (JAP 11).

An even smaller minority mentioned the necessity for the judicial system to eventually disengage from people's lives:

'I think that a number of things should not go through the judicial system. It's like killing a fly with a hammer' (JAP 17).

Others underlined that supervision as provided by PSC was similar to social work:

'You understand that I shall answer no. I am not social-work minded. I think that it should be each one to his own competence. If this was the JAP's job I would actually do something else' (JAP 40).

Two JAPs expressed their concern – in the same vein as Eric Miller (2007) – that this might lead to more intensive supervision, with a judge constantly 'on offenders' backs'. Still, most JAPs were enthusiastic about the American model, which is particularly interesting given the traditional French resistance to everything that comes from across the Atlantic.

One of the interesting features of PSC is that they allow judges to deal with obligations' violations with a large range of sanctions and to therefore avoid systematic recall, as is too often the case in traditional criminal justice. This is precisely how French JAPs operate.

H. A humane and fair handling of breach cases

It is often deplored that in many Western world jurisdictions, courts or other decision-makers revoke sentences or measures too easily. Such is particularly the case in Anglophone countries (Padfield, 2012; Padfield & Maruna, 2006; Blumstein & Beck, 2005), where a punitive context has led to an excessive focus on the systematic sanction of obligations' violations, even targets being assigned to services, such as automatic recall if the offender was absent to three, or sometimes two appointments, even though things are now becoming more reasonable in England and Wales (see Ugwudike & Raynor, 2013. It is precisely to the excesses of this un-individualised approach that PSC react. As stated above, one of their key features is that they use a large range or softer and more suitable sanctions. In line with this – or rather preceding PSC as they were invented decades before – JAPs are light years away from what has been called U.S. or England and Wales' 'revolving doors' [32]: they have a very progressive sanction system, take offenders' circumstances into account and put everything into perspective (their efforts as well as their violations). Their discretionary power, which might be cause for concern, is exercised humanly and intelligently. It nonetheless does raise serious legal issues pertaining to the presumption of innocence.

32. For a wider comparison please read the edition of 2012 n° 4(1) of the *European Journal of Probation*: http://www.ejprob.ro/index.pl/january_2012.

1. Gradual sanctions

a. First a reminder of the law

Interviews, hearings and the coding of 292 rulings which pertained to sanctions, showed that JAPs systematically – except of course in the case of an immediate danger – first used a '*recadrage'* procedure. *'Recadrage*" or '*reminding of the law*' is a procedure whereby the JAP convokes the probationer and firmly reminds him/her of the law and of his/her obligations. It is remarkable that JAPs have created, without any legal provision in this respect, a practice which is so systematic, to the point that one might attribute the label of 'custom', even though, in French criminal law, a custom can never replace or stand as a law (Herzog-Evans, 1998).

Interestingly, most '*recadrage'* hearings take place in a similar manner. First, the JAP reminds the probationer in no nonsense terms of the judicial mandate and his/her obligations. Then he/she asks him/her to express their own point of view on each of the violations. In these instances, the JAP always plays on the solemn context of the setting and the procedure: the person has had to go to the tribunal and not to the probation service; he/she has received a judicial convocation. The JAP then draws upon his judge's status – even if they do not all wear their robe as we have seen. All the JAPs require offenders to take their hands out of their pockets, their elbows from the table, to remove their chewing-gum; all demand that the person behaves in a dignified and respectful manner. This is how they set the tone which then allows them to move on to the second phase of their '*recadrage'* hearing, which consists of listening to the person and to get better acquainted with their difficulties and circumstances. JAPs try and assess whether the offender is going through set-backs or a rough patch – for instance if he has started using drugs again – or, conversely, if he is making fun of Justice and supervision. Here again, what JAPs endeavour to achieve is to put the person back on the right tracks, to obtain his/her adhesion to the measure and not merely his/her superficial compliance. They often give practical advice, check details on the spot, make phone calls; in short, they try to initiate concrete help with probationers' problems. When they come across a halftone case, as when the probationer breached some of his obligations or missed two appointments with the probation officer, but, on the other hand, has complied with other obligations which are significant (such as starting treatment, seriously looking for or even finding employment, paying damages), the JAP will congratulate the offender for his efforts whilst making clear that more is expected of him/her. These hearings make for a fascinating observation. Probationers often enter JAPs' offices looking at their feet; they leave it reinvigorated: first because they have been heard and listened to – an essential component of Tyler's model of legitimate justice –; second, because they have, at least this once, escaped recall. Justice itself emerges stronger: according to JAPs, '*recadrage*' is often enough to set things right. Probation officers also favour this procedure, and for the same reason. However, if probationers still fail to comply, we shall see *infra* that they would sometimes like JAPs to react in a harsher way, which JAPs will not necessarily do.

b. A large range of sanctions

We were only able to collect rulings which pertained to official sanctions such as recall or the prolongation of a probation order. We could nonetheless study various forms of leniency in these rulings which took the form of partial revocation or, as just mentioned, of the prolongation of an order. Conversely, we could not find in JAPs' rulings other sanctions because, strictly speaking, the law only authorises the three forms of sanctions which we just listed. Any other practice would have to be grounded on another basis. For instance, with measures under prison registry (Herzog-Evans, 2012 d) [33], JAPs will often use other sanctions such as **strengthening the obligations, denying or withdrawing furlough** over the weekend **or recalling remission**. This would take the form of a more discreet procedure, devoid of a hearing or formal ruling (see PPC, art. 712-5), which is the reason why I did not have any in our collection and could not draw statistics. However, I did find ample evidence of this practice during CAP [34] meetings and in JAPs' interviews.

JAPs also told us that they often used '**temporary incarceration orders**' (OIP: *Ordres d'incarcération provisoire*) in order to create a short prison shock of a few days, followed, as required by article 712-19 of the PPC, by a formal adversarial hearing [35]. In the course of the hearing that thus follows, they often merely cover the OIP period. What they only want is to create a short carceral shock in order to provoke a reaction from the offender who is going down a slippery slope; what they do not want is to revoke the measure. In doing so, JAP have created a system which is similar to the 'short incar-

33. In the French law system, three measures (semi-freedom, placement in the community and electronic monitoring) are called 'under prison registry' as the offender is legally considered as being a prisoner and receives a prisoner's number.

34. CAP are commissions in the context of which JAPs grant or withdraw remission and furlough. They are not a court, nor do they hold hearings: they take place in the prison and JAPs decide surrounded by prison staff, the governor and the prosecutor; the offender is not present nor is his attorney.

35. Art. 712-19 requires that the hearing take place after a maximum of fifteen days, although JAPs usually schedule the hearing within eight days.

cerations' which are frequently used by PSC. Gottfredson and *alii* have estimated that 60% of PSC used this system (Gottfredson et al., 2006: 178).

The 292 rulings which were coded, showed that even where **recall or prolongation** are indeed at stake, JAPs can still give the probationer **yet another chance** in a significant number of cases, especially when one remembers that he/she first benefitted from a '*recadrage*' – and sometimes even two. After such a '*recadrage*' and if the offender still fails to comply with his obligations or further reoffends, JAPs revoke the measure in 69.1% of the cases; pronounce a more lenient sentence (prolongation or partial recall only) in 8.9% [36] of the cases, and impose no sanction at all in 21.9% of them. In 52.7% of them, a legal reason explains the lack of recall. This may be the case because, *inter alia*, the person has been deported back to his/her native country, is deceased or has proved that he/she is insolvent (which only applies for day-fines). However, in nearly all the other cases, the JAPs are actually being benevolent. In 21.5% of them where they do not revoke the sentence or measure, the probationers often bring documented proof of his/her compliance at the very last minute and the JAP, albeit not duped, does not see the point in sending the person back to prison when he eventually complied with his obligations. Clearly JAPs dislike recalling someone to prison if it has the effect of annihilating efforts which have also been made; indeed this also explains why they use '*recadrage*'. For this reason, in 25% of the cases, they expressly note in their rulings that the person has made positive changes and that a return to prison would be counter-productive. Indeed, JAPs perceive recall as being a serious thwart to the desistance process. They are very aware of its zigzag nature, a term which is often used by desistance specialists (Burnett, 2003; Maruna, 2001; Maguire & Raynor, 2006). In 11.1% of the cases, JAPs also justify their leniency with the fact that the criminal justice system has already sanctioned the behaviour at stake and that adding a second one would not be opportune. This is particularly the case when the breach consists of a new offence. One knows that in the field of sentences' implementation the principle *ne bis in idem* (double jeopardy) is unfortunately not respected (Herzog-Evans, 1999 b); all the more reason to support JAPs' jurisprudence. Their criticism of the criminal justice system is even more apparent when they explain their lenient decisions by evoking its errors and faults, which is what they do in 5.5% of them. Some mention that the probation service has not helped with the offender reinsertion or has only arranged one meeting with him in the course of a very long period, or that they have only taken charge of his/her case after a great number of months. When the JAP nonetheless sanctions, they also take offenders' circumstances into account.

---

36. A prolongation was only possible in 93% of the files.

2. Taking circumstances into consideration

As stated above, JAPs do not easily recall probationers to prison. As we also analysed they focus on 'substantive compliance'. Therefore, when they eventually do recall it is because they feel that the measure at stake has run its course and has become meaningless, because the offender has understood its purpose for him/herself in terms of his/her rehabilitation or because there is an imminent danger. In this respect JAPs' interviews were fully corroborated by their rulings.

During their interviews, JAPs mentioned reasons which could – but would not necessarily – drive them to recall. Several of these reasons reflected the measure's **loss of meaning**. Such was the case if the person systematically breached his/her obligations; such was also the case when he/she committed another offence during the execution of the measure. In such a case, there was a strong risk of that the person would be incarcerated for this other offence, and the community measure would not be sustainable. Moreover, this new offence revealed, according to the judges, the person's chronic delinquency and that a community measure was not sufficient to stop it; therefore, this measure had lost its purpose.

'I have to revoke when there is a new offence; that's a no-go – that is taking into account its severity and the person's attitude though. It is a sign that the person has not understood the measure' (JAP 12).

'Reoffending is the first cause for revoking. We have to preserve a minimum of credibility and meaning for sentences' implementation measures' (JAP 15).

JAP also confessed that they tended to revoke even more if the person was not present during the hearing or behaved aggressively or seemed not to care. Here, JAPs are no different to their other judiciary colleagues who become very irritated when '*justiciables*' make fun of the justice system. However, in this respect, they are also sensitive to the confirmation that the justice system has had no success with him/her and that, as a result, it does not make any sense to perseverate. They hope that the sanction will make the offender realise that it is time to think about his/her actions.

In other circumstances judges take the **public and victims' security** into consideration. They said that they revoked when there was an immediate risk for the victim. They have also become extremely vigilant with domestic violence cases over recent years. They are equally vigilant with sex or violent probationers who are showing signs of imminent risks of reoffending. What the research showed was that they were fully aware of the types of signs which constitute such an imminent risk. For instance, sudden alcohol or drugs relapse or the sudden withdrawal or rebellious attitude towards supervision, were all identified as acute factors (Hanson et al., 2007).

'Clearly yes… much less tolerance for the authors of violent offences or dangerous personalities or those who are at obvious risk of endangering someone else' (JAP 15).

The analysis of their rulings corroborates the interviews and the reasons listed by JAPs for recalling a person to prison. The decisions which pronounce a sanction mention the risk for the person to reoffend in 24.8% of the cases – a risk which is also mentioned in 30.3% of all the JAPs' decisions. This is particularly apparent with sexual offences and domestic violence cases.

Most interviewed JAPs mentioned that they would recall when **obligations' violations** were **repeated** or when a person had an overall elusive behaviour (e.g. would not attend meetings). Here we can set aside the rulings which pertained to fine and day-fine defaulters, namely those where there was no obligations involved and those which prolonged a probation order which are considered as being soft sanctions and which have different causes (see *infra* Chap. 5). I had collected 163 decisions which represented true sanctions for non-compliance: total or partial probation order recall; probation with community work or parole recall. Of these decisions, 88.3% mentioned repeated violations or non-compliance. JAPs will tend to recall in such cases because, as was said *supra*, they will have first given the offender one or two chances in the form of a '*recadrage*' procedure. Moreover, before the '*recadrage*' is even organised, the probation service will have tried to solve the problem on its own, by sending formal convocations, by calling the offender, and, lastly, by convoking the person in front of the probation chief. It is only when all this has failed that they appraise the JAP of the violations that have been taking place, sometimes for a number of months. After a '*recadrage*' or two, the JAPs' feelings are that leniency has its limits and that it is their task to intervene as the offender is clearly on a collision course.

JAPs actually deplored that they are often informed by the probation service when things have been going downhill for a significant amount of time. They often discover this state of affairs by reading a message on APPI or a report. They would like to appraise such cases much more rapidly so that they can do something before things become fully jeopardised. In most cases, however, they do not need to be informed – or only other than via APPI message –, that a person has arrived five or ten minutes late to his/her meeting with the probation officer or has once returned home a little late whilst under curfew. Conversely this would warrant a *recadrage'* if it happened on a regular basis. JAPs are fully aware of the economic situation and of the psychological state and environment of their probationers. In terms of employment, for instance, they do not have irrational expectations. In this, they are in line with the law: both the penal (art. 132-25; 132-26-1) and the penal procedure code (art. 729): they now contend themselves with a temporary job or even the fact that the probationer is actively looking for a job.

The analysis of the rulings revealed that, just as they said in their interviews, JAPs take the person's attitude into consideration. Thus 27.6% of the decisions mentioned his/her lack of commitment with the measure, his/her nonchalant attitude, his/her lack of respect, and sometimes even his/her aggressiveness towards the probation officer or the judge. Here again, what is at stake is the aforementioned '**meaning of the measure**'. This is mentioned in 61.3% of the decisions, a remarkable percentage which is to be compared to the total lack of use of any punitive word or connotation in any single one of the 292 rulings which pertain to sanctions: in other words, the decision to sanction or recall is not about punishing the offender for not having complied; it is about putting an end to a measure which has lost its meaning. It is definitely the professional culture of JAP such as is being analysed in the present book, which can best explain this contrast. It also relates however to French legal provisions. Indeed, article 132-25 of the Penal Code states that sentences aim, *inter alia*, to punish offenders. However, article 707 of the penal procedure code, which formulates the guidelines that must be followed by sentences' implementation courts when they make their decisions, does not mention punishment at all; quite the contrary, article 707 refers to the prevention of reoffending, and to the insertion and reinsertion of offenders. In such a context, when an offender does not comply with a sentence or measure, JAPs analyse this as being caused by the criminal justice system and/or the measure's failure and they hope that the next time around, the offender will be ready to grasp the hand which is raised to help him/her. This is further confirmed by the way in which JAPs use the prolongation of probation orders. In such cases, it is clear that JAPs hope that by prolonging the measure, they will have more time to have an influence on the offender and to convince him/her to grasp the aforementioned hand. Indeed, in 92.2% of their prolongation rulings, JAPs expressly mentioned the need or the hope that the person will henceforward comply with the measure.

Some offenders are clearly **treated more punitively** in view of the higher risk they represent. Such is the case with terrorists. For instance, Mr Rouillan, a former member of the French terrorist group Action Directe, who was released on parole with a one year probationary period under semi-freedom – a measure where a person sleeps in the prison at night, but is daily released into the community for work, training, treatment or other activities (see Herzog-Evans, 2012 d) – was recalled whilst on semi-freedom even though he had fully complied for the first ten months. His recall was pronounced because he imprudently gave an interview to the national weekly *l'Express* despite having been banned, according to article 132-45-16° of the Penal code from publishing or speak publicly about his past offences. The journalist had asked him whether he regretted his crimes and in particular having killed one of his victims: 'I am not allowed to speak about this... but the very fact that I cannot say anything is in itself an answer. For it is clear that if we regretted everything we did I would be allowed to speak freely. But our obligation to remain silent does now allow us to fully draw critical conclusions about our past'. After his recall (Sentences Implementation Chamber of the Court of Appeal of Paris, Paris, December 4, 2008, *Recueil Dalloz*, 2009, n° 20: 1388-1393, obs. M. Herzog-Evans), he spent another year and a half in prison before being rereleased with yet another semi-freedom one year trial period before his parole started. Any other offender would have escaped recall given his consistent reinsertion efforts and this full compliance with the measure.

Conversely, JAPs can be **more understanding with vulnerable probationers** who cannot be expected to perfectly comply with their obligations. Such is particularly the case with '*justiciables*' who have a mental impairment, who are mentally ill, or those who abuse drugs and alcohol. JAPs understand the mechanisms of addiction. None of those who were interviewed, nor any of the rulings which were analysed would for instance revoke simply because the offender was taking drugs, except if he/she tried to smuggle them inside the prison, in the case of semi-freedom because of the security issues this might raise in the prison.

JAPs – and likewise the probation service – are understanding in situations where the person has faced an obstacle, providing he/she has notified the probation service or the JAP's service. Such will, for instance be the case with a person placed under electronic monitoring who arrives late and thus violates his/her curfew hours because the underground drivers are on strike or has to wait for his or her child's school bus which has been delayed or whose employer has asked him/her to do an extra hour after his/her shift, and so forth They even tolerate the probationer losing his/her job providing he/she then actively looks for another and even more importantly, does not lie about it, which does not mean that even in such a case the adequate sanction will be recall:

'The one who loses his job and does not tell us and, as a result, benefits from lots of leisure time, this chap who was under EM or semi-freedom well I will withdraw his morning free time' (JAP 10).

It is obvious that **the person's attitude** is an important factor in the decision. In particular, if the person comes out frankly with a relapse of violation, as opposed to trying to get away with it, this makes a big difference. In this respect, JAPs have similar expectations to problem-solving courts. The goal here is to maintain the supervision when it still 'means something'. This is why JAPs prolong the probation order of some nonchalant or even exasperating probationers, in the hopes of eventually making them comply. This happened with one of JAP 2's hearings. The person had to pay 5000 euros in damages to the victim who had been injured following his violation of a STOP road sign. Two years after his sentence he had done nothing to comply. The '*justiciable*' defended himself loudly and theatrically and interrupted the judge and the prosecutor several times. According to him, he did not earn enough money:

Prosecutor: We hear you loud and clear but you do not listen [the man tries to speak]. You interrupt people. What do you know about the victim's own circumstances? Doesn't he have his own problems? Does he not have his own financial difficulties? You have totally ignored his situation. I am asking for a prolongation, but this time I am demanding results.

JAP: Are you ready to pay 70 euros? [monthly]

Probationer: I wanted to pay 50.

JAP: we're talking about a sum total of 5000!

Probationer: I thought I would start with 50 euros and in a few months, when the situation allows, I'll go up to 70 euros.

JAP [exasperated]: If before the 6th of June I don't have a payment schedule which says 70 euros a month or 10% of your wages, it will be two months imprisonment and that's the end of it!

Probationer [equally exasperated]: 'If you send people who work to jail, if that's the French justice system well thank you very much! [he leaves the room but comes back later to know when the judge will make his decision]

JAP: You'd be better inspired to keep your comments about the French justice system to yourself. It is high time you understood you're not alone in this world!'.

JAP are harsher when **the person** is **not present at his/her hearing**, which was the case in 48.5% of the coded rulings pertaining to sanctions. When the offender is not present, he/she is recalled in 84% of the cases versus 42.5% when he/she is present with an attorney and 34.7% when he/she is present without an attorney.

Indeed, in such cases, the person loses the chance to defend him/herself, to be assisted by an attorney or, more prosaically to bring, at long last, the documented proof that had been expected of him/her for months – something which does save probationers from recalling in a great number of cases. It is also probable that JAPs are exasperated by what they perceive as being a frontal insubordination against the justice system. It is also probable that they consider, once again, that the measure has no more meaning – its meaning being, as stated above, JAPs' main goal – if the offender feels so little interest in its execution that he/she does not even bother talking to his/her judge. During the hearings, the issue of the absentees is constantly present.

JAPs would need to read the cards in order to schedule their hearings. If they convoke ten probationers for half a day hearings, there is a strong risk that they will only see three or four and will have wasted a lot of time. Conversely, if they convoke eighteen, they can expect to have approximately eight or ten, which is doable, or just as possible, thirteen or fifteen, which is not reasonable given the time each hearing takes. If most judges spend their idle time reading or dealing with other files or making phone calls, their exasperation is plain to see. They keep going back and forth to the waiting room and often return disappointed. Some resort to humour to deal with these situations. Thus, during our research period, JAP 3 had to deal with an offender who had obtained an electronic monitoring measure in lieu of his imprisonment sentence but had never sent the JAP the documented proof pertaining to his circumstances that he had promised, did not work. He had also failed to start paying damages and, according to the probation officer's report, still manifested great hostility, and aggressiveness even against her and, on top of this, was not even present for his hearing. The prosecutor jokingly said: 'I would be kind of tempted to request you revoked this measure!'; a comment which sent the JAP into a fit of giggles.

We also saw on several occasions that the offender, albeit present, was clearly on such a collision course that he actually considered this recall to prison as a good outcome. As an example, during a JAP 1 hearing, we saw a heroin addict who had committed multiple offences, and entered the room, displaying all the signs of withdrawal. He had already been sent back to prison for a short time in the course of a 'short incarceration order' after an umpteenth relapse. The JAP was wondering whether recalling him would be a good idea:

JAP: What do you think?

Probationer: It would be better for me to stay in jail until I get better.

Overall, if JAPs are 'good judges' when they deal with breaches, it is plain that the justice system they operate in is far from perfect.

3. The limits of this fair justice

The French criminal justice system has so far been based on a principle of individualisation of sentences (Saleilles, 1898) and of their implementation (Créan-Rivette, 2005). This is reflected in the law: article 132-24 of the penal code expressly refers to it. Contrary to their Anglophone counterparts, French lawyers are not shocked by the important discretionary power that their judges have when making their decisions. Like them, however, they do not seem to realise that there may be miscarriages of justice being committed in the decisions dealing with breach cases. Conversely, they are fully aware of the irrational delays between a given situation (for instance breach) and the decision they are eventually able to make.

a. JAP discretionary power: positive or negative?

Discretion is 'the freedom, power, authority, decision or leeway of an official, organisation or individual to decide, discern or determine to make a judgement, choice or decision, about alternative courses of action or inaction' (Gelsthorpe & Padfield, 2003:3).

Over the last decades, many jurisdictions, particularly Anglophone ones, have manifested a strong opposition to courts' discretionary sentencing power and have endeavoured to reduce it in a number of ways. Two fundamentally divergent reasons can explain this opposition. This movement has first been supported by punitive policies with complex causes themselves (Garland, 2001). With this in mind, the main goal is to make sure that courts are not too lenient with offenders (for England and Wales, see e.g. Thomas, 2003; for the U.S. see: Greene, 2002). France has not completely escaped this particular evolution, with for instance its mandatory minima for recidivists (Herzog-Evans, 2007 and 2009 a).

The second cause of the opposition against Courts' discretionary power is to be found in the desire to prevent discrimination (Blumstein et al., 1983; Tonry, 1996). This was at the root of the Consistency in Sentencing European Recommendation n° R(92) 17. This recommendation has had real influence in Europe, but none whatsoever in France. For instance, French criminal law manuals never mention it. Unsurprisingly the JAPs who we interviewed were totally oblivious to the risk of discrimination that they might manifest towards probationers. This risk has hardly ever been studied in France (but see Tournier and Robert, 1991) but has been elsewhere, including in the sentences' implementation phase (Lewis et al., 2006).

In our opinion, if the consistency in sentencing movement has had such an impact on the Anglophone world, it is because, beyond the aforementioned factors, in a common law system, courts do have powers which are by far superior to those they would enjoy in a written law system. In France, as in other written law systems, the need to control courts' power was never as strong, as the law already strictly framed criminal law and the principle of legality forbade courts to interpret and implement the law other than very strictly and even more so to create legal rules. JAPs may have an important discretionary power and we have indeed seen that the principle of the individualisation of sentences does allow them to choose measures and decide on the obligations attached to them according to the personality and the circumstances of the offender. Still, in doing so, they are strictly bound by the provisions of the law, which does go into great detail.

In addition, French judges are strongly persuaded that the risk of discrimination is being neutralised, for the most part, by the virtuous principles of individualisation and personalisation. In this respect, it is interesting to note that the advantages of probation officers' discretionary power is currently being rediscovered in England and Wales (Deering, 2011) after having been reduced by an inaccurate interpretation of what 'What Works' programmes entail. In fact, the What Works movement does emphasise the utmost importance of adapting supervision to the person's level of risk, of treating the exact criminogenic needs that each person presents and of adapting to his/her receptivity (Andrews & Bonta, 2010). In practice, there is indeed a collective dimension to programmes (group work or modules) but it does not mean that they must be 'one size fits all'.

On the contrary, justice, fairness and legitimacy inevitably lead to tailoring a decision to the person's context rather than forcing onto him/her a rough and ready measure. The more one takes a person's circumstances into account the more this person will tend to feel that he/she has been treated fairly. We know that people comply more with decisions they consider to be fair (Bezenko, 2011; McIvor, 2010; Padfied et al., 2012). In this respect, the judicialisation which occurred in 2000-2004 is reassuring: all the known parameters of legitimate and fair decision-making seem to be present: there is a hearing that the probationer can attend; he can thus express himself; has time to do so; can be assisted by an attorney; he can access the file; he can appeal the decision and can appraise the highest court (Court of cassation) if the appellate court decision does not satisfy him. The behavioural dimension of legitimacy, that is, Judges really listening to the '*justiciable*' and showing him/her respect (Tyler, 2012) was visibly present in most hearings we saw. JAP actually manifest a truly 'therapeutic', and to a lesser degree, problem-solving (Burke & Leben, 2007; Herzog-Evans, 2011d) attitude. This is particularly essential with sanctions (Collins, 2007; Digard, 2010c).

Because JAPs focus on the end result – desistance – they think that it is only by individualising and personalising their decisions that they will be efficient. Unfortunately, the French criminal justice system does not allow them to efficiently adapt to the concrete needs of offenders.

b. Lack of time

If JAPs focus to such a degree on the meaning of measures and decisions, it may be in part because they are alas conscious that, the criminal justice system is too often responsible for their loss of meaning.

By attending hearings, and even more so by coding rulings, my team and I were repeatedly exposed to situations where the person had been charged with continually breaching his/her obligations, not attending his/her meetings with the probation officer and this for months and sometimes years since the sentence was passed and even more so since the offence had been committed. An example can be found with one particular person who had been convoked for a recall hearing in 2011. This was for violations occurring in 2010 of a sentence which had started being executed in 2009 but was pronounced in 2008 for an offence committed in 2007. In one particular case the offender had been sentenced to six probation orders, two of which the very same day by the same court and the JAP was apprised of his reoffending – and had thus received a seventh probation order; none of the six former probation orders had led to a single meeting with a probation officer; none had led to a single report by the probation service; and in fact none had even started to be implemented. What can possibly be 'the meaning' of situations like this? In some cases, the offender, after all these months or years, may have turned his life around completely, and implementing a sentence at this point could cause more damage than good. On the other hand, like in the second case, his situation may have seriously escalated, and the criminal justice system is clearly partly responsible for this: it has neither controlled the offender nor reacted in time to his regression, nor helped him with his criminogenic needs.

The repetition of such situations made me very ill at ease. I did know that judges and the probation service were overloaded to the extreme; still, being constantly exposed to aberrant situations and to the total abandonment of offenders to their issues and difficulties – and, likewise, victims and society to the risks they thus encountered – was very disturbing. Yes court overload is one of the main causes of such delays: the JAPs interviewed by my team and I were in charge of 900 to 1,400 files; probation officers, supervised between 100 and 180 '*justiciables*'. However, their caseload does not explain all. Another major cause is the lack of communication and collaboration between JAPs and the probation service, which considerably slows down the circulation of information and their reaction time (see *infra*). Another cause is the extreme flexibility with which all practitioners deal with breach cases: delayed JAP appraisal by the probation service after numerous violations; '*recadrage*', and so on. If on principle this system is commendable, it would be much more credible and efficient if the '*recadrage*' occurred a lot earlier, if JAPs were systematically informed, and preferably, when needed, by phone or in person rather than on APPI the server which JAPs fully consult when they have the time. Better still, ideally, and much like in PSC, it would be indispensable that supervision started immediately or extremely fast after the sentence is passed and did not take the current usual shape of a merely 'administrative supervision' or something akin to it, where meetings are rare and can be merely formal, without much if any support with criminogenic needs or problem-solving.

c. Lack of means

We shall address the issue of supervision credibility *infra*. Let us nonetheless immediately stress that supervision '*à la française*' more often than not takes the following shape: very few meetings; no risks and needs assessments; no evidence-based practices; no evaluation to gauge whether or not it works; an overall philosophy whereby the probationer has to show his/her own ability to desist and is not supported (Herzog-Evans, 2012 a and forthcoming a).

Practitioners do not only have an exceptionally heavy caseload; they also have terribly dire work conditions, something we shall also return to. When I did field work in a Parisian region tribunal, here is what I saw: the minuscule window of the JAP's office would no longer be open; the only lavatory that worked in the whole tribunal was situated on the sixth floor; another one situated on her floor leaked out into the corridor where '*justiciables*' were waiting for their divorce cases to be dealt with; printers were constantly out of order; scanners had been out of order for months, never having been repaired; heavy parcels would not be posted by the mail services as we mentioned above even if they concerned dangerous offenders; there was no money left in the tribunal past the first trimester to pay psychiatrists experts that the JAP were by law required to appraise of the risk assessment of sexual and violent offenders (see Koskas, forthcoming) and so on.

Even in wealthier tribunals, there were simply not enough resources for the criminal justice system to be credible. Thus, unless an offender was clearly dangerous, or if he/she abandoned his/her residence without notifying the JAP or the probation service, very little was done to actually find him/her. He/she would be registered on the 'researched offenders registry' but would most of the time be arrested following another offence, in the course of a police road control or by sheer luck.

The issue of the treatment of alcoholics is a good example, which is unfortunately bordering on a caricature. The French legal system does not allow the JAPs or any other court of law to forbid an alcoholic to drink. Article 132-45 of the penal code, which lists all the obligations courts can choose from, only allows them to prohibit – and this is not a joke even though it sounds like one – this person from going to pubs and cafés. In other words, he/she will be legally compliant with his/her obligations if he/she buys enormous quantities of alcohol in the local supermarket. Indeed, the offender might be considered as having 'notoriously bad behaviour' (see, for parole, article 733 of the PPC and for other measures article D 49-24 of the PPC). Still, as this concept is so vague and hence is in violation of the principle of legality, it is seldom used by the courts. In any case, it does not send a clear message to offenders. Indeed, alcohol is a legal drug which can be purchased in supermarkets without any condition other than being of age.

Still, not giving people who suffer from this terrible addiction a clear message constitutes, in our opinion, a shameful along with a ridiculous abstention. In such a context, it is not surprising that France has not bought the existing technologies which allow for the measuring of whether offenders drink (Feuvrel et al., 2008 [37]; Boelens, 2009). Instead, probationers are sent, in the best of cases, to their local laboratory for blood tests, thus making it easy for someone else to go in their stead. Since JAPs cannot forbid offenders from drinking alcohol, when they then read the results judges are simply checking whether the results are 'in the norm', which is not a legally predictable criterion. Moreover, some judges have no idea how to read these blood tests. It is true that constant offender monitoring does contribute to the aforementioned revolving-door phenomenon since it sends many of them back to prison. Nonetheless, and conversely, the French approach totally abandons people who have an addiction to alcohol. This tells a lot of about the extreme poverty of France's criminal justice system, but also, in the case of alcohol, of its refusal to seriously tackle this issue, probably due to a collective cultural blindness.

This lack of desire to be efficient is also present with some of the JAP's partner agencies. Such is the case with The Mail (*La Poste*). This service is undergoing a slow but continuous privatisation process. As a result the very notion of public service and the former culture of result (where mailmen worked hard to find the addressees) has been replaced by differential treatment of clients: those who can pay for it can opt for a 'delivery guaranteed' system; the others have to make do with the minimum service which is less and less reliable. There is also no longer an incentive for staff to do their best in order to dispatch the mail to its addressee. Today, managerial demands (round length, and so on) prevail (Malaval, 2010). JAPs are at the forefront of the consequences this can have on probationers and many of them did complain about it during their interviews. If the envelope does not specify the letter which designates the particular building where the probationer lives, if his name has been deleted from his letter box – a frequent occurrence in some places – thousands of letters never reach their addressee. Technically speaking, probationers could be held in violation, since they do not appear to live at the address which they gave the court or probation service.

'You have to realise that we end up incarcerating people because The Mail does not do his job any longer!' (JAP 19).

---

37. V. see the video by one of these firms: http://www.youtube.com/watch?v=RVrn4J32KLM – accessed on September 9, 2013.

Other agencies with which JAPs must work can also create serious problems as a result of their intransigence. For instance, I learnt that the Parisian Treasury refused to let offenders pay their day-fine by instalments: it was all or nothing. Benevolent JAPs had to suggest that offenders would first save money and then pay the whole sum. This, however, delayed compliance with the court decision, which could be demobilising for offenders. We also know that even if a 2003 'Sarkozy law' (Sarkozy, 2003) allows a court to parole a foreign offender on French soil and thus suspend his/her ban from French territory, prefectures, i.e. the services in charge of delivering documents allowing foreigners to stay in France, often refuse to do so.

However, on occasions, JAPs are indeed responsible for the deficiencies of the criminal justice system.

d. Presumption of innocence in breach cases and the burden of proof

I have often advocated that sanctions in the sentences' implementation phase should be treated in the same vein as the sentencing phase, whether from the substantial point of view (for instance with the rule *ne bis in idem*: Herzog-Evans, 1999 b; or with the principle of legality: Herzog-Evans, 2012-2013 a) or from the procedural point of view.

With regard to the latter, if French law does organise a fair trial in such cases, it is however at fault when it comes to respecting the presumption of innocence principle, whereas the risk of committing a miscarriage of justice is just as real in probation as it is in the former phases of the criminal process. Judges and attorneys should be more careful than they actually are and should keep their minds open.

Attending hearings showed my team and I that in most cases, attorneys opt for a collaborative form of defence. This might indeed be the best approach in most cases, for instance when the offender has been elusive, but does bring the long awaited documented proof that is required of him/her because he/she was coached by an attorney. In addition, the attorney will often find excuses or mitigating circumstances for his/her client, by explaining his/her difficult financial or family circumstances, his/her alcohol or drug relapse, and so on. When, however, the offender denies having committed what he/she is charged with or has a different perception of how it happened, an adversarial stance would be more adapted. After all, the burden of the proof that the offender has not complied with his obligations should be placed upon the prosecutor; the offender should not be legally bound to prove he/she did not commit the violation.

Not one single interviewed judge mentioned that there was a risk of sending an innocent back to prison. When the question was broached with a handful of them, they admitted that offenders who were charged with committing an offence should be deemed innocent until sentenced by the sentencing court. As we have indeed seen, the law allows the court to revoke a measure because of the offender's 'bad behaviour' (PPC, art. 733 and D 49-24), which the Court of cassation jurisprudence has sometimes tolerated (Cass. Crim. 28 mars 2001, n° 00-82.284, NP; Cass. Crim. 21 mai 2003, n° 02-81.861, *Bull. crim.*, n° 106). Still, this is not the issue which we are trying to raise here: i.e. the risk that for a violation of the obligations, which will not be referred to the sentencing court, but only to the JAP, the person has actually not violated said obligation at all or it happened differently.

In the case of remission and furlough, things are even more critical. For these cases, there is no hearing even for breach cases (PPC, art. 712-5) and the offender is not even seen at any point (although it is legally possible it is extremely rare: see PPC; art. D 49-28, paragr. 3), nor defended by an attorney. Moreover, the JAP is usually appraised by the prison governor (PPC; art. 721, paragr. 3) – or, in practice by the clerk service of the prison (*greffe* – see Poinsignon, 2013) – who will have established, so to speak, the reality of the violation based on exceptionally loose investigation techniques and rules (Herzog-Evans, 2012-2013 b). The JAP will rule in a room where the prosecutor, the prison governor and several prison officers are present. Together they form a commission called the CAP (*commission de l'application des peines*); nobody is present to defend the offender's point of view. There is no doubt that France is at risk of being deemed in violation of article 6 of the Human rights convention as was formerly the case with the United-Kingdom [38].

JAPs also spend little time processing cases during the CAP, which does not leave time for doubting the facts as they are presented by the prison service. Besides, JAPs are placed in a difficult psychological situation: CAP are held within the prison walls and are surrounded by prison staff.

Coding the 292 rulings which pertained to sanctions was just as discouraging. Only one of them mentioned the principle of the presumption of innocence and decided not to revoke the measure. It would thus seem that JAPs are totally unaware of the risks. However, one should be cautious when interpreting these results. We were first told that on the aforementioned listserv '*Justpeines*', JAPs and prosecutors frequently discuss the presumption of innocence issue. Moreover, a number of interviewees did mention how ill at ease they were that the law allowed them to appraise themselves of

38. EHRcourt, *Campbell & Fell v/ U.K*, 28 June 1984, Serie A, no 80; EHRcourt, *Ezeh et Connors v/ U.K*, 15 July. 2001, applic. nos 39665 and 40086/98; EHRcourt, Gr. Chamber., *Ezeh & Connors v. U.K*, 9 Oct. 2003, applic. nos 39665 and 40086/98.

cases, even breach cases (PPC, art. 712-4). In order to attempt to overcome this difficulty, JAPs refuse to appraise themselves of breach cases and when they are informed by the probation service, they refer the case to the prosecutor and let him/her determine whether he should appraise them. However, this is a meagre procedural protection which also has a negative impact: it further slows down the process. In fact, in 63.7% of the rulings JAPs had actually appraised themselves of the case.

Whilst self-appraisal might be legally admissible when the offender is asking for release, it also violates the presumption of innocence principle in breach cases. This procedural context also leads to substantial difficulties. Firstly, it is conducive of a culture whereby practitioners focus first and foremost on obtaining documented proof and more often than not forget about the essence of the case, that is, offender supervision and the end result of the measure. This is also the unsurprising effect of the lack of resources and of criminological knowledge, even if some practitioners are aware of the aforementioned unfortunate consequences. Secondly, it is obvious that a great number of offenders do not read or write easily and that they have, as a result, developed elusive tactics. Focussing on documented proof is indeed coherent with the judicial context – one needs documents in the file and these should be presented to all parties to the trial [39] – but it does create a host of legal, human and concrete difficulties.

I. A good understanding of denial

Practitioners' lack of criminological training and ten years of punitive policies has had an impact: JAPs tend to focus on what is known in France as 'the person's position as of the offence' (Herzog-Evans, 2012 e). In fact, this focus is even stronger amongst probation officers, and this is in direct line with the increased 'prison thinking' which has contaminated supervision since probation services were annexed by the prison services in 1999. This conquest has had a progressive impact on their profession and has, in particular, led to the regression of social work and an exaggerated focus – but as we have seen a purely formal one – on whether the offender does comply with his obligations with the ultimate goal of preventing reoffending (Herzog-Evans, forthcoming a). This has, *inter alia*, led to the elaboration of a so-called risk assessment tool, which contains an entire section pertaining to 'the person's position as of the offence', even though the literature has now shown that denial, whether total or partial, minimisation, or rejecting respon-

39. This in turn creates a vicious circle: for instance in Paris and PACA (South East) regions there are organised trafficking of documents such as false job contracts.

sibility onto the victims are not predictive of a higher risk of reoffending and are not obstacles to treatment (Nunes et al. 2007; Yates, 2009; Andrews et al., 1990; Beech et al. 2009). This leads to an equally erroneous focus, whether in their interviews or in their reports on 'the person's position as of the offence' and their causal circumstances (Neuilly, 2010).

JAPs are not subjected to this institutional pressure and are consequently less amenable to this recent trend. Nonetheless, as we shall see, some of them do focus on the 'the person's position as of the offence'. Moreover, with some categories of offenders, such as violent or sex offenders, the law requires that they mandate an expert in order to assess the offender. These experts are for the most part psychiatrists – sometimes psychologists – and most 'assess' based solely on their clinical experience (Morali et al., 2011 ; Baratta et al., 2012). Indeed, this is despite the fact that the literature has long shown that unstructured clinical assessment leads to numerous errors due to heuristic and cognitive biases and because practitioners do not refer to valid items (e.g. Meehl, 1954; Ennis & Litwack, 1974; Blackburn, 1993). Most unstructured experts' reports occasionally refer to 'the person's position as of the offence' and it is obvious that this item constitutes, in their mind, the core elements of their risk assessment (Herzog-Evans, 2012 e). It is therefore inevitable that JAPs would be influenced by these constant – and increased given that the law has gradually made risk assessment mandatory in a rising number of cases – peremptory albeit erroneous references to denial or minimisation. This explains why over the last few years we have noticed a clear change in the way hearings are conducted. Most hearings start with a reminding of the offence and with the JAP asking the offender what his/her position is in this respect. Even if these never take much of the hearing time, it has nonetheless become a systematic ritual.

An important question relates to whether or not the addition of data (via the probation reports, the experts' reports, and the hearings) which focus on 'the person's position as of the offence' influences their decisions? As previously mentioned, offenders' questioning as to this position only takes up a small part of the hearing, usually at the beginning of it. Without exception, all JAPs then turn towards the future and concentrate on the offender's release plan, his/her supervision, and the psycho-social information which the law requires them to obtain (: work, training, education, housing, treatment, family, and so on). The offender is asked to provide documented proof and to try to assess how committed to desisting as opposed to offending he is.

The interviews also showed that only 43.2% of the JAPs actually thought that denial was an important decision factor, whereas 56.7% said that it was a complex issue but never constituted a reason to deny release. Thus only a minority, albeit a significant one, felt that denial, and the 'the person's position as of the offence', are important circumstances:

'Yes it is important, especially with sex offenders' (JAP 8; JAP 14) 'or domestic violent offenders' (JAP 20).

Only a very small minority told us that it was a decisive factor:

'I have this inmate who has been sentenced for domestic violence against his spouse and the expert's report is really bad. During the hearing he only talks about himself. He says nothing about the victim, which the expert has noticed. I denied him release based on this even though there were other positive elements in his file. I ruled that he had to work on his position as of the victim. And now he's just made another application. Apparently, he has started to see a psychologist. But during the CAP, I granted him even less remission than what the prosecutor advocated. Conversely, I have this youngster who is going to be traumatised until the end of his life because he has caused an accident. He really is emotional and gets treatment. This case is totally different. He heavily feels the weight of his responsibility and I have actually mentioned this in my ruling and have even submitted him to treatment for his own good' (JAP 62).

'What I am interested in is to see how the person perceives things afterwards; how he understands why he committed the offence and puts it into perspective in view of his priors' (JAP 71).

Conversely, other JAPs totally rejected any influence of 'the person's position as of the offence' on their decisions. One of them (JAP 3) aptly referred to the Court of cassation jurisprudence which has clearly stated that denial was not a legal criterion for rejecting a release application [40].

Two other JAPs pointed towards the possibility that a person might actually be innocent which meant it was not prudent to base one's decision on such a criterion. In this respect, we saw during the hearings and heard JAPs confirming in their interviews, that once the sentence has been passed, it is final and if the person denies his/her guilt then he/she should have appealed. They refuse to rule on the person's guilt and explain to probationers that they have to do their job and that they can only reasonably do this based on judicial truth. The most frequent attitude consists of asking the offender for his/her point of view about the offence during the hearing, but to then base the decision on other factors:

'Denial must never be a decisive factor if all the lights are green' (JAP 7).

---

40. Cass. Crim., 25 Nov. 2009, n° 09-82.971, *Bull. crim.*, n° 197, *Ajpénal* 2010, 90-91, comments M. Herzog-Evans, *RSC* 2010, 645, comments P. Poncela; Cass. Crim., 3 Feb. 2010, n° 09-84.850, *Ajpénal* 2010, 334-336, comments M. Herzog-Evans.

The research yielded fascinating findings: it showed that JAPs have a rather refined understanding of the psychological mechanisms of denial and that this explains why they do not consider it to be too important. They understand that denial is mostly caused by shame and that it is very difficult to come out of it:

'I accept denial… [it]can be caused by shame' (JAP 10).

'I have this probationer who screams that he is innocent to the point where we start having doubts. Except he did confess in front of the investigating judge, and then recanted. In front of the investigating judge he said: 'with my co-inmates it's just impossible to be a sex offender so I say I didn't do it' and 'with my family it's impossible too so I said I didn't do it.' So we know if he's in denial it's because of his family and we understand that this is not a reoffending factor. On the contrary, it shows that they are ashamed' (JAP 11).

'As far as I am concerned it is not essential. I can be satisfied with a pretend acknowledgement. One realises that having committed horrific acts is too difficult to take responsibility of and that we cannot blame them for that. That is for us, it is not because the person is in denial of the offence that the risks of reoffending are more important' (JAP 16).

Some JAPs referred, as we have seen, to legal reasoning. Like many attorneys, they considered denial to be a legal right.

'It is a very delicate matter as after all one may well consider himself innocent, even when one has been sentenced. As of discrediting the victim (: 'he had disrespected me with his look M'ster Judge') and minimising ('raping, raping, that's going too far, I just inserted a finger and also I was trashed') are classic defence mechanism' (Jap 56).

'As far as I am concerned, denial is a vested right. In such cases I tell offenders that they are totally entitled to their own feelings, but that I have to implement the 'judicial truth'. They will accept this much better, and also in any case they won't budge and I shan't either' (JAP 61).

Other JAPs mentioned the likelihood that offenders will feed them the expected lies, after have been coached by their attorney or know the drill. For this reason 'the person's position as of the offence' is nothing but an orchestrated choreography and is pointless.

'I remember this gendarme who had raped and the expert report was very negative. The first was negative that is, but he had asked for a second one and this time it was much more positive. He had been cunning enough to understand how to talk in front of the next expert' (JAP 64).

Conversely denial can be mere posturing destined to better present the offender's release application:

'Minimising the offence is only fair since the JAP will rule on releasing or not. Discrediting the victim is of course something else and this would make me harsher and would mean I would not grant the application. Denial is more complicated' (JAP 36).

As previously stated, we now know that denial can actually be, in some cases, more positive than admission of one's guilt, particularly for high risk offenders (Nunes et al., 2007). Luckily JAP 49 had benefitted from adequate training. She confessed that this had changed her opinion. Prior to her training, she said she paid a lot of attention to 'the person's position as of the offence' and in particular whether or not it consisted of denial, because she had worked in long term sentences' prisons where most high risk offenders were incarcerated. Her instinct told her that this did not augur well in terms of reoffending. After her training she radically changed her position.

JAP 9 actually had a positive view on denial:

'I tell myself that denying is a protective factor' (JAP 9).

Interestingly JAP 9 also told us how she dealt with offenders in denial. Without having read Marshall (Marshall et al., 2001), she spontaneously followed his very efficient (Serra and O'Brian) clue:

'Tell them: 'OK you deny the offence, still there is a problem. Surely you accept that.' And if they accept that then we can move on to something else'.

She also added:

'Sometimes you hit a wall, especially when the offence is very ancient and they have built this story in their heads. We do not have the time to start all over; this is a therapist's job'.

Judges are legitimately persuaded that one can work with an offender in denial:

'Denial is not necessarily synonymous with reoffending and can allow for the offender to be supervised upon release and to protect the victim by imposing bans or by making the offender pay damages' (JAP 15).

It was important to confront what the JAPs said they did and thought with their rulings. These rulings revealed that JAPs hardly ever took 'the person's position as of the offence' into consideration. More importantly they only mentioned it when they grant a measure; not when they reject an application as one might have expected. Decisions granting a measure (release or the conversion of the custodial sentence in the context of the procedure of article 723-15 of the PPC) refer to 'the person's position as of the offence' in only

8.6% of the cases. 0% of the decision which reject applications refer to it! This may be partly explained by the fact that JAPs usually have other – and sometimes plenty of – reasons to reject the application, including lack of credible project, the lack of documented proof, a remaining risk for the victim or the offender's behaviour during the hearing or whilst in custody. In other words, JAPs refer to 'the person's position as of the offence', although it does not influence their rulings, contrary to what attorneys think. In fact, they were nearly unanimous in complaining that JAPs focussed too much on denial. How can this contradiction be explained? It can probably be explained by the fact that attorneys are present during the hearings and hear JAPs asking their clients about his/her position concerning the offence, which puts them in an uncomfortable situation. When the JAP then goes on to reject the application, even if it is explained in the ruling by other factors, and particularly because of the lack of credible project or the remaining risk, attorneys remember the hearing and draw other conclusions. It is important at this point to understand how French rulings are drafted. By law, judges are required to first list all the data they have gathered (documented proofs; criminal records and so on), to present all the opinions they have heard (probation service's report, prosecutor's opinion, experts' written testimonies, and so forth) and to summarise what happened during the hearing. Inevitably they thus refer to the 'the person's position as of the offence'. However, this part of their ruling is not what they themselves make of the case based on all this data. Their own opinion is summarised immediately before their decision is expressed and usually takes the shape of one, generally two to three paragraphs. These are the only parts of the rulings which reveal why judges made such or such a decision. The rest is neutral presentation of the elements which were presented to them. For this reason, the percentages mentioned above (: 8.6/0%) were exclusively drawn from these final paragraphs. Despite the fact that attorneys should know better, they tend to get confused with what is said in the neutral presentation of the elements of the file and the final decisive factors which judges have actually made theirs.

Contrary to attorneys, and in line with the evolution of their own institution, probation officers generally have no objection with JAPs' focus on 'the person's position as of the offence':

'We are on a par with JAPs on this, because this is what we are required to pay attention too' (DPIP 6).

§ 2. JAPs as seen by their partners

At this point it is fitting to ask the question, how are JAPs perceived by other practitioners? According to one researcher (Mouhanna, 2011) there is currently a war going on between JAPs – who are unpredictable and irrational, and, on the other hand, the prison services, and particularly their probation service, which has uniform practices. Such a perception is contradicted by our research. However, we shall only elaborate on this subject in the next chapter: because of its complexity it requires separate developments. Indeed, none of the recent research focussing on probation (Lhuilier, 2007; Mouhanna, 2011; Dindo, 2011; Larminat, 2012) has raised the issue of JAPs and their other partners, particularly attorneys and prosecutors.

A. JAP according to attorneys

This research study has a section dedicated to attorneys. Thirty-two attorneys were interviewed and others were observed during the hearings. The aim was to determine what they had to say about JAPs and desistance. However, the research allowed us to present a striking classification between classic attorneys and holistic attorneys. Lastly, it yielded some tentative results pertaining to their usefulness in terms of offenders' defence.

1. Classic attorneys and holistic attorneys

From a legal viewpoint, the mission of attorneys is to assist rather than to represent (PPC, art. 712-6 and 712-7) (PPC, art. 712-13), with the exception of appeal cases (PPC, art. 712-13). This is a classic criminal justice mission: advising, gathering documenting proof, pleading and, occasionally appealing the first decision. The research showed that 'classic criminal attorneys' were patently different from 'holistic attorneys'. Just as a hospital midwife will be strikingly different from a homebirth midwife who supports the mother from the beginning of her pregnancy until several months after the birth, attorneys either provide a standard support which considerably varies in quality, or holistic and global support.

Classic penal attorneys represent by far the majority of cases (87.5%). Their knowledge of sentences' implementation varies considerably. Some are very well trained; others are completely ignorant; the majority fall into an intermediary grey area. Their knowledge of and commitment to the file follows a similar pattern. Many of these classic lawyers insist on the necessity for a speedy processing of cases – they deplore that it is not fast enough – and on their financial (legal aid amount is insufficient; it is very difficult to actually get paid) and material ordeals (e.g. having to travel far or to remote places – when they take place in prison – to access hearings). They have a limited knowledge of the desistance process. They also hold traditional views on what their professional obligations should be. They consider that their role is: to advise in the case or the file; in our domain, to tell the offender which measure (conditional release, electronic monitoring, semi-freedom, others) will stand a better chance of being accepted by the judge who is appraising their case; to coach their client how to best behave during the hearing; to convince him/her that he/she has to bring the documented proof demanded by the JAP. In terms of the latter, they do not seek the documents themselves – but for those held at the JAP's office, which they can access – they expect the client to provide them on his/her own. If he/she does not do this, it is his/her loss, nobody else's. On the day of the hearing, their plea is often devoid of passion, descriptive, and sometimes insignificant. It is also swift and adds little, if anything, to the understanding of the case. They perceive success as obtaining what they asked for, but quickly forget about their client after they have done their job. These attorneys are not always bad lawyers; and all legitimately try and keep their business afloat. They also try to emotionally protect themselves from the difficult situations they encounter. Unfortunately some of them do not seem to fully understand what the best interest of their clients is:

'One of my clients confided in me. He has asked this attorney's collaborator to be present at his recent hearing because he feared– these are his own words – that this attorney's 'charisma' might irritate the judge. What I think he was referring to was the classic ego of the local big criminal courts names who have no idea about the collaborative work one must do with the judge. This big name must have previously tried to be his usual clever self with the judge at his client's expense' (Attorney 16).

A significant minority (12.5%) are **'holistic attorneys'**. They see their job through radically different lenses. Along the same line as the American 'comprehensive law' (Daicoff 2011 a) or 'therapeutic jurisprudence' (Winnick & Wexler, 2003; Wright, 2010) movements – both linked to a school of thought which tries and humanise justice, its impact on citizens and outcome (Daicoff, 2011 b) – these lawyers have, as Susan S. Daicoff advocated (Daicoff, 2006) reinvented their craft. These holistic attorneys, when compared to their more classic peers, seem to be happier and even radiant, whilst, even though they do face the same financial and material ordeals, they never mention them. They thus seem to escape criminal lawyers' well-known stress, as studied in North-America (see *inter alia*: Benjamin et al., 1990; Dugin, 2004; Silver et al., 2004), but virtually ignored in France (but see Kneusé, 2003; Conseil National des Barreaux, 2010). This can have serious consequences such as depression, alcoholism and drug addiction. Some are even affected by vicarious trauma. The author maintained regular contact with four of these holistic attorneys (attorneys 2, 4, 16, and 18) in order to better assess what they might be adding to the job. The first difference with their colleagues was that they start preparing release or sentence management from the very beginning and usually as soon as the sentence is passed. They already start at that point in time to advise, coach and prepare their clients for their future in the community. This meant that they might continue advising their client in some cases for a great number of years. They also work in partnership with their client's families and coach and advise them. In some cases, I was struck by their incredibly deep knowledge of the family history, circumstances, psychological balance and links, and so on. They would meet family members regularly, gather documents; meet their clients in the attorneys' visitation room of the prison, and sometimes drive hundreds of miles in order to do so, thus becoming regular TGV (*high speed trains*) or plane passengers. They would also get in contact with the probation service(s), the JAPs, the prosecutor, charities and third sector agencies, Job-Centre plus administrations and so on. They would not hesitate to pester these agencies and their staff as they would not take no for an answer nor let these practitioners ignore their request for documents and other information. They would, in short, spend months or even years, preparing the offender's release project, in collaboration with him/her, his family and loved ones, and relevant agencies. Because they would know their client and his circumstances to a T, they would be sure to draft a perfectly credible tailored release plan for him/her and his/her family. They would never bow down to their clients' or families' unrealistic chimera, but would, au contraire, with time and collaborative coaching, firmly yet with care and support lead them to the right application. 'No this measure is not for you' or 'if you embark on such a project I can guarantee you that it will be rejected'. This approach can make a big difference to their client's fate:

'You saw this young man, born in 1990, who last week or a fortnight ago found, thanks to his attorney [vocational training]. I think it's great. Perhaps this will be the right path, the right project for him and it's great that his attorney has managed to shake him up a bit before the hearing. Because had he had a different attorney, with a different personality, he would have come to the hearing with two or three pieces of paper and we would not have made much headway; whereas in this case, we did. I don't know, only future will tell, but I hope we made some headway' (JAP 40).

Holistic attorneys are also capable of deploying the full range of their humanistic competence even when they have only met their clients a short time before the hearing. One of these attorneys, attorney 16, showed the author a ruling by the sentences' implementation chamber of a Court of appeal which granted her client, a desocialised drug addict, a conversion of his custody sentence into a community work sanction with probation, this, in spite of the fact that he had formerly lied to the JAP. Contrary to what he had told the JAP, he had lost his job, had no more income and had split from his partner. He did obtain the conversion for a good part because he had come clean in front of the appellate judges – who, as an exception to the normal appeal procedure in such cases, had heard the offender – and secondly, because in view of his lack of employment, converting his sentence into community work made a lot of sense; both things which were stressed by the attorney during her plea. When the author asked her about this positive outcome here is what she said:

'I met this client one hour before his hearing! We still had time to work on his case, to assess his personal and professional situation. More importantly, I pushed him to face reality. I felt that he had to present himself 'naked' in front of his judges rather than remain trapped in his mesh of lies; that we would restore the judges' trust if we admitted to having sinned; and that we might be successful in making them see the case with a fresh outlook. So I presented his extreme psycho-social difficulties and explained, at the very beginning of the hearing that he was so demoralised that he had come to the hearing empty-handed; that he had lost hope (and it is true that this man had arrived defeated). But I added that one had to give him credit for his coming out as of his former lies, and that the very fact that he did admit to lying was significant, that it proved that he now faced reality. I then suggested that the best way forward was to convert the sentence and choose one that would not compromise this new dynamic. In short, I think that my part in this was in helping him to present his true self and to suggest he should admit he had lied and explain why he had lied. I knew he would thus truthfully face his judges and they would understand him. It also was to make his judges understand the value of this acknowledgement, what it meant in terms of accountability – he became more responsible by admitting to his lies and by presenting himself as he truly was – and also, to make them think in terms of another sentence than the one he was caught in' (Attorney 16).

Holistic attorneys also have remarkable expertise in sentences' implementation law. Just as remarkable is their understanding of the desistance process. During the hearings, they are efficient interlocutors for the JAP: they bring in a global yet detailed understanding of offenders' context, personality and past. They too present a narrative of this past, present, and future. Because they are also excellent lawyers, they can suggest elaborate legal constructions and analysis which greatly pleases judges and are both intelligent and convincing. The personal commitment to the file is absolute. They are authentically disappointed when they lose – which is probably less frequent – but when they do, they revert to a new plan or project. In most cases they already have a plan B up their sleeve:

'I remember this fantastic release project that I prepared in collaboration with a probation officer in X; an extraordinary scheme for a lifer. We truly worked in partnership. I had found this man a driving school where he would learn to drive in X and how for him to pass his driving test. I had found him a shelter and the plan was for him to ask for semi-freedom. So if you want, this was an A to Z construction of a release plan in terms of housing, work, and a driving licence since in X he would need to drive. It's like a turnkey project in a sense. It is very different from what a classic attorney will sit his butt on the chair in front of the JAP and will intervene in a dossier he has had no part in' (Attorney 18).

It is important to stress that beyond the classic/holistic attorney dichotomy, most classic criminal lawyers, similar to JAPs, are also keen to interact with '*justiciables*' and really want to help the people they are in charge of. They are very different from their American assertive, domineering and sometimes even provocative counterparts (Daicoff, 2006). Most French criminal lawyers are closer to the stereotype and want to 'protect the weak and helpless':

'I always wanted to do this job. It's a conviction and a passion for human beings. I love the law and I want to defend those who are weak and helpless' (Attorney 25).

Nonetheless, because of their commitment and efforts, holistic attorneys are also very different from classic attorneys in terms of what they expect from JAP.

2. Different expectations

Holistic attorneys expect much more from JAPs than other attorneys. They first and foremost want JAPs to be humane. Because they are themselves very committed and collaborative, they expect JAPs to likewise be committed and to meet the same standards they impose on themselves – to the point of being at times unrealistic:

'Some [JAPs] are attentive to [*justiciables*] and accept that attorneys can teach them something or two, that he can convince them, or, at least to discuss the option which I am putting on the table, even if they end up rejecting it. Others are in their ivory tower and just don't listen' (Attorney 18).

When judges do not meet their expectations, they can be particularly vindictive. According to one of them, courts of appeal are particularly disappointing:

'Apart from that I always had presidents of sentences' implementation chambers [of the court of appeal – hereafter CHAP] who were total assholes who did not have a clue, who would not even attempt to apply legal reasoning. In particular the president of the CHAP of X is clearly an old moron. Conversely the ideal CHAP are A and B. I also like C, even if I am not very successful there. Y I absolutely hate and the same with Z. I totally hate having to plea in front of D, really hate it!' (Attorney 18).

Opposite to this, **classic attorneys depict JAPs very favourably**. Most say that JAPs have all the qualities they can hope for in a JAP, and are good judges, humane, competent and aware of their client's problems, who nonetheless know how to set boundaries and are rational. Most say that they have hardly ever met a bad JAP. They seem to consider that JAPs are overall quite similar people:

'A good JAP or TAP is one who understands that the road from crime can be an extremely difficult one' (Attorney 10).

'It is a humane magistrate, who is aware of the difficulties that some '*justiciables*' encounter' (Attorney 23).

'It is a truly, really humane person' (Attorney 11).

'They are fair and unbiased' (Attorney 26).

'A good JAP will focus first on reinsertion and on preventing reoffending; individualise the sentence and be attentive to all parties' (JAP 22).

'Judges are truly all rather good. One cannot say that they are bad, lazy or crazy ones. Most of the time we have good judges so I have good relationships with them' (Attorney 17).

'Yes JAPs know what they are talking about' (Attorney 21).

However, some of their colleagues have a more nuanced perception of JAPs or refer to individual differences.

'There are JAPs who are very competent and highly committed. Others...' (Attorney 32).

'The new generations of magistrates are clearly more punitive than their older peers' (Attorney 10).

'You have some JAPs who are extremely competent people and extremely committed. You have others who have become JAPs without really wanting to be a JAP. You know, being a JAP is like being a Youth Judge, it's a highly demanding job and one must have chosen it in order to feel happy about it. Some people have enough psychology and humanity to be JAPs. Others would rather do property foreclosures' (Attorney 14).

Previously we discussed the issue of 'the person's position as of the offence' and mentioned that a significant number of attorneys complained that JAPs focussed too much on this factor. We also mentioned that they had a biased perception on this matter which was contradicted by JAPs' rulings. As a perception, however, it is an interesting subject. It does tell a great deal about how attorneys perceive their role in most cases, i.e. essentially defending the 'justiciable' during the hearing – which is where offenders are asked about their 'position as of the offence' – to the detriment of other forms of support and counsel.

'It is always 'yes but you are not working on your responsibility in this'' (Attorney 14).

Attorneys do share probation services' views however, specifically that over the last few years, and particularly since punitive policies have started affecting sentences' implementation – and even more so since the Pornic case – that JAPs have become more cautious and fear reoffending more than they used to. It is however difficult to distinguish whether this actually comes from a changed perception or whether it comes from the host of increasingly punitive legal reforms which have forced JAPs to become ever more cautious (Herzog-Evans, 2012-2013 a : 04.91-04.117).

Still, most lawyers, whatever their category, cannot help but have a biased perception of JAPs. All of them are in a position where they have to plead for their client. It is their job to take on their point of view and perception, even if only for the trial. When the project is badly packaged and their client presents a rather worrying profile, they still believe in him/her or want to believe in him/her:

'A good decision, that's a bad question because the good decision is the decision which goes according to my client's wishes [laughter]. Yes a good decision is a decision which grants what I asked for, but that's totally biased! [laughter] (Attorney 19).

'A good JAP is a JAP who really listens to the argument you make if it's a convincing one' (Attorney 28).

'A good JAP is a JAP who takes his responsibilities and gives a second chance to offenders who deserve it, yet is demanding when it comes to supervising them' (Attorney 30).

In short, all think a good decision is a decision which is favourable to their client – whether they had a significant role to play in this matter is another subject – and when that happens all attorneys including classic lawyers, are happy:

'When one obtains release for an inmate, one feels useful' (Attorney 20).

'An immense satisfaction' (Attorney 25).

'Definitely the satisfaction of having done my job!' (Attorney 28).

Holistic lawyers use even more passionate and even poetic words to describe their pleasure:

'The immense satisfaction of emptying the sea with a teaspoon!' (Attorney 2).

3. 'Even an appalling attorney is a useful attorney'

Let us first evoke a general impression drawn from twenty years of constant exposure to sentences' implementation and hearings. This author has always summarised attorneys' role in this field to her students with the following joke: 'even an appalling attorney is a useful attorney!' Indeed, the minimum requirement for an attorney is, with his mere presence, **to counterbalance the inevitable unbalance** between his client, on the one hand, and the two representatives of the judiciary, i.e. the JAP and the prosecutor. Offenders will enter the office of even the most neutral and benevolent JAP with the idea that it is 'them against me'. Just by being present, the attorney adds to the head count and evens it: it becomes two (attorney and offender) versus two (JAP and prosecutor).

'It's a counter-power' (Attorney 24).

Secondly, and *a minima*, attorneys will have lawyers' reflexes and, for instance, know that when an applicant asks the court to grant him/her something, he/she bears the **burden of proof**. For this reason a lawyer will make sure his/her client arrives with documented proof, whereas had this client been alone, he/she would probably not have brought anything. Most offenders are not very much at ease with documents and paperwork or might simply have forgotten them at home. In fact, four lawyers responded to our question pertaining to the best way in which to convince a judge with this simple exclamation: 'Documents!!' In fact all attorneys referred at one point or another to documented proof. Their role is thus:

'To present a solidly supported file and to advise on the best way to adapt the sentence' (Attorney 30).

We also saw in the course of numerous hearings that attorneys are often **translator-interpreters**, for their clients: they speak the same language as the judges; they have the same social background, have been on the benches of the same universities and usually speak grammatically very correct French. Besides, they understand legal language. Their client – and there the contrast is often striking – speak an obviously less refined and educated French; some have a characteristic 'ghetto' youth accent. The different languages clearly constitute a barrier between offenders and their judges. Some offenders never learnt, be it at home or at school that one stands before a judge with one's hands out of one's pockets, does not stoop nor chew on gum. All these language and social codes can be quickly taught to offenders by their attorney. In all cases, attorneys are indeed their clients' interpreters. They are the social equals of the judges.

An attorney, who on top of this is competent, at least from the legal viewpoint, can also present a **well drafted written application** which contains legal arguments and solid legal reasoning. He can also prep his client so that he/she does not ruin his/her chances when speaking in front of the judge.

'We have to make our clients understand what it is that is important to bring in front of the judge' (Attorney 23).

During the hearing a good understanding of the file and the offender allows them to be **useful justice auxiliaries** [41].

'It is about presenting his life, his school and professional background, his flaws, his desire to turn his life around, his psychological treatment' (Attorney 25).

However, if one refers to their own criterion for success, i.e. winning their case, **our research did not show that their presence had a decisive impact**. It would have been too complex to try and determine whether they had played a significant part in the decisions to release, as too many parameters are involved in such matters. In addition, we were also unable to attend enough hearings to convincingly measure their impact at that point, nor assess how much input attorneys had had in the construction of their clients' project. However, our perception is that holistic attorneys are particularly efficient Despite the limitations of such an exercise, it was decided to try and measure whether attorneys made a statistically significant difference in terms of breach cases. Indeed, in such matters, nothing in the cases seemed to clearly distinguish the offenders who were assisted during the hearings from those who were not. Based on all the breach cases, 19.1% only had an attorney (versus 41.9% in other types of files); 55% were present but had no attorney (versus 4.9% in other types of files); 48.5% were not present (versus 0.2% in other types of files). When an attorney was present, recall was pronounced in 42.5% of breach cases; in 27.7% of the cases, *'justiciables'* obtained one or another more favourable sanction than recall; in 29.6% of the cases there was no sanction at all. Conversely, when the offender was present but had no attorney, he/she was recalled only in 34.7% of the cases, obtained a lighter sanction in 36.8% of the cases and was not sanctioned in 29.4% of cases.

41. In France, attorneys are called 'justice auxiliaries' which conveys the idea that they are not only counsels, but they also help with the judicial process itself.

Table 1 : Breach procedure outcome and offender defence

	A : Full recall to prison	B : Lighter sanction	C : No sanction	**Total of favourable decisions (B+C)**
Attorney and offender present	42.5	27.7	29.6	**54.3%**
Offender present – no attorney	34.7%,	36.8%,	28.4%	**65.2%**
Offender absent	84%,	7.5%,	8.3%	**15.8%**

When reading these figures, one must bear in mind that the cases where an attorney was present were rather limited (19.1%) thus meaning that our sample was actually rather limited. Nonetheless, the abovementioned table suggests that when breached an offender fears better without an attorney than with one. More importantly, this table shows that offenders take inconsiderate risks by not being present at their hearings, as they are at a much higher risk of being fully recalled. How can one explain these results? As we have suggested elsewhere (Herzog-Evans, forthcoming c), there might be several explanations. Firstly, if the offender fares worse if he/she is not present at his hearing, it is, to a great extent because he/she is not able to present his/her case and to hope for an understanding of his/her situation – it is more difficult to care for an absentee – , albeit somehow disillusioned in some cases. The offender loses the chance to bring documented proof at the very last minute. He/she cannot explain his/her difficulties, his/her despairing state of mind, his/her relapse, to judges who, when they are directly exposed to it are usually extremely understanding. To sum up, it does not allow JAPs to be exposed to the person's humanity; these judges will only rule based on the cold and objective truth as is derived from the file; a truth which, in breach cases, is bound to appear negative. It may also be true that those who are not present at their hearing are often those who are also going down such a slippery slope – a 'regression' that Spanish researchers talk about (Cid & Tebar, 2012) – that in any case, little could have been done for them at that point in time.

Apart from these highly compromised cases, as stated earlier, nothing in the rulings revealed any significant difference in terms of pros and cons, risks and needs, or other factors, between those with an attorney present and those with no attorney present – bearing in mind, however, that these results were drawn from the rulings themselves and not from the files to which I had no access. Could it be that JAPs pity '*justiciables*' who have no counsel? Indeed, during the hearings my team and I noticed that JAPs' demeanour changed significantly when there was no attorney, whether the hearing and particularly in breach cases where the prosecutor was also present. They sounded and looked more neutral and seemed to embrace even more the role of an arbitrator between the two parties (the prosecutor and the offender). They would more consistently look straight at the offender whereas when the counsel was present, he/she sometimes took over completely and his/her client would not dare speak up. In such cases, the attorney was like a shield between the judge and the offender and the JAP tended to listen to and focus on the attorney and less on the offender – even if no JAP would go as far as to ignore the offender. Conversely, without an attorney, the offender could, as normally befits, occupy centre stage. Lastly, whereas with release and other favourable measures' applications, 'even a bad attorney is a useful attorney' given the role he/she can play in these procedures (see *supra*). Indeed, this is not the case when the stake is recall. The research suggested that in most cases, attorneys may not be sufficiently committed and sometimes not sufficiently competent. We also already mentioned that many opted for the same collaborative form of defence which they used in application cases, despite the fact that in a number of cases, a more pugnacious defence would have been preferable.

The American therapeutic jurisprudence doctrine has wondered attorneys' best attitude towards PSC should be (Boldt, 2002). In France, rather than an adversarial principle, it is the '*contradictoire*' principle which governs all types of procedures. Whereas the adversarial principle has a bellicose connotation, the principle '*contradictoire*' suggests a more peaceful and moderate balance between each party [42], which is indeed closer to problem-solving courts' procedures (Stobbs, 2013). American attorneys might have originally had a hard time understanding what their role should be when they had to assist offenders in cases where the judge were benevolent and caring. They had to learn to work more collaboratively (Daicoff, 2009). They should not be passive, however (McColl, 2002: 21); they just need to learn to behave differently in the courtroom. French attorneys were already prepared to navigate easily from one stance to another, sometimes aggressive (usually during the sentencing phase), other times collaborative, and, as we have seen for some of them, participative. For this reason, Arie Freiberg is perfectly

42. In France, the legal doctrine has not shown too much concern for the role of attorneys in sentences' implementation, but, rather for their competence in this legal field, which, until recently, was not even taught at university (Bianchi, 2005).

right in saying that continental legal systems are more adapted to problem-solving forms of justice (Freiberg, 2011).

To sum up, like JAPs, attorneys are sometimes a link in the chain which may support the desistance process. Another link may be the prosecutor who can also behave collaboratively.

B. JAP according to prosecutors

The research did not focus on prosecutors' role in supporting desistance. Whilst several French studies have recently dealt with prosecutors in general (Milburn et al., 2007 and 2010), none have specifically focussed on their role in sentences' implementation. An earlier study showed that the first reform which partially judicialised sentences' implementation (Law of June 15, 2000), was a shock to prosecutors as it went against their professional culture; one where offenders should not be released lightly, where they were first and foremost seen as a risk to society, and where after the sentence was passed it should be executed (Herzog-Evans & Péchillon, 2003). It seemed incongruous that offenders should be allowed to appeal JAPs' decisions and benefit from yet another fair trial. More than ten years after this reform, it seems to us that what was then perceived as intolerable, has now become the norm [43] for most prosecutors who work in a sentences' implementation office (*service de l'exécution des peines*). Indeed, they have fully embraced this new culture and, like the JAP, do become acculturated when they work in such offices. Our sample, so to speak, was however far too small (N13) to allow us to draw any clear cut conclusion. Our research did not focus on prosecutors but on how they perceived JAPs. Indeed, more research is needed in order to better understand who prosecutors are and whether they have indeed, as we are suggesting, become more aware of the desistance process and more favourable to supporting this process. This is the PhD subject of doctorate student Clémentine Danet. Milburn et al. (2007; 2010) showed that prosecutors oscillated between, on the one hand, an increasingly managerial and administrative culture, and, on the other hand, the culture of magistrates, which they also are, since they are trained in the same universities and in the same Bordeaux school as judges. Our study, which involved interviews with 13 prosecutors and observation of many others during hearings and CAP, confirmed Milburn et al.'s findings.

43. Although as I was finishing reviewing this book the current French government was considering going back to the previous era.

1. Different concerns

Milburn et al. (2007; 2010) revealed how much prosecutors' jobs had changed over the last few years. In particular, they are today first and foremost in charge of the smooth processing of cases throughout the penal factory lane and things are no different at the sentences' implementation phase. This, as well as governmental injunctions [44] have contributed to altering their original opposition to release measures and the aforementioned 'management of sentences'. In this respect, they are now on a par with JAPs. Conversely, most JAPs are still strongly opposed to factory-lane justice; they still choose quality over quantity, which does not mean they are totally immune to the need to **move the docket**. Many JAPs would like to have more time to better supervise probationers. In contrast with classic prosecutors, prosecutor 7, who had been a magistrate for thirty-four years, and in a sentences' implementation office for sixteen years, was the president of a rehabilitation and community sentences charity. He started his interview by saying that what he expected from his job was to 'deal with humans and not what we're currently supposed to do, i.e. managing stock'.

There was also a second difference JAPs and prosecutors: the culture of **partnership work.** Indeed, JAPs do have a host of partners. However, and we shall return to this, each one of their partners' work is usually done autonomously and without much if any contact between them. Everyone (: probation service, JAPs, medical doctors, third sector agencies, and so on) take up part of offender treatment but hardly ever collaborate. Leaving aside their clerk services JAPs work solitarily. In contrast with this, prosecutors are used to partnership work, starting with their own service. They also work collaboratively with other practitioners and agencies, such as, for instance, with the police. In the course of this research they mentioned that this was one of the major appeals of their job. This also explains, to some extent, why they are not annoyed when JAPs do not follow their opinion. Most understand that this is part and parcel of the daily judicial routine, and that judges and prosecutors each have their own job to do. They are perfectly at ease with institutionalised professional disagreement. Moreover it was striking to see that when they told interviewers about success stories, they usually referred to collective successes or to the criminal justice system's positive outcomes rather than to personal triumphs.

'Someone was supervised by the JAP as part of a probation order for a domestic violence offence. He was incarcerated after a series of probation

---

44. And in particular the Ministry of Justice circular of 27 June 2007 NOR: JUSD2007.30042C. It is important at this point to remind the reader that in France, prosecutors may be magistrates, but that they have to obey the Ministry of Justice's orders.

orders were revoked. We worked really hard when he was released in order to prevent him from reoffending. He was particularly angry with the criminal justice system and against his former partner and demanded to see his children. He had been quite capable, including whilst he was incarcerated, to threaten to kill his ex and their kids. So the prosecutor's office decided to work with everybody on this, the JAP, the probation service, the gendarmes, the youth judge, so that his release would take place under better auspices in order to prevent his reoffending and put simply from doing what he had said he would i.e. kill everybody. Today we have a situation where a little more than one year down the line, things are starting to get better, where he can see his children and there are no more threats. We went from weekly supervision by the probation service to something which is now more spaced out. He now has an appeased relationship with his ex-partner and this is indeed only because every single judicial partner has managed to sit around a table and make sure our decisions were compatible' (Prosecutor 10).

Other differences between judges and prosecutors are classic. Prosecutors' core mission is 'to **protect society's interests'** and to make sure the law is strictly implemented. Linked to these two core missions are the prevention of reoffending, preserving social order and peace and public security. This is also what they like the most:

'It's operating at the very heart of society' (Prosecutor 6).

Nonetheless, both during their interviews and the hearings, it appeared quite clearly that these magistrates now consider that 'society's interests' are not necessarily linked to sentences being served to the full. They now focus on the long term and cases as a whole and are unanimous in saying that a good decision is a decision which is 'understood by everybody', i.e. all judicial partners, the offender and which citizens would be able to understand:

'It is a decision which is legally sound, and understood; which makes sense in terms of the person's circumstances and personality' (Prosecutor 12).

Whilst prosecutors may now accept 'sentence management' and measures they are nonetheless much stricter and demanding than JAPs. Instead of being *a priori* against release, they now focus on the credibility of the offender's project, on the nature of the release measure, and on the obligations which are attached to it. However, when it comes to breach cases, one would have a hard time finding the same understanding which JAPs currently have. As far as they are concerned a new offence should systematically lead to recall; and the violation of obligations warrants recall as far as they are concerned in more cases than JAPs would actually agree on. Still, several of them (Prosecutors 4, 5 and 6) said that they would not jeopardise on-going desistance. None had however heard of desistance and their understanding of the desistance process was far less advanced than that of JAPs. They were also more demanding with probation services. They were virtually unanimous in deploring that probation services could not or would not do their job any longer, whereas JAPs, as we shall see, had more contrasted opinions and were more understanding.

However, like JAPs, prosecutors are magistrates. As a result, they have a lot in common.

2. But a similar passion

It is important to remind the reader that in France, prosecutors being magistrates, they can and more often than not do, transfer from judging positions to prosecutor positions. Such was the case for a number of JAPs who we interviewed (see Chapter 1).

In their interviews, prosecutors mentioned similar reasons to JAPs for choosing their current position. Likewise, many spontaneously – the question was open – mentioned as an example of something pleasant in their daily work, examples of '*justiciables*' who were not in a good place (delinquency, drug addiction, and so on) whom they saw again, this time totally transformed, in a better health and having ceased to offend. Again, like JAPs, they mentioned how deep and humanly rewarding their job is and how interesting it is to have daily contact with probationers. Prosecutor 10 actually wanted to 'cross the bridge' and become a JAP. Like JAPs, a minority (4/13) also referred to the intellectual interest of sentences' implementation's legal complexity. Even more so than JAPs (9/13), they stated that they are extremely passionate about their position.

Just like their judge colleagues, prosecutors were convinced that holding fair hearings is essential and believed in their values in terms of human and legal rights and in terms of the information that they yield – and as a result of public security. They confessed that many a time they changed their minds after such a hearing. Indeed, prosecutors are also focussed on flows and are less fundamentally opposed to processing cases without a hearing (hereafter HDC procedures: *hors débat contradictoire*, i.e. without an adversarial hearing). They did however understand that in certain cases they are useful. Nonetheless, most of them were strongly convinced that maintaining these hearings is a necessity. For this reason they were unanimously hostile to the current executive attempts to partly dejudicialise sentences' implementation via so-called simplified procedures where the JAP is marginalised and fair trial disappears. They were fully aware that this represents an executive attack against the judiciary in general and against the JAPs in particular and in this, they reacted as members of a common profession, that of magistrates, who share the same values, namely a fair trial and qualitative work.

They were even more unanimous against dejudicialisation than JAPs, although one must bear in mind that our sample was smaller:

'Definitely not! It's not the role of probation services, but it's exactly what the legislator wants though' (Prosecutor 10).

Speedy so called 'simplified' i.e. dejudicialised procedures which require a less thorough investigation – in some cases virtually none – do not seek the offender's collaboration and involvement – things are done for him/her not with him/her – who will be less, if at all, supported with their needs and problems once released. However, they can also be more constrained in some instances [45], which may strongly hurt their professional culture and ethics. They see quite clearly that these procedures can be dangerous in terms of reoffending and are not efficient in terms of rehabilitation. When the prison services drafted what would later become the Prison Law of 2009 they expected they could rely on prosecutors' obedience with the executive tradition. It was hoped that unlike JAPs, who are at least in theory independent, prosecutors would simply obey the orders they were given. The prison services forgot that prosecutors are pragmatists who happen to be in charge of public safety. As a result of this professional culture they have decided to use 'simplified' and speedy procedures with parsimony and to keep focussed on the ultimate goals as listed in article 707 of the PPC. Precisely, these goals – preventing reoffending, offenders' reinsertion, public safety, and victims' interest – are the exact opposite of so-called speedy procedures – which are designed exclusively to free prison space. If some prosecutors implement them in certain jurisdictions, it is only because the Ministry of Justice insists they should. They nonetheless only do so sparingly [46].

This is probably because they work in close collaboration with the JAP and because they share the same goals and passion, and that prosecutors are very positive about JAPs in general and of 'their' JAP in particular. They

45. Such is, in particular the case with a speedy release of offenders under electronic monitoring four months before the term of their sentence: investigation is minimal, the JAP does not intervene and there is no hearing; offenders are not in the least supported upon their release and have no obligations but are restricted to their home for a minimum of twenty hours a day. Here, the focus is not outcome; it is only to free another bunk bed in a cell (Herzog-Evans, 2012 d). In these procedures, the probation service does the preparatory work and the prosecutor makes the decision. Despite being called 'simplified' or speedy, these procedures are in fact just as complex as the regular judicialised procedures and are not faster. Such will also be the case if the current government's Bill is eventually voted by Parliament:. The plan is to make JAPs decide in the context of a CAP as they did before the 2000 and 2004 reforms, without the offender preparing a release plan, without him/her being present or represented by an attorney, and without any appeal being possible.

46. Only 528 offenders were thus released in 2011 and 624 in 2012. Direction de l'administration pénitentiaire, 2012 and 2013: 6.

also praise their decisions and how they justify them in their rulings. It is only in a handful of cases that they appeal JAPs' decisions – something which the JAP confirmed. They consider that JAPs do abide by the law and make fair decisions. As we suggested above this also reflects the notion that they are used to working collaboratively with a host of partners and to accepting that others might not share their opinion.

C. JAPs as seen by other personnel

This research did not explore the perception of other practitioners and in particular prison staff and clerks. With regards to the first, we had started interviewing a handful of them but the prison services wanted to take over the control of our study. I refused this, since I investigated the judiciary, and because of the delays this would have generated for the students who did part of the field work. There was also the risk that access would eventually be denied, leaving students with no research material as had happened with another research study on prison guards' culture. With regard to clerks, it was the choice of the author to abstain from this. For one thing it was extremely delicate to ask them what they thought of 'their' JAPs when they were actually working right next door to them. More importantly, I had decided to conduct a research study which would focus on this profession in the near future.

A sociologist and his team recently conducted a study funded by the Mission *Droit et Justice* (Law and Justice), which partly focussed on the interactions between JAPs – but also prosecutors – with prison and probation services (Mouhanna, 2011 a). Just as we shall do *infra*, the authors pointed to communication difficulties between the judiciary and prison and probation services. It seemed to us that probation services' interactions with JAPs were too complex to include in the present limited paragraph, particularly since our findings were significantly different from Mouhanna's. Contrary to his team, mine found that many of the JAPs told us their relationship with the probation service was rather good – which probation staff confirmed. Conversely, JAPs said that things were much more complex regarding prison staff:

'With the prison services and the governor it's like we have to strongly defend our prerogatives in order to be able to work normally and it's virtually a daily battle. For instance I had battles about two things. Some prisoners worked for the prison '*mess*' [47] for instance and as a result could not access psychological treatment as the prison told them it was too burdensome to take them to both. So I refused to sign off for appointing these people to the '*mess*' if the prison service did not also take them to treatment. I also realised that those who had prison jobs outside the prison were unsupervised and one day one of them escaped' (JAP 64).

'It's more sensitive with the prison services. We can feel it with the type of information the prison services give us in view of release measures. Their philosophy with regard to these release measures is not the same as ours. Besides, the information they give us during CAP is biased depending on what outcome they want' (JAP 39).

The research confirmed, as did earlier work studying JAP practices when they were not yet judicialised courts (Herzog-Evans, 1994), that when they operate within the prison premises during CAP they have very little room for manoeuvre. There, because they are not at the tribunal and are not presiding over a hearing [48] and are surrounded by prison staff, they have a very hard time being assertive. In such a context there is a lot of pressure on them to also take into account the impact that their decisions will have on the prison's good order. Remission and day-leave (furlough) are measures which are immensely important in terms of good order. If a JAP does not grant enough, it can create many disturbances (Herzog-Evans, 1994). As was the case two decades ago [49], JAPs are totally dependent on the information that prison staff provide them with. Lastly, they only have a few minutes to rule on each case as they will typically process eighty to a hundred cases in half a day. Inevitably, prison governors expect, depending on their prison, either an important number of favourable decisions or the exact opposite, when the balance of power favours prison guards over offenders, which is particularly the case with prison hosting short term sentences. In all prisons JAPs are pressured not to grant remission or furlough to prisoners who exasperate prison staff.

'What prison staff say is respected in X. The JAPs follow my cue because this prison is me' (Prison Governor 2).

---

47. The prison 'mess' is a restaurant-café for prison staff, which is either situated within the prison premises or a few streets away in the community. 'Mess' staff are usually comprised of inmates.

48. They also hold hearings in the prison premises to decide on prisoners' release and there, no prison staff are present, unless they decide to invite the governor.

49. This will be the case with all release measures if the current government's Bill is enacted by Parliament.

As an illustration, I was present during a CAP which took place in a small prison for remand prisoners and sentences of up to two years. During this CAP, prison and probation officers kept reacting to files by saying 'this one is insufferable in the wing' or 'I really don't like this one' and expected the JAP to take such 'criteria' – which, needless to say are illegal – into account in order to determine whether prisoners should be granted remission or furlough. The JAP, who was probably one of the best I saw when he held his hearing at the tribunal due to this self-controlled, empathic, humane and problem-solving manner, became a much more submissive person who bent under the pressure of the prison services when he presided over the CAP. There, he had a rather rigid remission policy and did not display any of the humanity we saw in his tribunal hearings. He seemed to essentially follow the cue of prison staff, the governor and even the probation officers who, having worked for ten years at this local prison, had become fully prisonised and could not have been distinguished in any way whatsoever from prison guards. CAP remain settings where the JAP have a very hard time affirming their judicial power and, more worryingly where they find it very difficult to base their decisions on objective un-prisonised information.

Our research did not allow us to go beyond that. The very limited number of prison staff who were interviewed – that is five prison governors, three prison clerks and four JAP services' clerks – was not sufficient to investigate these issues further. It is nonetheless interesting that these practitioners were unanimously positive about the JAP they had worked with and added that they had good relationships with the JAP and did not seem to challenge their judicial authority. Conversely, they all referred to the material difficulties that currently prevail in sentences' implementation.

3

Obstacles in a JAP's way

> '*Judges are very frustrated.... I think the innovation that we're seeing is a result of judges processing cases like a vegetable factory. Instead of cans of peas, you've got cases. You just move 'em, move 'em. One of my colleagues on the bench said: "You know, I feel like I work for McJustice: We sure aren't good for you, but we are fast*".'
> (Berman, 2000: 80, citant le Chief Justice Kathleen Blatz)

PSC were created in reaction to a factory lane type of criminal justice. JAPs, who were created decades before PSC still resist, and in some cases with all their might, the development of managerialism in criminal justice (Danet, 2010) as well as the industrial way of processing cases. Just as serious, but probably not as irreversible, are the difficulties they face with probation services.

§ 1. Managerial and punitive criminal justice policies

In most Western world countries, criminal justice has been affected by a double movement: on the one hand, increasingly punitive policies (Garland, 2002 ; Danet, 2006) which eventually impacted probation (for France: Herzog-Evans, 2012-2013 : Chap. 04; for England and Wales: Deering, 2011) and, on the other hand, increased managerialism that is: 'Broadly defined, managerialism encompasses a pragmatic, technologically-supported, and quantification-oriented political construction which has subjected the police, courts, probation, and prisons to a regime of efficiency and value-for-money, performance targets and auditing, quality of service and consumer responsiveness' (Loader & Sparks, 2002; also see Cheliotis, 2006: 397). Managerialism is present in most Western world probations (For Belgium: Bauwens, 2011; for England and wales: Phillips, 2011 and Deering, 2011; for France:

Herzog-Evans, 2011 b). On top of these general trends, France also presents a series of specificities: on the one hand, extreme and dismaying poverty of the judiciary; on the other hand, increasingly virulent attacks against JAPs.

A. Enormous caseloads

The JAPs we interviewed were in charge of between 900 and 1,400 files. Such figures are naturally much higher than probation officers' caseloads as JAPs do not see probationers as frequently. In return, JAPs have a lot of additional tasks, such as numerous verification and judicial entries or writings and the preparation of files for the trials. It is important to remind the reader that these judges are not full time JAPs. In many jurisdictions, they also have court standby duties such as being assessors in correctional courts (the minimum being once a month) and in criminal courts [50]. In smaller courts, they may also have other part time positions as family judges or investigating judges.

What the two year field work revealed is that the correlative managerial pressure, the weight of the caseload, the absurd situations they often have to deal with, and the sheer impossibility to do qualitative work in such conditions is clearly more present in big urban tribunals than it is in smaller or rural ones. The smaller a court is, the easier it is for the JAP to carry out better and more thorough qualitative work, and in turn the more peaceful they appear. It was also easier to obtain appointments with these JAPs to contribute to the present research. The dichotomy between the two categories of courts is plain to see upon entering them. In the bigger courts, one can see on the floor huge piles of files in the clerks' and JAPs' offices; in smaller courts, files are neatly organised and are hardly even visible, as they still fit on the shelves or in the cupboards.

It is easier for JAPs working in smaller courts to get appraised of their environment and to spend more time with '*justiciables*', to get to know them and to interact more frequently with their usual partners (prosecutor's office, probation office, prison services and community agencies or charities). They typically seem happier with their job. One of the most obvious features of bigger courts is the number of cases which are dealt with '*hors débat contradictoire*' (hereafter HDC), that is, without a hearing. The law allows the JAP to grant an offender a favourable decision – release, *ab initio* transformation of a custody sentence into a community sentence or measure – with-

50. Being an assessor in criminal courts is particularly taxing for JAPs: it takes a very long time and during that time, they are not allowed to work in their office, which leads to sometimes insurmountable delays with their activities.

out a hearing if the prosecutor and the offenders agree (PPC, art. 712-6). The bigger and more urban a court is, the more cases there are to process, and the more they will be dealt with by HDC. For instance, in the course of a training session which the author took part in for the ENM at the beginning of 2012, a JAP from X, one of the biggest French cities, told us that in her court, 80% of cases were processed HDC; conversely her colleague from the small Western coast town of Y only performed around 15% HDC procedures. In Z, we were told by the JAP that they only did 5%. As can be expected in the Paris region HDC percentages tend to be extremely high. JAP 27, who worked in a big Parisian suburb court, told us that 90% of his *ab initio* aforementioned procedures of article 723-15 of the PPC were HDC. With the article 723-15 procedure it is actually a wide-spread method, although this does not mean that the JAP never sees the offender. The most common practice for the JAP consists of seeing the offender without his attorney for an informal meeting – which is thus not called a hearing – and to then ask him whether he would sign a form whereby he consents for his case to be dealt with without a hearing should the JAP grant his application.

'In fact we organise this quasi-militarily for things to work. It is precise to a fraction of an inch and this is what saves us' (JAP 27).

According to the law, hearings are the principle and HDC the exception. Clearly, in the Paris region it is the reverse:

'We have no choice here. Hearings are a rare occurrence here. We had to banish the odd hearing except exceptional circumstances. In the community we have about one a week and we alternate presiding over them. Each time we deal with twelve to fifteen cases. So hearings are our last resort' (JAP 71).

In the PACA region, that is the South East densely populated region where big cities such as Marseille, Nice and Cannes are situated, JAPs made similar statements. However, even in big cities including in the Paris region, we shall see *infra* that some magistrates manage to save fair trial.

Workload is thus a constant struggle. In fact when they were asked 'what is a good day' a significant minority (16%) immediately answered: 'a day where I can deal with all my files'. 10.6% more mentioned that they managed to deal with an emergency. JAPs' increased caseload is the result of the two legged judicialisation of sentences' implementation which took place in 2000 and which was completed in 2004. This has been very demanding in terms of verifications, attention to detail, contact with other agencies and personnel (e.g. experts). Moreover in recent years, law reformers have asked JAPs to be more cautious with high risk offenders (sex offenders but also domestic violent offenders). The constraints of fair trial are undoubtedly more demanding than the former informal procedures followed by the then 'super social worker' JAP. The fear of being held accountable for a mistake or negligence is also at the heart – and rightly so – of the increased attention and time they devote to high risk offenders. And yet JAPs would like to keep doing tailored and holistic work. In big jurisdictions, this has become mission impossible.

Increasing managerial demands make this even more difficult. Some JAPs are subdued by these demands, whilst others fiercely resist them and persist against all odds to give priority to quality over quantity. Inevitably they do not process enough cases or have to make equally exacting demands on their partners (particularly clerks, prosecutors, probation staff) and emerge as annoying. As a result, when the time comes for the president of the tribunal to grade the quality of their job, they are told that they do not process enough files and should get along better with their partners. Tribunals' presidents are now in charge of the management of the judiciary's meagre pennies and of the fast processing of the penal process lane – a term which does not seem to shock in France, unlike in the Unites States (see *supra*).

JAPs' complaints are confirmed by our observations. There is indeed a decreasing meaning of sentences' implementation measures. Their instrumentalisation in order to deal with prison overcrowding (Herzog-Evans, 2013 d) has led to strong pressure on these magistrates not to ask probation officers to write detailed reports, to do in depth investigations and sometimes even to bother worrying about the end result of these measures (Herzog-Evans, 2012 d). These issues were systematically at the heart of the JAP interviews. Another recent change has also contributed to the loss in meaning of sentences' implementation measures: the Prison Law of 2009 raised the threshold for the *ab initio* procedure of article 723-15 from one year imprisonment to two years. Whilst all the JAPs were strongly in favour of release and sentences' implementation measures, they did not agree they should be granted at all costs. This cost they find too onerous when it leads to a system where the correctional tribunal in charge of felonies in lieu of a sentence pronounces a rough and ready patron/sentence leaving to the JAP the task of adapting it to the offender (Gautron, 2013; Danet, 2013). The result is that correctional judges do not hesitate to sentence offenders to imprisonment as they can protect themselves emotionally against the brutality of such a sentence by telling the offender: 'don't worry! The JAP will put things right for you!' If this seems shocking it is important to remember that it is also the result of how the French criminal justice system works. If France needs article 723-15 procedures, it is because its typical penal trial never spends time on discussing the sentence. This time is devoted to determining whether the offender is guilty; the judge or court then swiftly determines the sentence. A second reason is that pre-sentence reports are not systematic [51]. In other words, the prevailing idea seems to be that it does not matter if the correctional tribunal functions like a factory-lane and as a result, that justice is far from perfect, often unsuitable and even inhuman (Ligue des droits de l'homme de Toulouse, 2012) so long as the JAP will eventually add depth and humanity to the process. Sadly, JAPs are themselves increasingly contaminated by this factory-lane logic and also have to operate in an exceptionally dire context.

B. Extreme poverty

The French budget for criminal justice is one of the poorest of the Council of Europe: 57.7 euros per year and inhabitant in 2011 versus 140.5 in Sweden, 114.6 in the Netherlands, 106 in Germany, 86.3 in Spain, 83.4 in Scotland, 79.7 in Belgium, 75.1 in England and Wales, and 71.8 in Italy. In France, there are 11 professional judges for 100,000 inhabitants versus 84 in Germany, 18 in Portugal and 15 in Belgium (Alternatives Economiques, March 2011, n° 300).

Even if this author is used to dilapidated and run down French universities, entering a few particularly ruined tribunals did come as a terrible shock. The first time I visited the tribunal of X I learnt that there was only one functioning toilet on the sixth floor of the building, with all the others having been out of order for months and one actually leaking out nauseous liquid into the corridor where *'justiciables'* were waiting. There were piles of files both in the paralegals' and the JAPs' office to the point where it was actually difficult to move around them; the judges' offices were overheated as the building's boiler had been dysfunctional for months and yet the windows, having been blocked for years, could not be opened. The tribunal cafeteria had been closed for months and judges and other staff had to either eat in their office or in local restaurants. Printers would regularly break down and the scanner had not been repaired for months even though judicial files are, by law, supposed to be dematerialised. Judges constantly had to be on the lookout for folders for their files and would have to steal old ones or buy new ones with their own money... On a number of occasions, I saw *'justiciables'* whose facial expression clearly expressed pity upon entering the office where these judges were made to spend their long working days. The tribunal of X was probably exceptionally run down. Yet the sheer poverty of

51. It is significant that there is very little literature on this subject contrary to neighbouring countries (comp: Tata et al., 2008 and the special issue of *Punishment and Society*, 2010, n° 12(3) – but see Brizais, 2006).

the French Justice System is well-known and was in fact denounced by the press during the year 2011 after the Pornic case and again in 2012, after another case, the Chloé case. In the latter case, the lack of means of the Justice system was one of the causes leading to this high profile case. Chloé, a fifteen year old teenager was abducted and driven by a repeat sex offender from the South of France to Germany, where she was saved by sheer accident from the boot of her abductor's car. The offender, who was under supervision had suddenly fallen off the radar and his probation officer had notified the JAP by sending her a fax which, due to technical failures never arrived at the tribunal. Due to the dysfunctional mail service, the JAP had never received the official file of this offender and as a result was not formally appraised of his case. This meant that she would not have been legally allowed to launch an arrest warrant. In other words the lack of a functioning fax machine and mail services led to the loss of crucial time, thus exposing Chloé to serious physical and sexual abuse. Most tribunals had no paper, ink and sometimes pens left (Vingt Minute, 23 Nov., 2012). Some judges told us that after the Pornic case and the superficial audits which were made in its aftermath, a few financial plasters were applied in a few places, with a fax machine arriving here and a printer arriving there. In reality, though, nothing fundamentally changed.

Poverty also contaminates professional activity. It goes without saying that staff shortage is also monumental to the point where a culture in which it appears normal not to do one's job has developed. There is also no money to pay experts past a few months as the yearly meagre budget of most tribunal generally runs down before the summer holiday. Experts who have indeed completed a risk assessment report are denied payment of their highway fees: the tribunal objects that they should have used free state roads. More seriously, we were told by JAP 13 that she had had to fight against her mail service for several weeks after they refused to post a high profile sex offender's file to the court where he was not to be supervised. This was because it was too heavy – of course it was given his profile! – and therefore expensive. She was eventually forced to illegally split up the file into several little parcels. Meanwhile, the offender was not supervised for several weeks.

Material and human poverty is one of the leading causes of the monumental delays in taking charge of offenders, something which was studied *supra* [52]. If judges usually keep a low profile regarding the issues of poverty as it directly impacts on their dignity and that of their '*justiciables*', they are

---

52. However, as will be seen *infra*, it is also caused by ill-adapted prioritising by probation services (they are for instance asked to focus on prisoners' fast processing out of prisons rather than on efficient and qualitative supervision – and by insufficient collaboration between JAP and probation services.

more eloquent about the impact of poverty on the heart of their work and the credibility of justice.

'When we see a person a month or two after a violation, we clearly arrive after the battle; we are not credible' (JAP 9).

'In order to keep up with my work, I sleep five hours a night... if I get little sleep and write during the weekends and holidays... but that's the sort of thing that drives my wife crazy' (JAP 56).

'A third [problem] is that we cannot know all our files. With some of them I just assume they are doing OK because I never hear from them, but if the person commits another offence it would be better if we had an overview of his case' (JAP 68).

'I feel powerless' (JAP 58).

It is important to note that the questionnaire did not contain a single question pertaining to the Justice System's poverty. This is something that we observed repeatedly on site, during the hearings and talked about during informal discussions. However, during their interviews, 20% of the JAPs spontaneously mentioned it and recalled particularly difficult and sometimes even dangerous situations.

Judges were even more concerned about the lack of staff. They all referred to the lack of clerks, the lack of JAPs and the patent lack of staff in probation services. In a small court on the West coast of France, JAP 42 told us that following the post-Pornic audits it was revealed that his service was the worst overloaded of the entire country despite its small size. Indeed, he was the only JAP working there and was in charge of two remand and short sentences prisons and had an enormous number of offenders supervised in the community. The audit revealed that such a workload corresponded to two full time JAP positions. If no other JAP was appointed at least he obtained the right not to continue having to take on other tasks in his court, which is an extremely rare luxury. Things can sometimes reach yet another level. For instance, in an East of France tribunal, there had been no JAP at all for an entire year and as a result the prison services had taken on the functions of a JAP, which was completely illegal. In a South-East tribunal there were only two probation officers left in a service where six were officially needed and this had lasted for more than a year at the time we conducted our interviews there. In another tribunal, there was simply no clerk:

'As of this Friday I have no clerk. New files cannot be created; I cannot hold a hearing without a clerk; I cannot rule without a clerk. Nobody has any idea how long it's going to last. The president [of the tribunal] has no solution to offer right now' (JAP 9).

On numerous occasions we noticed that such situations led to a collective acceptation of poverty, thus leading some practitioners who work with JAPs to consider that it is perfectly normal not to do a job they should normally do. During a CAP we thus heard a probation officer exclaim that she could not be expected to read the inmates' files which were examined that day for possible remission! Another JAP told me that her clerk, objectively overloaded to the extreme, retorted to her that she could not be expected to deal with the JAP's datebook, when in reality this is the very basic task of a clerk. Such attitudes inevitably lead to serious tensions within services and particularly when one of the practitioners operating along the line is a demanding professional who wants things done properly. Unfortunately, in some of the most dilapidated services JAPs themselves tended to give up and forsake the very notion of doing a thorough job and end up processing files rather than taking care of people. Indeed, this is a classic distant and purely legalistic magistrate's stance which is in direct contrast with the heart of '*Japperie*'. This guarantees them that if their partners have likewise given up they will not be aggravated by their demands.

However, this represents a minority of judges. In fact, as was mentioned at the beginning of this book, only a few JAPs want to leave this position. Precisely, JAP 7 did tell us that he had originally wanted to finish his career as a JAP but had changed his mind precisely because of the considerable poverty of JAP services – which is even worse than other services in tribunals. He added that he was sick of taking risks in terms of his reputation and career as a result of mistakes and negligence committed by his main partners.

The Justice system's poverty inevitably impacts on the quality of supervision and its outcome. French probation services have a professional culture whereby they expect offenders to make most desisting efforts on their own (Herzog-Evans, 2011 c; 2012 a); poverty makes things even worse. There are no beds in psychiatric hospitals; no places in drug treatment programmes, none in shelters or council housing, and, naturally no jobs. How can it be expected, in such dire conditions, that offenders will be supported in building what desistance specialists call 'social capital' (Farrall, 2002; Hattery & Smith; Mills & Codd, 2008)? JAPs consistently complain about these issues which makes probation services and themselves work in vain, or at the very least have a rather reduced level of efficiency:

'We lack programme and centre space. We don't always have what we would need (shelters, health centres), which would allow us to serenely envisage inmates' release' (JAP 75).

They all deplore this lack of means along with the decline in collaborative work (see *infra*) and the fact that the prison services have exclusively focussed on electronic monitoring and abandoned 'placements in the community' [53]. This is regrettable as everybody seems to agree that 'placement in the community' is a rare example, in the French offender supervision landscape, of true partnership and qualitative work (see e.g. the report by two M.P.s Raimbourg and Huygues, 2013 and Herzog-Evans, unpublished). The measures can only be sustainable thanks to the collaborative work of all partners (judges, probation services, third sector agencies, prison services) which is appreciated by JAPs. In the JAP 62 region, the prison service had nonetheless decided to put an end to these programmes forcing him to allocate all offenders to electronic monitoring, despite the fact that it was patently unsuitable to the profiles of those who were formerly allocated to 'placement in the community'. The prison services unfortunately tend to have 'one size fits all' policies and the very meaning of measures – and very likely their successful outcome – tends to be lost (Herzog-Evans, 2012d). Constant punitive law reform has naturally made things worse.

C. Schizophrenic policies

JAPs unanimously complained bitterly about the constant law reform. Indeed, since 2004, twelve law reforms – and at the time of writing a thirteenth bill was being drafted – were enacted, thus reflecting contradictory goals and policies and creating a terribly confusing tangle of legal rules, epitomised in 2005 by what the legal doctrine called a 'legal bug' (Herzog-Evans, 2005 a). Whereas the law of March 9, 2004 had been a model of technical expertise construction, which also reflected a coherent policy – with the exception of the amusing 2005 legal bug – the following laws and their inevitable convoy of decrees created nothing short of legal chaos. All seventy-five interviewed JAPs complained that they were exhausted as they constantly had to adapt to complex and often unintelligible new legal rules. Even if the technical complexity of this legal field is also a source of pride, as we saw above, for those who manage to understand it, judges unanimously condemn a legal complexity which serves no purpose and is only caused by reforming restlessness. Things have become so serious that the Constitutional Council has recently deplored in one of its ruling 'the complexity of the legal regime of sentences' implementation' (§15) [54].

---

53. As was previously mentioned 'Placement in the community' refers to a release measure or sentence whereby the offender is really supported via housing, employment or training, treatment and care (Herzog-Evans, 2012 d). It is essentially used for offenders who have a host of psycho-social needs and/or are released after serving very long sentences.

54. Cons. constit. 4 août 2011, décis. n° 2011-635 DC relative à la loi sur la participation des citoyens au fonctionnement de la justice pénale et le jugement des mineurs.

The sheer incoherence of the recent laws is *inter alia* the result of a schizophrenia that is plain for everybody to see. On the one hand, under the reign of Mr Sarkozy – first as minister of Interior, then as president – politicians put all their efforts into radicalising France's Criminal Justice System and making it evermore punitive with, *inter alia*: mandatory minimum sentences for recidivists, numerous procedural and other barriers to the release of offenders serving long sentences, sexual and violent offenders and recidivists; injunctions on public prosecutors to ensure all sentences are executed; reduction of remission for recidivists; and, lastly, the abolition – set in the marble of the Constitution – of annual collective pardon.

Unsurprisingly these reforms created terrible overcrowding which in turn, and on the other hand, led to the Prison Bill of November 24, 2009, which consisted of discreetly releasing inmates through the back service entrance – the expression back door measure is here perfectly adapted – this discreetly in the sense that it was done in the course of such a complex tangle of legal rules that no journalist saw through it. These so-called 'simplified release measures' – labelled SEFIP or PSAP; an indecipherable jargon which added to the opacity of these measures – evicted JAPs and focussed solely on freeing prison space. Offenders would be released without a real plan or supervision; whether these measures worked or not was plainly not the concern of reformers (Herzog-Evans, 2012-2013). The sheer aberration of this system is plain to see for all the practitioners who were interviewed.

'I think that SEFIP and PSAP are a substitute for former pardon and amnesty laws. I am strongly against this. I found this meaningless. I mean there is a sentence which bears some meaning and it is totally deleted… there was no point in pronouncing the sentence in the first place. No! Sentence management measures should not solely exist to free prison space. It's not at all what they're about' (JAP 41).

Many practitioners expressly used the word 'schizophrenic':

'We are told we release too much when they reoffend and not enough when prisons are full! This is schizophrenic for us!' (JAP 9).

'This is schizophrenic: mandatory minimum sentences but then we have to release them: prosecutors are told to boot people out of prison before the end. That's the principle but one must bear in mind that… we're talking about the shittiest files, the shittiest! And they tell you that these [PSAP and SEFIP] are not sentences' management measures [but another way to serve their custody sentence] and the person is only allowed out of his home two to three hours a day! Exposing people to such conditions creates a reoffending risk' [55] (JAP4).

'Incarcerating on Monday with mandatory minima and releasing on Tuesday without any inmate's agency or involvement in his release plan or minimum investigation [about his circumstances]: it's a huge hypocrisy!' (JAP 15).

JAPs' partners shared their views:

'What I really did not receive well were these paradoxical injunctions: mandatory minima and then systematic release measures. There comes a point where the message gets blurry. That it's blurry for us, too bad for us, but for offenders now that! Obviously I'm in favour of release measures, but not at any cost' (Chief of service 1).

'Conversely, some of the other legal norms, well that's schizophrenic' hey. Politically they don't show off too much about this, even though there is no shame in releasing offenders. I think that citizens aren't idiots. They're trying to make people believe that they are incarcerating people but they are released just as fast' (DSPIP 7).

'There comes a time where you wonder whether we're not schizophrenic: on the one hand mandatory minima and all sentences must be executed and then we realise that prison's walls are not elastic then we think 'ahem perhaps we should release people!' At times it lacks coherence; public opinion definitely feels that way too' (Prosecutor 2).

JAPs used other negative adjectives in order to describe the aforementioned 'simplified release procedures'. 'Schizophrenic' was approved by seven of them. Other labels were: 'hypocritical' (JAP 1; JAP 15; JAP 16); 'populist' (JAP 1); 'accountant's logics' (JAP 3; JAP 59) 'propaganda' (JAP 4); 'incomprehensible' (JAP 5; JAP 6); incoherent' (JAP 5 ; JAP 6 ; JAP 48) ; 'ridiculous' (JAP 17) ; 'meaningless' (JAP 18 ; JAP 32) ; 'anti-pedagogical' (JAP 20); 'illogical' (JAP 51); 'paradoxical' (JAP 40; JAP 42); 'absurd' (JAP 58); and even 'it leaves me speechless' (JAP 22) or 'it's crap'

---

55. See in this respect a recent court case where a JAP had to parole an offender as he was first released via a SEFIP scheme without medical treatment or food, let alone supervision. His fourteen year old son had to steal from his mother's fridge to bring food to his father (M. Herzog-Evans, « Libération conditionnelle sur « grâce électronique »: les avatars de la SEFIP », obs. sous JAP Bobigny, 8 juillet 2011, *Blog Dalloz*, 2011). All the JAP told us about such cases where they had to convert SEFIP electronic monitoring decisions into 'real' electronic monitoring release measures with much more time in the community or into parole in order to untangle the absurd consequences of SEFIP: the offender would not have the time to sort out his daily problems, to work, to get treatment and so forth.

(JAP 56), the latter being chosen by a full of imagery JAP who had consistently entertained us with his Audiard-like vocabulary.

What I previously labelled 'bathtub logic' (Herzog-Evans, forthcoming h) goes against JAPs' and many other practitioners' professional culture: they perceive sentence management measures as being measures which should work and should be meaningful for all concerned: the community, the Justice system, victims and above all offenders themselves. Recent reforms and in particular the prison law of 2009 – the aforementioned current government Bill which goes even more drastically in this direction – have created a system whereby it is not important whether sentence management measures work so long as they exist (Herzog-Evans, 2012 d); something which profoundly shocks JAPs, hence the reason why they strongly resist it:

'The 'Canada dry' nature of electronic monitoring is utterly ridiculous' (JAP 56).

Thus, virtually all the interviewed JAPs (98.6%) said they were strongly opposed to 'speedy release measures'. Still, most of them understood that the prison services do have a pressing need to find a solution to their overcrowding problem:

'I think it is an understandable reaction to try and find ways of emptying prisons. But then perhaps one should look for ways of not filling them up! [laughter]' (JAP 9).

Given the considerable pressure practitioners were under to implement the 'simplified release procedure' it is all the more telling that these procedures failed. In all the jurisdictions where all types of practitioners who were interviewed worked, we were told that SEFIP, and even more so PSAP, were not often used, or were not used at all. Practitioners who were interviewed after the Pornic case explained that it had had a 'freezing' effect and that probation services, in charge of SEFIP, did not want to bear the responsibility of fast processing offenders out of prison, even those with short sentences, since in the Pornic case a so-called low risk offender released after a short time in custody had then committed a horrific crime. Being chronically overburdened, probation services did not have the capacity to add yet another task to their load – a task which would interfere with their core missions, i.e. supervision, even if the recent reforms have indeed removed them from these missions. Moreover, the aberrant effects of SEFIP played against them: practitioners were not ready to implement measures which were so clearly criminologically and humanly absurd. According to our interviewees, a great proportion of offenders seemed to also reject SEFIP as they came with too much control and because they would rather have the right to see 'their judge' and have access to 'their fair trial' which was the only legitimate procedure for a number of them. This is coherent with legitimacy of justice literature findings (Tyler, 2006, 2012). As a matter of fact, such conclusions had already been drawn when a former – but more modest – partial dejudicialisation attempt had been made in 2004 (Garreau, 2004). The fact that the offender's consent must be obtained before these 'simplified release procedures' are put in place in a given case does not equate to the offender's personal commitment and agency, which is so important in terms of resettlement. Economist Kuziemko's studies showed that discretionary release measures worked better than fixed term release dates (Kuziemko, 2007 and 2012) as they created less reincarceration (Stivers, 2001) and reoffending (Solomon et al., 2005) [56]. In this respect, the recent proposal made by two French M.P. Mr Raimbourg and Huygues (Raimbourg & Huygues, 2013) to create automatic parole for offenders serving up to five years, which a consensus conference organised by the Ministry of Justice also advocated (Jury de la conférence de consensus, 2013) has caused concern (Herzog-Evans, 2013). In contrast with this, and as magistrates also believe, if discretionary measures work it is because offenders have put a lot of effort into preparing their own project, a project which, as a result really is their own, and which they then have to defend in front of the judge they appraise of their application to their judge:

'[with SEFIP] the formulation 'consents to' is interesting; it is not 'applied for' (JAP 9).

SEFIP and PSAP are the epitome of what they think does not work:

'A project which the offender does not commit to or which is based on the very same circumstances as the ones which led him to offending and which does not allow the offender to identify why he was incarcerated in the first place and does not offer him an escape route' (JAP 15).

'A measure during which nothing happens, where the person is not expected to commit to anything… I am not comfortable with that sort of thing. Can a sentence management measure be built on nothing?' (JAP 14).

Moreover, prosecutors whom the prison services expected would be obedient little soldiers in view of their hierarchical dependency with the ministry

---

56. To be exact, Solomon's study showed that there was no difference between those who served their full sentence and those who were automatically early released in terms of reoffending. It however showed that discretionary release measures fared better. Nonetheless, once all potential confounding variables were taken into account, discretionary measures only outperformed other forms of release by 4%. One must however bear in mind that the U.S. system is vastly different from the French system: parole criteria are above all behavioural and criminological, whereas in France they are centred on offenders' release plan and commitment to it.

of Justice [57] and would thus be key players in the implementation of SEFIP and PSAP – as they had the last word and were to control which cases were selected by probation services – also have, as was pointed out, a magistrate's culture (Milburn, 2007 and 2010). During our interviews prosecutors made clear that they were opposed to 'simplified release measures' as they were an attack against their fellow magistrates JAPs. They added that they were not ready to take insane risks in terms of public safety.

Crucially, whereas their proponents had tried to sell simplified procedures by saying that JAPs were too slow to process cases, what we saw in practice was that JAPs were actually quite capable of being just as fast whilst doing a better job.

Indeed, the logic behind automatic early release is nothing new. Most Western world jurisdictions have had to face the same fundamental contradiction between, on the one hand, continuous incarceration expansion caused by foolish punitivity (Garland, 2002; Waquant, 2009) and its consequences in term of overcrowding, inhuman detention conditions and its sheer inability to be effective on crime (Petersilia, 2003; Maruna and Immarigeon, 2004; Travis & Visher, 2005). As a result they are now turning towards community sentences; some, like England and Wales, have created a system which is rather similar to French SEFIP (Home Detention Curfew – Dogson et al., 2001). Others, like Belgium, have put on hold for an indeterminate time the implementation of a reform which was supposed to create Belgium JAPs and would have been in charge of releasing offenders sentenced to up to three years imprisonment [58] and have abandoned parole to the prison services which uses it for purely 'bathtub' emptying purposes (Beyens et al., 2010).

In a number of jurisdictions, 'bifurcation' – to quote Pratt (Pratt, 2002 – but see the critic by Matthews, 2005) or hybridisation to quote O'Malley (O'Malley, 2000) and which this author had used for France (Herzog-Evans, 2005 b) has been put in place. In France, it consists of splitting offender treatment into a number of categories to which different rules apply and in allowing for rules to hybridise in various complex forms. Fundamentally however, they also reflect a clearer dichotomy between, on the one hand, serious offences and dangerous offenders for whom sentences are harsher or early release more difficult to obtain and, on the other hand, short sentences

57. This is why the European Human Rights Court has refused to acknowledge their status of magistrate. See EHRCt, *Medvedyev & others v. France,* July 10, 2008, Applic. n° 3394/03. This contradicts French law and a former French Council Constitutional decision of December 11, 1993, n° 93-326 DC, *Garde à vue*.

58. Beyond that, a three JAP tribunal which has indeed been created is competent (Scheirs, 2013).

and non-dangerous offenders for whom if community sentences are not pronounced release measures become the norm. Translated into the French legal context, this does correspond to: on the one hand, a series of reforms which are considerably limited in various ways (: postponing the eligibility point for parole and other release measures; reduced remission quanta; multiple mandatory risk assessment by experts; jurors added to sentences' implementation tribunals, and so on…) access to early release for sexual and violent offenders and recidivists; and, on the other hand, dejudicialised (Herzog-Evans, forthcoming c) 'simplified' and speedy early release (Herzog-Evans, 2011c), accessible to offenders who have up to two years to serve without any consideration for outcome and meaning, particularly in terms of desistance. It is thus the entire release system which is at risk of losing its meaning as it is moving away from the fundamental principles laid down in articles 132-24 of the Penal code and 707 of the PPC as most JAPs deplored:

'I think it's lying to people to make them believe that it's panacea because we have no idea what is actually going on. All the person has to do is abide by his curfew hours whilst getting drunk and beating his wife. We make public opinion believe that we control people but in reality we do not control anything' (JAP 39).

Moreover, judges' professional culture, which implies judging with caution and based on objective data, rebels against supposedly swifter quasi-automatic systems. In fact, and as mentioned earlier, they are not swifter and are devoid of precision and content. Therefore, they resist what they perceive as being a collision course by remaining focussed on the aforementioned fundamental principles and by striving to make quality prevail and making the required verification and investigations. It is these high standards which lead the prison services to think they are a bother (Mouhanna, 2011 a and b – this author shares the prison services' views).

D. Constantly attacked and threatened judges

The increased institutional detestation of JAPs is the result of a nexus of factors which are both erstwhile and short-term and have been explained elsewhere (Herzog-Evans, 2012 g and forthcoming b). France has a rather peculiar understanding of the principle of separation of powers. Its 1958 constitution has flagrantly organised a system whereby the legislative power is shared between legislators and the executive. In fact, President François Mitterrand had denounced what he called a '*coup d'état*' (Mitterrand, 1964) before he unashamedly benefitted from it himself as a president. In France the executive has legislative competence of its own in certain domains. In these domains, it can adopt decrees without competition from Parliament. Moreover, when the Parliament enacts a law, this law never fully applies until 'application decrees' are enacted by the executive, which more often than not leads to violation and blatant deformation of the law itself. Prison and probation law were long exclusively based on decrees, leaving the executive – and in particular the prison services – to self-determine the rules governing themselves (Herzog-Evans, 1998). Indeed, it is only over the last thirteen years or so that things have – slightly – changed with the legislative at least defining the frame of sentences' implementation law (Herzog-Evans, 2012-2013 a: Chap. 02 and 04). Moreover, under the 1958 constitution it is virtually impossible for Bills presented by MPs to ever develop into enacted laws; there are extremely rare exceptions, with only bills presented by the government ever becoming laws. Worse even, in sentences' implementation there exists what has been called a 'norms' hierarchy reversal' (Commission Canivet, 2000; Péchillon, 1998). In a written law system, legal rules are supposed to abide by the Kelsen Pyramidal structure, whereby inferior rules respect superior rules. This rule has consistently been violated in French sentences' implementation law, thus further accentuating the executive domination over the legislative. An example consists of the prison services enacting – so to speak – mere internal circulars, which infringe on the strict domain of the legislator or contradict the laws it has enacted. After some progress was made with the judicialisation of 2000-2004, recent years have seen this shocking phenomenon begin to resurface.

'When I started working in '*Japperie*' I could never have imagined that I would have to get back to the good old Kelsen pyramid. Every two months, our good old Ministry of Justice produces circulars which are destined to the prison services and which are supposed to explain to its staff how to interpret such and such rules enacted in [recent laws]. Half the time, these circulars have been written with knives and forks or worse literally violate the law. This is not exceptional but happens very often and it has clearly contributed to the progressive degradation of the relationship between the prison services and the judiciary' (JAP 56).

This JAP brought up a fundamental issue: the prison services have, for a very long time, been able to rule virtually on their own – and as of 1999, when probation services were integrated into the prison services, this has included probation – and have thus been allowed to make their own policies and rules prevail over the legislative. As judges JAPs are independent, at least on principle, from the executive and thus insist that Kelsen's pyramid is observed, and that superior rules such as European law rules and laws prevail over executive decrees and circulars. This profoundly irritates the executive. The JAP is thus seen as a terrible nuisance who interferes with this super-powerful agency (Herzog-Evans, forthcoming a) and has recently become the enemy that needs to be taken off.

Since the dejudicialisation of 2000 and 2004, there has undoubtedly been a strong tendency for the prison services not to understand where its righteous place should be as an executive power in a modern democracy and to resent and resist the separation of powers. It is no accident that it was during the directorship of Napoleonic local prefects at the prison services headquarters (Herzog-Evans, 2012-2013 b: 111.20) that this resentment and resistance reached its peak (see in particular the presentation of two of them in Froment & Kaluszinski 2011: 59-87). It is no longer paranoid delusion to say that there is a clear design to eliminate the JAP or at the very least, to reduce his/her powers to recall issues. This was the official position of the recent conference of consensus (Report of the *jury de la conférence de consensus*, 2013) and some researchers with a patent prison service bias would definitely approve (Mouhanna, 20121 a and b). Thus, JAP 69 who had himself worked at the Ministry of Justice for several years made the following summary:

'I know for a fact that the long range trend is that the JAP would become the recall judge' (JAP 69).

Many of the JAPs felt that this has already become their fate since recent reforms have deprived them of a right to have their say in the determination of the intensity of supervision [59]. Such reforms are the result of executive norms such as decrees and circulars which are, for the most part, created by the prison services, since, as stated above, the French constitution thereby lets administrations self-regulate themselves, with no democratic control or supervision, including when they use it to deprive the judiciary of its own prerogatives. As we shall see *infra*, 'Who Works' – that is what JAPs, probation services and prison staff are in charge of – does need to be reconsidered to some extent. However, in order for such a change to be truly democratic and to be legitimate in the eyes of all parties concerned, it should have been put together and accepted by all of them and should have had clear and viable penological goals.

In our opinion, leaving JAPs in charge of only recall and sanction decisions would constitute a terrible historical mistake. Its most obvious effect would be to eliminate what constitutes the very usefulness of judiciary intervention and JAPs. As is the case with PSC judges, it is their culture and personality which makes them necessary and efficient. Should they become

59. Decree n° 2011-1876 of 14 December 2011 pertaining to the respective attributions of JAPs, other mandating judges and the probation services and Circular of 16 December 2011 pertaining to the respective attributions of JAPs, other mandating judges and the probation services, NOR :JUSK1140065C. This circular was recently partially abrogated by the highest administrative Court, the *Conseil d'Etat* (C.E., 13 fév. 2013, *Ajpénal* 2013: 230-231, obs. M. Herzog-Evans), but the Conseil d'Etat did not abrogate the decree.

recall courts they would lose this very culture and would start looking very much like their sentencing colleagues. This analysis was submitted to the JAP who had spent several years at the Ministry of Justice and his reaction was not optimistic:

'Indeed, there is a real risk of acculturation. Yes we have to fight tooth and nail against it. But it's complicated because we have a hard time realising just how monumental the strike force of the prison services is. And I do think my colleagues don't fully realise it. In fact from the public finances point of view JAPs are nothing. The prison services are a formidable force when it comes to imposing their views.'

The feud which the prison services have maintained against the JAPs is not limited to the national headquarters; it is sometimes transplanted at regional or local level. It then takes the shape of a denigrating discourse against JAPs and the relaying of national guidelines whereby probation services now refuse to do, or considerably reduce, pre-electronic monitoring investigations or house visits [60]. JAP 56 summarised this in his usual colourful language:

'Oh the prison services' tendency which consists of indoctrinating their staff and telling them that JAPs are just pompous pains in the arse sitting on their asses, who know nothing about 'the reality of the field', who make out they are lawyers when really "fuck the law!" since only circulars count and CRIMINOLOGY – well not Herzog-Evans' criminology, nah nah, it's more like Expert Manhattan's criminology! Meanwhile the very same prison service headquarters, for mean pecuniary reasons, go as far as to tell their probation officers that they should not do the pre-release under EM investigation that the JAP asked for. And as far as I am concerned incidentally I am thankful to my probation service because it does not take part in this dangerous game, even if the temptation is still there' (JAP 56).

In the field, as will be seen, probation officers do not usually fall into this sterile and counter-productive trap and do not take part in the institutional guerrilla. Things are however more complicated when it comes to their chiefs.

'I felt that I was deprived of my prerogatives. But it does not mean that the probation service or his chief talk big' (JAP 29).

Nonetheless probation staff must follow national guidelines and, since it is overloaded, it can actually appreciate being unburdened of some of its

---

60. The aforementioned December 2011 decree put an end to the reports that were formerly sent every six months to the JAP telling them how supervised offenders were doing.

missions, even if they are main ones. JAPs often mock policies which consist of progressively depriving them of the means to do their job and in annexing their attributions, particularly regarding the release of offenders. However, as JAP 42 noticed, they take only the easy cases 'where all the lights are green', whilst leaving them the 'dirty work' that is sanctioning probationers' violations and reoffending.

One thing is clear: JAPs are hurt and exasperated by these constant attacks from an institution which should be their partner. On a more fundamental level, many of them thought that neither probation services nor prosecutors should be in charge of release.

A few preliminary observations need to be made at this point. It is true that in a number of countries, things 'work' without judicial intervention in supervision and release. Nonetheless, this has been criticized by foreign lawyers on the basis that the executive was not independent and that executive procedures did not respect fair trial principles. The French JAP has been presented as a model by the English lawyer Nicola Padfield (Padfield et al., 2012; Padfield, 2011). Moreover, the position of JAP was transplanted in Belgium (Snacken et al., 2010) and whilst it currently only applies to sentences of more than three years, this is actually due to similar difficulties with overcrowding and the need to fast process inmates out of prison. Judicial intervention also exists in Finland, Germany, Italy and Spain (Padfield et al., 2010) and is present in Latin America. Indeed, the judiciary's attributions and the legal rules and procedures applying differ depending on the historical, institutional and legal context. Even more significant is the aforementioned PSC movement; a core element of which – and one which has been linked to its efficiency – is judicial intervention in supervision along with a mix of care and legitimacy of justice (Tyler, 2006 and 2012) which characterises them. We saw that French JAPs are in direct line with this movement, and in fact preceded it by several decades. This is precisely why probation staff would usually like to keep them, particularly as far as sanctions are concerned:

'Whether you like it or not we are in a society where the judge is an authority and the probation officer is not. Proof is that when supervision starts going wrong, probation officers ask JAPs to straighten things up as they don't manage anymore; they need the intervention of a socially recognised authority' (JAP 2).

'When we intervene, there is a before and after meeting the JAP effect; perhaps also because there is a real reaction of the judiciary. For some it's the first time that they see a judge who's not in a full blown decorum context and who's capable of hearing some of the things they have to say about the justice system' (JAP 71).

The JAP is the incarnation of a better procedural and criminological way of doing things and it would be absurd to replace it with a less performing and less human rights protective one.

Fundamentally, if JAPs are irritated by the attacks against their profession, during their interviews they systematically shifted the discussion to higher grounds: to the lack of content when it comes to 'speedy simplified procedures' such as SEFIP and PSAP; to the lack of precision when it comes to 'investigations' – if they can be called that – which are conducted, and so on. In short, they analysed the attacks against their profession as being attacks against what is most important for them, that is 'the meaning' of sentences' implementation measures. They also deplored that these attacks have gradually separated them from their probation brothers and sisters, i.e. probation service staff.

§ 2. Complex relationships with probation services

The research which led to this book was itself a sequel to another two year research study which pertained to probation services in the 2010 decade and particularly concerning their perception and actions to support offenders' desistance (Herzog-Evans, 2011 b ; 2011 c ; 2012 a ; forthcoming a). The previous study had drawn attention towards the gradual distancing of probation services and JAPs' culture, about the multiple sources of their misunderstanding and their increasingly different perception about offenders' desistance. The present research focussed more systematically on the state of JAPs' relationships with probation services and practitioners. It allows for optimism as it shows that despite of undeniable difficulties, these relationships are not irremediably compromised. It does however raise the alarm regarding a fundamental difficulty: the quality of offender supervision, a sore question about which some JAPs complain and which will be studied in a separate section. Lastly, in order to try and make sense of this complex situation, a problematising attempt will be made.

A. The nature of their relationship

A few years ago, Dominique Lhuilier commented that JAPs and probation staff got along very well (Lhuilier, 2007). Conversely, we saw that Mouhanna made a very unfavourable presentation of their relationship and nearly entirely blamed the judiciary for this. In particular, he accused judges of not complying with what he considered to be a positive change, i.e. so-called uniform probation services' practices (Mouhanna, 2011 a and b) – a uniformity which neither our aforementioned studies on probation services nor Dindo's (Dindo, 2011) ever observed. Had things changed so drastically since 2007? It was not impossible given the speed of the changes implemented by the prison services in supervision, particularly since 2008. Undoubtedly these changes, which were presented previously, were not conducive of harmonious relationships: anti-judiciary guerrilla; removal of JAPs' means to execute their missions; instrumentalisation of release measures, and so on. Was it possible that the people who worked in the field were actually falling into these traps and that this had a significant impact on their interaction at an individual level? What the present research actually yielded was even more complex. People usually do get along rather well, respect each other and would like to have more person to person communication opportunities. Nonetheless, some situations and questions create potential misunderstanding occasions. It is essential to hear both sides before an attempt at rationalisation is made.

1. JAPs' point of view

The questionnaire contained an open question pertaining to the manner in which probation services and JAPs got along and which both JAPs and probation staff had to answer. It yielded contrasted responses.

a. Global satisfaction

The most striking finding of the research was that 61.7% of JAPs felt that the relationship they have with the probation service is good. Only 17.1% of them stated that they have a bad relationship with the probation service and exactly the same percentage answered that it depends on the probation officer. This figure is coherent with a recent national activity report for sentences' implementation services of November 2012, which found that 69% of the services whom they had polled said they had good relationships with other penal services, including probation services but also prosecutors' offices (Direction des services judiciaires et direction des affaires criminelles et des grâces, 2012: 24).

In other words, in most cases JAPs were satisfied with their relationship with probation services. However, when these relationships are bad, there may be a host of reasons for this: drastically different philosophies; lack of coordination with the probation chief of service; the headquarters anti-JAP feud which can start impacting locally and generating provocative attitudes towards the JAP; probation staff's refusal to do the work the JAP requested, and so on. Indeed, we were the witnesses of rather staggering scenes during some CAP where probation officers behaved towards the JAPs in a very shocking manner. In fact, several JAPs did mention cases where because they felt protected by geographical distance and their institution, some probation officers could be rather disrespectful.

'The tone they use when they request the criminal record from us is discourteous' (JAP 29).

'I was against the three tier system so I told the probation service. They answered that it was not my place to talk about it' (JAP 21).

'Yes there is serious problem between the JAP and X the probation service. The probation service has filed a complaint for harassment against the JAPs' (JAP 69).

Locally compromised situations can cause bad relationships; they can nonetheless improve with effort and communication. Thus, JAP 46 told us he had arrived in a difficult service: there had not been any JAP for a year. Fresh out of the judge school he had had to take over a service which, in the absence of a JAP, had been completely – and illegally – engulfed by the prison services. Bad – and equally illicit – habits had been taken up, and these persisted for a while. For instance, the prison services would filter prisoners' applications to the JAP. A clarification was needed but it was equally important for it not to offend his interlocutors. Luckily this JAP was calm, cold-headed and diplomatic, yet assertive. In fact he too considered that his relationship with the probation service, and with the prison services was very good. Indeed, many JAPs actually felt that these relationships are not only good, but are actually excellent:

'They are very *very* good.' (JAP 65).

b. Variation factors

A first variation factor is **the size of the jurisdiction**, even if it is not always decisive. Unsurprisingly, in big jurisdictions, JAPs often have a negative perception of probation services' work (see *infra*) and in fact these judges are typically not in a position to do the qualitative work they would aspire to. This inevitably generates tensions between these two partners, each being tempted to cast responsibility onto the other for each other's predictable deficiencies.

In one jurisdiction, the relationship was particularly damaged. The probation service was overloaded and worn out to the extreme and it thus always acutely underperformed as we could see by checking their reports, which most of the time were useless and at times even non-existent. There was clearly a general sloppiness in this service and the JAP had reached such an exasperation level – his service being regularly paralysed as a result – that he could no longer find ways to communicate in a serene and effective way.

One of the Master Plus students who did an internship in this JAP's service for several weeks took the following field notes:

'During the last three days I have also seen the files and reports that were uploaded on the common server APPI – when it actually functioned – and saw a patent lack of dedication on the part of the probation officers. This morning all we did was ask the probation officers in charge of the files to please send the documented proof that were supposed to be attached to the files'.

The same student attended a CAP where she was exposed to the extremely shocking attitude of the probation officers. One of them displayed an exceptional level of disrespect for the JAP. In addition, during another CAP she noticed that the probation officers who officiated that day were not aware of the content of the files which were supposed to be processed that day and would nonchalantly answer for every single one of them: 'It's not my file, I cannot tell you anything'. In a third CAP, JAP 13 asked the probation officer a question pertaining to a specific file who answered: 'You can't possibly expect me to read the files!'

A second variation factor is **how far JAP and probation services are from each other**. Because they are both constantly under pressure and overloaded, JAPs and probation services do not have the time to work on their relationship and to maintain enough direct interaction with each other. Probation services left the tribunals when they became autonomous from the JAPs in 1999, although their actual moving sometimes took years. In certain cases, direct contact was still maintained afterwards.

'They first kept a committee room at the tribunal in order to avoid probationers' attrition. And when the prosecutor left, the prison services came and told the chief of the tribunal that this committee room would have to stop and he invoked fallacious reasons for it. The truth is that they wanted to cut the cord between the JAP and the probation service. Besides, it's idiotic because they don't even have enough room at the probation service. They really forced their way through in this matter and did not even notify me' (JAP 32).

In other cases, as with JAPs 8, 9, 20 and 21, the probation service had still been recently situated in the tribunal at the time they were interviewed and the move had just occurred. All these JAPs referred to cordial relationships and to authentic partnership. In another jurisdiction, the JAP told us that the probation service was situated across the street and that it was consequently very easy to simply cross it in order to have a discussion. In another, the probation service's building was actually in a building right next door to the tribunal so that communication and mutual understanding had been maintained. The probation service did understand how a court would work and problems could be solved immediately and directly. However, proximity is not always a panacea. JAP 43 himself worked outside of the tribunal in an office where his service was on one floor and the probation on another. Whereas this should have been ideal, he told us that in fact relationships between services had been bad for years and he himself had no idea what had started it. Nonetheless, he did say that he went along very well with older probation officers and could actively collaborate with them. This was confirmed by an instance which we witnessed, as the following field notes show:

'JAP 43 welcomes a probationer in his office who was released a few months back after a very long prison sentence for a series of counts of aggravated rape. He clearly has a mental illnesses and I am told he also has hepatitis C. When he committed his offences, he had only been in France for a short period of time. He came from Gabon where he was born and had lived all his life with his Gabonese mother. He has been staying in a shabby hotel found by the probation service for him but he's idle and terrorised by the Parisian crowd and unable to find his way around the metro and, as a result, never leaves his place and is very bored. The JAP worries that he might get worse and commit another crime. He both feels concern about the risk that this 'justiciable' represents and pity for this poor lost and ill-adapted soul who may have French nationality but who is a foreigner in France. He decides to call an 'old generation' probation officer to his office. Both of them have a long talk and try and find solutions. They talk to the offender in order to try and make him understand what they are trying to put together. I then learn that this probation officer has been driving the offender around Paris whenever he needed to get paperwork done. This has enabled her to put forward what is for the probationer a pressing question: according to him he only has French nationality and Gabon does not want him back but he has all his family over there and would really like to return to Gabon. The JAP and probation officer then try and find a solution to his legal and administrative conundrum. They mention applying for a passport and a visa. Caught in the collaborative atmosphere I suggest that this person probably has, without even knowing it, Gabonese nationality since he was born there, his mother is Gabonese and he has lived there all his life. When I return to my office I check it out and confirm to the JAP and probation officer that indeed their client is Gabonese'.

This scene shows how effective offender focussed collaboration between JAPs and probation officers can be. We shall return to this subject *infra*. It also shows that collaboration probably comes more naturally to probation officers who knew CPAL.

A third variation factor precisely pertains to **the generation to which probation officers belong**. Nearly 15% of the JAPs – a significant figure given the fact that there was no question on this subject – said they preferred working with older generation probation officers, who had been recruited before the 'probation and insertion councillor' status had been created in 1993. According to these JAPs, older generation probation officers who were former 'social assistants' and 'educators' did more qualitative work:

'Older generation probation officers used to get their hands dirty!' (JAP 43; JAP 45).

'Old school probation officers had a vocation, like social workers. They worked up a sweat to do the investigations and obtained more information.' (JAP 64).

This point of view was actually confirmed by a probation service chief:

'Based on the report that I have to validate, my impression is that there is this new generation which does put in content and does have a good command of computers, but what I deplore is that they do not check out the information and that their reports are full of 'Mister so and so declares that', whereas older generations would actually go and see people and did not hesitate to open up to new things. Building up networks of partners, finding ways to improve how we sort administrative problems for offenders, that's what we get with older generations. New ones are keener on checking formal compliance with obligations' (DPIP 5).

Some practitioners wanted to elaborate on probation officers' recruitment and commented that they perceived their work differently. Indeed they have an increased workload, but they also have a more bureaucratic understanding of their job. Indeed, those of them who are lawyers – that is an increasing proportion of them – are disconnected from the complexity of offenders' social and psychological issues, thus possibly explaining why they sometimes behave in a way or express points of view which are rather surprising:

'I have noticed that older generations behaved too much like social assistants; today that's not it at all and in fact it's exactly the other way around. I am shocked when I hear CPIP say 'Mister Such and Such has disappointed me. I don't care I don't want to see him again!' I tell them that they'll have to continue and that we have to work with this person. My colleague and I often have to warn the V service and tell them 'Mister X will be released in a year and it is a huge huge concern because nothing has been done yet and one has to get started right away.' Indeed they are overloaded as they only have seven interns and only one confirmed [CPIP] for 600 inmates, but still, they only care about those of the inmates who ask them for something. This is our pet theme here' (JAP 49).

JAPs also deplored the inherent logic behind French offender supervision where everything is expected from offenders who have to make reinsertion efforts entirely on their own (Herzog-Evans, 2011 c and 2012a):

'I fulminate quite a lot about some of the CPIP's discourse who say: "these people! One has to put an end to this welfare and dependency policy. They have to do things on their own"' (JAP 49).

Another JAP, who was himself a former probation service educator, made a similar analysis:

'Twenty years ago, all my former colleagues came from psychology and sociology [universities] whereas now 90% of them come from law faculties and sit a host of other exams. They do not have what it takes to be a social worker but at the same time this is not what they're asked to be anymore. I don't feel that these past years' recruits see the bigger context behind rehabilitation whereas in fact rehabilitation is a bigger picture issue. It does not just go down to whether the offender comes back at the end of his furlough' (JAP 69).

However, most JAPs were more nuanced: the important issue is not officers' background, but **how they do their job**. What counts for a JAP is that they can write good and thorough reports, and explain their opinion, check facts and do not merely take on face value what the offender says. In short, they like those who do their job well, which in turn allows them to do theirs.

'I personally have a good relationship with them, but it is true that there are some amongst them with whom I get along better. It is those who do a thorough job and write good reports' (JAP 23).

Another important variation factor is **communication between the probation service and JAPs**. This issue was the one JAPs were the most loquacious about. They pointed towards several obstacles to good communication. The first, i.e. geographical distance, was mentioned previously. Nowadays, communication mostly goes through APPI, the server JAPs share with probation services. A second obstacle lies in the barrier that probation service chiefs may erect between JAPs and probation staff, which was confirmed by several of them as we shall see *infra*:

'What I would like is for contacts between JAP and probation officers not to be interrupted so that they can talk directly to each other without having to run it through their hierarchy or at least for this communication to be easier and more direct than through writing numerous APPI notes which they then have to get validated by their chief before they can be forwarded to the JAP' (JAP 12).

In concrete terms, JAPs would like to actually see probation staff more often and participate in their meetings or some of their activities.

'I would like to participate in the meetings they organise between probation services, shelters, psychologists when it comes to the most serious cases' (JAP 75).

As we shall see *infra*, probation officers also aspire to more frequent and direct communication with the JAP.

'CPIP also complain about the split with JAPs. Older CPIP unanimously regret the pre 1999 era' (JAP 23).

Conversely, other JAPs seemed to have totally accepted the new situation to the point where they do not consider distance to be an issue nor feel the desire to communicate more. They stated that communication is direct since they give probation services their phone number! This might indeed be a means to reduce distance, although it has nothing to do with authentic collaboration, nor with a true relationship.

'Well not so much here because they know I am available for their calls. So yes perhaps that geographical distance means we have no more direct contact. We go once a year to the probation service to talk about the new law reforms and they talk to me about their difficulties. But we do have phone exchanges' (JAP 67).

'Well we the JAPs or the chiefs of service such as Mrs X don't go so often to the meetings. When I arrived here I went to the probation service. After that I did not need to anymore. I call them over the phone, especially if I have a question. I also issue general guidelines' (JAP 74).

They are indeed 'sentences' implementation commissions' (COMEX). However, they are only service meetings between the JAPs and the probation service and their goal is not to talk or collaboratively discuss files, but to sort out problems between their services by drafting protocol agreements. Increasingly, the prison services, caught up in their own logic of national uniformity over the whole territory – despite the vast differences between these territories – put the JAPs under pressure for them to sign up the **protocols** which the prison services have unilaterally designed. Some JAPs agreed to sign them up; others strongly refused to. It is in fact inadmissible and illegitimate for one of the parties concerned to try and impose onto another, protocols which have not been conjointly prepared by both. Some JAPs also pointed out that through the actual content of these protocols, their goal is to force them to sign for a significant reduction of the actual work that probation officers will do. For instance, they are pressured to accept the disappearance of pre electronic monitoring enquiries which used to determine whether such a measure was feasible given the offender's specific circumstances and this even though the literature has shown how indispensable they were (Beyens & Kaminski, 2013: 156). It may be important for both parties to organise how they will work together in order for their actions to reach a certain level of predictability. For instance, as will be seen *infra*, it can be important to determine in which cases the probation service should appraise JAPs of offenders' obligations' violations. Nonetheless, protocols, and particularly those which are unilaterally forced onto JAPs, are not conducive of good personal relationships between both parties. In fact, the absence of protocol has been cited by some JAPs as constituting proof that the relationship they had with the probation service was good:

'I have an excellent relationship with them. We are really close; we do not have protocols. We call each other; they have my direct line. They communicate well with me whenever there is a problem' (JAP 19).

c. The importance of human factors

More so than material and institutional aforementioned factors, the human factor is clearly crucial in understanding the local state of the relations between a JAP and a probation service.

When things get bad it is first and foremost because on either side, individuals are uncompromising and have neither the desire nor the skills to communicate. Conversely, when such skills and when flexibility are present, and particularly on both sides, good relations are possible.

As previously stated, the goals and culture of JAPs and the probation service have started to diverge over the last years. For this reason, it is particularly important that both parties try and understand each other's professional context and demands and difficulties – and they are numerous.

'Probation officers are a little disoriented. Most of them joined in order to help, to do social work and in fact they used to be called social workers. Then they're told they are supposed to do probation work and later that they are supposed to do criminology. It really is complicated for them' (JAP 18).

Creating and sustaining good relationships goes beyond being open to other's circumstances. It also requires **rising above the current institutional war** which is orchestrated at top level and reaching out to the other in order to work together.

'When I got here a year and a half ago I quickly gathered them all for a meeting and told them that I was not interested in this war between the judiciary and probation and that my job was to work in partnership' (JAP 19).

A core component of a good relationship is for a JAP to compensate for the geographical distance by giving probation officers and their chiefs the means to contact them directly. Many JAPs told our team that they had given their direct phone line and were reachable at any time. However, as will be seen *infra*, it is unfortunately frequent for local probation hierarchies to block direct interaction between the JAP and their subordinates.

'It is true that they asked me to at first and indeed a JAP can be mobile and I followed in my predecessor's footsteps here. It's thanks to this that we created such ties. Indeed we had to create boundaries: I told them not to call me every five minutes, except if there was an emergency and I told them to communicate via APPI. At the same time they know I am available and so are they' (JAP 39).

'Well it did happen to me that the PO did not have the same analysis of the file which I had and when there is a problem we have a talk over the phone or via email. I try and talk about it. I try and not let a communication problem linger and it's always informal; we have email exchanges' (JAP 74).

Even more important is the **establishment of a direct human relationship** where the JAP actually goes to the probation service and organises meetings other than those which are mandatory. Such was for instance the case in JAP 65's jurisdiction. Yet, when she had arrived in her new office, things did not look good. The probation service was in a bad shape; there was not a single probation officer left in it, whereas there had previously been four of them; only a secretary officiated who would act as a receptionist for offenders. Things improved a little with the arrival of two new probation officers; this, however, was not enough for qualitative work to be done. Such difficult circumstances could have badly affected the relationship between the JAP and the probation service. However, this was not the case as the JAP had decided to fully communicate and to create a system whereby phone calls and meetings would be frequent and always possible, and showed that she fully understood their persistent difficulties. She said that her relationship with the probation officers was 'very very good'.

The team observed several such success stories, where the JAP had managed to remain diplomatic, respectful and to accept the context in which their probation partners had to operate, by not being too demanding, but keeping focussed on what was essential. They thus displayed communication skills which were essential in most jurisdictions:

'One has to be firm yet diplomatic' (JAP 73).

Such an attitude also correlates with JAPs' institutional position. Probation officers are very sensitive to how JAPs treat them. In particular, they do not like it when they behave like 'I am the judge here' and 'you are the executant'. JAPs who behave or are thought to be behaving like this can be assured that they will immediately be badly perceived by their interlocutors. It is important at this point to remember that probation officers are increasingly lawyer-like; something which the annual demographic statistics drawn by the National School of Prison Services (the ENAP) confirm year after year [61]. Many of them would rather have passed the more prestigious national magistrate or attorney exams. I personally see these generations of Master Plus students in criminal law to whom I have been teaching for nearly two decades [62]: most students start out by wanting to pass these exams and either fail before falling back on the less prestigious probation staff national exams. Alternatively they may also change their mind during this last university year, because they are at long last caught up by the reality principle and realise they will probably be luckier with the latter ones. I personally also hope that I have managed to convince some of them that probation offers have great perspectives and that it is a fascinating line of work. It is however natural for those who turn to probation exams to feel envious of the 'first in the class' who have succeeded. If the latter conspicuously brandish their status in their face, this can only alienate their partners.

'Here things work rather well. I tend to treat my probation service for what it is: independent from me. I have no hierarchical authority over it. Often, my colleagues forget that they cannot give them orders. It's a little like my prosecutor colleagues with the police. The JAP has no power over the probation service. It must consider it as an external agency. It is hard and one has to be diplomatic and to have human interaction skills. But once you respect that and people, things go well. Sometimes one needs to shake them up, but in moderation. But one must bear one's goals in mind. Again, my colleagues often come out as 'I am the judge so I give the orders!' [laugh] (JAP 73).

JAPs and probation officers increasingly have the same background. Moreover, their aspirations are very close. As mentioned above, JAPs want to be close to '*justiciables*' and to help with reinsertion. In my aforementioned study regarding probation officers, I heard them answering in the same vein to this very same question. This was confirmed by the probation staff who were interviewed in the present research.

In several jurisdictions **'good practices'** were put in place. Their main advantage was to maintain a close enough proximity between probation staff and JAPs so that each would be more aware of the other's context and difficulties. These examples must be borne in mind as they relate to the three fundamental bullet point values in probation which I refer to consistently in

---

61 http://www.enap.justice.fr/.

62 First, as lecturer at the University of Paris X-Nanterre in 1996, then since 2000-2001 and until today at the Bordeaux IV-Pau-ENAP setting of Agen, and at the University of Nantes; and lastly, since 2006, as a professor at the University of Reims.

the present book: a) relationship; b) communication; c) partnership. For indeed:

'In order for things to work we need close ties between JAPs and probation services' (JAP 35).

A first example which takes place in several jurisdictions consists of probation officers being invited to JAP hearings. Such a practice was created a few years back in a Parisian suburb court, X. Rather than inviting, which is more frequent and actually envisaged by the penal procedure code itself (PPC, art. 712-6 and D 49-17), the chief of the probation service to the hearings which take place *in prison*, here it is probation officers who are invited to the *tribunal* hearings. There are several advantages to this system. Firstly, one can have an immediate response to a question pertaining to the file. JAP 28 actually said that this prevents probationers from lying in terms of the supervision they have benefitted from. However, this particular point raises concerns. Whilst, in most cases, these are indeed lies or defensive posturing, in rare cases supervision will have been dysfunctional; if a probation officer is present, this prevents probationers from voicing their criticism. Indeed the attorneys who were interviewed for this research immediately saw that this would be a problem if such a practice were to go to scale. Conversely, as the research showed in another jurisdiction, at times, the probation officer can actually give weight to what the '*justiciable'* says. Such was the case with this former addict who had not taken drugs or even alcohol in three years. The probation representative who was present did confirm that he was 'not the same man' as he was before, which then led the prosecutor to speak in the same vein. Both thus probably reinforced the person's desistance process (Maruna, 2001; Maruna, 2011).

The presence of probation officers in court makes JAP hearing even more similar to PSC hearings where every person who has contributed to the offender's supervision and care is present and can testify and find solutions to potential difficulties. It is also similar to England and Wales and Scotland's sentencing hearings (Tata et al., 2008). There is no doubt that international examples of good practice support probation officers' presence at court.

However, in order to avoid any infringement of probationers' defence rights other JAPs invite probation officers who have not supervised them. Their presence in court is thus not useful in terms of proof or direct information on the case; it is still very important from the second viewpoint, which is, in my opinion, essential, i.e. it does allow probation officers to see what goes on during these hearings. As we shall see later, a major source of incomprehension comes from a lack of understanding regarding unanticipated and misunderstood decisions because they are unaware of what can happen in court and oblivious to the fact that opinions other than their own are also expressed there. Letting them see hearings gives them a clue about what they are usually unacquainted with and, *inter alia*, that probationers do not behave and do not experience the same things in court as they do in the probation service. Hearings are instances where truths which no other setting allows to surface are voiced and discovered. Letting probation officers access them allows them to be made aware of JAPs' reality and, as a result, improves their relationship. Indeed, JAP 28 said she had excellent relations with the probation service. that she knew its staff well, communicated with them, and so on. When she was asked whether she was sometimes disappointed with the quality of the supervision done by the probation service there was first a telling long silence followed by strong denegation.

JAP 28 had inherited a system which had been put in place by a former JAP, who was also interviewed: JAP 69. JAP 69 added that he had also implemented it in his new court and also had excellent relations with the probation service, stating that they worked collaboratively, had regular meetings and a no nonsense and problem-solving approach to things. During the meetings, all partners – and not, as is too often the case, only the probation services' managers and JAPs – were present, that is: the JAP, the probation officers and their chiefs and managers, prison staff, clerks, and even - which is bordering on a miracle - medical staff, and so on. Here is how he depicted these meetings:

'Before the meeting, a month before, everybody sends me his suggestions for discussion and we make decisions there and reassess them every six months. And I write the minutes of the meetings for everybody to read the very next day' (JAP 69).

This collaborative and problem-solving culture which was created in X by JAP 69 still existed years after he had left. In the course of this research we learnt that in Y, a small West Coast court, probation officers also participated in hearings. One of the students who saw these hearings noted that the JAP presided over them in a classic way, but systematically allowed the probation officer to speak in order to express his/her point of view, then allowed the prosecutor to speak, and, according to the law, the last word was for the attorney and/or his client. We learnt of a similar practice in a prison which held long term prisoners. There, the main goal was to facilitate good communication and common understanding:

'Yes we have launched this new policy for both prison and community settings where we try and associate a maximum of people. Within prisons, it is not only probation officers who are present, but also a person from the prison services so that they all understand where our decisions come from' (JAP 73).

Unfortunately these good practices cannot be implemented everywhere nor in all circumstances. As we shall see, probation chiefs are often hostile to this as they analyse it as being unproductive for their own service. The undeniable extremely heavy caseload which their staff have to endure makes it very difficult to go to scale.

Simpler but nonetheless useful practices have been put in place in other courts. They aim to create a more convivial work environment with other partners and agencies than APPI and phone calls. For instance, in Z, the prison governor, the probation chief of service, the JAP and the prosecutor, were all newly appointed and had more or less arrived in their new job at the same time. This made it possible for them to create their own communication channels and style, which would not be pulled down by previous experiences. Regular work meetings were put in place, which, in the same vein as the CAP, led to a rather congenial 'new tradition' whereby they would take turns to bring a cake. A similar practice was in place in A, as JAP 69 and Chief of service 1 confirmed. In other jurisdictions, we heard about retirement, transfer, and birth drinks parties where everybody was invited. We also heard of the JAP knocking on each and every member of staff's door when he went to the probation service for a meeting, and so on. These modest good practices have little weight in view of stronger institutional factors; they nonetheless do smooth the edges.

d. Institutional factors

Recent changes in probation and in probation officers' work have profoundly destabilised practitioners (Herzog-Evans, 2011 b; Dindo, 2011; Larminat, 2012) and made them particularly vulnerable to their quotidian difficulties:

'Probation services are like drunken sailors. And their unions are super powerful. They are people who cannot be tamed; they have no methodology. You have people who work remarkably well and others who don't do anything! Others do weekend overtime and they are paid the same… clearly things have become worse since the recent probation services' reform [here he refers to the Decree of December 2011]. The judiciary cannot tell them anything anymore. It has to go through their chief and nobody ever answers' (JAP 27).

The very professional identity of probation services, the very meaning of their work, which was still stable a few years back (Lhuilier, 2007) is now being reconsidered. A form of consensus in favour of more evidence-based practices in probation may be emerging at the time I am finishing this book (Dindo, 2011; Herzog-Evans, forthcoming j). Indeed, this is demonstrated by the organisation of the recent conference of consensus for the prevention of reoffending by the French Ministry of Justice and by the Unions' contributions which were made public [63]. However, as the contribution of the headquarters of the prison services reveal, it also made even more visible their exclusive focus on preventing reoffending [64] as being the sole purpose of probation services. It has also made clear that the prison services perceive this purpose as excluding social work– and this is typical of the aforementioned 'prison thinking'. Superficial criminological knowledge has for instance led them to insert in the so-called assessment tool, the DAVC, items pertaining to how the offender perceives his/her own offence and denial whilst also demanding from offenders that they 'work on their offending' without, in most cases, helping them with their cognitive and circumstances issues, even if it may border on the absurd. For instance, in one file which I obtained for this research, pertained to a mentally impaired woman who also had behavioural problems and a severe alcohol addiction. In addition, she had not held down a job since 1992, had had no contact with her family in a long time and was in a severely compromised financial and material situation. In relation to this case, the sole conclusion of the DAVC was that she had to do 'a lot of work on her own responsibilities' and should also 'work on her relationships with her family and the way in which she dealt with her problems 'through drinking and taking medications'. At no point did this DAVC envisage that the probation service should help her do this monumental work. Luckily, and as seen previously, JAPs are usually more distant towards this so-called 'position as of the offence'. What they are looking for is first and foremost concrete information pertaining to employment, training, housing, treatment, family circumstances and serious and evidenced material details.

What is at stake here is that JAPs and probation staff who were so closed in the past and used to have the same goals and values are now drifting apart. Whereas JAPs are still attempting to be craftsmen and to keep focussed on the four pillars laid out in article 707, probation services are too often imprisoned in managerial figures and unfortunately, as a result, on superficial work in order to process more people and cases. This inevitably creates problems with JAPs who expect them to actually check the information they have to collect and to do qualitative supervision.

'Reports haven't been good in a long time. I know how they operate. Even if … it does irritate me at times I take things for what they are, I man-

63. http://conference-consensus.justice.gouv.fr/.

64. http://conference-consensus.justice.gouv.fr/2013/01/08/direction-de-ladministration-penitentiaire/.

age to sort of, well that is they manage to con me at times… when decisions are important I postpone them so that I can serenely rule' (JAP 52).

JAPs also criticised probation services' managerial and bureaucratic downward spiral which some of them analyse as being the price to pay for the aforementioned judicialisation of sentences' implementation.

'We immediately saw it coming before it actually happened as this was the price to pay for judicialisation. We knew we would fall into the trap of a much more techno-institutional functioning. Beforehand, we used to talk things through between doors and could sort things out on the spot. Judicialisation has formatted and formalised things with probation services which as a result has had to become an industry' (JAP 69).

Some also criticised the very insertion of probation services into the prison services because of all the red tape and stiffness it generates.

'It's often rather difficult to work with probation services. The prison service is a rather difficult agency to work with. If it does not come from them they won't do it. Take for instance the disappearance of pre-electronic monitoring feasibility investigations. In the past they had made it mandatory even in instances where it was not necessary and now it's the other excessive way around. So now if you need one you need to fight for it. So it's a very monolithic agency and it is very complicated to maintain room to manoeuvre. Currently I have the problem of unaffected files. We had a considerable number of such files. We saw their number increase up to 500. I found that they had set the maximum number of files per probation officer at sixty-five. Then the Pornic case occurred and the prison services suddenly decided to allocate each and every single file. Before we wanted them to take on more cases and we were told it was totally impossible and then, all of a sudden, their headquarters tell them to do it and it becomes miraculously possible' (JAP 71).

When the quality of the work done by the probation services is not good enough, a minority of JAPs admitted they ask the third sector to do it in their stead, which in turns leads to more tensions with the state probation services which brace themselves as strongly as they can onto the notion of public service and have the feeling that the third sector's ultimate goal is to steal their job.

'Personally I love the third sector, but if you start heading that way, well besides they are not better trained… Moreover it also has a cost. I did my internship in a charity and it cost seventy euro per mission. And these are people who are not necessarily competent. And they do not supervise offenders afterwards' (CPIP 37).

'They are competitors. If it's occasional... but for placements in the community, it's clear that the third sector and the JAPs perceive us as being the one too many partner. Also we see utter rubbish, such as the charity who asks for conditional release. It's constant and we have to clarify things on a regular basis' (DPIP 6).

'They constantly want to technically or even financially participate in our own missions. I feel this happening really strongly. It's a good thing to have partners. For instance charity based intervention is interesting, and so are local agencies. But it's a fact that probation services have to stroll along their territory, have to be convinced of what their missions are and also have to be convincing. I know for a fact that some of my colleagues are not ready to dialogue like this. If we had the capacity to do rapid pre-trial reports, well why not then' (DSPIP 5).

Conversely, given their extreme caseload, other probation personnel did not object to the third sector taking some of it off their shoulders. Such has indeed been the case with the March 27, 2012 law which transferred pre-sentence reports to the third sector:

'If they are able to take over such tasks, since we have so much work... We still do them in X, but not in Y, even if I have managed to reduce their number with the approval of the prosecutor...' (DSPIP 7).

In the Paris region, JAP 43 explained that he now only wanted to read reports from either one of two charities whose details he gave to couples involved in domestic violence who asked him whether they could live together again. He explained: 'I know my probation service. It will send me an empty report which will add nothing to the file and will not allow me to rule based on a minimum level of security guarantees. In such cases, danger is very real and responsibility huge'. Conversely, he added that the two charities carried out a thorough investigation which comprised of home visits, which, as we have seen, are rapidly disappearing from state probation.

There is a serious risk for state probation to be perceived with mistrust by some JAPs who tend to assimilate their staff to prison staff.

'In prison settings I have seen rather complicated things to deal with which could be explained by a number of things. For instance, a new semi-freedom wing had been created and for this institution it 'had to be filled in' and the DSPIP made it his personal endeavour and would build projects with his CPIP with which we the JAP might disagree' (JAP 64).

What transpires both through the interviews of JAPs and CPIP is that there may at times be **issues with probation managers**. According to the JAPs, probation management often prevents them from having good relationships with probation officers. To be more precise, DSPIP or DSPIP often oppose JAPs having direct contact with CPIP and vice versa as they want to be the only ones to benefit from such direct contact. As we shall see *infra*, this is an erroneous understanding of what management should consist of in order to be efficient and collaborative whilst at the same time remaining totally removed from what their subordinates actually expect from them. If, as a result, one simply relies on often unreliable technology (e.g. fax machine or APPI) to send the JAP crucial and/or urgent information as opposed to phoning him/her, catastrophes can occur. It is however important to note that of all the 'chiefs' we interviewed, only one seemed to correspond to this category.

What JAPs expect from probation chiefs is that they organise their service in such a matter that it is reactive and efficient, does supervise offenders in a credible fashion and carries out the investigations it is mandated to carry out. As we have seen, this is unfortunately not always the case. Probation officers, on their part, want their chiefs to really supervise them and also want them to be their 'probation referent'; a point we shall return to. In other words, they want them to be able to advise their staff in difficult or delicate situations and to represent an authority in terms of knowledge and how to do things. According to them they unfortunately more often than not come across pure managers instead. A few middle managers appeared to us to be rather fragile, which raises the issue of their recruitment and training. In this vein, a former probation officer who had been promoted to DPIP told us he regretted it, but for the increased wages:

'Supervising teams and different personalities is very complex. We are not trained in the least for this. This lack of training puts us in a difficult position when it comes to managing teams. We don't always make the right decisions. Besides, CPIP are not easy people to manage. They have a hard time with authority… It's easier to supervise inmates than CPIP' (DPIP 4).

Questions relative to the recruitment and training of probation chiefs are even more acute than those raised by the recruitment and training of probation officers. They go way beyond the issue of communication and partnership with JAPs. For instance, the literature has shown that probation chiefs are essential to the implementation of RNR programmes (Andrews & Bonta, 2010). Research has shown that their effective implementation is indissolubly linked to the quality of the chief or chiefs (Taxman & Sachwald, 2010; Geiran, 2012) and that a programme is more efficient when it has been supported by a competent, charismatic and enthusiastic chief (Pearson et al., 2010). The extant literature pertaining to the skills which such chiefs must have in order to obtain optimal results is still limited. However, a recent study drawing on existing human resources science has confirmed that 'leaders' rather than 'managers' were better at executing projects and at making their subordinates implement them (Lee et al., 2010). Another study has unfortunately confirmed that paramilitary contexts, such as for instance, the prison context, were unlikely to produce such leaders (Massood et al., 2006).

Whilst the aforementioned American research (Lee et al., 2010) found that, fortunately, there were more 'leaders' in the United States than 'managers', it is impossible to say what results would be found in France. The present research did show that JAPs are confronted by a significant minority of 'managers' who sterilely defend their territory and are hostile to collaboration – but a minority, to which one must add, as in most professions, a handful of different characters:

'The director of X has a peculiar personality. He is not very refined and has a hard time with the fact that I am a woman who is twenty years younger than him and that he has to be accountable to me. However I get along well with his deputies. And that being said, it's not that catastrophic; we're not at each other's throat. I do see that he speaks more with my male colleague though' (JAP 68).

In most cases, however, JAPs say they are happy with their relationship with probation services management, and some are extremely positive when they describe the qualities of their interlocutors:

'She is a remarkable lady. Unfortunately she will be leaving shortly' (JAP 47).

2. Probation staff's point of view

As we have seen, probation staff and JAPs are very similar on a number of points. Firstly, an increasing number of probation officers and their managers are lawyers. This relatively recent and increasing phenomenon will inevitably – unless there is a policy change in recruitment – eventually take over completely. Despite the potential rivalries it may engender, it still means probation staff and JAPs have a common background. Secondly, JAPs and probation officers have similar aspirations: they want to have close interaction with '*justiciables*' and to do socially useful work which contributes to the reinsertion and prevention of reoffending. It is thus not surprising that, just as in 2007 (Lhuilier, 2007), probation personnel usually like their JAPs and respect their job and that, just like JAPs, they would like to communicate more with them. However, from the institutional viewpoint, JAPs and probation staff have moved apart in recent years. They have yet to compromise the common respect they have for each other, although this has undoubtedly already created tension.

a. Global satisfaction

Probation officers' opinions regarding JAPs were glowingly positive; those of their chiefs were also, but to a lesser degree, positive. 76.3% of probation officers and 56.2% of their chiefs said they were happy about the JAP they had encountered – bearing in mind they might not have appreciated such or such an individual.

'Based on my short experience, I think there are more good JAPs than bad ones' (DSPIP 3).

'Oh they are good! [strongly emphatic] I have been lucky to work with some JAPs, even if I know that their status is not well respected... I have worked with young ones freshly out of school and they did this job with interest and dynamism. I have only met super people. Even now with their three different personalities, they try and do their job and to give meaning to it' (CPIP 34).

In fact, probation staff often agree with the decisions made by JAPs, with, of course, some exceptions.

'"My" JAP, because there are four of them. There are three working on community sentences. I would say that they are rather different and I think that they are often right. I rarely disagree... I find X's practice rather coherent: recall of a measure or parole only is a last resort and when a magistrate of X reaches that point, it means that all the possible solutions have been tried or that the risk for public order or the victim is too great. I find that they are often fair' (CPIP 2).

For some practitioners, the JAP is just as much an institution as he/she is an individual.

'The relationship is very good; we are work partners. Then again we try and work based on good terms. We are accountable to them, which is entirely fair. They are work partners, but not hierarchical authorities' (CPIP 37).

On the part of probation officers, there is clear respect for the fact that JAPs are first and foremost judicial authorities.

'That is if I can give my opinion on a judge's decision' (CPIP 2).

'Well I have no demands towards judges... the sentences' implementation judge is both the judge of legality and the judge of the incident. In this context, he is independent and I have no problem with his independence. Who am I to judge her? Things are okay the way they are' (CPIP 20).

However, this point of view was not shared by all probation officers. A minority clearly felt that they are rivals as lawyers:

'You are telling me about the relationship between young CPIP and JAPs, but it's also because young CPIP's initial ambition was to become judges themselves and have the same study level and this stiffens things a little. In the same vein, 80% of our hierarchy are former probation officers and I have had probation chiefs who were my former interns and it was not easy. I heard young lawyer colleagues saying that the JAP was not a very good lawyer, not as good as they were.... Ancients like me never competed on petty procedural issues with them; we did not see ourselves as rivals. On the contrary I ask them for advice' (CPIP 35).

As will be seen *infra*, it is particularly important for probation officers to be acknowledged by their JAPs both for the importance and for the quality of their job. They expect JAPs not to contradict what they state in their reports and to thus display his/her trust in them, and even, as will be explained later, that he/she praises their work. Most probation staff actually think that such is indeed the case.

'They trust us. There is a trusting relationship and they are approachable. They trust us; they need our reports. If they ask for them it's for a reason' (CPIP 8).

'What I really appreciate with this JAP, is that she is approachable, whilst respecting CPIP. Here, judges are really accessible to the point where we can call them without having to go through their secretary or asking for permission beforehand. That's pleasant... So honestly, for someone fresh out of school, she has had to take over an impressive amount of things' (CPIP 30).

'We are not competing agencies; we work hand in hand and we trust each other. If there are things we need to say, and there were times there were hard things to hear, the judge felt instrumentalised, well she told us and so we changed our practices. So we talk things through when things don't work. There is no bad intent' (DPIP 5).

'The privileged relationship with the JAP... works well. The courts trust us and I have to say that it's very pleasant to be praised for what we do and to be able to share information with them collaboratively... what I deplore is probation services' hierarchy. A lot of those who have been appointed as chiefs... are completely out of their depth, and sometimes even non-existent. One wonders what their use is... it's sad but as far as I am concerned, it feels that my chiefs are the judges' (CPIP 25).

'All DSPIP envy me. It really is a collaborative work. Information really flows.... I call if there are doubts or problems, to sort things out with her... With [JAP 42] there is real professional trust... It's serene work. She takes the time to really investigate during the hearings' (DSPIP 1).

Conversely, lack of collaboration, respect and trust was deplored by the same probation chief as far as another interviewed JAPs (JAP 37) were concerned. There can indeed be personal preferences, but this does not reduce the general satisfaction:

'Well we have a new JAP who has just arrived for the prison and he is a former investigating judge and he is a problem because he has preconceived ideas about the files and has these whims with others... But here this is an individual case, other than that I have nothing to say against JAPs' practices and we very very often communicate by phone. They appraise us... What they expect is very very clear' (CPIP 12).

Probation officers may be so happy to work with their JAPs that many of them mentioned it was difficult to adapt to a new one – and interestingly JAPs said the same about probation chiefs:

'It's really complicated because the two JAPs are newbies. Before I had one who had been a JAP for a long time and was a former president of the ANJAP [65], Mrs X and of course I base my experience on her. She was a fantastic JAP actually' (CPIP 10).

Probation staff were satisfied with the way JAPs do their job, and the speed with which they react to situations (what they call 'reactivity' – see *infra*), which, as we shall see, is crucial for them:

'I appreciate JAPs' reactivity. In particular in prison she really listens to people, she is reactive. Yet when it's time to decide, she decides. She tries and have a maximum of information in order to reach the best possible decision and I enormously like working with her' (CPIP 23).

Probation officers unanimously answered yes when they were asked whether JAPs clearly explained the reasons behind their decisions in their rulings, known in French law as 'motivation'. It is obvious that probation staff clearly identify JAPs as being judges who carry out their judicial tasks well. In other words, probation staff unanimously acknowledged JAPs' competence as judicial actors and their judicial legitimacy was never contested. Things are more complex, as will be seen *infra*, when JAPs go beyond these strict judicial borders.

Most practitioners (JAPs and probation staff) laughed heartily when they were told of our considerable difficulties and efforts in trying to find 'bad JAPs'. Only a handful of probation personnel were in fact able to give us an example of a JAP who was difficult, rigid and mean to offenders. As a matter of fact, it became rapidly clear that those who were mentioned were pre-

65. The ANJAP is JAP organisation.

cisely the rare ones which my team and I had managed to eventually find. 'Bad JAPs' are indeed a rarity. Why, in that case are they brandished to this degree, and particularly in certain prison services circles to the point where their future disappearance was at one point envisaged? A conversation with JAP 71 was very revealing. He had spent some time at the ministry of Justice. According to him, bad JAPs may be rare, but when they are present, one talks about them at length. Probation officers nor their chiefs write to the prison headquarters in Paris to mention that such and such a JAP is marvellous and competent; they only write to complain about the bad ones. This inevitably leads to a distorted perception at headquarters level:

'For instance in Lyon, we systematically transferred inmates so that they could avoid the local JAP' (JAP 71).

He also insisted that there is a risk, with other not necessarily bad JAP, for judges to invoke their judicial imperium and to be inflexible and haughty in their relationship with others, particularly probation staff. On the contrary, what the latter want is a reachable JAP who is respectful of what they do.

'Yes judges are often authoritative. We have to be careful not to fall into this trap. They have problems with all their partners. It won't show so much with a correctional or a civil judge. It will just make their clerks' life difficult. Conversely, in functions where one has to work with other services, it makes things very complicated' (JAP 71).

Undoubtedly, however, and contrary to what has been suggested (Mouhanna et al., 2011), judges do not have a monopoly on stiffness. What this research has shown, is that whilst in most cases humans who work on both sides mean well and know how to communicate, problems, when they arise, are virtually always caused by difficult individuals who can belong just as well to the judiciary as to probation services.

During the second year of the research, a specific sanction section was developed. This example was chosen as it was clearly a source of tension. We asked probation officers whether they thought we could get rid of the JAP entirely and in particular in this domain. Only one (CPIP 4) said he was hostile to keeping JAPs even for breach cases. However, he was also the only interviewed probation officer who was extremely virulent towards JAPs in general. It is clear that CPIP – perhaps as a result of their legal training – have fully accepted judicialisation and understand that it constitutes a fundamental right for offenders to be heard and defended during a hearing. This is even more apparent with breach cases. However, most interviewees then went on to talk about JAPs' other missions. A great number of them were aware that one cannot be, as CPIP 3 put it 'judge and party'. They think that the separation of functions (: to probation services the proposition and the information; to the JAP the decision) is perfectly legitimate.

'I think that we have a good system, because we are those who help the judiciary reach its decisions; we do not make decisions, so it has to be someone who is an equivalent judge to the one who pronounced the sentence' (CPIP 7).

'No I am not a judge. It's great I think that we advise and someone else makes the decision' (CPIP 10).

Most probation officers answered something akin to: 'but who could make the decision anyway?' We then suggested that they or their service could decide. Their reaction was even more negative on the basis of their lack of legitimacy as members of the executive to make such decisions:

'Certainly not! We have no legitimacy for that!' (CPIP 12).

'Definitely not! Definitely not! I am against and strongly so, moving from such a competence to an administrative body. I think this would be a permanent breach of the law.... I think this would open the door to dramatic things such as what was seen in other countries' (CPIP 18).

'Clearly no! It's not possible! I don't understand! That's a rather odd conception of things!' (CPIP 37 – who first burst into laughter when it was suggested).

'It is not for us to make such decisions. I had to put a CPIP in her place recently as she was telling the probationer that he would go to prison if... It's not our decision to make' (DPIP 5).

The fact that they usually have a legal background certainly contributes to their position:

'Because of my training, I think that this function must remain in the hands of a judge who is the guardian of individual liberties... I think that this must remain in the realm of the judiciary and not become a judicial administration thing, or the thing of the prison services' (CPIP 9).

Their legal background also explains why these probation practitioners are fully aware of the importance of judicial rituals at this stage of the criminal justice process; an essential theme which will be explored further in Chapter 4. Here, the necessity of solemn judicial intervention is acclaimed not only for breach cases, but moreover for release and other decisions which JAPs make:

'I remain persuaded that justice must remain solemn. It is pedagogical for people who have been sentenced to have hearings where they can express their point of view, and it is very important in my opinion. People who are imprisoned who apply for release and see that their case is studied [that way] understand the decision better. If their application is rejected in particular, then the reasons for this refusal are explained and he can express his views and defend himself. If the procedure is completely written (and bearing in mind the difficulties that inmates have to understand written documents) it becomes senseless. The decision will not be understood as well and in my opinion will not be accepted as well' (DSPIP 3).

Importantly, twelve years after judicialisation took place, probation personnel have fully assimilated judicial rituals which, importantly, comprise of defence rights.

'It allows the inmate to express his views and to have an attorney' (DSPIP 4).

Spontaneously, some referred to the risk of the pure and simple extinction of JAPs:

'It is great that JAP weren't made to disappear' (CPIP 8).

'It would be a serious blow to defence rights' (DPIP 4).

As pointed out above, most practitioners questioned how breach cases broadened the discussion and were adamant they did not agree with the idea that judicial intervention in sentences' implementation should be withdrawn.

'Before there were permanent contacts with "*justiciables*"... I find that they still have an individual approach to things; I find that interesting.... Meeting the JAP allows to personalise and adapt to the person; he meets a judge face to face... and this allows the judge to have a more exact vision of the people who are supervised' (CPIP 18).

There are however the odd exceptions. Apart from CPIP 4, who is very hostile towards JAPs, CPIP 36 suggested, in line with the current practice in Belgium and after all, with French so called 'simplified procedures', that the JAP could deal with serious offences whilst probation staff would deal with shorter sentences.

Still, most probation practitioners had very positive opinions of JAPs.

b. Positive view of JAPs and desistance

Given the main purpose of this research, probation practitioners were obviously led towards discussions pertaining to JAPs and desistance. Overall, they expressed **positive opinions** concerning the qualities required to work in the field of rehabilitation:

'Most JAPs choose this function knowingly and because, I suppose, they have some understanding of reinsertion' (CPIP 15).

'Yes they are not at all punitive and have a specific sensitivity. Also they have passed various exams. I don't think that this function has a high status amongst junior judges. Indeed it is not so natural to help others' (CPIP 37).

A significant minority nonetheless noted – incidentally in the same vein as JAPs did regarding probation officers – that it **actually depended on the JAPs' personality**. Thus, a DPIP (DPIP 6) had rather negative things to say about her current JAP but added 'Hum… [hesitation] without generalising that is. 'I don't know'. As it happened, she belonged to this category of probation chiefs who tend to defend their turf against the JAPs. However, despite being rather critical of everything, she also added that probation personnel were in fact less favourable to reinsertion than JAPs were:

'Sometimes they lack that social vibe and see things through a rather theoretical prism. They do not realise what the real problems of people are.'

Some practitioners recalled instances where the JAP had had unrealistic expectations of what the offender could actually provide or of his circumstances:

'It depends. They are very tuned in reinsertion… but sometimes the obligations they set in their ruling are absurd. For instance a person has to work when that person is manifestly unfit' (CPIP 37).

'Well I would say that without being a statistician, some have a hard time understanding, that even if the Code contains certain obligations…. they have a hard time seeing what the global picture impact of their decisions is' (DSPIP 5).

Other practitioners seem to confirm an overall impression which former aforementioned studies (Herzog-Evans, 2011 b and c ; 2012 a) pertaining to probation officers showed, that is, that probation officers might be currently **drifting from a reinsertion culture** which they used to share with the JAP as they did complain that the JAPs were in fact too focused on reinsertion.

'Sometimes a little too much… [laughter]. I don't know if it is the new sociology of JAPs. Beforehand, probation officers were the hippies. The classic educator was pictured in flip flops. But here we are back to standards. But sometimes we are surprised how lenient some JAPs are. Sometimes they put us in a bad spot because they don't tend to make the right decision at the right time. It varies considerably, but I think that they are more lenient than CPIP' (DSPIP 4).

Conversely, they sometimes criticise JAPs for being too inflexible concerning the release of inmates.

'First they are not very humane. Second, it's more a matter of them being judges and having to take into account a number of different parameters and it is difficult for them to release given the political climate. What the legislator asks them to do is complicated and paradoxical and it's difficult to make sense of it' (DSPIP 7).

Here one comes across a rather **classic schizophrenic perception of JAPs**: sometimes 'Santa Claus'; other times 'Mister Bogeyman'. This schizophrenic perception should not come as a surprise: probation staff themselves have very diverse personalities and philosophies and what they expect from a JAP will vary accordingly and will also depend on where they work. There is nothing similar, for instance, between a probation officer who works in the community and a probation officer working in a high security prison. As a matter of fact JAPs' practice will also differ correspondingly. It is only natural that a JAP who works in a high security prison would release offenders more cautiously and it is what they are increasingly expected to do by policy makers.

Furthermore, contrary to probation personnel, JAPs have to embrace and implement all the guiding principles of article 707 section 2 of the PPC. If probation services are also theoretically bound by this rule, they also have their own objective as laid down in article 13 of the Prison Law [66].

There is an important difference between article 707 and article 13: the first refers to **victims**, whereas the second ignores them. In fact, the probation officers who were interviewed never mentioned victims once, contrary, albeit in a rather limited way, to the JAP. If of all the rulings which were studied not one refused to grant a favourable measure or release based on the sole point of view of or because of the victim, when the victim did express his or her point of view, it was, as it should be by law, reported in the ruling and as a result did play a part in the decision. More importantly (Herzog-Evans, 2008), the victims' concrete needs or interests are taken into account in order to shape the modalities of supervision. This factor is completely off the probation services' radar. Today, such pragmatic interest for the needs of victims at the sentences' implementation phase of the criminal justice process (Herzog-Evans, 2012-2013 a: 01.181-01.189), which, in my opinion is perfectly legitimate (also see Nellis, 1999: 237) is not restricted to victims of serious crimes. This research has shown that JAPs are extremely concerned about the security of women and children in domestic violence cases. It is a recent phenomenon and a rather welcome one that France would now be

66. Article 13 states that: 'Penitentiary probation and reinsertion service staff is in charge of preparing and implementing the decisions of judicial authorities pertaining to the insertion or reinsertion of people under judicial mandate who are awaiting trial or have been sentenced. In this capacity, it implements insertion and reoffending prevention policies, supervises or controls people under judicial mandate and prepares the release of detained persons'.

concerned with the physical security of victims beyond the sentencing phase. Indeed, taking victims into account in their rulings would inevitably colour JAPs' decisions in a sense which could, because of their own differing focus, be considered as null and void by probation practitioners. Other questions may also be the bones of content between probation staff and JAPs.

c. A first bone of content with breach cases

As previously mentioned, probation staff may well be currently **drifting from the former common goals and principles** they used to share with JAPs. Some are clearly more punitive than them. For instance, we never heard a single one of them speaking in the following vein:

'I had been misled concerning offenders' personalities. I mean most of the time it is a choice, even if in their lives they had a difficult life course. But they did choose to become offenders'(CPIP 31).

'Wait a minute M. you can make the effort in favour of the victim according to your means, but here you, according to what you are telling me, can definitely pay fifteen euros a month; and on the other hand the prosecutor will say 'oh no poor thing!' Oh Come on! She chain smokes fags and does not care that you are being made a complete moron here. I mean you cannot work anymore here and you cannot make the person budge' (CPIP 3).

As a matter of fact it is the entire criminal justice process which is accused of being too lenient:

'At times I have a hard time understanding that people who benefit from a series of measures (two probation orders, two community sentences, a community sentence mixed with a probation order, day-fines, and so forth) can escape custody. I think that at times there is a lack of punitivity with this addition of various measures: two probation orders, two probation orders mixed with community work, day-fines, and EM on top of it! Comes a time, in my opinion where incarceration cannot be avoided' (CPIP 15).

Crucially, and radically contrasting with the JAP (see *supra*) was the rather unexpected reaction which most probation staff who were interviewed had: despite the Pornic case, which at the time was still recent [67], virtually all of them said they were **indifferent to public opinion** in their daily practice and in particular when the time came to referring a breach or violation to the

---

67. The next high profile case (the Chloée case) had not yet occurred at the time of the interviews. It even more strongly shows that public security should in practice be made the equal of the other principles laid down in article 707, notably reinsertion and the rights of victims.

JAP. Surprisingly, most interviewees used the same strong language: 'I don't give a toss!' As can be expected, however, their chiefs did not share their logic. It is important to point out that in the Pornic case the probation chief of service was eventually sacked.

'It is true that there is still the syndrome of the Angers case and practitioners have been deeply affected by this case' (DSPIP 5).

'[laughter] Ha! I am afraid too [of the evening news syndrome]; it's not just the JAP. I have fun with the JAP about this: "so we'll be in the 8 O'clock news!" It's not so bad if you're aware of it. It's something at least' (Chief of service 1).

The handful of probation officers who worked in high security prisons also had a different opinion to that expressed by the majority:

'We want to have a maximum of information. So we take more precautions and I have to say that I too, with experience, feel responsible for giving [the JAP] a maximum of things, for placing the person in a place where he will not be in danger or won't put anyone in danger. I have known the era before judicial surveillance [68] where we did not know what the address of the person was once he was released' (CPIP 39).

However, this difference in penological perception is not in my view what explains the core of the dissensions between JAPs and probation staff pertaining to breach cases. More subtle yet crucial things are actually at stake. Firstly, it is **difficult for** probation staff **to continue supervising an offender who was referred to the JAP** for not having complied with his obligations if the JAP decides not to revoke the measure or, at the very least, does not do a convincing '*recadrage*'.

In the course of the research I thought of a metaphor which I then went on to present to practitioners on both sides. Indeed, there was unanimous agreement over it: the probation officer represents the mother who is exhausted with having to daily educate her children and, because of her closeness with them, loses the necessary credibility when it comes time to show authority. The JAP represents the father, who spends less time at home, but has a bigger voice and therefore, has more authority and obtains compliance more easily. When the mother/probation officer loses control during the day over her offspring/probationers and they take advantage, she threatens them: 'you'll see when Daddy/JAP comes back tonight!' When father/JAP returns home and refuses to punish his children/probationer, mother/probation of-

---

68. Judicial surveillance is a mandatory supervision measure for sex and violent offenders sentenced to at least seven years imprisonment which applies upon their release. It was created in 2005 (Law of Dec. 12, 2005) (Herzog-Evans, 20009 a).

ficer completely loses face and it becomes even more difficult for her the next day.

'This metaphor completely works for me [laughter]. I get a lot of that both at home and at work!' (CPIP 34).

Some JAPs were actually quite aware of this. For instance, JAP 46 told me that when he arrived in his court, the probation service apprised him of their needs in this respect and with the prosecutor, he thus decided that even though the Prison Law of 2009 allowed him to do so, he would not rerelease someone whose sentence had been revoked. When the JAPs respond to their needs, probation staff are very happy:

'For instance I had asked for the '*recadrage*' of this guy because he would not show up. This guy lied to him and told him: 'it's the probation service's fault. Mrs C never set up the appointments on the days I asked her to!' She answered: 'Mrs C always convoked you on Fridays' and he said that I would never convoke him on Fridays and at ridiculous hours before 5 P.M. She told him: 'No! Mrs C did convoke you every Fridays after 5 P.M. You took me for an idiot; you took the probation service for an idiot! You'll be convoked to court for a hearing!' Bam! Well I found that this was great. I found that this was coherent. The guy takes her for an idiot, whereas the other one [JAP] would, I don't know, do three '*recadrages*' and there would be no probation appointment he would respect and we would ask her eight times for a recall and she would never follow through' (CPIP 3).

Nonetheless, JAPs also have to take the file and what goes on during the hearing into account, thus possibly including victims' point of view. The prosecutors' requisitions and the arguments developed by the attorney and or the offender will also be important denominators. In other words, the JAP cannot base his/her decision solely on the probation services' advice or hopes and has to consider a great number of facts along with legal constraints. It is therefore inevitable that at times he/she will make decisions which will not satisfy the probation service: their perspectives are simply different. What is striking is that since probation personnel do not attend hearings – except in the aforementioned jurisdictions – they do not have access to part of 'sentences' implementation truth' to which JAPs do have access. Some probation officers are aware of this fact, and this even included CPIP 4, who, as stated above, was particularly hostile towards JAPs.

'But most of the time judges have the same opinions as probation services. Judges do see things that we don't see' (DSPIP 3).

'The judge sees things which we do not see' (DPIP 5).

Probation services also want JAPs to act quickly whenever they are apprised of an incident. Here, again, two logics may be opposed which remind us of the aforementioned metaphor. **When a probation officer refers an incident and this incident**, after the chief of the service has put his stamp on it, is referred to the JAP, it **often follows a series of problems**, delays and absences or repeated violations. The probation officer and often his/her hierarchy have already tried to sort things out on their own, without success. When they decide to appraise the JAP, it is because they have tried everything under the sun and they thus strongly expect that he/she will react swiftly and punitively.

'When we get to the point where we refer a case to the JAP it's by then time to thump the table. If then the person still gets yet another chance! It depends on the JAP. Some of them are very reactive, phone us, whereas with others nothing happens and in the end they don't take into account what we say. They have to understand that there comes a point where things don't work' (DPIP 6).

Legitimately, French JAPs have a progressive practice of recall and other sanctions, which prevents them from falling into the trap of the aforementioned 'revolving door'. When a JAP is apprised of an incident for the first time, it is indeed his/her first time dealing with the offender's non-compliance. As mentioned above, the JAP will take into account the whole file, all the points of view and what happens during the hearing which, again, is something the probation personnel are not confronted by. In these recurring situations, each party, JAP and CPIP are both functioning in a perfectly legitimate fashion. It just so happens that these two legitimate ways contradict one another. There is no doubt that their extreme workload is also at the heart of JAPs' delays in responding to the considerable number of incidents they are apprised of. For a JAP this is an emergency amongst many other emergencies; for the probation service it is the only emergency that JAPs should consider.

'Yes it's normal, because that puts us in an awkward situation and tells the probationer that he can continue acting the way he is. So it's important for JAPs to be reactive... but then again talking about reactivity, it's important indeed but we do not control his timetable. If it takes months, and we are asked to re-assess the situation, it means we are all wasting time' (CPIP 37).

Some probation officers actually do understand that JAPs, just like themselves, cannot respond to situations as swiftly as would be desirable:

'Then again, with serious incidents, a majority of JAPs are very reactive. For small ones, much less because there are, there are a lot of them and I think that they consider that it is not necessarily a daily priority and that they have a lot of files and a limited amount of time. In X, there are no full time JAPs. They also have social security tribunal sessions and a host of other tasks which have nothing to do with this and I imagine that it is not easy to find the time' (CPIP 10).

As previously mentioned, the adjective which probation officers used the most was '**reactive'**. They all expect a swift response, not necessarily always a sanction though, as most, if not all of them, agree with the *'recadrage'* system. However, most of them expect a swift enough reaction so that their own work will look sufficiently credible in the eyes of probationers.

'It's a fact that when delays are too long or when the probationer can think that he won and it just drags on, we are not credible' (DSPIP 5).

JAPs themselves actually also expect more direct (by phone) and in particular swifter transmission of information when an offender starts drifting. They often deplore that they were not put in a situation where they would have done a *'recadrage'* earlier as they think that, in most cases, it would have prevented this drift.

'Beforehand I was not apprised often or early enough. When things went wrong in a reinsertion shelter and the probation service only informed the JAP after three massive alcohol intakes, it was not right. I asked the probation service to inform me immediately. I told them I did not mind being flexible, but I wanted to be able to warn the offender before a second alcoholisation' (JAP 11).

A chief of service told us that her viewpoint was that *'recadrages'* were unfortunately too superficial, only focussing essentially on the production of documented proof, but not enough on the deepest issues.

'These are things which never come up. *'Recadrage'* only pertains to documented proof not about the real issues' (DSPIP 4).

This question was mentioned previously: there is a risk that JAPs and the probation service will lose track of their common goal, and the core meaning of supervision. Indeed, this is particularly likely in a system where, on the one hand, for the JAP, documented proof must be produced and must be in the file in order to be considered in the case, and, on the other, for the probation services' managerialism and focus on figures and documents.

However, DSPIP 4's perception was not confirmed by the *'recadrages'* my team and I attended. This does not mean that there is no global risk where practitioners will indeed focus excessively on what is formal and written whilst forgetting individuals and processes. Nonetheless, the hearings and *'recadrages'* which were observed may have marginally focussed on documented proof – and probationers had been warned in advance by various means, including, *inter alia*, a written list with everything they needed to bring – but they also focussed and, for the most part, on the person, his/her circumstances and life course, and his/her current state of mind.

Protocols between services are rather useful when it comes to dealing with these questions. They allow for discussion regarding what the issues and expectations are and reaching a common agreement. Protocols which come from top (Ministry of justice) to bottom are in this context a very bad idea as the needs and possibilities vary considerably from one site to another, as does the type of delinquency which practitioners have to deal with.

Probation services are sometimes rather unrealistic. **Some practitioners** thus **expect the JAP to have a predictable and uniform jurisprudence**. Those who mentioned this did so spontaneously as there was no question on this subject. No less than 15.7% of probation officers and 18.7% of chiefs voiced these expectations; but it is not impossible that others had identical ones. The illusion that everything must be totally even and identical, which is coherent with the prison policies of the last few years, has unfortunately left a mark on practitioners (and sometimes even on researchers: Mouhanna, 2011).

'I cannot accept that CPIP A does one thing whilst B does another. But they do things differently. They do not have a service culture beyond a few people' (DSPIP 5).

The issue of JAP discretionary power has been previously presented. I developed the idea that the issue was not to justify the capricious whims of the judiciary whose enormous power would be rendered totally incoherent, but to remember that the French legal system's fundamental principle was the individualisation of sentences and their implementation. Precisely, humans and contexts vary and decisions need to take into account a number of parameters. Local contexts also differ considerably. This research focussed on deserted rural areas with very poor public transportation and very little employment and services, on Oversees islands, on Paris close and faraway suburbs, on Paris itself, on the East, West, South-West and South-East, on the Massif Central, on the PACCA region, and so on. There was nothing in common between these regions, these cultures, these employment opportunities, and their third sector networks; all these were as greatly diverse as France's territories are. Despite this, there was indeed a desire for uniformity:

'Sometimes it will be a youngster and the judge will tell you: "yes but you must understand; he's young; he needs an educating context'!' (CPIP 4).

'I would like JAPs' practices to be more uniform' (DSPIP 4).

There is an undeniable paradox in this since **probation services** and their staff **have greatly diverging practices** themselves (Dindo, 2011); some justified, as with the JAP, by local contexts and individual circumstances, others not so much. It is thus obvious that probation personnel demand discretionary power for themselves but have a hard time accepting that it is also a necessity for JAPs. My team did see that probation officers had significantly different practices, at an individual level, when it came, in particular to determining what sort of incident they would refer to the JAP and how fast they would do it. The following examples will illustrate this point. CPIP 8 explained that she would systematically refer to the JAP cases where a person who had previously been a drug addict for years suddenly started drinking three beers every night, but would not tell the JAP if this person would smoke 'a joint'. Such was her own perception of what constituted or did not constitute a dangerous slope. CPIP 7 said he would not tell the JAP if a person who had been sentenced for driving under the influence of alcohol suddenly started drinking again and would then go on to drive as 'there are just too many of them'. Indeed, this was despite the considerable danger that such behaviour represents to the community. Conversely, CPIP 6 said he would systematically refer such a case to the JAP. Others said they would wait until it had happened two or three times.

Some probation officers have concocted their own sanction policy and distinguish between categories of situations. For instance, CPIP 18 said she was particularly attentive to the payment of damages and mandatory treatment, but did not focus so much on other obligations. Others, such as CPIP 5, said they would react swiftly concerning former prisoners who had been released into the community than for those who had been sentenced to community sentences. Others still said they were more reactive when it came to the violation of general obligations, as laid down in article 132-44 of the Penal Code and less about the optional ones chosen by the judge from the list of article 132-45 of the Penal Code. No logical argument justifies any of these dichotomies, and in fact in most cases individualising according to the personality and circumstances of the offender would have been preferable, albeit less predictable, than positions such as these.

Other probation officers decide on a purely discretionary basis without referring to any criterion. Thus CPIP 6 explained that he systematically informed the JAP when *he* thought things were going downhill. CPIP 11 explained that the waited 'a little' to see 'how things were going' before she did.

JAPs were well aware of the great diversity of practices amongst probation officers. Some referred to the classic opposition between social control and social work (Lhuilier, 2007; Rintaud, 2008; Dindo, 2011):

'Some are more controlling and the supervision has to be straightforward and they refer more incidents. For instance the guy is ten minutes late and they refuse to see him. They get quickly conflicting and oppositional. Others, on the contrary, forget all about the penal and judicial context and are uniquely focussed on social support. These are the two classic mistakes.

Indeed some of them manage to reach a balance between these two extremes' (JAP 71).

In my view this is typically the case where national protocols would be dangerous, as they would mean a higher risk of recalling offenders to prison as was the case in England and Wales (Padfield & Maruna, 2006). If it is indeed important to keep intact a sufficient level of discretionary power (Deering, 2011), local protocols would conversely be useful. However, they may not always totally eliminate sources of confusion. As CPIP 34 told us, in his service a protocol stated that the case would be referred to the JAP every time the offender would miss two interviews:

'Some CPIP think it means they can ask for the person to be recalled; others understand that it means they only have to inform [the JAP]' (CPIP 34).

An even greater paradox is that the ruling's coding revealed that the domain in which **JAPs have the more consistent and uniform practices** was the domain of **breach cases.** For instance, they unanimously used '*recadrage*' procedures despite the fact that they are not even mentioned in the PPC (see *supra* and Herzog-Evans, 2012 c and forthcoming e). Indeed, at an individual level uniformity and predictability may not be absolute, particularly in view of the different reasons explained above. Moreover, there are probably differences between, for instance, young JAPs who have just arrived and have to get used to '*japperie*' and JAPs who have years of experience, as mentioned by a clerk:

'I think that people who have years of practice take more risks' (Clerk 1).

There are also predictably different personalities as probation officers have told us. However, it is difficult to appreciate whether what they tell us is solely based on how they perceive the individual contact they have with JAPs or whether it is based on an analysis of their jurisprudence. For indeed the analysis we made based on a number of cases showed that in fact there was great uniformity between JAPs:

'Well we have three JAPs. We have a nice soft one; we have the moderate one and I like very much working with her; and then there is Crushator' (CPIP 3).

Indeed, when illustrating JAPs' different practices, CPIP usually referred to JAPs' different personalities, whether the JAP listens to them, communicates well with them and so on. From this point of view, there is no doubt that they do encounter a great variety of individuals with very diverse personalities, despite the aforementioned common aspirations of JAPs. As mentioned above, some, albeit rare, but nonetheless dangerous JAPs, are clearly not fit for this job and leave very bad memories behind:

'The first I met here, in practice he was a tyrant. He took immense pleasure in incarcerating people. For instance, when we wanted a measure to be revoked, he would not revoke it; and vice versa when we did not want him to, he revoked it. As far as he was concerned, CPIP were "idiots" and "I do the exact opposite to what they ask for". He had no respect for us. With him it was zilch partnership. He loved incarcerating a person on the 24th of December, in particular if he had kids. He was not liked by other judges' (CPIP 28).

CPIP 9, who had nineteen years' experience and had known a number of JAPs, despite saying that JAPs were 'good people' complained about the time it took for each new JAP to become accustomed to his/her functions and his/her service. She confirmed that '*juges placés*' or former investigating judges had a harder time with this.

There are times where probation officers simply contest JAPs' decisions because they **disagree with the fact that they did not follow their advice**:

'And this other JAP, well how can I put it, she is a little peculiar as she does not always follow our advice' (CPIP 4).

In the same vein, CPIP 31 candidly said that a good decision was a decision where the JAP followed her advice. Beyond the patent humour of such statements with some probation officers, there is also a lack of maturity or hindsight concerning the separation of powers and functions and the fact that one may not always share their analysis of a case or that legally their advice cannot be followed. A small minority of probation officers have a hard time dealing with such disagreements:

'In some services, we have colleagues who maybe have different attitudes towards the judicial mandate and judicial authorities. But here I think we all accept the law' (CPIP 9).

'Yes, it's something which I marginally perceive in CPIP's discourse pertaining to JAPs they consider as being too lenient, when they have reached a point of no return with a measure and the JAP still wants us to continue. I feel as if this perception, which I don't share, because as far as I am concerned when a decision has been made by the JAP it is valid... We have to deal with it; it is a new fact and we have to deal with it' (Chief of service 1).

However, a majority of probation officers are more mature. Thus, when the JAP does not follow their advice pertaining to a breach case, CPIP 5 will talk it through with the JAP in order to understand why. She said that each one explains his/her opinion and this allows her to think about the validity of her own and sometimes to amend it. Given the common capacity, in this instance to discuss it is then easy for each party to accept that the other may have a different opinion; For instance, when the JAP seems to dispute her presentation of a case:

'Yes it happens. It is not frequent, but it is always rightful and diplomatic' (CPIP 5).

If JAPs do not always follow probation officers' advice it is also because they have a higher burden of proof.

d. A second bone of content regarding the issue of proof

As previously mentioned, there is a fundamental difference between the perception of JAPs and probation officers and their chiefs, pertaining to the question of documented proof. We explained in depth the reasons why JAPs had to be demanding and cautious about the existence, the credibility and veracity of the documents which had to be inserted in the files. Probation staff, on the other hand, tend to consider that this is too finicky and time consuming, as is for instance the case when the JAP wants them to check whether the offender really has employment as opposed to merely writing 'Mr X declares he has employment' in the report.

'It's a lot about documents. Sometimes they go as far as to obtaining accountants documents and balance sheets. Sometimes they push it too far…' (DPIP 6).

Such demands are also perceived as contesting their statement, in particular when they have written in their report that a given fact was objectively present (for instance, Mr So and So has found a job), whereas the JAP needs tangible proof (a hiring letter, an employment contract, a payslip, etc.).

'Sometimes I deplore that they do not believe enough in our word and what the service's position is' (CPIP 2).

Nonetheless, in the judicial context, the demands of the JAP are perfectly normal in terms of public security, credibility of justice and defence rights:

'When we want to see a copy of their convocations in the file, when they tell us that people did not go to their meetings, they don't get it. They say we contest their statement. Our answer is that this is an adversarial hearing and that the attorney wants to see the convocations and we need to have them. They see this as challenging their competence' (JAP 71).

In fact, most probation officers found that JAPs' demands are completely legitimate. Some actually grounded their analysis in the legal context which is just as much theirs as the JAP's:

'It does not shock me because it's linked to the supervised person's rights, otherwise I could be writing rubbish. So it seems to me that it's a guarantee in terms of liberties... I don't feel as if I'm being suspected' (CPIP 18).

Probation officers also complain that, according to them, JAPs listen to what probationers say even when they lie about how supervision went on. Because they are not present during the hearings, they are not aware that the JAPs will not necessarily believe the probationer, but are required by law to let them speak freely and to mention what they say in their rulings. Moreover, even if the decision the JAP makes is not what probation officers expected, it is not necessarily caused by what the probationer said:

'They have to stop challenging what our service says and believing the guys during the hearings' (DPIP 6).

'Yes the biggest problem is trust. If the offender says something and the JAP is influenced by what he says, then it's difficult...' (DSPIP 7).

This shows that probation officers also expect JAPs to respect their work.

e. A strong desire to be respected by JAPs

This research yielded a surprising finding. It became clear that a great number of probation officers expected that the JAP would conspicuously acknowledge the quality of the work which they individually accomplished. They expected him/her to show them visible and strong signs of their respect through **congratulations in person or by phone** and by reproducing their statements in the rulings.

Some officers spontaneously mentioned that they – in other words they only and not their colleagues – had no problem with JAPs because their work was thorough. We already know that this is precisely what JAPs expect from them and on this basis that they rate probation officers' competence. When such is the case, we also saw that JAPs can indeed use very positive adjectives to describe their admiration for them. Clearly they are well inspired to mention their admiration to their interlocutors who will be extremely proud to receive them. Pride was clearly present in the following quotes:

'Well once they see how you work, the quality of your writing and how you perceive your work, if you are consistent, then they know that when you want a recall it means it is really justified and proportionate and documented and it's not something you say because yesterday the Olympic of Marseille won [a match]' (CPIP 3).

'I rarely have problems. For instance, the other day, the JAP called me to tell me she had discussed with her correctional tribunal colleagues and that they were very happy with the quality of my reports. Since it's rare for us to be complimented in general, it really is pleasant. And the same ones say they don't read what my colleagues write' (CPIP 35).

Probation officers also perceive as being a **strong sign of acknowledgement** of their work the fact that JAPs **often quote verbatim in their rulings portions of their reports**:

'What is clear is that in some rulings we find part of our reports. So clearly they use them. And this in all sorts of rulings [satisfied tone]. In my opinion, judges expect us to help them reach a decision, so we give them facts. I personally try and present all my reports exactly in the same way so that the JAP can always read them in the order she chooses to and to select which part she wants to read' (CPIP 37).

During the interviews some probation officers conversely mentioned with contempt in their voice that JAPs would 'steal' their words from their reports without acknowledging they came from them. Positively, but in the same vein, CPP 39 thus said that she appreciated when JAPs used quotations marks before quoting their reports rather than simply copy-pasting part of them. What is obvious is that, even though a great number of CPIP are lawyers, they are not familiar with the customs of drafting ordinary courts' rulings [69]. Indeed, in their rulings, judges are required to reproduce the elements which were gathered during the investigation phase and which were produced and said during the hearing. Probation officers' reports are naturally one of these elements, but no more and no less than, for instance, relevant experts' testimonies, prosecutor's requisitions, prison services' advice, and so on. I did explain this to several probation officers I interviewed myself and they were all indeed very surprised to hear it. However, when I coded the rulings, I realised that JAPs could send more subtle signs of acknowledgement for good CPIP reports, such as reproducing longer portions, and concluding their rulings with elements taken from the report. Conversely, when they did not find the report useful, they would only mention them in one or two sentences. JAPs' interviews confirmed that when reports are good, they are indeed this support to decision-making which CPIP 37 mentioned. However, when the quality of reports is poor, do not add anything tangible to the case, when they do not contain proof which can be used in court because nothing has been checked out, JAPs indeed do not use them. They then quote them because they are legally bound to do so, but they confide that they do not take them into account at all: they simply cannot use them because they are useless.

69. Law faculties are clearly responsible here as they only train students to study supreme courts' rulings (Court of cassation, Conseil d'Etat, Constitutional Council and European Court of Human Rights).

We also perceived that probation **managers expect similar acknowledgement from the JAP**. However, what they want is for him/her to respect their turf and competence and to be identified as the JAP's equals.

When the JAP on his/her part has an arrogant judge *imperium* attitude, managers understand that he/she wants them to feel he/she is superior in status. Conversely the managers who do not think in turf terms and who work with a JAP who is not stiff or arrogant can enjoy their partnership. Thus, pride was audible in this middle manager's voice – and she did not belong to the category of turf-focussed managers – who mentioned that what she wanted and obtained was acknowledgement through **harmony with the JAP**.

'In any case I have always worked well with JAPs [emphasis and pride in her voice]. Currently I work with four JAPs as I work between X and Y. I have always had good relationships with them as I have never based my work on turf and power. JAPs with whom it does not work, it's all a matter of power. And it is often difficult for our hierarchy' (Chief of service 1).

It may come as a surprise that probation staff expect acknowledgement from the JAP despite having conquered their autonomy from this position fourteen years ago at the time I am writing these lines. Those who work in the community used to be JAP subordinates; today, there is no subordination relationship between them. Fourteen years later, however, most **JAPs have totally accepted the autonomy of probation services** and only two interviewed probation officers wanted the old system back:

'It is positive to be independent. But it can also come with a host of problems and the one who pays the price is the supervised person' (DPIP 4).

Nonetheless, **probation personnel work under a judicial mandate**. They would obviously have no right to intervene without such a mandate. As a matter of fact, even though the Prison Law of 2009 was drafted by the prison services and personified their lack of deference towards the judiciary, article 13 nonetheless states that 'Penitentiary probation and reinsertion service staff is in charge of preparing and implementing the decisions of judicial authorities pertaining to the insertion or reinsertion of people under judicial mandate who are awaiting trial or have been sentenced'. The aforementioned decree n° 2011-1876 of December 14, 2011 pertaining to the respective competence of the JAP, other mandating judges and the probation services was a unilateral attempt on the part of the prison services to reduce the powers of the JAP and increase those of the probation services. Despite this however, the PPC still refers to the judicial mandate (see art. D 575 and D 577). It is thus a fact that probation services and their personnel are accountable to the JAP, not of course for the organisation of their service nor for their supervision policies, but for the individual supervision of each individual case, and for the investigations they are asked to conduct.

'I consider that I am accountable to the judge. I type all my meetings so I can swiftly send the JAP full reports' (CPIP 37).

It may be that this acknowledgement expectation that probation personnel have towards the JAP and the fact that they are indeed accountable to him/her, does at times generate resentment on the part of managers who are protective of their own authority. They might have a hard time establishing their authority over their subordinate in a context where, ultimately, it is first and foremost the JAP's appreciation which counts for them. Unfortunately, they do not feel his/her appreciation as much now that they are not in the same buildings. It logically follows from this that they aspire to have more direct contact with the JAP.

f. A desire for more communication

For JAPs and probation staff communicating better and more directly appears to be equally crucial. However, they do not always agree about their modalities and what they should talk about. **'Ancients' who knew the former system** are often nostalgic:

'We are far from the tribunal. In the [previous era] we were in the same building and used to get together for coffee. They wanted to separate probation services and JAP. We lost a lot. There are many older colleagues who are nostalgic of when relationships were very different even if we weren't buddies' (CPIP 35).

Because they have a long habit of communicating directly with the JAP, these 'ancients' often maintain this habit through time and regret the geographical distance even if some like having more space. Some seem to only acknowledge the JAP as a legitimate authority to the detriment of their own hierarchy, which in turn, does not help the latter when it comes to getting along with the JAP. Conversely, probation officers who have been recruited after the reform of 1999 fully accept the current situation and like working in their own building, clearly separate from the tribunal:

'It was too small. Then again [before] we could share things' (DPIP 6).

Still, objectively **delocalisation has made communication much more complex** between JAPs and the probation service, particularly when their buildings are very far from each other. However, communication is a necessity; as was seen *supra* it may at times be vital in terms of public security. Both sides have had to create new communication channels, apart from the common server APPI.

'Ha Ha [laughter]! I was the one who presided over our move. Some JAPs have yet to finish grieving over the presidency of our service. So yes there was a physical and geographical proximity and all we needed to do to get a file was to do a few steps. Our service did not have its own files: our service worked on the basis of the JAP's files. It was important to bring the flock back to the barns. It does not mean we cannot work together. It's true though that before APPI we used to communicate person to person. Now we have lost a bit…' (DSPIP 4).

I previously mentioned channels such as calling the JAP on his/her direct or personal line, meetings, invitation to be present at court during the hearings. However, each party is absorbed by numerous tasks and is severely overloaded. As a result, communication tends to be the first thing to suffer.

With a handful of services the geographical separation was yet to occur or took years to do so. For instance, the probation service of Z was in the same tribunal until 2008 and the JAP bitterly regretted the loss of the easy flow of communication and partnership which existed beforehand; the probation service had been transferred far away in a suburb of Z. In the same vein, DSPIP 5 explained that they had indeed moved, but that their building faced the tribunal so that all they had to do to talk or have a coffee was to cross the street. Conviviality and human interaction were thus maintained and consequently, she was very satisfied with her relationship with the JAP. Still, the research also showed that proximity does not always guarantee that people will get along as human relationships are in essence complex. In one of the jurisdictions, where the probation service and JAP service shared the same building, the relationships only existed with some probation officers.

'One can be 200 metres away and yet not be in tune' (DSPIP 5).

Good practices, as mentioned above, can include sharing meals or 'cake' traditions. Probation services who share such good practices are as satisfied with them as the JAP:

'We have always been positively surprised by their reactions. The last trainee judge came on her last day with cakes and fruit juice and another one had invited us with the judges for his leaving party before he was appointed elsewhere. I was on holiday at the time so I could not be there but that kind of thing tends to disappear. Before there were leaving parties two to three times a year. Now it has not happened in three years I think. Since we moved away and grew apart, everything is frozen and it's different' (CPIP 35).

More generally, many practitioners felt that it is important to find the time to see each other and have conversations:

'In the area of X, we have no problem. We manage to work harmoniously; we find the time for discussions' (DSPIP 4).

Unfortunately, and as we have seen, probation services' managers can sometimes prevent their subordinates from having direct contact with the JAP as they think they should be the only ones in contact with the judiciary. Here the issue of professional status is obviously central. This particular category of manager wants its status equality with the JAP to be ostensibly respected to the detriment, unfortunately, of the smooth circulation of information. In other words, these managers want to 'monopolise' contact with the judiciary. This attitude is fortunately not shared by the majority of managers; it does however represent an important minority. For instance, DSPIP 1 complained that one of 'his' three JAPs communicated directly with the probation officers instead of going through her. It was obvious that she considered this to be an intolerable infringement on her authority.

In other words, an important minority of probation managers give priority to the **assertion of their turf and status** rather than to dialogue and partnership. Separation, autonomy and sequencing tasks are various ways in which to re-enforce their own authority – just as it can be for some JAPs, who unfortunately work along the same lines.

'Each step of our independence, some people had more or less of a hard time, but hey [laughter]! They have a hard time accepting the fact that the propositions they make for offenders' supervision have to be validated by their hierarchy. We try real hard to remind them of that. They can ask for reports pertaining to a person's situation and supervision, but how many appointments there are, that belongs to us [firm tone of voice] and these are natural things that need to be reminded' (DPIP 6).

Other managers are not focussed on turf issues and rivalry with the JAP but legitimately raise the question of their respective roles:

'I think that the turf issue is an important one. If we trespass on each other's territories it does not work well. It's an important thing and that's why legal norms have to be precise. Up till now, in my opinion, they were not' (DSPIP 7).

Fortunately, most managers are intelligent enough to think in terms of content rather than status and legitimately perceive JAPs as being collaborators rather than competitors. Such was for instance the case with DPIP 5 who described the long-life learning sessions she organised with the JAP: regular meetings, frank and open discussions in order to reciprocally adjust each other's services' tasks, in a context where, and this is crucial, both parties were flexible enough and accepted to amend a point of view or position.

A previously mentioned example of **good practice** consists of **probation staff** and sometimes their managers **attending JAP hearings**. Just as with the JAPs who were interviewed, the probation personnel who had experienced this were very satisfied:

'Well in X, not in the community as they are too many cases, but in prison yes. It is really interesting as each one plays his part and it prevents probationers from talking rubbish' (DPIP 6).

This allows them to develop a better understanding of what a judicial hearing is and what it can add to supervision:

'It is rare but I have done it for release measures. Or when we wrote breach reports I asked for us to be present. Some colleagues do it, but it cannot be systematic. It is interesting to see what these people say when they are in front of the JAP. If we write a breach report and the person is seen by the JAP, it gives us some feedback too and we see that what people say there is different than what happens in reality [laughter]. Probationers aren't silly. In front of the judge, they are more respectful. The documents we have a hard time obtaining them but the judge does get them' (CPIP 37).

'I have done this in TAP. I think it is an added bonus for the hearing. So I am really interested in doing this and I have found my spot there and I think it is essential that we do this in prison settings. But indeed we do stumble across issues of availability. But it is not possible to be present for all the hearings' (Chief of service 1).

Time is often scarce. Indeed, many of the interviewed probation practitioners said they would be interested in such practices but dismissed them regretfully in their case for this reason.

'We have tried to do it. Precisely because we noticed that there were misunderstandings. We suggested they came as witnesses in those cases. Only one or two showed up. I was very surprised because I expected that they would all want to come. It was an opportunity for them to see for themselves why we do '*recadrages*' (JAP 71).

Again, unfortunately, some managers have vetoed such initiatives due to understandable issues relating to human resources. It seems that their subordinates' participation in hearings would take them away from the office and the person dealing with the daily tasks.

'Oh no we don't do that. But there is a JAP who asked me the other day… whether I would allow a CPIP to attend a hearing. I said: "No. I would like to know more. It cannot be the probation services which answer but the prison services. We write the reports in the name of the prison services and I would like to know what your expectations are". He told me: "but what if we have a last minute question?" Putting someone on stand-by for half a day just in case is simply impossible' (DSPIP 5).

However, this economical argument was rejected by this JAP:

'Our reasoning was also economical. If the probation officer is here at the very heart of things, then we all gain time in terms of supervision efficacy. With the DSPIP who was their chief then, we saw this as saving time in broader terms. A hearing lasts thirty minutes' (JAP 69).

As previously mentioned, letting probation officers attend hearings may at times raise issues in terms of supervisees' defence rights. However, things can go either way:

'The risk is for us to be instrumentalised by the prisoner's attorney and I did experience this in the high security prison of Moulin. So what we did was to organise a pre-hearing meeting with all the prison service staff and this allowed us to prepare a synthesis of our position which went deeper into things. But I don't think that it's particularly useful' (DSPIP 4).

It is important to remember that even if probation officers appreciate that it makes it more difficult for the probationer to lie, every '*justiciable*' is by law entitled to base his/her defence on lies (see e.g. the special issue of the journal *Actualité Juridique Pénal* of March 2008). It is down to the judge to try and see through it. Conversely, this is precisely why it is important for the probation officer to be present. In addition, and as previously mentioned, in some cases the probation officers or managers who attend the hearings are not those who supervised the offenders whose cases are studied that day. This may nonetheless be valuable for them in terms of status.

The difficulty here is the key issue of **the appropriate distance between probation personnel and JAPs**. It is indeed impossible to return to the former system which is still perceived by some practitioners working on both sides of the fence, as representing a golden era. The autonomy of probation services now seems to be set in marble. Unfortunately, whilst these services have gained independence from the judiciary, they have fallen prey to a much stronger institution whose culture was vastly different from their own, namely the prison services.

'Yes the pity is that we manage to have meetings and things with some prison governors and the like but not with the JAPs. We don't have such tools. We have concentred everything onto the cooperation with the prison services but not with the JAPs. They take the time to write individual instructions in the files but it's impossible to get general guidelines from them, for instance do we need to develop placements in the community, how flexible should we be with electronic monitoring?' (DPIP 6).

Probation officers who work in prisons see the JAP at least twice a month – and sometimes more – during CAP meetings and when they come over for formal hearings. This was, for instance, the case with CPIP 39 who worked in a high security prison. She explained that she attended two hearings a month and regularly communicated via email or phone with the JAP and also often saw him for meetings. She was very satisfied with this collaboration.

A good proportion of the managers who were interviewed had fully integrated the institution official discourse which their institution had embraced as of 2008, i.e. that probation officers are **clinician criminologists** and, as a result, have skills which the JAP does not share. This manager thus stated that JAPs had no idea whatsoever about desistance, contrary to her subordinates:

'No. Not at all. In the sense that they have no training in this. And just a handful of them are interested. They are not at ease with the social sciences of criminology' (Chief of service 1).

The reality is completely different and probation officers are actually well aware of it (Herzog-Evans, 2011 b, 2011c, 2012a). If it is indeed urgent that these personnel learn evidence-based practices so that they can implement them, it is putting the cart before the horse to affirm that this is already the case. In reality things are much more complicated than this manager sees them. Many JAPs have had criminology training of some sort, as was seen in Chapter 1, whilst most of them also have a fairly good understanding of the desistance process. Conversely, this is not always the case with probation officers (Herzog-Evans, 2011c; 2012a). However, the present research showed that things were already changing and that there was now a greater interest in science and international best practices as the Unions' contributions at the aforementioned conference of consensus has revealed. Things are not fully stabilised. This is why it now seems necessary to try and problematise the issues studied here.

3. Problematising attempt

In this section I shall remind the reader of the essential issues related to the relations between JAPs and probation services. I shall then attempt to present a series of recommendations. It is important to point out that any attempt to solve problems would require an authentic and equal commitment on both parts and an equal balance of powers when the time for negotiation would come, which has not really been the case thus far (despite the Lemaire and Camu report, 2011).

a. Preliminary observations

For some authors, things are quite simple: they are not going well and this is nearly exclusively the fault of judges, who have the utmost bad taste to be by virtue of the Constitution an independent power – and this, despite their actual independence being rather limited in the context of the French Fifth Republic. The issue relates particularly to their independence from the executive, namely, in our domain, the prison services, which have put considerable effort into trying to rationalise and standardise their subordinates' work over the past few years. JAPs are accused of unrealistically resisting this trend as they are obsessed with their own turf. These authors accuse them of being 'overprotective of their independence' and probation chiefs would try in vein to overcome this apparently major obstacle, since 'any little too strong attempt on their part can lead to an adverse result' (Mouhanna, 2011b: 8 – my translation).

My team and I made very different observations. Clearly 'it takes two to tango' and things are in fact considerably more **complicated**, as we saw previously. For instance, we saw that, for the most part, things actually work quite well between JAPs and probation staff, which is rather positive given the current context. We also saw that there are tensions in specific areas, such as how breach cases are dealt with and with documented proof. At a deeper level, we also saw that two key issues were at stake: firstly, the management of the **enormous caseload** that both parties have to process; and secondly, the **coexistence of two cultures** which whilst still close, are drifting apart.

Conversely I share, for the most part, the following summary by Mouhanna: 'But the majority of judges want to avoid at all cost to get entrapped in the 'automation' of decision-making with targets for release which would become mandatory. All defend the need to adapt to the personality of each individual and in this they are close to the preoccupations of prison governors. From their viewpoint one of the problems inherent to the reforms of sentences' implementation of the last few years is that it has 'drifted' towards a system whereby sentences management measures are granted virtually systematically without sufficiently taking the person's circumstances into consideration. They also refuse to fall into the easy trap of automatic release measures because they know that if there is a problem, they will be held accountable even if this happens in a process which for the most part is no longer under their control' (Mouhanna, 2011 b : 9– my translation). It is interesting to note that the jury of the conference of consensus has precisely advocated the automation of parole, which would become the one size fits all measure – when France had the interesting tradition of having a large range of different measures to better suit the person's circumstances – in spite of having also said that it was important to maintain the principle of individualisation of sentences (Jury de la conférence de consensus, 2013). However, the current government has decided in its stead to maintain JAPs' competence to release offenders and still allow him to opt for the wide range of release measures available in French law; however, in most cases, the JAPs would decide in the context of a CAP, as was the case before the laws of

2000 and 2004 and not of an equitable trial, which would, as with this previous era (see Herzog-Evans, 1994), inevitably lead to prison-data and prison-criteria decision-making, as opposed to desistance-oriented criteria and thinking.

Lack of time is also at the heart of the aforementioned difficulties as it all too often leads to one party criticising the other for not having done its job properly. Probation services can thus criticise the JAP for not reacting fast enough to the incidents and breaches referred to him/her; JAPs' usual complaint is that some reports are mediocre and that information has not been checked nor documents obtained.

Human nature is also an essential factor. Communication and flexibility are indispensable to the quality of relationships and of the work done. Signing local protocols can contribute to speeding the flow of the criminal justice system, which is too often slowed down, thus discrediting justice and probation. It is important that each party prioritise its tasks first separately and then jointly. For instance, my team and I noticed that a lot of difficulties appear at the clerk's office level. JAP clerks' services (*greffes*) are overloaded like all criminal justice practitioners, but also tend to have individual practices which differ considerably and are not always rational, nor processed in acceptable ways.

JAPs should also understand and accept that the credibility of justice and the future of offenders also depend on the rapidity with which they deal with cases. Equally, probation services are key to how slow things currently are, and the intervals between meetings with offenders are clearly too important.

From the institutional viewpoint, the issue of probation officers' **recruitment** cannot be avoided. The current way of dealing with scarcity of personnel is to ask prison guards to supervise offenders in the community. This does not seem to be such a good idea given the aforementioned example of Australia. However, the evaluation of this experience in the French context has yet to be made. More interesting would be to create a corps of probation technicians as has been done in England and Wales – not without controversies however – and to ascribe to them the less complex tasks and/or the supervision of what is called in France the 'segment one' i.e. the low risk offenders.

The most important finding of this research is that there remains **strong and common respect** between JAPs and probation staff. The latter actually even expect acknowledgement from the JAPs. Most probation personnel who were interviewed did not want to get rid of the JAP and adhered to the ethos of judicial decision-making, with its consequences in terms of fair trial and defence rights. Lastly, the entente at a personal level between practitioners is usually satisfactory, and probation staff told us that 'bad' JAPs were a minority.

Spontaneously, practitioners found various ways in which to compensate for the distance: direct phone line, leaving parties, being present during the hearings, meals, biscuits and cakes and so on. Conviviality, especially of a culinary nature, can do wonders in a country like France.

However, good intent is necessary on both parts in order for things to work. What has now become urgent is to go beyond turf issues.

b. Going beyond posturing and turf

Whilst I did criticise the intent and the manner in which the aforementioned decree n° 2011-1876 was enacted, it is nonetheless now part of the French legal system. It needs to be read in light of article 13 of the Prison Law. Both have delineated **the precise boundaries of each party's roles**.

What these legal rules have firstly made apparent is that probation services must abide by JAPs' and other judicial authorities' requests for investigations (PPC, art. D 574, s. 1); as a matter of fact they are only allowed to supervise or investigate based on a judicial decision. Secondly, probation services help with the decision-making process (Prison Law, art. 13; PPC, art. D 575, s. 3), particularly by writing reports (PPC, art. D 575, s. 4 &5). Thirdly, they are in charge of the daily supervision and control of probationers (PPC, art. D 574, s. 2); the JAP only intervenes to make the original decision to release, or to transform a custody sentence into a community sentence (PPC, art. 712-6) and to shape and later transform these measures' main contours (PPC, art. 712-8). The JAP lost the ability to issue recommendations in individual cases pertaining to the intensity and modalities of supervision, but is still competent when it comes to determining the frequency of meetings as France's supreme administrative court recently ruled (Council d'Etat, Feb. 13, 2013, n° n° 356852, *Ajpénal* 2013, obs. M. Herzog-Evans, p. 230-231) and issue recommendations pertaining to the goal of the measure at stake (PPC, art. D 577, s. 1). The current government's Bill is also planning to make clear that the JAP can also determine the intensity of supervision. The probation service is thus in charge of delineating the modalities of supervision, whilst the JAP can impose changes pertaining to the intensity of supervision – if the Bill is enacted – and the frequency of meetings. With regard to other issues, he/she can only make observations (PPC, art. D 577, s. 2). Besides, JAPs do not receive the bi-annual reports which probation services had to send them prior to the 2011 decree, but can ask for an *ad hoc* report and are also entitled to receive a report whenever there is a significant change of circumstances with a case (PPC, art. D 575, s. 5). JAPs can also still issue general guidelines (PPC, art. D 576); something which they seldom do. In my opinion JAPs were more legitimate in issuing individual recommendations pertaining to a given file which they are also in charge of than in issuing general guidelines pertaining to probation services' policies. Lastly, JAPs cannot ask probation managers to remove an officer from a case and be replaced by another when he/she is creating difficulties. They can only mention that there are difficulties or incidents for the probation manager who is then free to make whichever decision he/she sees fit (PPC, art. D 577, last s.). In practice, both parties are clearly aware that some individuals cause difficulties and managers spontaneously remove them from cases when it generates incidents.

I had email exchanges with my colleague Gwen Robinson (University of Sheffield, UK) who is a renowned specialist of probation issues. We discussed the respective positions of JAPs and probation officers (mail exchange of May 25, 2012). She asked me the following question: 'Do JAPs see themselves as being the "supervisors" of offenders and as in charge of a supervision process, or do they see themselves as being the 'supervisors' of the supervision process itself?' The legal answer to that question is clear: JAPs participate in the supervision process, but not in supervision itself and, in fact, they are now only co-pilots of the supervision process.

'JAPs do not supervise people; they supervise cases' (JAP 7).

'Supervision itself is more the job of the probation service' (JAP 36).

'The probation service does an important job with reinsertion. I don't think that's my job. It is to remind people of the law and so forth' (JAP 54).

Roles have been clarified by the decree of 2011, albeit imperfectly and illegitimately. We now know what the respective tasks of each *service* are. The decree cannot, however, solve all *individual* problems such as when JAPs and/or probation managers focus exclusively on issues of turf, which actually reveal broader issues relating to status. The key issue here is that of the nature of management which probation services need. As previously mentioned, they need leaders rather than managers. Such leaders – and my team and I met some of them – are more useful both to the collaboration with judicial authorities and to the quality of supervision. They will become essential assets in the qualitative mutation of probation services which is to be expected in the near future. Unfortunately France **recruits** all of its civil servants via national exams which essentially select good students with good grades rather than people with the skills which are required to be a good probation officer or a good manager. As far as the managers are concerned, individual skills such as the ability to communicate and leadership should prevail over legal knowledge, which can always be learnt later.

For JAPs, **mutation** has already happened. In less than a decade they went from being 'super social workers' to becoming fully-fledged tribunals

(PPC, art. 712-1) whose decisions can be appealed (PPC, art. 712-11-712-13). If JAPs do take part in the supervision of offenders it is now only to determine what the content and the contours of the measure shall be and to sanction violations and breaches. The key issue with American PSC has been how to mainstream what is still a parallel system (Fox & Berman, 2002); in France, JAPs were mainstreamed from the very beginning, although when they were judicialised the price to pay was that they would not be involved in supervision on a daily basis. It is not surprising that the JAPs who were especially attracted to this job because they wanted direct interaction with '*justiciables*', and to play a role in desistance and loved hands on and problem-solving positions, regret and resist the new context. However, such an attitude can only alienate probation staff:

'But that's why we have to make our boundaries clear; because if the JAP starts doing the job of a CPIP and vice versa it cannot work. But when things are clear it works fine' (JAP 69).

'Judges lose human contact, and lose a great part of their job. I would prefer to have more time to see people... the more you see them the better things go' (JAP 31).

A personal desire to do social work and to have human contacts with '*justiciables*' – and here we are pointing towards the very opposite desire to the one mentioned above, i.e. where a JAP would actually be better off being a probation officer – can lead to a **temptation to directly supervise offenders**. This can also happen with very serious cases, such as recidivist sex offenders. In some jurisdictions, the supervision of such offenders cannot be sufficiently intensive nor sufficiently regular, and thus they may find it hard to actually understand that they have obligations with which they must comply. JAPs who take over the supervision of these offenders violate the strict boundaries laid out by the aforementioned rules; yet given their difficult context, one can understand why they would resort to this. As a matter of fact, these legal boundaries must not lead to extremely rigid attitudes. In some cases it might be useful for the JAP to intervene directly in order to help sort out a difficulty and my team and I saw all the JAPs occasionally doing exactly this. Some will also take over the supervision of a given file when a probation officer clearly mishandles it and this can be a way of bypassing the fact that they cannot ask probation chiefs to remove this probation officer from the case.

'For instance I learn that the CPIP wants me to jail this man and I can feel that this CPIP cannot stand him. In such a case I take his supervision over' (JAP 19).

It is precisely because such cases are a minuscule minority that they are tolerable. Conversely, none of the JAPs we interviewed and observed perceived that they were in charge of the daily supervision of probationers. The research did show, however, that there was a dichotomy between two categories of JAP: first, those who were very hands on and wanted to intervene directly in supervision were not satisfied with a purely judicial and written intervention; second, those who first and foremost wanted to be judges were much more distant with probationers and probation personnel. The first category is clearly still a majority. Some JAPs did complain that they lack the time to play a bigger part in supervision so that for instance, one does not let things go too far before they deal with non-compliance. They do not however want to supervise offenders on a daily basis:

'It would be interesting if we could meet offenders once or twice a year and systematically at the end of a measure and not only when things go wrong' (JAP 75).

'Ideally, indeed, if we could be more present during these measures, it would be interesting. But I think one should not confuse things… I think that one has to find the right attitude, whilst being more present. For instance a social-judicial supervision, well during our last meeting with the probation service we suggested, Mrs S, my colleague and I that we would meet them periodically… but this gets us back to the issue of JAPs as being the judge of incidents. It's clear. Ideally if we could meet the person during his supervision when there is no incident, it could be useful' (JAP 41).

Two JAPs (JAP 5 and JAP 13) intervened a great deal in supervision. They clearly wanted to go beyond this but ran the risk of infringing upon probation services' missions.

'My natural tendency is to be an interventionist. I am interested in offender supervision and what I liked when I was a youth judge was to see people on a regular basis and I saw how important it was' (JAP 5).

Inevitably, though, this irritates probation services:

'Well it happened several times with domestic violence cases and that made us talk in our service! She convokes the man and the woman. Well for us she is trying to do our job because that's what the probation service's job is. But doing this in a judge's office, and for a judge to do this, she went beyond her domain and she obtained the woman's agreement to attend couple's therapy. That's complete rubbish! I mean what she is doing is to make sure the probation services cannot do things; only the probation service is legitimate to do that kind of thing' (CPIP 9).

'For instance a judge with a small workload has kept all the alimony cases for himself and we cannot do a thing. He's a man and he keeps these files. I don't know why. He says it interests him' (DSPIP 4).

Another slightly different issue is that JAPs who can afford to given their caseload, do the initial mandatory notification of obligations or at least for serious cases in order to make it a solemn moment. They all think that supervision usually works better when they do this notification themselves. Indeed, it seems that for delicate or serious cases or recidivists it is useful whilst not infringing upon the probation services' territory. Here again, being flexible is the best approach. And flexibility is present in most areas, such as when the JAP is required by the probation service itself to see an offender who, whilst not having violated his obligations, is creating trouble:

'It's clear that we are often the managers of incidents. So the JAP is more the person who reacts to incidents rather than the person who convokes people when there is an incident. However, if there is no incident and the probation service wants me to clarify things I do it willingly. That is if the probation service tells me that this supervision is complicated or it would be good if I re-explained things to the person who does not seem to understand or hear; I also convoke people in these circumstances. So I do it when I am asked rather than [on my own]' (JAP 42).

What this JAP means here is that because the JAP is a judicial figure and because the offender has to go to the tribunal to see him/her, the context is more solemn than it would be at the probation service and this can at times be a necessity with certain probationers or at some point of an offender's supervision. This is why it is not appropriate to have a rigid conception of the role of each party. Clarifying each party's role was an important step; being uselessly stiff and defensive about professional boundaries is neither realistic nor efficient. Much more useful is partners' collaboration.

c. Recreating partnership

France is not a country which is famous for its partnership culture. In numerous areas of the economy and public services, work is often solitary and the skill to work collaboratively is rarely given much value. Unfortunately things are no different in probation. Such collaboration would however be crucial in terms of supervision outcome (Herzog-Evans, forthcoming f). Here France's practice singularly contrasts with the policies which were launched by Tony Blair in 1998 which consisted of developing partnerships and multi-agency work.

In France, **work is done individually without** much, if any, communication and even less **collaboration**. The JAP determines what the measure and their content should be, and can notify the obligations; probation officers supervise; and community agencies, particularly from the third sector, and individuals support desistance. Not much is done in partnership or collaboratively, which is the exact opposite of one of the core principles of PSC.

Likewise, other experiences such as MAPPA (*multi-agency public protection arrangements*) in England and Wales (Home office, 2006) or COSA in Canada and elsewhere (Wilson, 2007) for the supervision and treatment of sex offenders or Pathfinders in England and Wales (Haslewood-Pocik et al., 2004) for the resettlement of released prisoners have shown that partnership is, in most cases, more efficient than individual, separate work, even if it may be complex to fully implement.

Partnership works better because information comes from various sides and each participant brings in his/her own professional culture which allows the whole team to have a better perception of situations. Collaboration is also indispensable in order to deal with humanly and socially complex contexts which are precisely of the kind one encounters in probation (Rumgay, 2004). It also constitutes a more efficient way of using public funds (Sloper, 2004; Sullivan & Skelcher, 2002) and can facilitate innovation.

To sum up, partnership works best. It would be indispensable for the French government to have the courage and the political depth of a Tony Blair, to place partnership at the heart of probation rather than to resort to its antediluvian tradition of amending laws all over again – which is unfortunately what the current government is about to do. Indeed, there are important difficulties, particularly since, as we have seen, things have been going downhill over the last few years with the delocalisation of probation services. It is first important to bear in mind that most of us react rather defensively when we are asked to change our habits and work methods (Sloper, 2004). Foreign practices confirm that a classic obstacle to collaboration is when agencies or people think in terms of turf and status (Pycroft & Gough, 2010; Sloper, 2004; Sullivan & Skelcher, 2002) as is unfortunately often the case in France as well. It is consequently an obstacle which has to be overcome. Another obstacle is when one of the partners is much more powerful than the other (Hannah-Moffat, 2002). This is one of the reasons why I am in favour of the creation of an independent direction for probation services. Currently, their insertion in the prison service not only contributes to a tendency for prison thinking, but also means that prisons services are more powerful than they were when they had no control over community sentences. This would thus help with yet another obstacle: when partners have vastly different professional and institutional cultures (Sullivan & Skelcher, 2002). Whilst this can contribute to the added value of partnership, if it is too important, it can also endanger it.

It is therefore indispensable to systematise communication, to develop a partnership culture and for the institutions at stake to nurture it. It is equally necessary to recruit people who are capable of working in such a context and to exclude fierce individualists. Numerous avenues for improvement have been suggested (Mattessich et al., 2001); they are transferrable to France

(Herzog-Evans, forthcoming f). The quality of supervision would be re-enforced and the justice system and probation would be more credible and legitimate, in the eyes of policy-makers, public opinion and supervisees.

§ 3. The quality of supervision

Beyond relationships, **French probation suffers from numerous ailments** and in this, JAPs are both first witnesses and contributors. This study did not endeavour to investigate these ailments in depth. It will suffice to list some of the most salient ailments, some of which have already been explored *supra*:

- The delays with which both probation services and JAPs take charge of a supervision and react to incidents or difficulties;

- The very limited number of meetings with offenders. In England and Wales normal supervision consists of one meeting a week; in France intensive supervision consists of one meeting a month – in some cases once a fortnight (Herzog-Evans, forthcoming i);

- The lack of evidence-based practices (Herzog-Evans, 2012 a and forthcoming h);

- Solitary separate work and fruitless practitioners' opposition;

- The idea that probation excludes social work, where the offender is expected to prove he wants to desist (comp. with Farrall, 2002) and is hardly ever supported in doing so (Herzog-Evans, 2011c) – even if, of course, the agency is also important (Herzog-Evans, forthcoming j).

It is therefore not surprising that **JAPs**, who one has to remember generally analyse their relationships with probation services as being good, are **critical about the quality and credibility of offenders' supervision**. Only 12.9% of them said that supervision quality was good, to which one may add the 3.7% who answered that they trusted probation services. Conversely, 25.9% said that supervision quality was poor, to which one may add the vast majority (57.4%) who said this depended on the probation officer.

'What I see is that some reports are superb, whilst others are disgraceful' (JAP 1).

What my team and I were told, and what we saw in the files, was that there was a real decline in the quality of reports: no more bi-annual reports; virtually no more home visits; information which was not uploaded into APPI; 'bordering on the dangerous' according to JAP 11; offenders left three months without any contact with the probation service upon their release as cited by JAP 20, which as JAP 13 and JAP 43 added, equates to useless supervision.

'Sometimes, in two years, two or three meetings in two years one wonders whether that's serious!' (JAP 14).

'It's surreal with some stuff, where documents simply don't reach us, in spite of them being on the floor below me' (JAP 29).

The sentence or the sentence's implementation measure makes little sense with such indigent supervision as some JAPs told us, and as we witnessed for ourselves:

'I had bi-annual reports where I could see that the sentence had no meaning at all because of the nature of supervision' (JAP 21).

JAPs are **especially critical about the supervision carried out in the community**. They are conversely much more satisfied with the work done in prison settings, which corroborates a former research which found that probation officers did more support and concrete support in prisons than in the community (Herzog-Evans, 2011 c).

'As a matter of fact yes, because we cannot supervise all our probationers on a daily basis and we need them. Indeed it is especially in the community that there are problems with probation services. [At one point] they were up to 150 files per CPIP' (JAP 74).

This **impacts on their own work** as well, since they depend on the content of probation officers' reports in order to make their decisions.

'It would be better if they had more time and their work was more thorough. The probation services' report is essential to our decisions' (JAP 33).

Some JAPs pointed to the fact that probation services put more effort into dangerous profiles. However, even with these cases, other JAPs felt that what probation services are in a capacity to offer does not match the level of risk or the complexity of the files at stake. JAP 24 told us that even though more attention should be given, in principle, to terrorist cases, on more than one occasion he had had to remind some local probation services of that in no uncertain terms.

Whilst JAPs were critical, most of them were also fully **aware of the considerable difficulty** their partners face when it comes to conducting qualitative work given their enormous caseload. 54.8% of those who criticised the quality of supervision spoke in terms similar to their following colleagues:

'I learn that they have a hundred and fifty to a hundred and eighty files per person!' (JAP 20).

'If I don't write that supervision should be intensive, they won't supervise at all. Currently they have too many files' (JAP 21).

'If they only had thirty files instead of a hundred and thirty… we would have quality work… I would like them to do more home calls, because there are more substantial things that come out of it… The man who is sentenced for domestic violence and has a probation order and tells us he lives with the victim, I would like to have a better picture of things' (JAP 41).

Time and workload are essential here. Six JAPs **accused policy-makers** and the prison services of having taken insane risks by transferring part of the decision-making in release to the probation services, thereby removing them from the tasks which should constitute their core missions, i.e. offender supervision.

Some link this to the **poor quality of management** (JAP 16; JAP 43).

Others (e.g. JAP 40; JAP 43) reminded us that since the Pornic case, all files were theoretically affected in order to give the impression that all offenders were supervised. In reality this is merely 'a **fake allocation** in a lot of cases' according to JAP 43, as once the so-called allocation has been made the file will 'stay in a cupboard exactly like before Pornic'. According to JAP 40 this had considerably increased the number of cases attributed to each probation officer: a hundred and sixty to a hundred and eighty in her jurisdiction to the point where CPIP had been on strike for two months at the time she was interviewed.

Probation officers' **reports and investigations reports** which are uploaded and sent to the JAP via APPI are essential to their decision-making process. In the worst case scenario, there is no report at all. For instance, I was in a big urban tribunal where the JAP was seeing a person freshly released on parole by another JAP who had arrived in her jurisdiction because of his address. His offence was rather serious: he was one of these middle range drug traffickers which are plentiful in Parisian suburb ghettos. He had been sentenced to four years. The JAP showed me the file in question and its content: her colleague from the other jurisdiction had had to try three times to grant the conditional release this person had applied for. For indeed, the probation service had not issued the investigation report the first time around, nor the second time around thereby disabling the judge who had had to adjourn. By the time she had held her third hearing, several months later, the probation service had still not produced a report. She then decided that, since by now the offender only had three months to serve, it made more sense to release him without the report which would have given her an idea about his circumstances and release plan – if he had one – in order for him to have at least a few weeks' worth of supervision rather than to max out. The executing JAP could only approve. However, she noted bitterly that since we were by now in May and that the end of the sentence was in August, mid-holidays – and since her colleague had not taken the risk of prolonging the supervision beyond the end of the sentence as French law allows, as she feared he might refuse to be paroled – the offender would not be supervised at all by the probation service. In other words, the only supervision he would have was the notification of his obligations which she was doing that day.

Other JAPs told of similar stories. For instance, JAP 38 explained that in Paris his office had decided never to ask the probation service for a report in the case of the aforementioned article 723-15 of the PPC procedure, as this would mean that the person's situations would remain on standby for several months. In order to go faster, JAPs would gather evidence on their own as best they could. In the same vein, JAP 43 showed me a manifestly indigent report and told me: 'what do you expect me to do with something like this?'.

Several JAPs, such as for instance JAP 48, added that in any case, reports were often useless, particularly with regard to employment since, as previously mentioned, probations services and sometimes even the police, would only check whether the firm actually existed but never verified whether it had the financial capacity to hire somebody. There are notoriously a great number of duplicitous job offers and in several regions, important networks of fraudulent ones. JAP seemed to be the only ones worrying about this which is rather revealing of a system whereby sentence management measures become virtually automatic whatever the context.

A minority of JAPs operating in rather drab regions said they contracted out to the third sector in order to conduct the most sensitive investigations. As previously mentioned, JAP 43 told us that he would only use two of them in cases where a man had been sentenced for domestic violence and the couple wanted to obtain an authorisation to live together again. He showed me a report which had been written by such a charity: it was clear that it was significantly more thorough than what one will typically find in a probation services' report. Moreover, facts and circumstances had actually been checked *in situ*. During one of his hearings pertaining to this exact type of circumstance, the husband's only documented proof was a letter handwritten by his wife – according to him – asking to get back with him. I was then a witness to the following discussion:

Judge: 'I am sorry but I cannot rule if I don't have a report from the charity X'.

Attorney: 'But why don't you ask for a probation service report?'.

Judge: 'Because I know my probation service and what they are able to do. I cannot contend with this given the risk I would take if Mr X lived with his wife again on the sole basis of what they would deliver'.

He then brandished a probation service report which had advocated that another domestic violent offender could return to his wife when he had in fact only seen a probation officer three times in one year and this was advocated in a two paragraph report which did not contain a single verified piece of information. 'How can they support the application of someone they have seen every four months?!' he asked with a regretful tone.

Indeed, we have already come across this issue: some JAPs complained that reports do not contain objective verifications and merely repeat whatever the offender has said; this was confirmed by several probation chiefs.

'It's also hard for probation services. Increasingly they contend themselves with what the probationers declare and what their families tell them. But of course we can always order a police or gendarme investigation, but...' (JAP 64).

'And with the probation services it's sometimes not thorough enough. They only superficially check how credible and viable the employment is. Some social workers used to do this very well. When I arrived in 1999, there were still social workers who used to go on site; now they sit behind a desk' (JAP 67).

However, most JAPs said that there is a clear dichotomy between, on the one hand, good probation officers who write solid and well-sustained reports and relating to these they do not hesitate to use laudatory adjectives such as 'remarkable' or 'exceptional' and, on the other hand, those who do not take their work seriously.

'Hum... our relations are person based. With some people there is total trust and I give them a case in total confidence, without any fear or worry, whereas with others, it's much more complicated.... It can be younger or older people; their common denominator is that they are thorough in what they do. They are very thorough. They know to a T the ins and outs of their job, care for people, and know how to build a trusting relationship and a good rapport with probationers without falling into the trap of becoming friends. They have a clear positioning both with us and with offenders and it really makes things much easier. They also have a good feeling. All this derives from doing their work thoroughly' (JAP 68).

As mentioned *supra*, JAPs expect CPIP to do a good job as their own work depends considerably on the quality of their reports in order to rule serenely and securely.

'It only takes for them not to convoke the person... in X the population is unstable; there are a lot of people without a fixed abode who keep moving from one place to another. So the population is not stable and the probation service is rigid as they refer people for incidents after they missed two appointments… Beyond the complexity of their functioning in particular because of the prison services' headquarters' policies… I have to say that I don't understand what they're doing. They don't always put in much effort… they don't always upload data onto APPI as they should' (JAP 30).

Because of their judicial **culture**, JAPs tend to **pay attention to each detail** of their files. For them it is out of the question to leave out an error, an omission or a contradiction. This detail and authentication culture is not present in the probation service. This is both a matter of training (this is not something they focus on at the ENAP) and yet another manifestation of the crushing workload of the French probation service. There is also, at a deeper level, the idea that a sentence management measure is in any case a positive thing which has to be supported on principle, even if in order to do so one must cut corners in far from perfects cases. This lack of attention to detail sometimes leads to monumental mistakes. For instance, in the jurisdiction of JAP 13, the probation service had recommended that Mr X, a Guinean citizen should be deported on parole to his native country, Guinea Bissau as it had clearly not read the file properly. Indeed, Mr X had no ties with this country whatsoever as he had left it when he was a small child, twenty-six years before. He had spent all his life in Portugal, a country where all his family and other relatives and friends lived. The offender had signed and thereby accepted the documents, written in French, which the probation services had handed him, even though he only understood Portuguese. Only the JAP's attention to detail allowed her to discover this mistake. In another case, attorney 18 recalled that the CPIP had declared that she had searched in vain for the existence of the firm who was promising employment upon her client's release on Google and one other source which was just as inappropriate rather than on easy to find official databases. One minute of searching on the official French firms' registration site allowed the attorney to find evidence relating to the existence of the firm and its credibility. Out of politeness, and also in the hope that the report would be amended– so far negative for her client because of the so-called lack of credible employment –, she called the probation officer on the phone who was very vexed that she would 'challenge her statement'. Such examples show that it is important not to rely solely on one practitioner – whichever he or she is – and useful that other people such as attorneys, for instance, are in a position to cross examine them. This is only possible when there is a fair trial.

4

JAPs and fair trial

Since the reforms of 2000 and 2004 fair trial has become the norm when it comes to the decision-making process of sentences' implementation courts. At the time, sentences' implementation finally became compatible with the professional culture of the JAP and with the principles which are consubstantial with democracy and with a justice system which aspires to fairness. All the practitioners who were interviewed in this research were persuaded that hearings were absolutely indispensable (§1) and that they had to carefully explain in their rulings how and why they reached their decisions (§2). However, their practices were particularly diverse. Despite the 2000-2004 proclamation that there should be fair trials in sentences' implementation, contrary to PSC, French courts do not hold public hearings (§3).

§ 1. The 'magic' of hearings

Fair trial is not only a democratic and legal necessity; it is also useful in terms of sentences' implementation outcome. All JAPs and other practitioners felt that fair trial is essential, even though, in practice, they cannot always hold hearings and, in to some extent, videoconferencing is gaining ground.

A. Equitable hearings: a fundamental principle

In France, fair trial is summarised by the following expression; ***'contradictoire'* principle.** This principle cannot be adequately translated by 'adversarial' trial. Even if the term '*contradictoire*' does imply that there are two parties which are supposed to be equally treated from the procedural viewpoint, it is also a more balanced principle, which does not necessarily include aggressive tactics, or a pugnacious defence. It allows French lawyers to adopt softer tactics whenever it suits their clients' needs. Beyond defence practices, it is also a principle which guides the entire procedure – and is common to all legal fields (Ascenci, 2005). Just like fair trial, it has numerous implications and, *inter alia*: oral procedures; defence rights; equality of rights between parties; separation of antagonistic functions and impartiality; right to appeal; and right to access supreme courts. For a French lawyer, the '*contradictoire*' principle is essential both to the legitimacy of justice and to the establishment of truth: it is deemed that when the judge is exposed to several opinions and viewpoints (: contradiction) rather than a single one, he/she stands a greater chance of finding the truth, which, in essence, is always complex. Discovering the truth is just as important in sentences' implementation as it is in sentencing or civil procedures. In these particular cases the goal is to ensure that the person does meet legal conditions for obtaining sentence management measures, whether he has understood what he was sentenced for, and whether the guiding principles of article 707 of the PPC are met.

From the **legal** viewpoint, the '*contradictoire*' principle is **a general principle,** thus meaning it applies even when a written law states otherwise. It also transcends all legal fields and procedures. It shows how cardinal it is. However, whilst it finally made it into written law in 2000-2004, soon after, the Prison Law of 2009 created competitive non judicial and not '*contradictoire*' procedures (Herzog-Evans, 2012-2013, n° 01.122 and 01.231 s.). Moreover, if most practitioners have rejected these so-called 'simplified' procedures, it is partly because of the virtually 'natural' nature of the '*contradictoire*' principle which, as a result, has easily become the norm after little more than a decade. Offenders, and particularly inmates, want 'their' hearing; attorneys, JAPs and prosecutors, also think they are a necessity.

Indeed, European jurisprudence does not demand that member states put fair trial into place in sentences' implementation cases (EHRCt, *Kafkaris v. Cyprus*, 12 Feb.. 2008, n° 21906/04) but in a few exceptional cases (EHRCt, *Weeks v. United-Kingdom*, 2 March 1987, *A Series,* n° 114, n° 9787/82 ; EHRCt, *Singh v. United-Kingdom*, 26 Jan.. 1996, . n° 23389/94 ; EHRCt *Del Rio Prada v. Spain*, 12 July 2012, n° 42750/09, *Ajpénal* : 494-496, obs. M. Herzog-Evans : 494-496- Padfield et al., 2010 : Chapter 1). Nonetheless, this jurisprudence was adopted due to the fact that there were not enough member states who had reached this level at the time. There is no doubt that if more jurisdictions had fair trial in sentences' implementation, then European jurisprudence would also progress. In the French legal context, it is sufficient that the '*contradictoire*' principle is a general legal principle to justify its application in this domain.

Importantly this principle also has value in terms of outcome. As the **legitimacy of justice** literature has shown (Tyler, 2006 and 2007), lawyers were right in considering that fair trial was fundamental. '*Justiciables*' tend to comply more with judicial decisions, even those which are not favourable to them, when they have been listened to fairly (Liebling, 2007; Crawford & Hucklesby, 2012). As Tyler recently put it himself (Tyler 2012: 21), there are four major components to the legitimacy of justice: Firstly, 'people want to have a forum in which they can tell their story, that is, they want to have a voice. This first component corresponds exactly to the '*contradictoire*' trial during which the person can express his viewpoint and can be assisted by an attorney in doing so. The concept of forum is more complex to implement in a context where, as is the case in France (see *infra*), hearings are held on camera; still, the solemn – to a degree – atmosphere of the hearing compensates for it - again to a certain degree. According to Tyler, a second principle is that 'people react to evidence that the authorities with whom they are dealing are neutral'. This refers to the European law principle of impartiality and in French law, of separation of functions which is only respected in formal '*contradictoire*' hearings but not during CAP or so called 'simplified' procedures. Tyler, thirdly stated that '*justiciables*' are 'sensitive to whether they are treated with dignity and politeness and to whether their rights as citizens are respected'. In my opinion this actually contains two principles. On the one hand, it refers to the usual implications of fair trial. On the other hand, it refers to the attitude which judges have towards '*justiciables*'. This research has clearly shown that most JAPs adopt such attitudes. Tyler finally stated, in part redundantly, that 'people focus on cues that communicate information about the intentions and character of the legal authority with whom they are dealing'. Is the court interested in their case, and is it trying to do its best? The analysis of rulings and the observation of hearings along with the interviews of practitioners who attended such hearings (prosecutors and attorneys) showed that these were indeed qualities that most JAPs possessed. They use a tone which is at times firm, but always problem-solving, at times empathic and always containing yet caring and respectful; this is all in line with the legitimacy of justice literature.

What constitutes legitimate justice is thus the combination of fair trial and the ties between a probationer and the judge, through his/her interest for him/her and his/her case, but also through the boundaries he/she sets. This certainly has more weight on the offender than what a civil servant working in an office or in a non-judicial commission would. The 'therapeutic' humanity of the JAP has been well summed up by Charles Amrhein, an American psychologist who works in a mental health court in the Bronx à propos of PSC: 'In problem-solving courts, the fact that the judge will connect with the participant in spite of the unequal relationship, has been shown in the procedural justice literature to have meaningful impact. In psychology we might call this a "violation of expectations," in this case the expectation of unfair treatment is violated by the surprising experience that one's case has been heard and recognised with respect. The positive effect, I imagine, may for some be magnified if the participant feels understood by a judge in the full costume of authority, and for others the positive effect may be equal to a judge who does not wear a robe and is not sitting on en elevated bench. However, we can say that this positive effect is created by the actions of the court rather than staging. In my experience though, having a judge in full judgely attire does seem to magnify the effect of positive connection when the judge does not confirm an expectation of unfair treatment. So many of our clients in mental health court have had very positive experiences with someone in authority, and while this is just a guess, I suspect they like the robe and the elevated bench as it offers a chance for a pleasant surprise' (email on the 'therapeutic jurisprudence' listserv).

The '*contradictoire*' principle is a balance principle which, contrary to the American 'adversarial' principle does not imply that the parties prepare to go to war against each other. Arie Freiberg is in this sense perfectly right in saying that continental Europe legal systems are probably more adapted to judging in a PSC key than adversarial systems (Freiberg, 2010). What is certain is that for French JAPs, '*contradictoire*' hearings are essential.

B. '*Contradictoire*' hearings: an essential tool for JAP…

JAPs were nearly unanimous in saying that they were extremely fond of '*contradictoire*' hearings. 92.6% of them said they were essential: 4.8% said that it they were not; 2.4% said it depended on the circumstances. This was close to a **plebiscite**.

Indeed many JAPs were, on principle, protective of the '*contradictoire*' because of their **legal culture**:

'It's the ABC for a judge!' (JAP 21).

All of them regularly experience what the solemn context of a hearing adds to compliance with obligations (particularly through their '*recadrage*' procedure) and what it represents in terms of legitimacy of justice.

'Absolutely and this is why I only use HDC procedures with parsimony. A hearing is a solemn moment which allows the person to express himself' (JAP 6).

They add that, as was mentioned *supra*, adversarial hearings allow for one to **get closer to the truth** than a discussion in an office based on an informal interview and documents. For this research, my students and I did attend numerous hearings and I have spent the best part of the last twenty years attending even more. I have always been struck by the turnarounds, the candid comments, the emotions and the revelations which occur in these courts:

'I think that there is a truth that comes out of a '*contradictoire*' hearing, just like in correctional or crime courts' (JAP 52).

The truth, precisely, is in essence multi-faceted and complex. It is not constituted by the sole probation service reports, nor by the point of view of the prosecutor or the offender. It is based on the confrontation of all the points of view and facts that the judges of the entire world make their decisions:

'Yes and in the '*contradictoire*' hearings, prosecutors may say something which is pertinent and they have made sure not so say something in front of their CPIP, but here, they will talk about it. We can ask embarrassing questions... they will react. And by definition I like for inmates to understand that CPIP write the report but that it's a human thing. Besides we see huge differences in how the CPIP and prison staff see things. So I have to take all this with a pinch of salt. I see that at times there can be very different things depending on the person' (JAP 64).

For some, during the hearings **very strong and deep moments occur**, which are only made possible because of these hearings' mix of solemnity and intimacy. Here, we come across 'therapeutic jurisprudence' findings:

'Yes, some probationers are intimidated but once they start feeling at ease they open up more. You cannot get any of that by reading a file' (JAP 13).

'In any case it's a meeting between humans' (JAP 15).

'We are emotion shakers' (JAP 19).

'For the probationer, justice has a human face. He knows 'his' JAP and it's important' (JAP 61).

The, albeit modest, solemnity, may well, as I have argued above and as advocated by Maruna (Maruna, 2001 and 2011 b), **symbolically re-enforce the desistance process**.

'Sometimes you see people and you tell them: "Hold on a minute, you look fifteen years younger since the last time I saw you because you quit drinking." And some people are proud to go to the hearing and to say: "my application was granted without me seeing the judge, but I wanted to show him my good blood screens and to show him my hiring contract!" Some are proud to come with their documents and to tell: "you see, before I was not getting treatment, things weren't going well; now I get treatment and you see my Gamma GT have gone down; I can see my kids because my wife allows me to visit them." It is true that it is an important moment for them to say "see I have proved I could do it!"' (JAP 9).

The hearing is, for the person, **proof** that his/her **case** is **dealt with seriously and with care**. Moreover, with regard to prison settings, JAPs were unanimous in saying that prisoners would feel they were dealt with using second-rank justice if the judges would rule without a hearing (: HDC procedures). JAPs are not the only practitioners who are present during these hearings: there is also a prosecutor and an attorney whose roles are just as important:

'When I did 723-15 procedure, I also missed hearings. I really felt that it was missing. And when I supervised these measures I realised that when I had ruled HDC things were going way worse. If there is no hearing, not a bit of that solemnity... hearings are a bit like a rite of passage. All the practitioners will make their point of view clear. And the prosecutor! I have never seen an offender who would not religiously listen to what the prosecutor has to say; whether they pull a face when he is harsh or have tears when he says something positive' (JAP 49).

Unfortunately, time is precious and in big and densely populated jurisdictions, JAPs must frequently resort to HDC which they bitterly regret as they do think that offenders take less formal forms of justice less seriously.

'Processing everything HDC or via dejudicialised procedures gives a feeling that a sentence management measure is delivered like a hamburger. We feel it in the attitude of probationers' (JAP 56).

Indeed, several JAPs told my team and I that they had abandoned **systematic HDC procedures**. For instance, JAP 13 explained that in her former court, she notified obligations on her own and had much less problems with compliance than when it was decided that she should increase the number of HDC procedures and delegate the notification of obligations to the probation service. Since she was about to be transferred, she had not opposed this new system, but had immediately started seeing difficulties and non-compliance increase. JAP 40 told a similar story: the time that one saves by avoiding '*contradictoire*' hearings is then lost, she said, because one must then convoke the person to court in order to set things right with him and make him understand what his/her obligations are.

'Yes for me it is essential. I got back to hearings [after having processed a lot through HDC procedures] because I realised that without them I missed a lot of information. The prosecutor has the same opinion. Because often he will write that he's against the measure in the file, but during the hearing he changes his mind' (JAP 39).

Several JAPs mentioned that they had changed their policy in the same vein. After having delegated and done a lot of HDC, they took over again and felt that it improved offender compliance with their obligations [70].

'When the Pornic case occurred I put an end to it and reinstated the notification of obligations… if the sentencing court had not done it. The probation service told me that things now work better and people are better contained' (JAP 23).

For this reason, all the JAPs who have enough time prefer to notify the obligations themselves.

For most JAPs it is not possible nor professional to do justice without holding a hearing.

'I think that one must really see people. It is very difficult to reach a decision solely based on a file. We are dealing with humans here and I don't like that. It's rather hazardous' (JAP 68).

'In prison settings it is impossible do to without; in the community neither because we do not have that many cases. I am lucky enough to have an excellent prosecutor. We both prefer to see people' (JAP 73).

It is mostly because they eliminate fair trial that most JAPs are hostile to the aforementioned so-called 'simplified' procedures and to the extensive application of HDC. Unfortunately, at the time I was completing my last interviews, the minister of Justice, Christine Taubira, issued a general penal policy circular [71] whereby she recommended the more frequent use of HDC, including in prison settings, which, as made clear by all our interviewees, was heretic in terms of prisoners' expectations:

---

70. This point of view can be shared by some probation officers. In this vein one can read the contribution of Isabelle Semelet for the conference of consensus: 'For offenders being first convoked by the JAP for a first meeting, in particular for the notification of their obligations is symbolically important. Offenders then see the ties between JAPs and probation services because this first meeting prior to the beginning of supervision clarifies what the rules are in a containing and strict context. People thus know that being sent back to the JAP will have serious consequences from the judicial viewpoint. Thus the judicial mandate warranted to the probation service is clear and significant from the get go and people are made to understand the serious impact of their not respecting their obligations. The fact that probation services are allowed to notify obligations leads to a loss of meaning for people placed under supervision' (my translation).

71. Circulaire Garde des Sceaux du 19 Septembre 2012, JUSD1234837C de politique pénale, article 6.2: 'I recommend that you prefer no-hearing procedures in prison settings and only request that a '*contradictoire*' hearing takes place in cases where the content of the JAP file is not sufficient to assess the offender's circumstances or when is release plan is not adequate' (My translation).

'Recently again, I saw Mrs Taubira's circular which is favourable to HDC including in prisons. Yes during hearings things happen that one does not see elsewhere based on the file; and it can go one way or another actually. I am very favourable to '*contradictoire*' hearings' (JAP 74).

From the viewpoint of fair trial and **defence rights**, it is clear that essential things happen during hearings of which my team and I were repeatedly the witness of. Rulings are also the reflection of what goes on during these hearings. For instance, in a decision dated of February 25, 2010, JAP 14 contradicted the conclusions of an expert who said that the prisoner was not committed to the elaboration of his release plan for a 'placement in the community' measure and that this was only a pretext for him to be released. Based on what happened during the hearing, as well as how the prisoner had presented and prepared his release plan she decided to release him. She wrote that this prisoner had been able to make clear what his reasons for this project were, what was its context and why it fitted his personality and circumstances; he also pointed out that he had been incarcerated four times before but had never benefitted from a release measure and added that this 'placement in the community' was a tailor made construction built with the support of the charity which would house and support him upon release. This was, he concluded, a one off chance for him.

Since probation services reports are often too mediocre to help the JAP rule, the hearing is necessary in order to learn more about the case, and the circumstances, which five JAPs expressly told us during their interviews. It is therefore unsurprising that a number of JAPs also said they could not conceive of ruling without seeing the person.

Sometimes, in lieu of a hearing, the JAP **informally convokes the person in his or her office**, without an attorney or the prosecutor. Such is often the case, for instance, with 723-15 procedures. The JAP first sees the person informally in his/her office, presents to him which measures are possible in his/her case, and hands him/her a list of the documented proof and actions which are required of him/her. Whenever it appears upon this meeting that the JAP will probably grant the conversion – from custody to a community sentence or measure – the JAP hands another document which the offender is asked to sign whereby he accepts that the decision will be made HDC. Indeed, it is probably preferable that the JAP does see the offender once rather than not at all. However, I would argue that it is regrettable that the meeting with the JAP is totally devoid of any solemnity when we know that a pinch of solemnity is precisely important in terms of compliance and legitimacy of justice. Equally important, it deprives the offender from being assisted by an attorney.

Lastly, '*contradictoire*' hearings are a form of **protection against the prisonisation of decision-making**. When I completed my PhD (Herzog-evans, 1994), JAP decisions were exclusively made in CAP without a hearing and even without the offender being seen or heard. At the time, my research had showed that JAPs were often unwillingly under the influence of, and sometimes even under strong pressure from the prison context. As a result, prisoners' behaviour was *de facto* a key factor in the decisions to release, as it is today in Belgium (Snacken, 2010; Beyens et al., 2010) or in Spain (Cid & Tebar, 2010; Cid & Tebar, 2012) whenever the prison services directly or indirectly intervene in the granting of release. Conversely, in France, judicialisation and '*contradictoire*' hearings had allowed for a move away from this obsolete prison thinking and to place at the heart of the decision factors such as insertion, security, victims' rights, release plans and offender motivation. There is unfortunately nothing of the sort with the decisions still made in CAP to this day that is remission, furlough and furlough under escort (PPC, art. 712-5). With regards these decisions, the JAP still makes his/her decisions inside the walls of the prison, surrounded by prison staff, and without seeing the offender. In such a context, it is very difficult to resist the aforementioned prisonisation. Thus, JAP 46, who was otherwise one of the most remarkable JAPs I saw during his hearings was conversely rather severe in his jurisprudence pertaining to furlough and remission, since the prison where the CAP took place only gave him behavioural information about prisoners (: 'he has had three disciplinary incidents so in our opinion he should not have more than a third of his remission' [72]). Indeed these were all too often purely subjective (: 'this one is insufferable with the guards') and probation officers would alas concur. Because he was fully aware of the risk of being under the influence of prison staff, JAP 52 told us that he would never rule on the spot when the CAP were held, but would systematically postpone his decision 'in order to escape the prison services' pressure'. Unfortunately, the aforementioned current government Bill is planning to revert back to the era when all JAP decisions were made in CAP, with the risk of prison data, criterion and logics prevailing over release plans and reentry planning, as was unfortunately the case prior to judicialisation.

There is no such pressure in a '*contradictoire*' hearing. This is why it is favoured by both prosecutors and attorneys.

---

72. This is despite the fact that the law distinguishes between credited remission, which is automatically granted by the prison itself and withdrawn by the JAP whenever there is bad behaviour (PPC, art. 721) and supplementary remission – the one we are talking about here – which is solely based on reinsertion efforts on the part of the prisoner (PPC art. 721-1). In other words for the latter, behavioural factors are not relevant.

C. ... and for other practitioners

Prosecutors and attorneys were unanimous in saying that they were strongly in favour of '*contradictoire*' hearings. **Prosecutors** put more emphasis on the discovery of truth and admitted that they had on numerous occasions changed their mind about a case when they had heard the offender himself, as our own observations *in situ* confirmed:

'There are files which on paper seem like a done deal, where revocation is certain or release is surely going to be denied. And then you see the guy and he starts telling you about his life, and we realise things are not as clear cut as they seem. But then it also is an issue with ruling 'motivation' because when a file goes one way and then the ruling goes another, it had better be explained' (Prosecutor 4).

It is particularly for this reason, that in some jurisdictions, prosecutors are in principle against going the easy HDC route. They do not trust this decision-making process and do not think it allows for them to get close to human realities and circumstances.

U-turns are exactly what **attorneys** hope for. They are persuaded that hearings can go their client's way, in particular thanks to their intervention, in cases where the file itself would probably not have been sufficient for their client to get his application granted.

'I really do believe in the magic of hearings. Extraordinary things happen there. I remember in X, this hearing lasted for two and a half hours. There was a religious atmosphere. We were two attorneys and we could see that the president of the tribunal and all the judges had an atypical perception of the case, where the innocence of the person appeared to be quasi certain despite what the Court of revision [73] had said, and so on... I also had hearings like that where we felt the authenticity of the applicant... Hearings where there is that magic when people are more at ease, when we can have a laugh as well because that can happen too. From the moment you have a bit of complicity with the judge who faces you or when there's trust, when you can feel he's listening and you can add things to the case, that kind of stuff is rather magic!' (Attorney 18).

This is in fact where those who invented dejudicialised 'simplified' procedures made a fundamental error: the hearing will often save a case which, on paper, was so and so, and had it been processed solely on its content,

---

73. The Court of revision is a court which is competent to deal with miscarriages of justice.

would not have had a favourable outcome for the offender, as, in particular, the prosecutor would not have allowed it:

'Example: a multi-recidivist woman is sentenced for the tenth time for shoplifting in a supermarket. The sentence is five months; a SEFIP is prepared but is rejected. During the hearing that follows she brings in a certificate written by a doctor who states that she took care of her mother and there she gets her release' (Attorney 15).

Unfortunately, '*contradictoire*' hearings face numerous obstacles.

D. The obstacles to fair trials

As was mentioned *supra*, there is a fundamental dichotomy between **small and big jurisdictions** where there is respectively still enough time to do qualitative work and where there are conversely masses of cases to process. However, this opposition cannot be generalised. Thus, we met a minority of JAPs who worked in smaller courts but who nonetheless used HDC extensively. Such was the case with JAP 17 who, however, did see offenders in an informal meeting without the prosecutor or an attorney before he made a decision. Such a practice has adverse consequences for the offender who loses a chance to be defended and advised by an attorney. Similarly, JAP 39 who also worked in a rather small jurisdiction, did 53% HDC but changed his policy after the Pornic case. He said that 'one would nit-pick at' him. Other JAPs were opposed to HDC on principle and despite both working in Parisian suburb tribunals, both JAP 13 and JAP 28 only did about 10% HDC.

Thus the question must be asked - how can a JAP deal with his/her caseload in a context such as **the Paris region** whilst keeping a very low HDC rate? Firstly, these judges obviously do not work on a 9-5 basis. None leave work before 6.30-7 p.m. and JAP 13, for instance, often leaves at around 8. All write their rulings at home over the weekend. Secondly, these judges can actually get into trouble with their chief of tribunal if, for this reason, they cannot process enough cases swiftly enough. In France, being civil servants, judges are annually graded by their chief of court. They cannot be dismissed, but their career can be put on hold indefinitely if their marks are not satisfactory. Moreover, and I shall return to this, these judges only write brief rulings: they prefer spending time interacting with '*justiciables*', rather than being the best possible case writers, at least for the majority of ordinary non dangerous and simple cases.

Sometimes the organisation of '*contradictoire*' hearings comes across rather **ridiculous obstacles**. Such is for instance the case in Paris itself. Indeed, JAPs have been sent away to a building situated in the 13th arrondissement, rue Fourier, twenty minutes – when they is no traffic jam – away from the tribunal. As prosecutors refuse to travel all the way to rue Fourier, JAPs have to rule HDC in most cases – the presence of a prosecutor is mandatory for formal hearings – except for breach cases. With breach cases, JAPs have to travel all the way to the tribunal, and to hold the hearings in an ordinary court room (the 12th correctional chamber), rather than in the typical intimate office of a JAP. The Parisian JAPs who were interviewed told me that they hated both the lack of hearing and having to hold breach hearings in a formal courtroom. Unfortunately there was nothing that could help them hope for a better future. As a matter of fact I learnt at the end of the field work for this research that Bobigny, a Parisian suburb court was at high risk of being submitted to a similar bleak and unpractical situation. In other courts, this sort of conundrum has been solved, so to speak, by way of videoconferencing.

E. Modalities: the issue of videoconference

The PPC authorises judges to use videoconference for their hearings (PPC, art. 706-71). It also authorises sentences' implementation courts – JAP (PPC, art. 712-6, s. 1) and TAP (PPC, art. 712-7, s. 2) and sentences' implementation chambers of Courts of appeal (PPC, art; 712-13, s. 1) to use it as well. For antiterrorist sentences' implementation courts, videoconferencing and direct hearings are an exception (PPC, art. D 49-80). On such a basis, videoconferencing has expanded at Court of appeal level because of the distance between these courts and prisons and because of the inherent reticence of courts of appeal judges to travel.

It is certain that a hearing with videoconferencing is better than no hearing at all. Precisely, the principle in Court of appeal cases was originally not to organise a full hearing in the sense that the offender could not be present, but only represented by his attorney (PPC, art. 712-13, s. 1). In this case only, videoconferencing is a bonus. In all other cases, it freezes faces, expressions, looks, silences, sighs, and **takes all the intimacy and humanity** of typical JAP hearings **away**. In sum, it eliminates the very thing which makes JAP hearings useful from the human viewpoint. After I completed the present research, I attended such hearings with a JAP and it was one of the most shocking I have ever seen: the JAP would not look the offender in the eyes – clearly one cannot look a person in the eyes on a screen! – and her entire attitude was contaminated by the technological context she found herself in. She hardly listened to the offender, whom she could not hear very well anyway as the audio system was atrocious, and dealt with these cases as fast as she could. In such a context neither the hearing nor the very existence of a JAP makes any sense. With another previously mentioned case, the JAPAT, antiterrorist JAP, had initially chosen to follow PPC rules and all his hearings were conducted via videoconference. After having travelled all the way to a Southern prison and having held a hearing in situ, he realised he dealt with the case in an entirely different manner and had, - and this is essential - been at long last made aware of an offender's humanity. Following this, he decided he would systematically travel.

In a recent opinion the prison ombudsman [74] has pointed to the risks of the excessive development of videoconferencing because of the pressure placed upon judges to process more cases more swiftly and because it was next to impossible for the prison services to find the staff that would be available to constitute escorts. He stated that in most cases, videoconferencing reduced the rights of the defence. As a matter of fact, in such matters a rather difficult choice must be made: must the attorney sit next to his/her client in order to better support and reassure him/her but lose influence over the court or must he/she go to the tribunal to be in front of the judge, but then leave his/her client alone to face his judges?

It was also clear to my students and I that sound and image were not only frozen but often timed extremely bad. I once sat for nearly an hour before the connection was restored by a technician as it had been brutally cut mid-hearing.

Unfortunately, videoconferencing is embraced by a minority of courts who do not necessarily have the excuse of being far from a prison from which prisoners cannot easily be extracted. Such was, for instance, the case with X. In November 2010, that is during the first year of this research, I had interviewed JAP 10 who then told me that in her court, which comprised of seven JAPs, there were now two opposite camps: those (3/7) who had decided to conduct all their hearings from the comfort of their tribunal, by connecting with the prison; and those (4/7), as was the case with her, who adamantly opposed the systematic use of videoconferencing. I contacted this JAP again in May 2012 and asked how things were. She said she was still opposed to videoconferencing but that she understood why some of her colleagues used it:

'In my office, there are still two opposite practices: some JAPs regularly use videoconference for their hearings; others ask the prison to transport their prisoners to the tribunal and rarely use it. But it is difficult to organise escorts as the police do not have enough staff in this jurisdiction [75]. As a result these hearings take up a lot of our time as we have to wait for the es-

---

74. Contrôleur général des lieux de privation de liberté, Avis du 14 octobre 2011 relatif à l'emploi de la visioconférence à l'égard de personnes privées de liberté, J.O. 9 nov. 2011.

75 On principle, JAPs actually travel to the prison themselves, but in this court, the prison is very far away from the tribunal.

corts to arrive. So even if we prefer escorts in terms of qualitative work, it means hearings are too long, and inmates get back very late to prison and have long waits in the tribunal cells. In other words the prisoners leave [the prison] very early in the morning and can sometimes return to it at the end of the day or in the evening' (JAP 10).

Pursuing the same line of research I learnt that, but for one, no other tribunal from which JAPs had been interviewed had the same practice. However, in this particular one, the JAP actually travelled to the prison to be with the prisoners; only the prosecutor and the clerk who would take the notes for the minutes of the trial, stayed at the tribunal and attended the hearing via videoconference. This can constitute a good compromise. It is precisely such compromises which JAPs must invent in order to be able to write their rulings, despite their enormous caseload.

§ 2. The practice of 'motivation'

'Motivation' is for a judge the act of explaining the legal and factual reasons why and the decisional process whereby he reaches his decision. It is an essential part of judicial activity. Analysing the content of rulings, both with the eyes of a lawyer and empirically yields a lot of information on the professional culture of judges and in particular on their goals and values.

A. The grounds of 'motivation'

'Motivation' is in European law the consequence of fair trial (EHRCt, 19 Dec; 1997, *Helle v. Finland*, n° 20772/92). Under French law, judges have to explain their decisions because they are held accountable to the nation: indeed they rule 'in the name of the French people'. This allows the French people to control the effective application of the rule of law and ensures that judges and courts do not use their power arbitrarily. Secondly, and accurately, the precise 'motivation' of rulings allows appellate courts to control the application of the law and the correct interpretation of the facts. It lastly allows the Court of cassation to control the application of the law by appellate courts. If there was no such 'motivation' superior courts would not be able to know the reasons – right or wrong, correct or erroneous – which lead inferior courts to rule in a given way. Thirdly, 'motivation' is pedagogical towards '*justiciables*'. If they are denied release, for instance, they must understand the reasons why and what is now expected of them. If a sanction is pronounced, they must decide either to abstain from the same behaviour in the future or to dispute them via an appeal or seizure of the Court of cassation.

elements in the file to add to the case. Moreover, she added that a great majority of attorneys were not specialists of sentences' implementation and did not say much during the hearings – something also noticed by my team and I – thus meaning that the defence's point of view could not take up much space in the ruling.

Most judges, regardless of whether or not they write meticulous rulings, and whether or not these rulings pertain to complex, dangerous cases, have created **templates**. Most of the interviewees explained they first used their internship master's templates and gradually distanced themselves from them throughout their career, eventually making their own. Less than a handful used the imperfect and incomplete ones which were uploaded onto APPI. Some JAPs insert typographic or presentation embellishments into their own templates so as to personalise their rulings even more. Naturally, though, these templates and rulings cannot fundamentally differ from one another: they all contain the mandatory information which is required by law and thus, follow the same standards.

Delving deeper into these rulings, I attempted to understand who the JAPs had in mind when they wrote them.

C. Who is 'motivation' for?

De jure, the grounds of 'motivation' are, as mentioned above, societal (: justice accountability, pedagogic impact), individual (: informing '*justiciables*', defence rights) and procedural (: appeal and cassation). At a personal level judges were asked whether they wrote their 'motivation' for society, for the prosecutor, for the 'justiciable' or for the appellate court. Very few judges included the courts of appeal in the list of addressees. 60% of the JAPs answered that they were motivated by **society, the prosecutor and the '*justiciable*'**.

'Because the JAP and all his judge colleagues render justice 'in the name of the French people', writing a 'motivated' decision which is available to all citizens, even if it is not always understood, is to me a normal thing' (JAP 15).

A portion of the judges who answered that they were also 'motivated' by society explained that they had the aforementioned 'eight O'clock' news syndrome in mind. As far as they were concerned a meticulously 'motivated' ruling could be a defence tool if they were later to be held accountable. Several JAPs added that since the Pornic case, one of their precautions now consisted of writing even more meticulous rulings.

40% of the JAPs said they were essentially 'motivated' **by '*justiciables*'**. Several of them explained that when they wrote their rulings they tried and sent messages to them:

'Yes, sending him a number of messages. Yes I have that in mind. However… we have people who, for some of them, are very limited and sometimes cannot even read or write. But I think that the probation service and the person himself can work on the basis of the ruling… We rule 'in the name of the French people' so it's something we have in mind' (JAP 41).

'I try to make my decision understandable by the inmate and I 'motivate' consequently, even if I know that they will not read everything; especially when I reject their application. In such a case the offender may appeal' (JAP 64).

One JAP (JAP 13) explained that she also used 'motivation' to send messages to the probation service, in particular when she had not been able to rule correctly because of the indigence of the report, or its lack thereof.

Another JAP (JAP 51) explained that he first and foremost 'motivated' **for himself**. This point of view was also shared by another JAP, who explained that 'motivation' also allowed him to have reflective time – which is incidentally what the American Judge Association recommends (Casey et al., 2012) – and thus, go beyond his after hearing impressions.

'Hum, well mine are rather long and I write for everybody and even for myself. Sometimes I am not sure of my decision and 'motivation' is what helps me decide in one direction' (JAP 74).

Whatever the response is, most judges are perfectly aware that '*justiciable*' do not often read the rulings and that if they do, they do not understand them much. For some, this explains the standardisation of their rulings:

'Precisely, I know who I write them for: my clients, half of them can barely read or write for starters so I am not going to write Super Duper rulings Master Plus student style' (JAP 1).

'I know that people do not read our rulings' (JAP 20).

This is particularly interesting in light of the literature which pertains to judicial decision-making according to which legal reasoning does not precede the decision, but is only its *a posteriori* clothing (Klein & Mitchell, 2010). Several JAPs conversely told my team and I that their first intent was often contradicted when they wrote their rulings as they realised that their instinct was not rational or that the decision they were about to make was not legal. Legal clothing will, at times, include strong reference to fundamental principles.

D. Mention of article 707 fundamental principles

The research yielded interesting information: some JAPs abundantly quoted legal norms, whilst others only quoted the minimum required. Beyond patent personal preferences as lawyers, there were clearly many more legal references in rulings dealing with long sentences or with higher risk offenders.

I chose to focus on the reference to the aforementioned article 707 of the PPC. For indeed, contrary to specific norms, which must be referred to in order to present the frame and the conditions for making each type of decision [76], article 707 is a general and introductory norm and its mention in rulings is not mandatory. Therefore, judges choose to refer to article 707 in their rulings. I wondered why some of them did and some did not. Before I present the results of this line of questioning, it is important to mention that even if not all the JAPs mentioned article 707 in their rulings, they were unanimous in saying that article 707 perfectly laid down the goals of sentences' implementation and of JAPs' work, along with the desired objectives and outcomes of sentences' implementation and what should guide JAPs' decisions.

The coding of rulings revealed that article 707 is **always present in TAP's decisions** and the decisions pertaining to **long sentences**, such as, in particular those pertaining to the shortening of tariffs. Conversely, this is not often quoted in rulings which deal with short sentences, community sentences and article 723-15 procedures. As with meticulous 'motivation', article 707 is thus a norm to which courts refer in order to ground the rulings which pertain to difficult decisions or those which involve more risks. Clearly, sentences' implementation courts refer to article 707 as a justification shield, particularly when they grant offender's applications. It may be brandished as a 'defence' as it shows that legislators want them to release offenders and that custody sentences should not be served to the full and should be followed by a supervised period in the community.

However, **some JAPs systematically use article 707** even for less important decisions. When I asked them why they often answered that their internship director had inserted them in his/her templates and that they had simply followed in his/her footsteps. With others, my question was followed by a silence and they had to check in their computers whether or not they referred to article 707 and in which cases. Article 707 is referred to either because it makes for a better legal reasoning (: it is always better to intro-

76. For instance, a ruling will remind of article 729 & sequel of the PPC before dealing with the parole application; it will refer to article 132-25 of the Penal code before dealing with the application for semi-freedom, and so on.

duce a legal reasoning with a general introductory rule, before moving on to specific ones) or at the time simply by pure coincidence.

JAP 13, who was often atypical both in her rulings and analysis, referred to article 707, but also to article 1 of the Prison Law. She started referring to article 1 [77] when she transferred from one court (small and rural) to another (very big and urban) and was not alone in this: JAP 46 also referred to article 1. JAP 13 referred to article 707 and article 1 in order to make apparent that legislators had reversed the traditional discretionary logics of sentences' implementation measures, particularly for article 723-15 procedures: from now on she would not examine the merit of a case, but would only quote a handful of social factors (family, housing, work) and would conclude her rulings by using the following sentence: 'there is no obstacle to the implementation of this measure'. In other words, now that, according to the law, sentences management measures had virtually become a right, in particular since the Prison law, she would only look for counter-indications and not for merit. She explained that she also opted for this attitude when she transferred from her previous small court to her new immense one where preoccupation for moving the docket was deemed essential.

Other JAPs, such as JAP 11 and JAP 28 had started quoting article 707 very **often, albeit not systematically**, since the Prison law. As a matter of fact all the interviewed JAPs were perfectly aware that it was from now on expected of them that they would release and transform via article 723-15 as many people or sentences as possible.

Interviews showed that 26.9% of the JAP **never quoted article 707;** the same number said they sometimes referred to it; and 46.1% said they always did.

The reasons given for not quoting article 707 were numerous: often it simply derived from their templates. JAP 45, who was one of the very rare JAP who did not use APPI templates, said he did not because these templates did not refer to article 707. Others, such as JAP 20, explained that they did not refer to article 707 and in fact, only referred to an absolute minimum of rules, because probationers did not read rulings and were not at ease with reading, and as such it made no sense to make the decision even more complex than it already had to be. Conversely, JAP 20 did read the decision to the sentenced person and explained it orally. Other JAPs, such as JAP 47,

77 Article 1 states that: ' Custodial sentences' implementation aims at balancing the interests of society, the sanction of convicted persons, the interests of victims, the necessity to prepare the insertion or reinsertion of the detained person and to allow this person to lead a responsible life and to prevent reoffending' (my translation).

explained that they preferred to simply explain the facts and reasons why they ruled in a given way, rather than spending a lot of time on legal norms.

E. Respect for '*justiciables*'

I have referred to the **legitimacy of justice** literature and its findings in terms of respect for '*justiciables*'. According to this literature, respect is an essential component of the legitimacy of justice and has a direct impact on compliance with judicial decisions.

Other authors have worked within a different theoretical frame. This is firstly the case with authors who belong to the '**therapeutic jurisprudence**' school of thought which was also mentioned *supra*. For instance, Carrie J. Petrucci (Petrucci, 2002) has focussed on what a 'therapeutic' judge, focussed like JAPs on accountability and desistance, says during his/her hearings. She looked for manifestations of respect such as speaking directly to the 'justiciable' and calling him/her by his/her name (Mister Smith, for instance) rather than calling him/her 'the defendant' or referring to the file's number. She also noted that some judges tried very hard to pronounce the names of people with foreign origins. She also studied the judges' tone of voice. They displayed no contempt, no pity, and no condescendence. She also noted that these judges really listened to '*justiciables*', looked them in the eye whilst they talked and hardly ever interrupted them. She noted that these judges called people 'Sir' or 'Madam', which was yet another form of respect. Another study, pertaining to the emblematic Red Hook community court, confirmed that '*justiciables*' were sensitive to this type of behaviour and perceived that the way their case had been dealt with was significantly fairer than that of a control group who had been dealt with by an ordinary penal court (Frazer, 2006).

'**Convict criminologists'** have also drawn attention to the fact that American politicians, media, academics, or penal courts excessively use terms such as 'inmate', 'criminal', 'delinquent' or 'offender', 'recidivist' or 'drug dealer', and so on (Richards, 2009; Jones et al., 2009).

These various theoretical frameworks led the **American** Judges Association to issue a series of recommendations. In particular, it recommended that judges should pay attention to their non-verbal language and learn to better listen to '*justiciables*' and to be more patient (Burke & Leben, 2007). Similarly, the Canadian National Judicial Institute recommended that Canadian courts should refer to '*justiciables*' by their surname preceded by 'Mister' and 'Ms' or 'Madam' and pronounce their names correctly (Goldberg, 2005: 11).

During the hearings which we attended, my team and I noticed that the **JAP** never departed from a **respectful tone**. They never used terms such as 'criminal', 'delinquent', 'offender', 'recidivist' or even more neutral French legal terms such as 'sentenced person' or 'probationer', nor to any word or expression which would reduce a person to his/her act. This actually does not conform to the French judicial tradition. None manifested contempt, pity or condescendence. Just like their American counterparts they all seemed genuinely interested in the *'justiciables'* and their lives, really listened to them, looked at them when they were speaking and hardly ever interrupted them. Moreover, all used the French 'Monsieur' and 'Madame' before their surname whilst their language, body-language and postures constantly reflected respect.

I wanted to verify whether **the rulings** also reflected such respect. This proved to be a delicate endeavour as in essence, judicial language is formal and neutral and does reflect formal respect which is not necessarily the exact translation of what judges actually think. I tried to look for additional details which might be interpreted as signs of respect compared to the rules which judges are taught at the ENM. Indeed, at the ENM, they learn to draft rulings in a way which allows them to instantly see the person's name. At the beginning of a ruling, they mention *'justiciables''* basic details: first name, surname, birth place and date of birth and address. First names and names are standardised in postal format as with Martine EVANS. This format was adopted in the totality of rulings which were coded. However, with regard to the decisions themselves, I decided to see whether this format remained or if the judges would add **'Monsieur' or 'Madame'** to these names. I am not arguing that this has a profoundly significant meaning in terms of respect. As a matter of fact, when I contacted some of my networks (in particular therapeutic jurisprudence, European society of criminology and convict criminologists) I was told that no research had, to their knowledge, specifically explored this subject. There was no clear theoretical framework within which this question could be explored. Besides, it also became clear that how *'justiciables'* were referred to in rulings had, above all legal, cultural and historical roots. For instance, as Judge Leben told me (email dated November 11, 2011): 'my sense is that in American English (as known by the vast majority of newspapers) most use a somewhat less formal style in which these titles aren't used.' Conversely, Doctor Astrid Birgden, an Australian forensic psychologist wrote (same day) that Australian drug courts always called participants 'Mister' or call them by their first name. None of my contacts referred to the language used in rulings.

For this reason, it appeared useful to complete this research by checking the rulings to assess whether or not judges departed from what they had learned at the ENM and in particular, whether or not they had decided to add these additional mentions. I discovered that only 14.8% of the rulings did add to the ENM frame, 'Monsieur' or 'Madame'. Those who did repeated it systematically in all their rulings, regardless of the offence. For the aforementioned reasons, I cannot draw significant conclusions from this. I do suspect, however, that this is a welcome additional sign of respect for '*justiciables*'.

'Therapeutic' and legitimate justice also imply that the judge **really cares about the '*justiciable*'**. The hearing my team and I attended did show evidence of such a feature. More surprisingly, some of the rulings also contained, whenever possible, encouraging comments. These were particularly perceptible in the decisions which granted release or article 723-15 conversions, or decided it was not opportune to sanction a person.

Encouragements or acknowledgements of the efforts made by the person, pertained, in all the decisions which granted release, to the behaviour whilst in custody and/or on the commitment to their release plan, since these are the very conditions required by the law. However, JAPs also focussed on the person's motivation and psychological progress. For instance, JAP 13, in an October 13, 2010 decision which granted parole, noted that the person had 'deeply reflected on his past actions' and seemed to 'have gained maturity'. Another JAP, B, who was not interviewed, noted in a ruling dated April 15, 2011, that the person seemed 'to have matured and thought about his offences'. Some JAPs used very strong adjectives to congratulate or encourage '*justiciables*'. For instance, in a ruling dated September 2009, JAP 11 noted the 'exemplary behaviour' of the detained person.

Judges were also keen to point to positive elements in contexts which are otherwise complex or not very positive; For instance JAP 13, noted in a ruling dated July 3, 2008, which granted parole that 'in spite of a serious addiction to this medication [subutex], which he acknowledges he has, with the consent of his doctor, managed to reduce the doses of this treatment by half'. JAP 28, in a ruling dated March 1, 2011 mentioned that Mister L, sentenced for DUI, had 'recently realised that he was addicted to alcohol'; something he had been denying for years. She added that although it was recent, the treatment he was now submitting to constituted 'a serious reinsertion effort which needed to be encouraged'. Here, the encouragement took the shape of both psychological reinforcement (as mentioned in the ruling) and in the decision itself (a custodial sentence was converted into probation with community work). The measure itself rewarded the person's merit, albeit minimal; it also was a necessity to try and sustain the efforts he had manifested.

JAPs can conversely also mention negative signs. For instance, JAP 14 mentioned in a ruling dated February 25 2010, that the person did not seem to 'have much consideration for the victims' (police officers who had been assaulted) but added: 'however, he also is very committed in his parental role, and is genuinely trying to succeed in the treatment of his addiction to alcohol'.

JAPs can even be encouraging in decisions which deny applications. Such was for instance the case with a non-dated ruling from JAP 11 which denied parole because the applicant had not provided documented proof pertaining to his circumstances, but did note that there were 'important improvements in his personality'.

To sum up, a JAP's office does indeed provide a therapeutic environment (Herzog-Evans, 2011 d; Berman & Feinblatt, 2005 ; Winick & Wexler, 2003).

§ 3. Intimate hearings

A foreign specialist of PSC might be surprised by some of the features of French JAP hearings: In PSC, hearings are always public and this is in fact considered to be essential; in France JAP hearings are not public.

A. Comparative law: PSC's public hearings

PSC are mixed courts: they are both sentencing courts and supervision courts. JAPs, conversely, are only supervision and release courts, with, to be fair, the capacity to convert a custody sentence of up to two years into a community sentence or measure (art. 723-15 PPC). For this reason, the reasons which traditionally explain why hearings should be public have to apply to PSC, whilst not being held indispensable for JAPs (Herzog-Evans, 2012-2013: n° 01.251-01.255).

Several years ago, the daughter of Jeb Bush was trialled in a Drug Court and asked whether, given her notoriety, the hearing could be exceptionally held on camera. The Supreme Court of Florida rejected her application by precisely referring to the traditional principles guiding the publicity of penal hearings. It referred, in particular, to the pedagogical virtues of public hearings for the general population. Going beyond the **general preventive impact of the criminal justice system**, the Court stated: 'Open access is critical so that the public can see that the drug court is working to reduce recidivism rate and to return individuals to a productive state' [78]. Precisely, it

78. Circuit Court of the Ninth Judicial Circuit for Orange County, Florida. State of Florida v. Noelle L. Bush. Case No. 48-02-CF-6371-0. October 10, 2002 accessible on http://www1.spa.american.edu/justice/documents/3419.pdf. I want to thank Caroline S. Cooper, BJA Drug Court Technical Assistance Project and Research professor and Associate Director à the American University, for referring this case to me.

seems that in certain cases at least, it would be useful if the French population was confronted by the reality of sentences' implementation, in order to better understand why judges release prisoners, which is always a contentious subject.

In France, traditional penal principles governing the publicity of hearings were more easily ignored in the case of the JAP because it is not a sentencing court even if he/she can transform a sentence as mentioned above.

However, in PSC, the publicity of hearings has other grounds which could be of interest in the French context. Indeed, it also contributes to their outcome. Other people and other offenders who are waiting for their case to be heard, are 'witnesses' of sorts, and often react when other cases are discussed. There is thus **interaction** between offenders, particularly in the American version of these courts, where judges often let the audience react to what is going on, and at times applaud. This was also something which the Supreme Court of Florida mentioned: 'Drug court is a team approach, and group advice, encouragement, admonishments and sanctions are involved in the treatment process. Having all drug court participants observe each other's court proceedings is also key because they can learn from each other's mistakes and by viewing other's successes, they realise that they too can overcome their addiction'.

When the person is in the process of desisting, the solemnity of the hearing, albeit limited as is the case with PSC, does constitute a desistance ritual which probably reinforces it (Maruna, 2001). If he/she relapses or goes backwards, the audience, and in fact the judge, constitute a small community of people who are worried and care for him/her.

B. France: hearings on camera

Conversely, France has from the start chosen to hold its hearings on camera; a principle which has also been renewed with the reforms of 2000 and 2004 (PPC, art. 712-6, 712-7, 712-13). This is indeed to a degree **a legacy of the former CAP** which were, as mentioned above, the mandatory setting for all JAP decisions.

Hearings on camera are also the **legacy of** another procedural context, namely that of 'disputes relative to sentences' implementation' based on **article 710** of the PPC. Article 710 governs disputes pertaining to the exact length of sentences and was, for a long time, the only existing procedure allowing offenders to contest decisions in the sentences' implementation phase. It was however never used for JAPs' decisions as '*justiciables*' were expressly banned from appealing them by another article (PPC, art. 733-1 in its former version). Article 710 still states that hearings are held on camera.

Another influence was the **prison context** in which JAPs made most of their decisions before 2004. Legislators thought it would be too complicated to organise a public hearing inside a prison. As a result, even '*contradictoires*' hearings are to this day held inside prisons. In other words, it is essentially practical reasons which explain why the principle of non-public hearings persists to this day.

A deeper reason also explains this persistence: the '**right to be forgotten**', which is a subliminal guiding principle in sentences' implementation (Herzog-Evans, 2011 a). According to this principle, a person who has served his/her sentence or is about to complete his/her sentence should be allowed to have his/her private life respected. In addition, if attention was drawn via a public hearing to his/her offence(s) this might constitute an obstacle to housing or employment. A diametrically opposite argument was raised in the aforementioned decision of the Supreme Court of Florida. It was stated that it was vital for the community to be in a position to observe that the PSC worked due to the fact that '*justiciables*' would become abstinent, law-abiding and productive, as citizens would be less reticent to offer them housing and employment. It is however difficult to transpose this line of reasoning to the French context, since JAPs do not meet offenders on a regular basis and daily supervision is carried out by the probation service. Thus, the French population would only see the 'before' and would not be exposed to the more positive 'after'.

In fact, JAP hearings have their own advantages, as my team and I repeatedly witnessed. It is patent that the absence of an audience creates an **intimacy** between the JAP and the probationer. This intimacy is even more perceptible when the JAP is alone with the probationers as is the case when he notifies them of obligations or for the informal first stages of the 723-15 procedure. As previously argued, this intimacy often leads the probationer to reveal very personal information and also shows him how much the JAP is concerned by his case and cares for him. Here I submit an example of what an attorney told me, pertaining to one of her clients who had been sentenced to life, and who had already served twenty-six years and applied for parole:

'This hearing lasted for four long hours, which is enormous. Everybody had the time to really listen to the others. And there, a miracle occurred. My client, who is usually virtually mute when he is stressed, who had come without any hope of being listened to, or to be understood and accepted for who he is…, was moved by the easiness and the familiarity of the debate and opened up' (Attorney 2).

During French JAP hearings, the judge does **not sit on an elevated bench** as his American PSC counterpart does. He sits by his desk in his office, and the probationer sits face to face with him. When it is a '*contradictoire*' hearing, the prosecutor and the attorney sit next to the probationer on a similar chair. Each person is extremely close to the other. As mentioned above, in Paris, unfortunately, hearings have to take place in a formal traditional courtroom, that of the 12th correctional chamber. The JAP bitterly complained about this and confessed that he was not a good JAP during these hearings and that despite the absence of an audience, the attitude of all participants was extremely similar to those of participants in a sentencing hearing. There was no intimacy: the JAP was more a judge than a problem-solver. When I attended this JAP hearing in the 12th correctional chamber it was obvious that what he complained about was true. As mentioned previously, he had spontaneously chosen to wear his robe, whereas in practice, JAPs do not. However, as we also saw this question was highly cultural and contextual.

It is, to sum up, impossible to formulate conclusions regarding this issue. Both systems have their advantages and their disadvantages. In the French context, the lack of publicity works rather well and reinforces the intimacy which is one of the JAP hearings' fortes.

The very complexity of the situations at stake will be even more apparent in the following chapter, which focusses on specific decisions which JAPs have to make.

5

An analysis of JAP rulings

I had initially collected 1,300 rulings. In order to do so, I used various approaches. I first asked the JAPs who were interviewed to send me their rulings. Since not all of them did and because I also wanted to obtain additional data to cover a maximum of individuals, I also asked attorneys to send me decisions. Finally, I also went to legifrance.gouv.fr, the national website which hosts French courts' rulings. I eventually decided not to use all the decisions I thus obtained for this chapter. However, I did use some of them for the former chapters. First, certain decisions had been anonymised to such an extent that it was impossible to fully code them. For instance they would not mention the offence or the sentence, which I precisely had decided to code. I also left aside decisions which only represented a handful of their kind and could not be quantitatively analysed. Such was the case, unfortunately, with humanitarian medical sentence suspension, with decisions based on article 721-2 of the PPC [79], and with the removal or reduction of safety periods – i.e. tariffs. I also left out the rulings with very little 'motivation', if any, such as ordinances pertaining to remission or furlough. I also decided to leave out decisions which would have been interesting for legal court comments but not for the present research. Such was the case with the rather important number of decisions pertaining to inadmissibility or procedure withdrawals. Lastly, I also left out decisions made by TAP and CHAP. With regard to TAP, this was because they differ from the JAP inasmuch as they are a collegial court and as they deal with serious crimes. Since the research

79. This article allows JAPs to impose minimal conditions on offenders who max out and would on principle not be otherwise supervised. These obligations are: paying damages and not getting in contact with victims. This minimal probation lasts for the time covered by remission. JAPs however use this rule very rarely as the very limited sample which I obtained proved.

pertained to the quotidian work of JAPs it seemed to me that it would not be relevant. I decided to leave out CHAP decisions for a similar reason: it is very likely that the judges who officiate in CHAP have a very different culture than JAPs and as such, should be subjected to a specific research. After such a drastic 'filtration' only 776 could be used for the present chapter. Whereas I used extracts in the previous chapters, I shall now analyse each type of decision, starting with recall and other sanctions.

§ 1. Breach

A. General findings

I had gathered 292 workable recalls and other decisions pertaining to breach cases. I had to leave aside a few decisions pertaining to the revocation of decisions under prison registry, such as semi-freedom, 'placement in the community' and electronic monitoring as my samples were too small.

As mentioned *supra*, it is with breach cases that offenders are, predictably, the most elusive and at risk of flight: 48.5% of them were not present at the hearings and only 19.1% were assisted by an attorney.

It is important to remember that in virtually all the cases, **people's behaviour and context** will have **gone downhill** and will have already benefitted from one – and sometimes several – *'recadrages'*. In other words, the peoples' situation is usually rather jeopardised and yet, JAPs only pronounce a sanction in 69.1% of them. They opt for a softer sanction than total revocation, such as partial revocation or extension of the order in 26.8% of all the cases [80] and for no sanction at all in 21.9% of them.

When studying all the decisions pertaining to breach cases one is struck by the abyssal delays between, firstly, on the one hand, the time when the sentence is passed and, on the other hand, the time when the person is taken charge of by the criminal justice system. Indeed, secondly, between the moment where incidents start to occur and the moment where they lead to a judicial decision. I have already dealt with the issue of delays and their main causes, namely the overload of JAP offices and probation services' overload, along, unfortunately, with very poor coordination between the two. One will remember that prior to the Pornic case, many of the so-called low risk files – this being based on non-evidence-based assessment – were not allocated and are now supposed to be – but are actually supervised 'administratively'. What follows is a lack of meaning and a loss of credibility of sentences'

80. Bearing in mind it was not legally possible in all cases – but only with the French equivalent of probation orders.

implementation and the criminal justice system. This also leaves vulnerable and difficult offenders to themselves thereby contributing to their going downhill and *in fine*, to the sanctions pronounced against them.

B. Fine and day-fine defaulters' incarceration

1. Presentation

In French law 'judicial constraint' is a form of incarceration which applies to people who have not paid their fine or day-fine. It does not apply to taxes, customs' fees or other public debts. Its goal is to convince a reluctant offender to pay his/her fine (Herzog-Evans, 2012-2013: 751.11). It is the last case of debtor's incarceration in the French legal system. Following the condemnation of France by the European Court of Human Rights (June 8 1995, *Jamil v. France*, applic. n° 15917/89) and the following Law of March 9, 2004, a '*contradictoire*' hearing must take place in the JAP's office and he/she is competent to make judicial constraint decisions (PPC, art. 749 to 761-1). In practice, it is essentially in the case of day-fines default – day-fines usually being the result of the conversion of a custody sentence into a day-fine sentence by the JAP in the course of a 723-15 procedure. Of the forty-three defaulter incarceration cases I had collected, forty-one pertained to day-fine defaults, one to a fine default and oddly another did not specify.

2. Procedure

In 8/43 (18.6%) of the cases, the offender was assisted by an attorney; in 19/43 (44.1%) of cases he/she was present but alone at the hearing; in 23/43 (53.4%) of cases, thereby exceeding the general statistic mentioned *supra* (48.5%), the offender was not present. I did not have such information in one of the forty-three cases.

As with other sanctions, most offenders are not present at their hearing and when they are, they rarely have an attorney. However, when they at long last hand to the judge a document which had been required of them in order to obtain a favourable decision, this is precisely when an attorney is present. As previously mentioned, attorneys are useful whenever they manage to convince offenders to comply with their order and provide the evidence.

However, when the attorney is present, the JAP still pronounces defaulter incarceration in 62.5% of cases; in cases where the offender is present but has no attorney (N8) only one defaulter incarceration was pronounced and in the seven other cases, another, more favourable decision was made: adjournment or even case dismissal. This confirms the aforementioned general findings: when an attorney is present, this is not necessarily an advantage for the offender. Conversely, when the offender is not present, he/she is more likely to be sanctioned: eighteen defaulter incarceration decisions were made in such cases, versus six other more lenient decisions.

3. Offences

People who are eventually condemned to defaulter incarceration – and who have thus been formerly sentenced to a fine or, more frequently, a day-fine – have generally committed non serious offences [81]. In most cases, these offences corresponded to the most frequent felonies which correctional tribunals and JAPs have to deal with. The sample did not contain many alcohol or drug related offences as these felonies rarely benefit from day-fines, except in the case of driving under the influence of alcohol or drugs (hereafter DUI). The offenders who were concerned by fines or day-fine defaults procedures had committed the following offences [82]:

- Against property (including checks, bank or credit cards, and swindling): 11/43 (25.5%);

- Violence: 5/43 (11.6%);

- Road offences (including DUI): 8/43 (18.6%);

- Drugs or alcohol as the main offence (includes again DUI) [83]: 7/43 (16.2%);

- Destructions and deteriorations: 2/43 (4.5%);

- Contempt and insults to public authorities: 2/43 (4.6%);

- Miscellaneous: 5/43 (11.6%);

(including possession of dangerous dogs without the appropriate authorisation)

- Sex offences: 1 (2.3%)

For 7/43 (16.2%) of all cases, the ruling did not specify what the offence was.

81. In the case of defaulter incarceration as with all the other breach decisions, I only coded for the offence(s) which was the object of the breached sentence and did not code for priors as they were not always mentioned in the decisions. For this reason it was impossible to draw statistics on reoffending.

82. The sum total is naturally superior to 100% since offenders may have been sentenced to fines or day-fines for a series of offences.

83. I counted DUII twice, once with road offences, and once with drug and alcohol related offences, as I wanted to draw attention, on the one hand to road offences and, on the other hand to offenders with addiction issues.

Only 4/43 offenders were incarcerated at the time of the hearing and this was actually held as being an excuse for not having paid the debt in one of them, whilst another benefitted from a case dismissal by proving he had eventually paid his debt entirely. In the other two cases, the *'justiciable'* received defaulter incarceration decision despite being currently incarcerated; in such a case, detention is prolonged accordingly. This shows that the consequences drawn by JAPs from a current incarceration of offenders in breach are not uniform.

4. Decisions' analysis

As with other sanctions, when the offender's case eventually leads to a hearing with the JAP, he/she will have benefitted from numerous chances to pay his/her debt. It is therefore not surprising that in a majority of cases the decision did pronounce judicial constraint [84]:

- 26/43 (60.4%) incarcerated the defaulter;

- 11/43 (25.5%) dismissed the case;

- 6/43 (13.9%) gave the offender more time or pronounced an adjournment.

All the decisions were **standardised to the extreme** and very similar in shape and form, whoever the JAP was. There was thus **considerable uniformity** between the JAP with regard to the presentation of the decisions. Standardisation can be explained by the fact that judicial constrain applies to low risk offenders for whom, as I have previously mentioned, JAPs do not spend a lot of energy and time explaining their rulings. Decisions always adhere to the following order. As with every single ruling, they first mention the person's identity and offences and the procedure which is to be followed during the hearing (e.g. did the person have an attorney, when did the hearing take place, was he allowed a final word as is mandatory, and so on). Secondly, the JAP mentions, as he/she is obligated by law to do, that the person has indeed been formally commanded to pay his/her debt according to the mandatory procedure for fines and day-fines (PPC, art. 754 - Herzog-Evans, 2012-2013: 751.52). Thirdly, JAPs must confirm that the person is

---

84. When presenting all the decisions made by JAPs I shall only hereafter focus on the two to three paragraphs which immediately precede the decision itself. For indeed, the developments which precede these last paragraphs pertain to the presentation of other practitioners' points of view (probation service, prosecutor, in certain cases, experts' testimonies, prison services' recommendations and so on) and a summary of what the offender and, when relevant, his attorney said during the hearing. JAPs are required by law to present these in detail, but they do not represent what he/she actually thinks of the case. His/her own point of view on the case is summarised in the last two or three paragraphs.

not older than sixty-five or is not a minor, which would constitute an obstacle to defaulter incarceration (PPC, art. 751 – Herzog-Evans, 2012-2013: 751.45-751.46). Fourthly, he/she must indicate that the person has not paid and has not demonstrated that he/she was insolvent as this would also be a legal obstacle to defaulter incarceration (PPC, art. 752 – Herzog-Evans, 2012-2013: 751.43). Generally speaking, after listing this mandatory factual and legal information, the JAP concludes that the conditions of defaulter incarceration are all met and that it is thus necessary to pronounce it. JAPs do not describe the person's circumstances any further since, in practice, he/she would have had numerous opportunities to pay his/her debt and, even though he/she is not insolvent, he/she has chosen not to. Moreover, since in most cases he/she is not present at his hearing, he/she loses a chance to defend him/herself.

Despite this, JAPs are still rather lenient. They have to be lenient when the law commands them to dismiss the case. Such was the case in 11/43 (25.5%) files:

- Because of technicalities such as when the file did not contain the Treasury's formal default notice to the offender, this in 4/43 (36.3%) of cases;

- Because the person proved he/she had paid – most of the time at the very last minute – his/her debt in full, this in 5/11 (45.4%) of cases;

- Because he proved he was insolvent, this in 2/11 (18.1%) of cases.

However, the JAP was not legally bound to be lenient in six cases (13.9%). Clemency took the form of adjournment of the decision or of a further delay for the offender to comply, which actually had the same result. The reasons invoked by the JAP in such cases were at times social and objective: in two cases, the offender had just found a job and was now in a position to pay his debt; in another case, he was not per se insolvent, but was rather impecunious and needed more time to raise enough funds; in other aforementioned cases, he was incarcerated and had no means. In yet other cases, the JAP simply decided to give the offender another chance. Two cases expressly referred to a second chance; three pointed out that the person had already made partial efforts [85]. As we shall now see, the concept of effort is often at the heart of decisions pertaining to probation revocations.

85. This terminology is directly inspired by England and Wales' legal system as the term 'community' is usually viewed rather suspiciously in France. For instance community work is called 'work in the interest of all'.

C. Probation revocation

In France, so far, probation sentences do not take the shape of a probation order. They consist of two parts: a suspended custody sentence; a period under probation (Herzog-Evans, 2012-2013: Chap. 421). This sentence can be either total, i.e. the custody sentence is entirely covered by the probation order or partial – called in practice a mixed sentence –, i.e. the custody sentence is only partially suspended (e.g. a three year sentence, where only eighteen months are suspended).

The current government will, however, create a new probation sentence called 'sentence in the community' [86], which will first exist for other community sentences and will replace them in three years. The government expects to reduce imprisonment by creating a new sentence, which seems rather unrealistic (Herzog-Evans, 2013: contra Tournier, 2013 a). Whatever the future holds, this study only pertained to the currently existing sentence of suspended sentence with probation.

I had collected a great number of decisions pertaining to breach cases relating to the French probation order (hereafter SME for *sursis avec mise à l'épreuve*): 155 in total. This can be explained by the sheer number of SME pronounced each year in France. In 2010, 55,759 SME were pronounced to which one also must add 29, 174 partial SME (Tournier, 2013 b).

1. Procedure

Similar to the general aforementioned findings, with SME, offenders in breach rarely attend their hearing and when they are present, they rarely have an attorney.

- In 28/155 (18% - and 18.9% if one leaves out seven files where the information was missing) of cases, the probationer was present and assisted by an attorney;

- In 72/155 (46.45 - and 48.6% if one leaves out seven files where the information was missing) of cases the offender was present without an attorney;

- In 79/155 (50.9% - and 53.3% if one leaves out seven files where the information was missing) of cases the offender was not present;

86. This does exceed the total of six as some decisions may have referred in several causes to leniency.

- As mentioned, in 7/155 (4.5%) of the cases, the information was missing or not clear enough, which is surprising as this is ground for quashing the decision.

We are indeed close to the general findings as presented *supra*. I mentioned then that some judges were not at ease with the self-appraisal (*ex-officio*) procedure, but noted that, in general, they nonetheless did use this procedure. This is confirmed by SME: they ruled *ex officio* in 65.7% of the cases and were apprised by the prosecutor in 34.2% of them. This is logical: most cases, as we shall see, pertain to obligations' violations or non-compliance with the supervision. Prosecutors are not directly informed by the probation service of this type of non-compliance; probation services directly inform the JAP via their common server APPI.

The rulings were all standardised, but not as much as with defaulters' incarceration. JAPs only referred to a few legal articles, which represented a maximum of one to two paragraphs, and sometimes to none [87], as if it was in any case legitimate in the eyes of public opinion, politicians and the media, to pronounce revocation and did not require further justification. This is striking when compared with release decisions, which usually contain at least two paragraphs, and in many cases more, of legal justifications.

2. Offences

I coded, as previously, for the offences for which the SME was originally pronounced. People had committed offences:

- Against property [88] (including checks, bank or credit cards, and swindling): 30%;
- Violence: 25.8%;
- Road offences (including DUI): 23.8%;
- Drugs or alcohol as the main offence (includes, again, DUI): 11.6%;
- Destructions and deteriorations: 10.3%;
- Contempt and insults to public authorities: 3.8%;
- Absconding or illegal correspondence with a prisoner: 0.6%;
- Death threat: 5.8%;

87. By law all courts are required to provide the legal grounds of their reasoning and this includes quoting the legal articles which allow them to make their decision.

88. Robbery (in French law: theft with violence) was counted twice: once with theft cases; once with violence cases. What I wanted was to underline the violent potential of offenders, regardless of the legal context. For a similar motive, theft with destruction was counted with thefts and then again with destruction/deteriorations. The same shall apply hereafter.

- Alimony default: 1.9%;
- Miscellaneous: 54.5%.

I then studied whether these probationers had an addiction issue of some sort, and whether or not they had been sentenced for this addiction. Indeed, there were many people for whom the rulings mentioned addiction to alcohol (23.8%), to drugs (16.7%) or to both (1.2%), i.e. a total of 41.8%. This may mean that their illness had been one of the main causes of their SME sentence or that it had made it more difficult for them to comply with their obligations and in particular the mandatory treatment which is frequently pronounced with SME.

Only 2.5% of the people charged with non-compliance with their SME were women.

3. Decisions' analysis

It must be repeated that when a probationer is trialled for non-compliance, the probation service and the JAP have tried everything possible to avoid recalling him/her to prison. By that time, the situation is usually irremediably compromised. It is therefore not surprising that 69.6% of the decisions pronounced a **full revocation** and in 1.2% of the cases, they actually revoked several sentences at the same time, i.e. a total of 72.2%. It must however be noted that in two of these cases, the judge had added to the full revocation a convocation for a 723-15 procedure, which meant that if the probationer had by then complied, the custody resulting from the revocation could be transformed into a release measure.

JAPs can also pronounce a **partial revocation**, but do not frequently use this tool. They did so in only 11.6% of the cases – 12.3% if one includes a decision which pronounced a partial revocation and another sanction, the extension of the order. In these cases, the partial revocation was of:

- Half the probation sentence: 33.3%;
- Less than half of the probation sentence: 38.8%;
- More than half of the probation sentence: 27.7%.

JAPs referred to a **large number of causes** to explain why they fully or partially revoked the sentence. Some of these causes correspond to the legal grounds for revocation. Such is first the case of **non-compliance** with the obligations. In 30.9% of the decisions which pronounced a revocation the JAP referred to an overall disobedience with the obligations. In 26.1% of the decisions, a partial violation of the obligations was mentioned. In 27.7% of the decisions, the judge referred to offender absconding, his disappearance or his elusive attitude (for instance he would miss some appointments but would attend others, would systematically take a long time to provide documents, and so on) in 18.2% of the cases. In 0.7% of the cases, the person had to serve a mixed sentence, and had not complied with its custodial part. Similar to such cases, in 1.58% of the cases, the offender had not attended the 723-15 procedure hearing which would have allowed the judge to dispense him of the custodial part of his mixed sentenced by transforming it into a release measure or community sentence.

In a minority of cases (23%), the person had committed **another offence** and was sanctioned by a total or partial revocation.

Other causes pertained to the risk which the person represents or his/her **overall behaviour**. Such causes were usually mentioned along with the aforementioned ones:

- The risk of reoffending in 1.5% of the decisions;

- The person's fault (its deliberate nature): in 1.8% of the decisions;

- The person's bad faith: in 8.7% of the decisions;

- The person's oppositional or aggressive attitude: in 1.5% of the decisions.

A minority of decisions referred to the necessity to **force a person to actually comply** with his/her supervision. JAPs mentioned the fact that the person needed a strict supervision in 0.7% of the decisions and the necessity to make sure the victim's damages were paid in 1.58% of the cases.

In many more cases (69.8%) the decision referred to the fact that the **meaning of the sentence or measure** had disappeared. Three JAPs (JAP 23, 13 and 28) used exactly the same phrase: 'the probation measure is no longer justified'. Moreover, 3.9% of the decisions referred to the aforementioned notion of substantial compliance.

Decisions only **exceptionally** referred to **psychological considerations**, which were encountered, as we shall see *infra*, more frequently when the court granted release or another favourable measure. Most rulings merely described the case and generally ended with a similar phrase which stated that the person had deliberately put him/herself in this situation. In other words, judges insist on the person's responsibility. I found more empathetic phrases in some of the decisions which only partially revoked the sentence, but this was exceptional.

Some decisions did not sanction the offender at all. There were however only 14.8% (N23) of such **revocation dismissals**. Their causes were in some cases legal: in one case out of twenty-three, the person had died and in another he had been deported. In three other cases, a legal mistake had been made and the case had to be dismissed by law: the prosecutor had apprised the JAP of the case even though the person had already been sanctioned before for the same violation. Other decisions clearly sanctioned the criminal justice system's own mistakes. Thus a decision dismissed the case because the prosecutor had taken months to react to the violation and to appraise the JAP and in five other cases because the probation service was responsible for the offender's drift as it had not sufficiently supported and/or supervised him.

Other decisions were simply designed to give the offender yet another chance. Such leniency was granted without other further reasons in two of the twenty dismissal decisions; in other cases, it appeared to be deserved. For instance in four cases, the offender had made an effort at the very last minute by paying the damages or starting therapy. In two cases, the judge realised that the offender had actually displayed mixed behaviour, with some positive actions and negative ones. In six other cases, the judge took the difficult circumstances of the person into account: his illness, his fragile psychological state or his young age.

In yet other ones of the twenty-three dismissal decisions, the judge still wanted to try and make the offender comply. Such was the case in two decisions, where he wanted the offender to pay the damages and in five others where he wanted to make sure that the person would actually be supervised. However, when the JAP has such a goal in mind, he is more likely to extend the order.

D. Probation orders' extension

I had collected forty-six decisions pertaining to the extension of an SME, forty-two of which actually pronounced it whilst four dismissed the case. One must bear in mind that in all of these cases, the offender also risks the full or partial revocation of his/her sentence and that by extending his/her probation, the judges are actually being lenient. The four dismissals constituted exceptions whereby, contrary to the general rule, the JAP had specifically been apprised of an extension request by the prosecutor.

1. Procedure

Similar to the general findings, 20% of the probationers were assisted by an attorney; 80% were present at their hearing, which is logical given that softer sanctions are typically pronounced when the person is actually present at his/her hearing thereby showing that he/she is respecting the criminal justice system and being able to defend his case.

We also found that JAPs' self-appraisals dominated (: 69.7%), in particular because probation extension is usually not granted to people who have committed another offence, but exclusively in cases where the offender has not complied with his/her obligation or supervision.

Rulings are just as standardised as those which revoke the SME, which is not surprising given the offences they apply to.

2. Offences

It is predictable that the offences originally committed by the offender whose orders are extended are similar to those mentioned above in relation to probation revocation, since these offences led to the same measure which the offender has not complied with, i.e. the SME. Since, however, our sample was smaller there was in turn a smaller range of offences, that is:

- Offences against property (including checks, bank or credit cards, and swindling): 27.2%;
- Violence: 15.9%;
- Road offences (including DUI): 31.8%;
- Drugs or alcohol as the main offence (includes, again, DUI): 40.9%;
- Destructions and deteriorations: 9%;
- Contempt and insults to public authorities: 2.2%;
- Miscellaneous: 6.8%.

It is to be noted that the offenders who benefitted from an extension of their probation order rather than a revocation, were less violent (15.9% versus 25.8%) but had more addiction issues (40.9% of cases where the offence was related to an addiction versus 11.6%). Other than that, the offences represent the quotidian of correctional tribunals.

3. Decisions' analysis

The JAP pronounced an extension in forty-two decisions out of the forty-six I had collected. A **case dismissal** – which is by definition a rare occurrence – was pronounced in four cases. In one of these four cases, the judge thought that the offender's behaviour had actually been partly positive and thought he deserved yet another chance; in the three other, the person had brought at the very last minute – i.e. at his breach hearing – the documented proof of his equally last minute compliance.

When the **order** was **extended** it was for different periods, which varied both according to the court's objective and the maximum possible length of time the law allowed it to opt for:

- For eighteen months in 4/42 cases (9.5%);

- For twelve months in 32/42 cases (76.1%);
- For six months in 5/42 cases (11.9%);
- For eight months in 1/42 cases (2.3%).

Probation extension may be a **softer** sanction than revocation as it does not send the offender to prison. However, it is also far from lenient as it extends the duration of a probation order, which, even in the rather loose context of French supervision, does imply some form of control over the offender. The literature has shown, albeit in other jurisdictions where control is much stricter, that beyond a certain length of time, offenders may prefer incarceration to probation or another community measure (see e.g. May & Wood, 2010).

Even in the French context, in most cases, the judge did want **more control** – to be fair, at times, some control full stop – over the offender. Thus in 95.2% of the decisions which pronounced the extension of the order, the ruling made clear that the aim was to make sure that the offender would, at long last, truly comply with his/her obligations (typically, the payment of damages and treatment). In 26.1% of the cases, the judge clearly gave the offender yet another chance – but this was often added to the desire to make the offender comply – because he/she may have breached the order, but he/she had also complied with some of the other obligations or his/her situation had improved (for instance he/she had found employment) so that revocation was not opportune. In some cases, the judge expressly mentioned the nocebo effect that the person's incarceration would have on his/her situation. Such a risk is also present when a suspended custody sentence with probation and community work is revoked.

E. Community work with probation revocation

1. Presentation

Under French law a rather interesting combination exists which comprises a suspended custody sentence of up to six months, probation (supervision and obligations), and a community sentence. This forms a sentence called suspended sentence with probation and community sentence (hereafter STIG for *sursis avec mise à l'épreuve et travail d'intérêt général*)[89]. It allows for the supervision and support of a person and his/her desistance through obligations which meet his/her criminogenic needs (employment, treatment and so on) whilst getting the offender's foot on the – employment – ladder. It is

---

89. I did not collect decisions pertaining to violation of community work as these cases are dealt with by correctional tribunals and not JAPs.

an interesting sentence for people who have not worked for years – in some cases never worked and/or have addiction issues. Despite its usefulness it is rarely pronounced by correctional tribunals. In practice, it is the result of a decision made by the JAP, in the course of an article 723-15 procedure, to convert a custody sentence of up to six months into a STIG as is expressly allowed by article 132-57 of the penal code. Such a decision, which shall be studied *infra*, is called a 'conversion-STIG'. It is important to note that a STIG, be it the result of a sentence by the correctional tribunal or a 'conversion-STIG' by the JAP is only possible for sentences of up to six months, or, when the sentence is a mixed one comprising a custody period and an SME period, the custodial period which can be converted into a STIG must not itself exceed six months. Such quanta are much lower than those which normally prevail for the procedure of article 723-15, i.e. two years for first time offenders and one year for repeat offenders.

The natural sanction of the violation of the obligations attached to STIG – which includes the non-execution of the community work – is the revocation of the TIG itself. It is legally impossible to extend the order in this case (on all these issues, see Herzog-Evans, 2012-2013: Chap. 423 and 711.141).

I had only collected thirty such cases. In all but one of them the offender had benefitted from an STIG via a conversion granted by the JAP. In other words, before he breached his order, he had already benefitted from a favourable decision which enabled him not to be incarcerated.

2. Procedure

The analysis of the procedure revealed that an attorney was present with the offender in only 4/30 (13.3%) of cases, which is lower than the general figures (19.1%). It also showed that in thirteen cases (43.33%), the offender was present at his hearing. Given the small size of the sample, the difference with the general figures may not be significant.

Offenders were more likely – but again, with necessary caution – to have been breached based on a self-appraisal (*ex-officio*) decision of the case by the JAP (24/30 cases, i.e. 80% versus 20% appraisals by the prosecutor). This can probably be explained by the fact that the revocation was never caused by a new offence.

3. Offences

In five of the thirty decisions I had collected, the original sentence – for which the STIG was eventually pronounced – was not mentioned or not clearly specified. The other cases mentioned:

- Offences against property (including checks, bank or credit cards, and swindling): 7/25;
- Violence: 1/25;
- Road offences (including DUI): 11/25;
- Drugs or alcohol as the main offence (includes, again, DUI): 7/25;
- Destructions or deteriorations: 2/25;
- Contempt and insults to public authorities: 2/25;
- Miscellaneous: 3/25.

These offences were not very serious and the offender had typically not been charged with several of them, which is coherent with the smaller custody sentence which was pronounced. There were many road offences. Eight rulings mentioned that the offender had an addiction to alcohol or drugs and in seven cases his sentence was related to this.

4. Decisions' analysis

Revocation was pronounced in 22/30 decisions. In two cases, a partial revocation was pronounced and in five cases the person benefitted from a case dismissal. In another one, he benefitted from an adjournment.

The analysis of the main and secondary causes of these decisions yielded interesting findings. As was previously mentioned, **total or partial revocation** (N23) was never pronounced for a new offence. Consequently, revocation only pertained to non-compliance with the obligations or supervision itself. In no less than nine cases, the person had purely and simply disappeared and had not been found at the time of the hearing. Several reasons for revocation could be present at the same time in the same decision.

The JAP also referred to secondary considerations. Most of them revealed a form of moral judgement: fifteen decisions mentioned that the offender was clearly of bad faith or was making a mockery of his/her sentence. In three decisions, JAP were less judgmental and mentioned that the offender had not understood the meaning of the measure and that it consequently had no more grounds.

Revocation dismissal (N5) was sometimes pronounced for legal reasons. In two cases, the sentence itself was illegal so that it could not be revoked. In one of these decisions it was illegal because the STIG was supposed to last twenty-four months when the legal maximum is eighteen (Penal code, art. 131-22 – Herzog-Evans, 2012-2013: 422.173). In the other case, the person had not been present at his original penal hearing and could not have been sentenced to a STIG, which is a measure requiring that the person is present (Penal code, art. 131-8, sec. 3 – M. Herzog-Evans, 2012-2013: 422.81-

422.94). This meant that the sentence had not been registered by the National Criminal Record Service as such.

As is classic, in two more cases, the offender provided last minute documented proof of his compliance. As we have seen, this profoundly irritates probation officers who try so hard to make the offender provide such proof, whereas the JAP obtains it more easily be it with a '*recadrage*' or a revocation procedure. In another ruling, the JAP noted that the offender was incarcerated and it was thus preferable to suspend the TIG in order to make sure he could benefit from the supervision attached to this sentence, upon his release.

Lastly, the only decision which **adjourned** the case noted that the person had at long last started to comply with his obligation to work, but was, probably mistrustful, and given the offender's clear lack of enthusiasm, had decided to check on his progress three months from then.

F. Parole revocation

I had collected a rather small sample of parole revocations (N18). Conversely I had obtained 142 decisions which granted parole. This very small sample does not allow me to draw any significant conclusions.

1. Procedure

Bearing in mind my cautionary note, I found that a greater proportion of the decisions, compared to the general findings or other types of sanctions, were made in the course of a hearing where an attorney was present (7/18 cases). Only 5/18 offenders were present without an attorney, whilst 6/18 were not present at all.

JAP appraisal modes were more balanced than in other procedures: prosecutors had apprised the JAP in more cases (9/18 versus 7/18 self-appraisal by the JAP – in two cases, the decision did not make this clear). In other cases, self-appraisal by the JAP was dominant. This can probably be explained by a greater vigilance of prosecutors for this type of measure, thus giving quite a lot of freedom to the offender. Indeed, this can apply to very serious offences, and therefore, long custodial sentences. It can also be explained by the fact that a greater proportion of revocations were pronounced in cases where the person had committed another offence.

2. Offences

Unsurprisingly, since parole is not a sentence but a release measure, which can also be granted to the authors of serious crimes, the offences which led the prison sentence of the people who were eventually paroled represented a greater variety of offences than what was mentioned *supra*. In one of the rulings, the offence was not mentioned. For the seventeen others the offences were:

- Offences against property (including checks, bank or credit cards, and swindling): 9/17;
- Organised crime: 2/17;
- Violence (including violent offences against property): 3/17;
- Road offences (including DUI): 2/17;
- Drugs or alcohol as the main offence (includes, again, DUI): 11/17;
- Destructions or deteriorations: 1/17;
- Contempt and insults to public authorities: 2/17;
- Sexual offences: 1/17;
- Homicides: 2/17;
- Prison escape: 1/17 ;
- Miscellaneous: 3/25.

A detailed analysis of the rulings, and particularly into the offenders' circumstances, showed that eleven offenders (11/18) had an addiction to alcohol and/or drugs.

3. Decisions' analysis

Fourteen decisions out of eighteen pronounced a revocation; four dismissed the case. All revocations were full revocations but could only by law apply to the portion of the sentence which had not been executed.

The causes of parole revocation were slightly different than what has been encountered thus far. No less than six rulings pertained to the commission of a new offence. Nonetheless, ten decisions out of fourteen referred to a violation of the obligations. In other words both causes could be present in the same case. In two cases, the offender had disappeared and had not been found at the time of the hearing. Lastly, in another case, recall was caused by the revocation of a probationary period attached to the parole decision. Indeed, in French law, parole can be granted providing the person first complies with a probationary measure which is typically one of the three measures under prison registry, i.e. semi-freedom, placement in the community or electronic monitoring. Since this measure is probationary, if it is revoked, parole is also automatically revoked.

JAPs also referred secondarily to other causes. In nine cases they mentioned that the parolee had not understood the meaning of the measure so that it no longer made sense. In one ruling, the person's bad faith was pointed out by the judge.

Revocation dismissal was pronounced in three cases because the person brought documented proof of his last minute compliance with his obligations. In one instance, the offender had been charged for a new offence but had not yet been sentenced and the JAP decided to dismiss the case based on the presumption of innocence principle (see *supra*).

§ 2. Release and other 'sentence management' decisions

Release and other 'sentence management' decisions represent the core activity of JAPs. They can either release prisoners using a variety of measures or transform a custody sentence before it is even executed into a release measure or community sentence, in the course of the aforementioned article 723-15 procedure.

A. General findings

I had collected a vast number of decisions which granted a sentence management measure: N391. It is important to note that in 2012, 39,289 measures were thus granted, representing an increase of 13.2% compared to the previous year (which represented a 5.2% increase compared to the one before that) (Direction de l'administration pénitentiaire, 2013 and 2012).

In the following paragraphs I shall only present the results which pertained to the main decisions: parole, electronic monitoring, placement in the community and semi-freedom. In the presentation of the general findings I shall however include other measures, namely conversion-STIG and conversion into day-fine, which will be studied in greater detail in §3. I also include in the following lines seven decisions pertaining to the anticipatory expunging of the criminal record of offenders serving SME as their small number did not warrant any further developments.

1. General procedure findings

Here the general procedural findings are in clear contrast with what we found with sanctions. There were:

- 73.2% cases where the person was present and had an attorney;

- 32.3% cases where the person was present at the hearing but had no attorney;

- 0.5% cases where the person was not present at the hearing;

However, these figures applied to cases where a hearing was organised. In 44.5% of the cases, however, there was no hearing at all – this was an HDC procedure.

There is thus a greater proportion of offenders who are present and assisted by an attorney than with sanctions, which is unsurprising given that offenders who breach their order are usually going downhill and tend to be elusive. Let us indeed compare with our findings pertaining to sanctions:

- Only 19.7% (versus here 73.2%) were present and had an attorney;

- 56.5% (versus here 32.3%) were present without counsel;

- 48.5% (versus here 0.5%) were not present.

We shall also see that the applications which were rejected comprised of 34.2% no show cases (versus here 0.5%). It is patent that the presence of the offender is of enormous importance, not that it is the cause per se of the denial (see *infra*), but also because no show offenders typically have not put their heart and soul into their release plan or other project, might have a plan which is not credible and/or do not provide documented proof.

In all HDC cases, the person is seen by the JAP during an informal preparatory meeting. Such information could not be gathered for sanction and denial of the application decisions as these decisions require a hearing. Nonetheless the percentage of HDC decisions is troublesome. One might wonder what the added bonus of judicial decision-making in release is if what constitutes its essence is eliminated.

It is important to note that it was not useful to mention how the JAP was apprised of the cases as contrary to breach cases, self-appraisal (*ex-officio* decisions) and prosecutors' appraisals are exceptional and no such instances were found in the rulings I collected.

2. General analysis

The rulings' analysis yielded interesting common denominators for the various types of measures which were granted.

For instance, it is clear that, as mentioned *supra*, JAPs explain their rulings (ruling 'motivation') more in depth than they do when they sanction a probationer for being non-compliant. The longer the sentence, the more legal references are found in the ruling. When the sentence is long, judges will also tend to refer more frequently to the principles laid down in article 707 or, for parole, in the similar principles laid down in article 729 of the PPC. When the person has recently been sentenced or incarcerated, the judge might feel that it is premature to release him/her; when, conversely, the end of his/her sentence is approaching, the judge will often mention this as an argument for granting him/her the measure he/she has applied for as they may feel it is now high time to prepare his/her reentry.

With medium length sentences, that is longer than two years [90] but below the level of competence for the TAP (i.e. ten years), JAPs concentrate on the person's criminal record, the quality and the credibility of his/her release plan, and on his/her sincerity. They hardly ever mention article 707.

With shorter sentences below these quanta, and in particular with very short sentences, time is of the essence. JAPs tend to think that the person will soon be released in any case, and that it is urgent to prepare his/her reentry and at least a minimal form of supervision along with some support for the person's desistance. In such cases, decisions tend to reflect the human misery and difficult circumstances of offenders and to take their hardship (: social difficulties, family issues, addiction, homelessness and so on…) into consideration. Because they often lack enough information, they will also check how previous incarcerations or community sentences were executed and how the offender then fared. 'Motivation' is however very standardised. JAPs typically first present the offences, project, probation services' and, when relevant, prison services' point of view, the prosecutor's recommendation and what was said during the hearing by the offender and his/her attorney. The few paragraphs which immediately precede the decision itself on the matter is usually only one paragraph long. JAPs hardly ever refer to article 707, with the exception of JAP 28.

In a number of decisions, JAPs use the exact same expression to indicate that the offences 'can be considered as old'. It is very likely that this identical wording reflects some form of deliberation between JAPs, particularly via their common thirteen year old listserv *Justpeines* or via their training at the ENM. In any case, the length of time since the last offence is favourable to the offender as it seems to indicate that he/she is currently desisting. When the last offence was indeed committed three or four years ago, this does seem pertinent. Such was for instance the case in this decision where the judge had placed a former drug addict female under electronic monitoring and had pointed out that her offences had been committed in 2006 and 2007 whilst the decision, based on an article 723-15 procedure was made in

90. Two years (sentence or term left to serve) is, as was mentioned previously, the maximum quantum for all the measures under prison registry (semi-freedom, placement in the community and electronic monitoring) and for the procedure of article 723-15 of the PPC.

2010 (JAP 28, 19 Nov. 2010). Conversely, in a number of cases, the offence was committed the year before. It is difficult to accept that it is 'old'. In general, however, if JAPs tend to grant favourable measures to '*justiciables*' whose offences are 'old' it would be particularly uncalled for the criminal justice system to at long last execute sentences which were pronounced years before for offences which belong in the distant past, when in the meantime, the person's circumstances and life may have changed for the better and he/she may have changed as well. It would indeed be inappropriate to implement a sentence in its custodial form when the person now has a stable life, has desisted or is showing very positive signs such as having stopped drugs or is taking methadone. It seems that the criminal justice system – in this instance represented by JAPs – has a guilty conscience for suddenly wanting to execute a sentence years after the offence was committed, especially in with non-serious ones.

B. Parole

I had collected 142 parole (conditional release) decisions. In 2012, 7,980 parole decisions were made in France (Direction de l'administration pénitentiaire, 2013: 6). After a long decline – to some extent due to the prison services pressure on JAPs to use electronic monitoring – this measure is on the rise again (+ 6.7% compared to the previous year).

1. Procedure

In thirty-two rulings there was no indication pertaining to the procedural circumstances (whether there had been a hearing, whether there had been an attorney…). Leaving these decisions aside, it is interesting to note that no decision to parole was made in no-show cases, except, of course for HDC decisions. 19% of the decisions were HDC. This is much less than the average (44.5%). It is indeed difficult to imagine that such a contentious measure – with its tendency to leave the offender with much more freedom than release measures under prison registry - could be habitually made without hearing the offender. Two MP suggested that offenders sentenced to up to five years should be automatically conditionally released (Raimbourg & Huygues, 2013). This proposition was also made by the jury of the conference of consensus (Jury de la conférence de consensus, 2013; Herzog-Evans,

2013 c) and this seems to be seriously envisaged by the Ministry of Justice at the time I am completing this book[91].

2. Offences

Parole, called conditional release in French, is accessible to all offenders, whether they committed serious crimes or not, whether they have long sentence – including life; even true life – or short ones. TAP are however competent for sentences exceeding ten years, when the offender has more than three years to serve; for sentences below this quantum or with long sentences with three or less than three years to serve, JAPs are competent (PPC, art. 731, sec. 1). For this reason, my sample does contain crimes. Offenders committed the following offences:

- Offences against property (including checks, bank or credit cards, and swindling): 31.6%;
- Organised crime (including terrorism): 4.9%;
- Violence (including violent offences against property): 29.5%;
- Road offences (including DUI): 12.6%;
- Drugs or alcohol as the main offence (includes, again, DUI): 38.73%;
- Destructions or deteriorations: 3.52%;
- Contempt and insults to public authorities: 1.4%;
- Sexual offences: 11.9%;
- Involuntary homicide and other unlawful killings: 1.4%;
- Voluntary homicide: 3.5%;
- Prison escape: 1.4%;
- Miscellaneous: 2.1%.

I then looked into the rulings in order to detect how many offenders had addiction issues, and whether or not they had been sentenced for these issues. I found that 11.2% were addicted to drugs, whilst 36.6% were addicted to alcohol. In other words, a total of 51.4% paroled prisoners suffered from addiction. Linked to this 38.7% had been sentenced either for drug trafficking, DUI or for other related offences.

91. See the daily *Le Monde*, August 26, 2013: http://www.lemonde.fr/politique/article/2013/08/26/christiane-taubira-se-presse-d-annoncer-sa-reforme-penale_3466450_823448.html (accessed on Sept. 13, 2013). Also see the Ministry of Justice Bill and my comments: http://herzog-evans.com/commentaire-du-projet-sur-la-peine-de-contrainte-penale-french-probation-order-bill-a-comment/.

There was also a significant proportion of sex offenders. Generally these offenders are sentenced to medium or long sentences and cannot benefit from other release measures which are under prison registry (semi-freedom, placement in the community and electronic monitoring), with the exception of pre-requisite probationary periods before they benefit from parole.

3. Decisions' analysis

a. The reasons behind the decision

As with the other types of measures, I shall hereafter focus on the two or three paragraphs which summarise the JAP's personal opinion on a given case and which explain why he/she made the decision. The preceding paragraphs simply contain a summary of the facts, other practitioners' opinions and the offender's statement. Only these two paragraphs can explain the decision to release or not to.

The law defines rather precisely what the conditions and criteria for conditional release (Herzog-Evans, 2012-2013: chap. 442) are. Article 729 of the PPC states that as a general condition the prisoner must make 'serious social resettlement efforts'. It is therefore not surprising that 43.6% of the rulings expressly mentioned '**reinsertion efforts**'; this shorter and, in the French language, more modern expression is actually preferred over article 729's longer one.

Article 729 then goes on to list what type of effort the offender should make. The list is non-exhaustive as is always the case in French law when it is preceded by the adverb 'notably'. The list refers to five **criteria**: employment; the essential participation in family life; the necessity to get treatment; efforts to pay the damages due to the victim; commitment to any other serious insertion or reinsertion project. All the rulings are thus required by law to refer to at least one of these criteria and they do indeed. However, when one only focuses on the last relevant paragraphs [92], three main categories of criteria stand out. Such is the case with treatment. JAPs will mention that the offender is undergoing treatment or needs treatment in 10.3% of the last two to three relevant paragraphs. It may come as a surprise that given the number of addicted parole applicants, JAPs do not refer them to treatment more frequently. However, JAPs will have also mentioned treatment in the former more descriptive and neutral parts of their rulings and will in such cases typically impose treatment obligations. Such is also the case with regard to

92. It is important to remember that the last two to three paragraphs of the rulings which immediately precede the decision itself are the only ones which actually represent what the JAP him/herself thinks of the case.

the damages due to the victim and the offender's obligation to pay these damages, which are mentioned in 14.7% of the cases. Lastly, JAPs refer to offenders' families and the need for their presence in 10.5% of the cases.

In all the cases, judges also refer to **article 707** of the PPC **principles**, since it is a general guideline which applies to all JAP decisions. In 7.7% they thus refer to the need to prevent reoffending – a principle which is incidentally also mentioned in article 729 of the PPC in the case of parole. Article 707 also refers to insertion and reinsertion, i.e. the French legal equivalents to desistance. As an example 2.8% decisions refer to the fact that the addiction is now under control or is a thing of the past.

Judges also explain their decisions with other reasons than the criteria and principles laid out in the law. Some have little criminological relevance as is the case with the aforementioned **'person's position as of the offence'**. 11.9% of the parole decisions refer to it. It is a minority, but a significant one. 9.1% of the decisions further refer to the person's behaviour in prison, which is no longer relevant – unless it is understood from the offence paralleling behaviour point of view (McDougall et al., 2012 and 2013) which is not the case with JAPs' decisions. Prison behaviour is however usually mentioned with the objective factors which JAPs have to list in the first part of the decision, but are seldom mentioned in their final personal summary which precedes the decision itself, and never as a sole decisive factor. In other words, it is a factual element which they have to mention and take into account, but it is never decisive. The rather modest percentage of decisions which nonetheless refer to prison behaviour in these final paragraphs reflect a positive evolution of JAPs' jurisprudence and practices which are for the most part due to the judicialisation of 2000-2004. Before that, JAPs made all their decisions, including parole, in the aforementioned prison commission, the CAP, and were thus much more influenced by prison culture and context (for this period see Herzog-Evans, 1994). Should the current government's bill be enacted, most JAP decisions would be made in CAP, as they were before 2000, and prison behaviour would inevitably return to the forefront.

Lastly, and more aptly, JAPs refer to criteria which reflect **what would** in their opinion **make sense for the case** at stake. Thus, 2.1% of decisions paroled the '*justiciable*' because another measure had by now become too burdensome for him/her. Thus they pronounced the conversion of a semi-freedom or placement in the community into conditional release. An even greater number of decisions clearly meant to strengthen a still fragile desistance process. Thus 2.8% of the rulings expressly referred to a test, and in some cases even a risk which was taken by the JAP, destined to see if the offender was actually ready to or would continue doing well. Even more significant, 23.9% of the decisions indicated that parole was necessary in order to better control or contain the offender once he/she was released, and this was clearly related to his/her reinsertion first steps, and 7% of the decisions did mention the necessity to support his/her reinsertion whilst 6.3% mentioned the need to support his/her efforts. In the same vein, 4.6% of the decisions mention the need to force the offender to respect such or such an obligation; in French law, most obligations are reinsertion related.

A number of JAPs also wrote that **it is now time** in the course of a sentence **to move on**. Thus 10.5% of their rulings mentioned that the person will soon be released and that it is now time to start preparing his/her reentry and supervision. In 2.8% of the rulings they did not hesitate to say that the sentence has by now produced its expected outcome and that it is time to put an end to it. 3.5% of the rulings referred to the aforementioned concept of 'old offence'.

A minority of decisions (8.4%) ostensibly **congratulated** the offender for his/her progress – during their hearings, they are less shy and congratulate offenders on a regular basis – whilst 4.2% of the rulings displayed some form of **pity** for the offender or granted him release because of his ill health or for other humanitarian reasons.

It is interesting to now focus on the **concept of risk**. Adding the decisions where the JAPs refer to the necessity to control the person when he/she will be released, those that mention that he/she will soon be released and it is now time to make sure he/she is supervised in the community, along with those which refer to the necessity to make sure he/she complies with an obligation, and those which expressly refer to the need to prevent reoffending or to the person's position as of the offence', yields a percentage of 66.1% decisions. In other words, parole is not only an insertion tool; it is also a public security tool. In fact, JAPs seldom take enormous risks in contexts where there is considerable doubt even if, of course, most cases are not clear cut and contain their load of positive and greater elements. In order to grant parole, positive elements must either be in greater number of bear more weight.

However, a small number of decisions are cause for concern, such as the one made by JAP 23 (decision of October 18, 2010) which pertained to a forty-four year old man who had sexually assaulted four of his young relatives (they were all aged less than fifteen, which is the legal age for sexual consent in French law) and had been sentenced to four years, which included thirty months on a probation order. Since the custodial part of his sentence (eighteen months) was under the legal limit of two years he was by law entitled to present his case in a 723-15 procedure in order to avoid being incarcerated altogether. He was then granted *ab initio* parole without going to prison even though there had been no risk assessment made in his case and he had never had any treatment, nor was obligated by the decision to get treatment.

As we have seen throughout this book, JAPs seem to have an understanding of what is a **delinquent career** and a **desisting process** along with what their contribution and their decision can achieve in this respect. Thus they do not hesitate to positively enforce the person's desisting motivation, in particular during the hearings; very much like PSC. As mentioned above, 8.4% of the written rulings do congratulate offenders in the final two to three paragraphs which, thus meaning that this is the basis of their decision and that they want to draw special attention to the person's merit [93]. Some JAPs make a habit of it. Such was the case with JAP 11 who, for instance, in a decision on September 22, 2009 referred to 'exemplary behaviour in prison'. In the same decision, he referred to the offender's efforts, progress and his strong release plan which 'allows one to foresee a much more peaceful future than his judicial past'. In a May 11, 2010 decision he ostensibly referred to the person's agency, a vital component of the desisting process. He wrote that the person 'seems to have decided to become the master of his own life'. This judge sometimes used a terminology which reminds us of the 'reentry' movement (Petersilia, 2003; Travis & Visher, 2005) as in this February 23 2010 ruling: 'Mr P.'s release plan is elaborate and coherent with his progress in prison and his professional projects... and is likely to participate in his transition to' the community. JAP 11 also referred to the transition process of adolescents to adulthood (see Lösel et al., 2012) when he stated: 'his delinquency seems to be correlated to a difficulty to transition to adult life'. Other JAPs, such as, for instance, one who was not interviewed, seemed to refer to Maruna's self-narrative (Maruna, 2001) when he said that the offender 'has declared that he analysed his past behaviour with a critical eye and' wanted to 'extricate himself from it'.

JAPs are usually aware of the difficulties which probationers encounter and the demands that, as a result, one can reasonably make of them. Such was, for instance, the case with a particular JAP who was not interviewed. This JAP referred in a decision of December 1st, 2010, which pertained to a psychotic '*justiciable'*, that he had made immense efforts given his context and could not have done any better because, as a result of his illness, he was isolated.

A significant number of decisions refer one way or another to the aforementioned **meaning of the sentence**. When one adds the decisions which state that the person has spent enough time in prison and that the sentence or incarceration has produced its expected outcome, and those which state that

93. They will often praise the offender in the former parts of the rulings, when, for instance, they describe the person's social and personal context. In the present lines I am however only focusing on the percentage of decisions which include such praise in the last paragraphs which present the very cause of the decision as summarised by the judge.

the offender will in any case be released soon and if parole is not granted, will max out, 13.3% of the decisions thus reveal that the JAP consider that the custodial part of the sentence to have lost its initial sense and will only make sense if the person is prepared for his/her transition to the community. Thus JAP 11 – again! – ruled on August 31, 2010, that psychiatrist experts made a rather negative assessment of a psychopath, but that this can be explained because he is arrogant and assertive. However, JAP 11 then noted that he did receive treatment, had a job whilst in prison, had made serious insertion efforts, and that his release plan was coherent and serious; in short he ticks every single legal box. One might indeed wonder what the future will hold for a person who, because of his personality disorder, has a strong propensity to reoffend (Milton et al., 2003; Patrick, 2006: Chap. 24 to 27). In this instance however, the JAP was right to consider that he was a few months away from maxing out and it was now more useful to prepare a release plan.

A few rulings are actually amusing. This was certainly the case with JAP 11 on March 17, 2011 who for the most part granted release because this Anglophone 'justiciable' had learnt French. Other rulings are clearly militant, such as one by JAP 13 which stated that the offender should be granted release because as a homosexual inmate he had been submitted to bullying bordering on the violation of article 3 of the European human rights convention (Ruling of May 2011, *Ajpénal* 2013: 113-114, obs. M. Herzog-Evans).

b. The decisions' content

With measures other than parole, post release supervision only lasts as long as the original sentence. If, for instance, the offender had two months left to serve and is granted semi-freedom, he/she would only be submitted to semi-freedom and the supervision it implies for these two months. Conversely, with parole, supervision can be extended for one more year (PPC, art. 732). 22.5% **decisions** thus **prolonged supervision**. In 12.6% of the total of parole decisions, the judge prolonged supervision for the maximum of one year; this represented 56.2% of all the decision which prolonged supervision. The other decisions were distributed as follows:

- Three months: 2.8% of all parole decisions; 12.5% of the decisions which prolonged supervision;

- Four months: 0.7% of all parole decisions; 3.1% of the decisions which prolonged supervision;

- Six months: 4.9% of all parole decisions; 21.8% of the decisions which prolonged supervision;

- Seven months: 1.4% of all parole decisions; 6.2% of the decisions which prolonged supervision.

Law-reforms have extended the number of situations where the offender must first go through a period under a stricter form of supervision in order to then benefit from conditional release, both being however pronounced in the same decision. For instance, the offender is paroled but must first spend a year under electronic monitoring surveillance and will only eventually benefit from parole if he/she is not recalled whilst on electronic monitoring. This essentially applies to longer sentences and is mandatory with the more serious cases. In many instances, it plays in favour of the offender as is allows him/her to apply for parole one year before the usual mid-sentence or two thirds (for recidivists) term. In such cases a **probationary period** under one of the three measures under prison registry is mandatory (Herzog-Evans, 2012-2013: 442.241-442.248).

Mandatory probationary periods were only present in 1.4% of our decisions. This can be explained by the fact that JAPs share competence with TAP and TAP are competent for long sentences for which probationary periods are precisely obligatory. 17.6% of the decisions contained a form of optional probationary period, which may be the result of the influence of the recent legal developments which made probationary periods more prominent.

Only 7.7% of the parole decisions were **'parental parole'** decisions, i.e. specifically granted to offenders who are guardians of children up to ten years and who have up to four years to serve. They were either sentenced to up to four years or are serving a longer sentence and have up to four years left to serve. Recidivists are excluded from this special type of parole (PPC, art. 729-3). This is not a great deal of time when one remembers that many offenders have children. However, we saw that ordinary parole rules – governed by the rules laid out in art. 729 – also refer to offenders' families. However, in such cases parole is not granted exclusively in view of the needs of children.

Only one person mentioned in our sample benefitted from the specific **parole for elderlies** – aged more than seventy – which was created by the Prison Law of 2009.

However, 14.8% of offenders 'benefitted' from mandatory **deportation-parole** [94] a form of parole which exists in virtually all the European jurisdictions (Padfield et al., 2010). It is important to bear in mind that most foreign-

94. In all the other cases, parole is optional and even if a prisoner applies for parole, he/she can eventually decide not to accept it.

ers will obtain one of the aforementioned forms of parole. Only those who are illegally in France can be submitted to mandatory deportation-parole (PPC, art. 729-2). In practice, however, offenders often apply for this type of parole in order to be spared the price of a plane fare. Even in some of these cases, 'Sarkozy law' n° 2003-1119 of November 26, 2003 (Poncela, 2004) allows the JAP to parole these illegal foreigners to remain in France and execute an ordinary form of parole; if they comply with all their obligations and are not revoked, they can then avoid deportation. Only two of the rulings I had gathered pertained to the application of the Sarkozy law. Another conversely allowed the offender to settle abroad. Rulings which do deport and parole offenders are typically under-'motivated'. Judges typically only mention that the application is admissible, refer to the offender's prison behaviour and verify whether the offender had a custom fine to pay and if the Customs accepted to reduce it to a lesser – often ridiculously lesser: at least ten times less – amount. Sometimes, they merely check whether the OFPRA (*Office Français de Protection des Réfugiés et des Apatrides*), the agency which charters planes for deportation currently has chartered one going to the exact location where the offender is to be deported. Conversely, some applications are rejected for their lack thereof, thus meaning that the person cannot be deported.

In none of these decisions does the JAP pay attention to the person's insertion or release plan. This was regrettably caused by two decisions of the French highest court; the court of cassation which ruled that when a judge ruled on a deportation-parole of article 729-3 of the PPC, he should not pay any attention to the social criteria laid out in article 729 – the article which governs ordinary parole (Crim. 6 March 2002, n° 01-85.914, *Bull. crim.*, n° 59, *D.* 2002. IR, 1405, *BICC* n° 557; Crim., 1er June 2002, n° 561, *RSC* 2002. 812, obs. B. Bouloc, *D.* 2003, Chron., 925, M. Herzog-Evans). Most of these decisions pertain to offenders who have no European Union origins, so that the Framework decision 2008/947/JAI (Morgenstern, 2009) – which is incidentally still not implemented in France – would be of little help. One thing is certain: this Framework decision does invalidate the Court of cassation jurisprudence when it comes to offenders who are entitled to stay in a European Union jurisdiction.

C. Electronic monitoring

I did not collect as many electronic monitoring (hereafter EM) decisions (N63) as I did with parole, which is not representative. Indeed in 2012 there were 11,790 offenders who benefitted from EM – to which one can add 624 SEFIP, i.e. this swifter purely administrative home detention curfew without supervision – and 7,980 persons who benefitted from parole (Direction de l'administration pénitentiaire, 2013: 6).

EM is either a measure whereby the offender has to stay at home during curfew hours, which is controlled via a static electronic device. It does use the GPS-system (see Nellis et al., 2013), a system which is reserved for sex offenders and serious offences and is neither a release measure nor a sentence: it belongs to the aforementioned category of 'safety measures'. Whilst submitted to a static EM measure, the person can spend time out of his/her house and have various activities, such as employment, job seeking, training, treatment, and so on. The judge adapts the hours to the person's activities and circumstances in a manner which is never too rigid. The person can also be granted furlough over the weekend and bank holidays (Herzog-Evans, 2012-2013, Chap. 443). In French law, EM can either be a sentence or a release measure; in rare cases, it can also be prepared by the probation service and merely signed off by the JAP and, lastly, it can result from a SEFIP [95]. In the latter case, hours are however much stricter (Herzog-Evans, 2012 d). Naturally my sample only contained release decisions by the JAPs. None of the decisions pertained to EM as a probationary measure before parole (see *supra*) as these were analysed with parole decisions. The sixty-four decisions which were collected corresponded to the two cases where a JAP can grant a release measure: either in the course of the execution of a prison sentence or *ab initio* via article 723-15 procedure.

1. Procedure

32.7% of the rulings were made HDC, which is a rather important percentage. If one excludes these situations, in 37.8% of the cases, the person was present and assisted by an attorney and in 56.7% of the cases, the person was present but unassisted. It is noteworthy that none of the decisions which granted EM were no-show cases. When the JAP rules HDC, the person is not present but has in most cases been informally seen beforehand by the JAP.

82.5% of the rulings which granted EM were made in the course of a 723-15 procedure. This does not fully embrace the cases where an inmate has indeed been submitted to EM. Indeed, as we have seen, on the one hand, in an increasing number of cases, EM is a probationary condition to parole and on the other hand, some benefit from a so-called simplified executive decision (e.g. the aforementioned SEFIP – even if as we mentioned earlier, in 2012, only 624 offenders were released under that scheme).

---

95. The current government Bill is planning on cancelling these procedures and replacing them with a semi-automatic release system, which has been presented *supra*.

2. Offences

The offences at stake in the sixty-four decisions were rather diverse and even included some sex offences. There were however no other types of crime:

- Offences against property (including checks, bank or credit cards, and swindling): 12.6%;
- Violence (including violent offences against property): 20.6%;
- Road offences (including DUI): 36.5%;
- Drugs or alcohol as the main offence (includes, again, DUI): 28.5%;
- Destructions or deteriorations: 4.7%;
- Contempt and insults to public authorities: 11.1%;
- Sexual offences: 7.9%;
- Involuntary homicide: 3.1%.

When compared in particular to offenders who are paroled, offenders who are released under EM represent the daily mass of felonies which are overrepresented in correctional tribunals: road, violence, property and drug offences. However, there were five sex offenders in the sample who benefitted from this measure which is theoretically reserved for offenders who have short or medium sentences to serve (see penal code, art. 132-26-1). Indeed, despite their offences, these '*justiciables*' had been sentenced to relatively short sentences, thus allowing them to benefit from article 723-15. There were two eighteen month sentences, one of six months suspended which had been revoked, one of fifteen days, and one of two years eighteen months; all of which were suspended.

As with the other measures I studied the rulings in order to see whether the offenders, regardless of their offences, had addiction issues. 31.7% had a problematic consumption of alcohol; 28.5% were dependent on drugs: 9.5% were addicted to both. In total, no less than 69.8% of the offenders had an addiction of some sort, which better reflects than with parole decisions, what the interviewed practitioners said about their 'habitual clientele': most estimated that they were in charge of 60 to 70% of addicts. Placing a person who has addiction under EM does raise serious concern, given the degree of agency and control that this measure requires. The pressure which has been put on the JAP both by law-makers and the prison services to focus on EM to the detriment of other more adapted measures has definitely led to a sense that it does not matter so much anymore whether these measures will hold or 'work' so long as prison space is freed (Herzog-Evans, 2012 d).

3. Decisions' analysis

The conditions of EM are virtually identical to those of parole (Penal Code, art. 132-26-1). It is therefore not surprising that the analysis of the two to three paragraphs immediately preceding the decision itself yield similar findings.

41.2% of the decisions thus referred to the **insertion or reinsertion** efforts made by the offender, or, with article 723-25 procedures, that they have **social capital** which must be sustained or reinforced. In 7.9% of the decision, JAPs mentioned that the person has a strong release plan. It is logically a rather small percentage because in most cases EM is granted via the procedure of article 723-15 i.e. for offenders who have not been incarcerated and do not need to present a release plan. In fact, article 723-15 aims to preserve and protect whatever human and social capital, even meagre, offenders may have. In addition, as EM is more constraining than parole due to the fact that it comprises a curfew and the means to control compliance with it, it can be granted to offenders whose context is not as favourable as parolee's.

Rulings then refer expressly to the **legal** aforementioned **criteria**: the payment of damages to the victim (9.5%); on-going treatment or treatment which can be imposed thanks to supervision (42.8%); and a family which requires the presence of the person or a stable family context (34.9%).

Significant progress with the offender can also strengthen insertion factors. They were mentioned in 11.1% of the decisions. In terms of **merit**, they sometimes refer to the fact that the addiction is under control, that the offender is receiving treatment for it or that he/she is no longer addicted (6.3%). Indeed, as we have seen, in a number of cases, there is a rather long period of time between the sentence and the JAP's decision to grant a measure in the course of an article 723-15 procedure. This may be regrettable in terms of the credibility of the criminal justice system and in terms of 'the meaning of the sentence', although it can actually be positive with many offenders: since he was sentenced and by the time he saw the JAP many offenders stabilise their family and professional circumstances, make efforts on their own, the JAP can then use these positive elements in order to grant them a community measure. This could be labelled a **curriculum vitae** logic. Rather than being merit based (: 'do you deserve this?') it could be expressed as follows: 'what have you done and who are you?' From the criminological viewpoint however, this does reveal a rather depressing situation whereby the French criminal justice system virtually abandons offenders when it comes to their social and personal difficulties whilst expecting that, in the meantime, they will solve them and make efforts on their own. It then uses these solitary efforts in order to avoid incarcerating them, whereas it would make more sense to support them with their efforts.

JAPs also referred to **article 707** principles and in particular to the necessity of preventing reoffending or, conversely, to the absence of such risk (: 15.8%).

A minority of JAPs referred to the '**person's position as of the offence**'. This appears in 7.9% of the rulings. In 4.7% of their decisions they also referred to offenders' **prison behaviour**.

They only exceptionally (in 0.4% of the decisions) seemed to be taking a **risk**. They more frequently referred, conversely, to the need to control the offender upon release (12.6%) – a percentage which is hard to understand in the light of the small proportion of offenders who obtain EM whilst they are incarcerated (: 17.4%) – or the need to make them comply with an obligation (6.3%) or to the fact that this is necessary for the person's reinsertion (9.5%).

EM is usually granted to **avoid incarceration**. 9.5% of the rulings indicated that incarceration would damage the person's human and social capital or would even be dangerous in their case. Conversely, for offenders who are inmates, one decision referred to the fact that the offender would soon be released. 4.7% of the decisions mentioned that the offences are 'old and 6.3% mentioned that a former community sentence was pronounced in the past and worked well. With recidivists, we saw *supra* that JAP always take former sentences into consideration, how they were executed and whether the person ever benefitted from a release measure. 3.1% of the decisions noted, to the credit of the person, that he/she was a first-time offender.

Humanitarian considerations or health circumstances explained release under EM in 11.1% of the cases.

In most cases, several reasons were mentioned. However, in no less than 20.6% of cases, the JAP did not refer to favourable social or personal circumstances but merely stated there were **no arguments against granting EM**. Such was even the case in one ruling which pertained to a sex offender. This can be explained by the Prison Law of 2009 which all but wrote in the guidelines of article 707 that sentence management had become a right and in any case, did state that in most cases it was the right decision (see PPC, art. 707 sec. 3). It has thus opened a large avenue – sometimes excessively – for all sentence management measures and in particular for EM which has increasingly become a one size fits all measure favoured by all the recent governments (Herzog-Evans, 2012 d). This also explains why JAPs, compared with conditional releases, do not look for as many or as convincing elements proving that the person is truly motivated or committed. Paraphrasing penal law terminology one could say that intent is required with regard to parole, but is not with EM.

Conversely, and this is rather unfortunate, placement in the community has been largely abandoned by law reformers, governments and the prison services.

D. 'Placement in the community'

As with semi-freedom (see E) and EM, placement in the community is a community measure which takes place either at the person's home or, in most cases, in a setting hosted by a third sector agency. The person is considered to be a prisoner (Herzog-Evans, 2012-2013: Title 43). It is pronounced in the same circumstances but cannot constitute a mandatory probationary measure – it can only be an optional probationary measure –; nor can it be pronounced in the pre-trial phase.

Placement in the community requires strong partnership and collaboration between the judiciary, probation and prison services and the third sector. It consists of a host of supportive interventions where the offender is generally offered housing, employment and/or training and social and psychological support. For this reason, and because this measure has been neglected in favour of EM over the last years, judges are forced to reserve it for highly dissocialised offenders –particularly offenders with personality disorders and/or addictions – or offenders who are released after long sentences and need a protected transition period (Herzog-Evans, unpublished).

Placement in the community is thus similar in many respects to Canadian halfway houses (Nafekh et al., 2009) and U.K. hostels (Cowe & Chery, 2010), but are very different from American half-way houses which are in fact closer to French hostels, and are not very useful in terms of reinsertion (Department of Corrections of Pennsylvania, 2013: 28-36).

1. Procedure

I only collected twenty-two decisions which granted placement in the community, which is representative of the marginal place of this measure. In 2012 only 976 placements in the community were pronounced in France, versus 11,790 EM and 7,980 conditional releases (Direction de l'administration pénitentiaire, 2013: 6).

As they have become marginalised this measure has been cornered in occupying a rather limited sphere. In particular, in direct contrast with EM, it is now more likely to be pronounced as a release measure (N17/22) than via an article 723-15 procedure (N2/22) (but for a local difference: Herzog-Evans, unpublished). Unfortunately, three of the rulings I had collected did not specify. In any case, placement in the community is indeed perceived by practitioners and offenders as a transitional period towards the community (Herzog-Evans, *Ibid*).

2. Offences and offenders

Bearing in mind that I had a rather small sample, which invites the utmost caution, it is nonetheless interesting to mention what offences were found in the rulings:

- Offences against property (including checks, bank or credit cards, and swindling): 11/22;
- Violence (including violent offences against property): 11/22;
- Road offences (including DUI): 2/22;
- Drugs or alcohol as the main offence (includes, again, DUI): 8/22;
- Contempt and insults to public authorities: 1/22;
- Prison escape: 2/22;
- Miscellaneous: 2/22.

Given the small number of decisions, it is difficult to draw general conclusions. It is however important to note that drugs, property offences and violence represent the bulk of the sample. Similar findings were as a matter of fact yielded from a local research in the West of France (Herzog-Evans, unpublished). Since I did not include in this sample placement in the community as a probationary measure attached to parole, there were no long sentences in the sample. The result is a rather classic correctional felony sample, with the important exception of DUI cases (only two cases). This can be explained by the fact that DUI offenders are typically socialised with a family and employment and are more likely to benefit from EM or, in some cases, semi-freedom.

However, a closer study of the rulings does reveal that a considerable number of people under 'placement in the community' – called the '*placés*' ('the placed' or 'the allocated') in practice – have addiction issues – again, a finding which was confirmed in the aforementioned local study. Indeed, 4/22 were alcohol dependent; 6/22 were drug addicts; and even more striking, 7/22 were dependant on both. In other words, 17/22 of 'the placed' had an addiction (i.e. 72.2%), which is way above the usual findings with other measures.

Offenders who are 'placed' typically have a rather difficult background, with several or more sentences, increasing in length due to their reoffending or to the addition of several smaller ones, or because they have sold drugs, without being exceedingly long – with the exception of one offender who had served sixteen years. Many of these probationers are in great need of treatment. Indeed, ten received treatment whilst in prison; others did not have any treatment, either because they were in denial of their needs or problems, or because they were not susceptible to treatment. Three out of twenty-two cases had a psychopathy diagnosis, which is extremely high since our overall sample revealed that in France, this diagnosis is rarely made.

3. Decisions' analysis

Despite the specificities of placement in the community, its conditions are *de jure* identical to those of semi-freedom; they are in fact mentioned in the very same legal rule: article 132-25 of the Penal Code. Therefore, JAPs' rulings reveal similar motives for the decisions [96].

6/22 rulings referred to **reinsertion efforts** and an identical number of decisions mention a **solid release plan or project**. The usual criteria for reinsertion are generally present in the rulings, with the exception of the payment of damages. However, payment of damages may be mentioned in the other parts of the decision. Only one ruling justified the decision by mentioning treatment, although two of them mentioned that the addiction is under control and 16/22 contained treatment obligations. Reference to the family being in need of the offender's presence was made in 2/22 decisions. One must bear in mind that placement in the community first and foremost applies to offenders who are isolated and have neither family nor, in most cases, housing or employment, but for what is offered by the charity which hosts 'the placed'.

Placement in the community is thus a measure which **applies to people whose reinsertion is going to be difficult and complex**. For this reason, the need to control the offender whilst offering him/her support was present in 9/22 rulings. 3/22 decisions stated that placement in the community is a necessity in order for the person to comply with specific obligations; 4/22 that it is necessary for the person's reinsertion; and 3/22 that it will support his/her efforts. Indeed, placement in the community is a package which comprises probation, obligations, active support for the offender with, in many cases, the permanent physical presence of the third sector agency social workers, housing, employment and or vocational training, treatment, drug treatment and sometimes, an impressive list of other interventions (see e.g. Herzog-Evans, unpublished). For instance, a JAP who was not interviewed stated in his ruling of October 14, 2011, that the 'sheer length of his incarceration has strongly dissocialised him'.

---

96. As with all the other measures, the sum total can exceed twenty-two as several reasons are typically mentioned in the rulings.

Indeed, placement in the community benefits offenders who are particularly fragile and JAPs are fully aware of this; something which is apparent in their rulings. For instance, JAP 11 noted in an October 12, 2010 decision that Mr R.'s progress in custody is still fragile and perhaps relative' and in a decision dated January 14, 2010, that the person's 'judicial path has been particularly chaotic'. JAP 14 noted in a decision of October 28, 2009 that the person is 'not very open to introspection and indifferent to his own situation during the hearing'.

Despite of these difficult contexts, most inmates will in any case be released and it seems logical to supervise and give them the strong support that they need. Precisely, 2/22 rulings expressly mentioned that these persons would soon be released.

Risk was not absent from the decisions. One of them showed that the JAP made a bet on the person's future and another noted that he never benefitted from a release measure, even though he was sentenced several times so that it may be opportune to try it this time. 5/55 decisions mentioned that placement in the community is a necessity in order to prevent reoffending or to ensure that the person does not present a reoffending risk. 2/22 referred to the 'person's position as of the offence'.

Importantly the decision is seldom granted because of the offender's merit even if 4/22 rulings did mention that the person has made progress whilst 9/22 clearly contain encouraging messages, which is more than the average. For instance, JAP 23, in a decision of January 11, 2011 mentioned that the 'considerable efforts both from the insertion and treatment viewpoints' and the necessity to encourage and support these efforts. Two decisions were conversely based on the person's psychological fragility, whilst two others were motivated by the offenders' ill health.

It is probably because of the excellent support and psychological work which is at the heart of placement in the community, that JAPs seem to consider that this **measure** is ***a priori*** **positive**. As a result they tend to ignore or minimise clear deficiencies, for instance in terms of behaviour (e.g. being consistently late whilst returning from furlough) and of their future plan's credibility. They are ready to take more risks because they deeply trust the high quality intervention of placement in the community. They either mention in this respect placement in the community's strong social components (housing and work and vocational training) or social workers' supervision and constant support. 15/22 expressly mentioned that this measure is more adapted to the person's needs.

With semi-freedom, they will focus more on the level of control and supervision.

E. 'Semi-freedom'

1. General presentation

Semi-freedom, like placement in the community and EM, is a measure under prison registry: 'the placed' person is still legally a prisoner. It is characterised by a daily alternation between prison time, generally at night and over the weekend (either in the special wing or division of a prison; or in a special semi-freedom centre or in an open prison equivalent) and time in the community, usually for an activity (work, vocational training or treatment) or with one's family. Over the weekend, the JAP generally grants offenders furlough when 'the placed' comply with the measure (Herzog-Evans, 2012-2013: Title 43).

I had more semi-freedom decisions than placement in the community (N82), which is coherent with general statistics. In 2012, there were 1,785 decisions in all (Direction de l'administration pénitentiaire, 2013: 6).

A relatively small number of decisions (31.7%) were made in the course of an article 723-15 procedure. In our sample, semi-freedom was essentially a release measure (86.2%) which is a very important percentage given that I did not include offenders who had been paroled with a probationary period of semi-freedom. As we shall now see, this can be explained by the fact that semi-freedom is perceived as being a more constraining measure and, as a result, offers better support for released inmates, particularly those who have served medium sentences and have multiple issues.

2. Offences

The analysis of the offences committed by the offenders mentioned in our ruling sample confirms the complexity of their profile. These offences are rather varied even though the majority pertain to the classic correctional clientele: property offences, violence, and road offences:

- Offences against property (including checks, bank or credit cards, and swindling): 41.4%;
- Organised crime: 4.8%;
- Violence (including violent offences against property): 25.6%;
- Road offences (including DUI): 20.7%;
- Drugs or alcohol as the main offence (includes, again, DUI): 29.6%;
- Destructions or deteriorations: 4.8%;
- Contempt and insults to public authorities: 8.5%;
- Sexual offences: 4.8%;
- Miscellaneous: 6%.

In depth analysis of the rulings reveals that an important number of these offenders suffer from various addictions (54.8%) – but less so than with placement in the community. 25.6% have alcohol problems; 28% have drug issues: 1.2% are addicted to both.

3. Decisions' analysis

The legal conditions of semi-freedom are the same as those of placement in the community and EM. In fact, they are laid out in article 132-25 of the Penal Code, which also pertains to placement in the community – and is identical to article 132-26-1 of the same code which pertains to EM.

For this reason, 41.4% of the rulings pertain to **insertion efforts** and 13.4% to the **credibility of the project**. We then encounter the usual criteria of insertion efforts and credible release plans or projects: payment of damages due to the victim in 4.8% of cases; treatment in 8.5% of them; and the indispensable presence of the offender with his family in 4.8% of them.

Risk, public security and reoffending are at the very heart of this measure; something to which I shall return. Perhaps only 7.3% of the rulings expressly referred to such risks one way or another. However, 65.8% of the rulings justified granting semi-freedom by saying that the person needs being contained. Thus the necessity to support reinsertion – which is not identical to observing that the person has made efforts – takes the second seat behind reoffending prevention. It nonetheless is present since in essence semi-freedom precisely allows offenders to spend their days in the community in order to work, find employment, take vocational training classes or get treatment. Still, JAPs explained that they grant semi-freedom for the person's reinsertion in only 4.8% of rulings; in order to provide him/her with a transition period after his release in only 2.4% rulings; the necessity to make sure he/she complies with a specific obligation in 0.1% cases. Despite of this, and in depth study of the rulings reveals that they represent risk taking on the part of the JAP – who thus grants semi-freedom when the person's circumstances are rather fragile – in no less than 21.9% of cases.

'*Justiciables*' who obtain semi-freedom often have complex and difficult trajectories. Therefore, it is unsurprising that JAPs do take their **behaviour in prison** into consideration in no less than 17% of their rulings. This comparably important focus on behaviour can also be explained by two other factors. Firstly, 'the placed' are usually inmates and data obtained from the prison services tend to focus on such factors; secondly, JAPs probably think that prison behaviour is an important criterion since semi-freedom comprises of periods of time spent behind bars or a closed centre. JAPs also referred to the '**person's position as of the offence'** in 9.7% of the cases. Still, in 2.4% of decisions the ruling concluded that custody would damage the person's social capital – which is classic with article 723-15 procedures – and for those who are detained, that the person will soon be released in 3.6% of the files.

As was seen above, the JAP will often look into the person's past to see if he/she previously benefitted from a community sentence or measure and how things went. This constitutes grounds for granting semi-freedom in 3.6% of the cases.

To a small extent, JAPs focus on the person's efforts (4.8%) and congratulate them (4.8%) for this. A diminished form of **merit** is also taken into account when JAPs mention that the person is a first-time offender or that it is his/her first incarceration (: 6%). They also focus on the fact that the person's delinquent behaviour is 'old' in 3.6% of their rulings.

Lastly, **humanitarian** reasons were visible in 4.8% rulings. They either mentioned that the person is fragile and that he/she is immature or has ill health, with this latter cause being mentioned in only 0.2% of rulings.

Like placement in the community, semi-freedom benefits from a very positive *a priori*, albeit for very different reasons. Here, the most frequent expression found in the two to three paragraphs before the decision, is that the measure is '**sufficiently containing**' or that it is a 'containing measure'. They also often used the verb 'to contain' or the adverb 'containment'. In total this represents 65.8% of the rulings. These expression or words were used particularly with addicts who are still fragile or those for whom semi-freedom represents risk-taking on the part of the JAP. This can be the case, for instance, when a person is detained due to the revocation of his/her probation order following his/her obligations' violations.

One of the JAPs – JAP 13 – systematically used a concluding phrase which expresses this idea: 'Considering the containment which it represents, semi-freedom seems the most appropriate' decision for Mr or Ms Such and Such. As a matter of fact she seldom ever mentioned other reasons than this when it came to explaining why she grants semi-freedom. Other JAPs also gave little in the way of explanation for their decisions. For instance JAP 25 in an October 15, 2010 ruling where semi-freedom was granted to a drug addict in the course of an article 723-15 procedure – and incidentally did not add a treatment obligation – only mentioned that he has employment and that the measure is containing. The in depth study of the rulings shows that in 21.9% of them, a serious risk was actually taken by the JAP, and the decision was in fact based on very loose grounds. Thus, semi-freedom benefits people who are difficult, aggressive, immature and/or fragile, in denial of their offence or their responsibility or of their addiction, repeat offenders and have very little, if any social or human capital; in many cases their sole project is to look for employment. Behind this surprising risk taking is the idea that since semi-freedom is containing and has a custodial or quasi custodial component meaning that violations and other incidents can be detected more systematically and swiftly. In rare instances it can even pertain to sex offenders. Thus, JAP 13 granted semi-freedom to a person who had committed a sex assault under armed threat and who had only been sentenced to sixteen months, twelve of which were suspended with probation and who, having thus only six months to serve, was allowed to present an application under article 723-15 (Ruling of December 10, 2010). As a result, this person did not spend a single day in prison despite the seriousness of the offence, whilst his only plan for his future was his desire to find public gardening employment and he had no other insertion circumstances.

However, as we saw previously, when they deal with **longer sentences**, JAPs tend to **'motivate'** their rulings in much **greater detail**. This was again the case with JAP 13 who granted semi-freedom to a person who had been sentenced to nine years for international drug trafficking and whose ruling (December 13, 2010) was nine pages long (i.e. a good third longer than the typical semi-freedom decision) and presented the cases' facts and context in much deeper detail than she – or other JAPs – would usually have done. She referred to the details of his release plan, the work he would have, how much money he would thus earn, and the fact that he would go to live in his own apartment. She even mentioned that he had learnt Spanish whilst he was incarcerated in Spain for his offences. The rulings further listed the activities he had had whilst he was in prison, and what his position pertaining to the offences he had committed was. She added that a police investigation had checked the credibility of his release plan, whereas in most cases, JAPs only asked for a probation service report.

The **nature of the jurisdiction** where JAPs work is also a factor which can explain how much time they devote to justifying their rulings. In big urban jurisdictions, particularly in the Paris region, they do not have much time to spend on it. Contrasting with their standardised decisions, JAP 3, who works in a small jurisdiction wrote, for example, a very detailed ruling on February 1, 2011 whereby he verified all the offender's assertions in terms of distance between his residence and his workplace and between his workplace and the semi-freedom centre in order to determine which was the closest to his work.

As with placements in the community, **treatment** was rarely mentioned as a cause for granting semi-freedom. Conversely, treatment was imposed in 29.2% of the decision, which is on par with the actual needs of offenders, in terms of their addictions and alcohol issues (54.8%) or the seriousness of some of their offences, particularly when one adds violent and sexual offences (30.4%). Some decisions are clearly so standardised that the JAP does not verify whether the person is receptive to treatment, should have treatment or even whether the person's addiction is under control. It is also important to note that offenders, even with serious alcohol issues are seldom subjected to the bars and café ban of article 132-45 of the Penal code (: 12.1%). Even if this obligation is rather ridiculous as French law does not allow for an offender to be banned from drinking, nor from buying alcohol elsewhere, e.g. in supermarkets (Herzog-Evans, 2012-2013: 613.121-613.125). However, in the case of semi-freedom, the person is regularly tested and if drunk will easily be detected upon his return at the detention or semi-freedom centre. Still, such decisions send a rather unclear message to offenders.

§ 3. 'Conversion' decisions

A. General findings

'Conversion' or 'novation' are decisions whereby a JAP transforms a custody sentence into another type of sentence, namely either a STIG (see supra) or a day-fine. In the first case it is called a 'conversion-STIG'; in the second case a 'conversion-JA' (for conversion to day-fine, in French *conversion-jours-amende*). Only sentences up to six months or mixed sentences comprising a custodial part of a maximum of six months can be thus converted. Day-fines can be also transformed into STIG and vice-versa (Herzog-Evans, 2012-2013: Title 62; Penal Code, art. 132-57; PPC, art. 733-1). Conversions are essentially pronounced *ab initio*, i.e. before the original sentence is implemented; this in the course of an article 723-15 procedure. Despite their common name, they apply to very different situations. Conversion-JA is used for solvent offenders who are typically desisters or on-going desisters; it is feared that incarceration would damage their desistance process. Conversion-STIG conversely applies to offenders with many criminogenic needs, who need social support (probation) and employment (community work). For this reason, I shall study these measures separately. Nonetheless, a first general analysis of all the rulings enlightens JAPs' practices.

Firstly, there are more **psychological or psychoanalytical references** in this type of rulings than with other decisions; this can be to the credit or to the debit of the offender. For instance, JAP 28 mentions in a ruling the 'lack of introspection on the offence'.

Another striking point is that both in the case of conversion-JA and conversion-STIG, alcoholics are treated differently than drug addicts. As long as alcoholics have a job, income and a family, clemency is often in order so that they do not lose these **insertion factors**.

With conversion-JA, alcoholics are not even required to seek treatment. It is true that there is no probation with day-fines, so that it would be legally impossible. Still, this leaves offenders to their illness and does not solve the crucial criminogenic need. With drug addicts JAPs are much harsher and if they do take into account reinsertion factors (social and personal), they also look for the person's motivation, signs of his/her progress, for on-going treatment and for the person's realisation or understanding of his/her addiction and difficulties.

As with other sentence management measures, a number of decisions take **former community sentences** into account and how they were complied with, this, in order to try and assess whether the person can be trusted. In the same vein, with conversion-JA, judges can check whether the person already had a similar measure in the past and whether he paid his fines or day-fines. If previous sentences were complied with and the offender did pay the damages he was owed, this is put to his credit. This is particularly true with mixed sentences: when the offender applies for the conversion of the custodial part of the sentence it is logical that the JAP first looks at how he/she has complied with its probation part.

We have seen that '**motivation**' tends to be **standardised**, and in some cases very standardised, when short sentences are at stake. With conversion, only very short sentences are concerned. For this reason, and because legislators have clearly indicated that whenever possible sentences should be 'managed' – thus implying that short custodial sentences should not be executed – (PPC art. 707, sec. 3 and 4), JAPs feel that it is not necessary to spend too much time nor too much energy on justifying why they convert them. The minimal requirement is clearly for them to mention the few reinsertion elements which allow them to save the offender from custody. It is patent that there is an *a priori* against custody both in general as these are short sentences and in particular in the offenders' case. Some JAPs, such as JAP 13, did not hesitate to write it expressly in their rulings.

B. 'Conversion-STIG'

I had collected a total of forty-five decisions which granted conversion-STIG.

1. Offences

The offences committed by conversion-STIG beneficiaries represent the mass of felony cases which correctional tribunals deal with. Only one ruling pertained to a serious offence, of a sexual nature. Most offences were road, property offences, violence and in a great number of cases, offenders suffered from addictions:

- Offences against property (including checks, bank or credit cards, and swindling): 11/45;
- Violence (including violent offences against property): 11/45;
- Road offences (including DUI): 20/45;
- Drugs or alcohol as the main offence (includes, again, DUI): 3/45;
- Destructions or deteriorations: 4/45;
- Contempt and insults to public authorities: 6/45;
- Sexual offences: 1/45;
- Miscellaneous: 3/45.

Very few offenders had specifically been sentenced for an addiction or a drug related offence which can be explained by the fact that none were drug traffickers or had sold drugs. However, the in depth analysis of the rulings revealed that conversion-STIG mostly benefitted offenders who had addictions. 23/45 were addicted to alcohol; 8/45 were addicted to drugs; 2/45 were addicted to both. This represents an impressive total of 33/45 (73.3%), which is nearly the equivalent of the results found for placement in the community; the difference being that placement in the community seems to mostly be used in order to release prisoners, whilst conversion-STIG seems to be obtained by people who can benefit from article 723-15 of the PPC and whose custodial sentences are also shorter. Conversely, supervision can be much longer with conversion-STIG than with placement in the community. For instance a four month sentence can be converted into eighteen months probation with seventy hours of community work.

2. Reasons behind the decision

As with all the other measures, I coded for the main reasons behind conversion-STIG and which were expressed in the two to three last paragraphs of each ruling. Social insertion and treatment clearly dominate amongst apparent causes. This is important given that law-makers have not taken the time to list in the PPC or Penal code, the conversion-STIG causes and conditions. The only legal indication is the maximum length of the custodial sentence. It is thus all the more important to study JAP jurisprudence. In line with the goals of an article 723-15 procedure, they look for **social insertion 'embryos'** and state that it is necessary to supervise, control and support the person.

Rulings refer to classic signs of insertion, or rather, as I just put it, to 'insertion embryos' in 15/45 decisions. They referred to on-going treatment in 13/45 decisions and to the person's indispensable presence in his/her family in 4/45 cases. They also referred to the necessity to supervise the person in various ways: in 8/45 decisions JAPs referred to the need to control the person; in 5/45 to the need for long-term supervision; in 11/45 cases to the need to make the person comply with his/her obligations; in 1/45 cases to the need to make him/her pay the damages.

JAPs also take into account the necessity to prevent **reoffending** in 8/45 decisions. They focussed on the person's former sentences and noted that a former release measure (6/45) or a former community sentence (5/45) has been executed satisfactorily (i.e. for a total of 11/45 of cases). They also mentioned that the offence is 'old' in 7/45 cases.

Merit is hardly ever mentioned in these decisions. JAPs' goal is to protect the offenders' desistance factors and to support people in great need. Four rulings did however contain encouragements and congratulations.

Two other considerations are apparent in the rulings and warranted specific developments: the exchange rate between prison and community work and the focus on on-going desistance protection.

3. Prison day/work day and probation exchange rate

I have borrowed the expression used by two American authors (: 'exchange rate') albeit in an entirely different context (May & Wood, 2010). Surprisingly, for a written law jurisdiction which usually goes into intricate and miniscule details, French law does not tell JAPs what criteria and principles should guide them when they determine how many community work hours '*justiciables*' should do and how long their probation should last. The law thereby gives them **full discretionary** power. It only refers to regular rules applying to community work and probation orders. This means that supervision can last up to eighteen months and that community work hours can range from twenty hours to two hundred and ten hours and that the community service must be executed in a maximum length of time of eighteen months.

Probation and time to execute the work are related. Virtually all the decisions in our sample referred to the legal **maximum of eighteen months.** This can be explained by two reasons. Firstly, it is often difficult to find community employment in a reasonable time and eighteen months is actually not such a long time to execute all their hours. Secondly, and importantly, eighteen months of probation is a rather significant period of time during which to have an impact on the person. Particularly with addicts, it seems foolish to expect that they would change in a few months. From this viewpoint, the short custodial sentence which is thus converted into a STIG seems like a rather unrealistic decision compared to eighteen months on probation. Yet clearly, in most cases, the exchange rate (maximum of six months custody transformed into a maximum of eighteen months on probation with a probation order) does not seem very appealing.

In my sample, only one decision made by JAP 2 ordered the offender to do his community work hours – in this case seventy – within six months.

With regard to the **total number of hours**, decisions ranged from a minimum of forty hours (which was the minimum before the Prison Law of 2009) to the maximum of two-hundred and ten hours. In other words, JAPs make full use of their discretionary power.

Beyond the net total of hours, I calculated the **exchange rate between one month in prison and one hour of community work**. What was striking, especially compared to all the other decisions which were studied for this book, was that, in fact, it was rather difficult to understand how they decide in each case to opt for one exchange rate or another. There is no doubt that legislators are responsible. This shows that when the law does not give JAPs enough details pertaining to conditions and criteria, there is little consistency in their decisions. Since French law practitioners are used to having rather strict guidelines they are not in the habit of referring to the proportionality principle.

The unfortunate result is that **exchange rates vary considerably**. They range from the smallest of twelve (: i.e. a sentence of ten months transformed into a hundred and ten hours) to the maximum of two-hundred and ten (two decisions transform a one month sentence into two-hundred and ten hours). Between these two extremes I found all types of exchange rates.

On average, the exchange rate is 58.72 hours of community work for one month custody. Nothing in the decisions allows us to understand how they reach their decisions as they never explain how they opt for a given exchange rate. It is thus impossible to analyse which logics and principles – if they are any – guide their decision-making. Only one decision gives us a hint: it converts a one year sentence into one hundred and ten hours – which is very far from the maximum and even from the average – and takes the time to explain that this quantum must 'be adapted to the person's reoffending… in order to give meaning to the sentence'. Another decision does not link the rather small exchange rate (forty hours for a one month custodial sentence; which is still an exchange rate of forty) with its observation that the offender is not a true delinquent but a father who could not pay his alimony and, rather than stopping his payments, should have asked the family judge to change or suspend it. Still it is obvious that the judge empathises, and in fact took the time to write, in the ruling, that the family judge is competent for such matters.

I then tried to assess whether there were recognisable patterns with each JAP's jurisprudence. For this part of the research there were six JAPs: JAP

1, JAP 2, JAP 3, JAP 13, JAP 14, JAP 28. The decisions of JAP 1 and JAP 2 could not be used in order to compare exchange rates as I only had one decision for each one of them. I also decided to leave out JAP 3 as there were only two decisions with an exchange rate of thirty-five.

I was left with the in depth analysis of JAP 13, JAP 14 and JAP 28's conversion-STIG decisions. This is indeed not sufficient to draw general conclusions. However, it does constitute an interesting basis and another more systematic research which would specifically focus on conversion should perhaps try and obtain more systematic data. Besides, it was not possible as I did not have access to computerised tools in order to formulate a more complicated hypothesis based on the people's offences or psycho-social circumstances. More importantly, there were not enough details in the decision pertaining to these crucial factors. There may have also been other factors linked to the environment in which these JAPs worked, although the three JAPs worked in difficult Parisian region jurisdictions.

In other words, different jurisprudence may have simply reflected different personalities and sensibilities.

	JAP 13	JAP 14	JAP 28
Minimum exchange rate	14	18.33	12
Maximum exchange rate	210	80	140
Average exchange rate	80.56	59.79	51.06

This rather limited comparison nonetheless reveals tendencies. Thus JAP 13 is clearly the harsher judge and presents the biggest range of exchange rates. Conversely JAP 14 is the one whose exchange rates are the most consistent and the least large. Lastly, JAP 28 is the less punitive. She is also the one who explains her decisions with the most detail. We saw that JAP 13, as with most JAPs, but to an even higher degree, had standardised her rulings in order to save a precious time in order to devote it to offenders and hearings or other meetings. However, another factor is at play here: JAP 28 is also a JAP who told us that she managed to have probation officers coming to her hearings. This is likely to have improved communication between her service and the probation service, and, as a result, she obtained more detailed and more precise information. Conversely, JAP 13 was given virtually no information by her probation service or received it too late. In other words, one particular factor may be that the less information a JAP has the more he/she tends to be punitive; the more information he/she has, the less he/she is punitive, a fact which has also been observed with sentencing correctional courts (Ligue des droits de l'homme, 2012). This strongly questions the current prison services' tendency to reduce the number of reports and investigations made by its probation officers.

I later communicated these results to JAP 13 who made the following response: 'It's funny because this is a debate we often have on *Justpeine* and it seems that there's unanimity in saying that one month equals thirty-five hours'. This, she explained, was because 'the official week comprises of thirty-five hours work and it is easier to deal with full weeks'. What we found in reality however was that JAP rulings are completely removed from such an exchange rate. JAP 13 explained that JAPs also had a tendency to be harsher when the sentence was actually the result of recall. She added that individual psycho-social considerations were additionally at play and explained why exchange rates were not consistent. Thus, the more insertion a person needed the more hours he/she would have to do:

'Community work will then be the spine of this insertion (: he works, learns to wake up early in the morning, and not to say 'f.' to all and sundry…) and it may thus be pertinent to give him the maximum payback hours in order to support this insertion' (JAP 13).

4. Preserving primary desistance

Most researchers now acknowledge that desistance is a process and typically takes time. The literature distinguishes two types of desistance: primary and secondary. Primary desistance is a temporary period of time with no offending; secondary desistance is longer-term non-offending which is accompanied by a change in identity (Maruna & Farrall, 2004; Maruna et al., 2004 – and for recently published studies: King, 2013b and Carlsson, 2013, the latter with a life-course approach).

The present research shows that conversion-STIG is a measure which is considered by JAPs to be particularly adapted to people who have **serious psycho-social issues**, and need both supervision – often time treatment – and to get work experience. These are very fragile people whose fate is still very uncertain; people who have seldom made the first footsteps towards desistance and for whom STIG constitutes an attempt to make them experience such footsteps.

In such a context, **employment** holds a very **special place**. In a lot of rulings I found a conclusive sentence which stated that conversion-STIG would allow the person to 'renew their ties with the working world'. 19/45 decisions referred to work as being a necessity for the offender who has not worked for months, at times for years or who, being a young adult, has never worked at all. In one ruling, for instance, a person aged forty-five had not worked at all in the last sixteen years.

However, offenders' social needs go beyond employment. Rulings refer to other reinsertion efforts' items such as treatment, or the necessity to make the person comply with specific reinsertion-related obligations. JAPs pronounce conversion-STIG at a point in '*justiciables*' lives when they do not have any or many reinsertion factors or social capital, but in some cases, for a first attempt at treatment which had long been overdue. JAPs lean on the **first signs of** what could be labelled **'desistance contemplation'** (Prochaska & DiClemente, 1982) or the first tangible act in this direction. In this vein JAP 3's February 11, 2011 ruling explained that he granted conversion of a six month sentence into 210 hours of community work and eighteen months probation in order 'to preserve, in the long term, the insertion factors – albeit embryonic – such as treatment, which appear likely to prevent reoffending.' In other words, JAPs' approach to conversion-STIG is that it supports desistance's first steps, rather than rewards more advanced desistance. As an illustration, in thirteen decisions, they referred to on-going treatment, which has in fact just started, and in eleven rulings, they wrote that it is necessary to sustain treatment's durability.

At times, JAPs also dismissed other measures which offenders apply for, such as EM, which will also not deal with the person's risks and needs, nor put him/her back on track, particularly in terms of employment, over the long run.

Conversely, people who benefit from conversion-JA have no such social issues.

B. Conversion to day-fine

When a felony is punishable by imprisonment, the sentencing court can pronounce a day-fine in its stead (Penal Code, art. 131-5). In most cases, however, day-fines are the result of a conversion by the JAP of imprisonment sentences of up to six months custody (PPC, art. 733-1), this in the course of the procedure of article 723-15. The JAP can also convert a STIG measure into a day-fine.

I only had a rather limited sample of such decisions (N15). For this reason, the following results are only tentative.

1. Offences

As with other measures, I coded for the offence which led to the sentence which was eventually converted into a day-fine and found:

- Offences against property (including checks, bank or credit cards, and swindling): 2/15;
- Violence (including violent offences against property): 4/15;
- Road offences (including DUI): 6/15;
- Drugs or alcohol as the main offence (includes, again, DUI): 2/15;
- Contempt and insults to public authorities: 1/15;
- Miscellaneous: 1/15.

This is clearly a rather limited range of offences. This is probably the result of the small sample I had. It is also probably the consequence of the fact that this measure, which is most likely the most lenient of the French legal system – but for sentence exemption – applies only to people whose delinquency is not serious – although one might find surprising that DUI are considered as not being serious – and who are socially integrated or not too dissocialised and are rarely recidivists. In this sample, one finds no crime (serious offence), and very little in the way of drug-related offences (N2). Indeed, even these offences were not drug trafficking cases per se, but simply addicts; one was carrying drugs for his own use and the other was found in possession of cannabis. In both cases, the offender was a rather young woman – they were aged twenty-seven and twenty – who may have benefitted from a 'chivalrous' reaction (see, *inter alia*: Moulds, 1978; Crew, 1991) in particular since the oldest one had a child.

With regard to the violent offences (N4), they had been committed by: a first-time offender; a well-integrated businessman; a former drug addict who at the time of the offence had stable employment, a child who was taking responsibility for it; and an alcoholic who was getting treatment and had a job.

As usual I looked into the files to verify whether the offenders suffered from addictions: 6/15 were addicted to alcohol; 4/15 were addicted to drugs; the total was thus 10/15 (66.6%), which was very close to the general figures. However, more of these addicts were receiving treatment.

2. Reasons behind the decision

The **law does not give any indication** of what the causes of conversion-JA should be. It merely mentions that the maximum custodial sentence which can thus be converted is six months or that this sentence can be a STIG (PPC, art. 733-1). Judges thus had to create their own criteria.

JAPd understand conversion-JA as being a very lenient measure which should apply to **on-going desisters** for whom probation or custody would be meaningless and very possibly damaging. Thus, 4/15 decisions mentioned that the offender has made progress in terms of reinsertion; 3/15 mentioned that the addiction is under control, under treatment or a thing of the past; and 1/15 decisions expressly stated that imprisonment would damage this on-going reinsertion whilst 2/15 mentioned that the person presents very little reoffending risk. For instance, in a ruling of October 20, 20101, the judge noted that the '*justiciables'* reinsertion effort 'significantly reduces reoffending risks'. 2/15 rulings also noted that the person has previously served another community sentence which has been complied with. One ruling also referred to on-going treatment. Two decisions congratulated the offender, such as this October 19, 2010 ruling which declared that he 'has consistently made insertion efforts' and that 'he changed very positively'. Only one decision granted conversion-JA for humanitarian reasons. Three decisions converted STIG into a day-fine: in these three cases, the offenders had found employment and it had become difficult for them to complete their community work. In such cases, judges clearly made desistance prevail over punishment. Their reasoning was that a 'real' job is more important in terms of desistance than doing community hours and serving the sentence.

The '**motivation'** of the rulings was usually **rather short**; it often only comprises two pages. Two decisions actually contain no 'motivation' at all other than the expenses and revenues of the person. Precisely, in most cases, 'motivation' merely consisted of an assessment of the person's capacity to pay and how much he/she is able to reasonably pay. The judge however usually briefly referred to the person's reinsertion path, in a few lines.

My sample was rather limited and it is thus difficult to draw any definite conclusions. However, the very short 'motivation' does reveal that judges have a favourable *a priori* with regard to conversion-JA. It may also be a sign that only offenders who have a sufficiently solid context have the Gaul to apply for it.

These offenders are clearly on-going desisters. Most of them have employment – and this is why three STIG are converted into JA. Conversion-JA is thus a measure which appears appropriate when it is not necessary or no longer useful to impose supervision. This is perhaps why I did not find in the rulings the aforementioned items pertaining to the need to control the person or to make him/her comply with specific obligations – which is actually impossible since there is no supervision attached to day-fines – or to help him/her desist. When a judge does pronounce a conversion-JA it is because no supervision is needed as, since the offence or the sentence was passed, what was expected of the person (reinsertion/desistance) has already occurred or is close to being achieved or because the offence was clearly just an incident in an otherwise law-abiding life.

3. Exchange rates

As with conversion-STIG, I wanted to know what the exchange rate for conversion-JA was, and to see how much money was exchanged for a month of imprisonment. This time, however, the **law** has given a few, albeit general, **indications** pertaining to the maximum sum for JA. Article 131-5 of the Penal code, states that JA are determined, on the one hand, based on the person's revenues and expenses and, on the other hand, on the offence's context. This article then states that the absolute maximum is 360 days multiplied by 1000 euros per day. *A maxima* a JAP could thus impose the considerable total number of 360,000 euros. In practice, as far as can be assessed based on my very small sample, JAPs are thankfully much more reasonable. As previously mentioned, JAPs focus on conversion-JA desistance-supportive nature and punishment takes a back seat. It is also important to note that none of the offenders who benefitted from conversion-JA in this sample were wealthy.

In the following paragraphs I shall leave aside one decision which imposed 3,000 euros in total, since this was an atypical ruling based on humanitarian reasons: the offender's ill health – but higher revenues. In order to calculate the exchange rate I also left out, for logical reasons, the three decisions which converted a STIG into JA since the exchange rate pertained to the link between each day-fine and each month in prison. I was left with eleven decisions. The **average exchange rate** was 180.68 euros. The minimum was 75 euros for one month imprisonment and the maximum was 450 euros for a month – but in this case, the sentence was only of one month.

With the three conversions of STIG to JA, I calculated how many euros were exchanged for one hour of community work. I found an average of 5 euros per hour, although this result is not significant as it was based on a very small sample.

Beyond these results, nothing in the rulings indicated the nature of the **factors which guided JAP**, apart from the rather vague prescriptions of article 131-5. This question was not raised during the interviews. However, JAP 3 referred to a very interesting practice:

'I think that my practice goes as follows:

- *A punishment approach*: I take the maximum of what can be taken (requisition of the National Bank Account Databank and of bank accounts) so that it strongly impacts their finances;

- *A clearing approach* as the sentence has become meaningless and there is no need for supervision. Union's tariff in such a case (I have at times applied the minimum that the law allows i.e. one day-fine at one euro per X month imprisonment). For this I need a strong case though'.

The need for a strong case is at the heart of the French sentences' implementation system, even if this has been reduced following the Prison Law of 2009. If the case is too weak, the application is denied.

§ 4. Decisions rejecting release applications

A. General presentation

The Prison Law has established a principle according to which release and other sentence management decisions are not so much destined to favour desistance, but first and foremost to free prison cells. JAPs are therefore asked not to focus on the efficiency of the decisions they make – but for dangerous offenders – but to think in terms of a supposedly intrinsic positive nature of release and other sentence management measures. The current government, as it was presenting its penal reform strategy, stated that the lack thereof was the cause of prison overcrowding – a blatant mistake. For their part, two MPs, Mr Raimbourg and Huygues (2013) issued a report whereby they suggested that conditional release should become automatic, and they were soon followed by the jury of the conference of consensus' report (2013 – also see Herzog-Evans 2013 c). Lastly, On August 30, 2013, the Ministry of Justice has confirmed that it had indeed prepared a Bill whereby it planned to create a virtually automatic release on probation – which was shrewdly labelled 'penal constraint' in the hopes of not sounding too lenient [97]. In this case, the French discretionary system would virtually disappear and the JAP would be rendered useless. It is also doubtful that such a system would be efficient in terms of overcrowding, since sentencers would probably adapt to the new system; it is equally doubtful that it would convince public opinion (see Beyens et al., 2010, à propos of Belgium). The truth is that sentences' management measures have consistently increased over the last few years as the annual report by the prisons service shows (Direction de l'administration pénitentiaire, 2013, 2012, 2011, 2010…) and that sentences have become longer and more punitive due to a decade of right wing governance, when Mister Sarkozy was first minister of interior and then president (2002-2012 - Herzog-Evans, 2009 a). My own opinion is that when there is not a minimum of either motivational or social factors or

97. See my detailed legal analysis here: http://herzog-evans.com/commentaire-du-projet-sur-la-peine-de-contrainte-penale-french-probation-order-bill-a-comment/.

public safety guarantees, and without offenders' participation and agency, these measures are meaningless.

Coherent with this analysis, the sample of application denial was much smaller than with favourable decisions (N91). It included applications for:

- Conditional release (parole) (N29);
- Article 723-15 procedures without further specification on the offender's part (N17);
- Placement in the community (N2);
- Furlough (N2);
- EM (N20);
- Semi-freedom (N11);
- Medical sentence suspension (N2);
- Miscellaneous (N3).

The small number of decisions for each type of measure did not allow for the distribution of my analysis for each one of them. I thus decided to present them together.

B. Procedure

In 36.9% of the rulings the person was present and assisted by an attorney. He/she was alone at the hearing in 30.1% of cases. There were many no-show '*justiciables*', which is one of the explanations for their applications being denied.

43.9% of all the decision pertained to article 723-15 procedures.

There were no ex officio cases, but exclusively procedures whereby the offender had filed a release application.

C. Offences

Because of the diversity of measures at stake, and since no less than twenty-nine decisions pertained to conditional release, it is not surprising that the offences were equally diverse. One finds the typical felony cases processed by correctional tribunals (property offences, violence, road offences and destructions), along with a few serious criminal offences:

- Offences against property (including checks, bank or credit cards, and swindling): 32.9%;
- Organised crime (including terrorism): 1%;
- Violence (including violent offences against property): 27.4%;

- Road offences (including DUI): 35.1%;
- Drugs or alcohol as the main offence (includes, again, DUI): 13.1%;
- Destructions or deteriorations: 10.9%;
- Contempt and insults to public authorities: 8.7%;
- Sexual offences: 10.9%;
- Homicide (voluntary and involuntary): 3.2%;
- Prison escape: 3.2%;
- Miscellaneous: 3.2%.

There were seven sex offenders in the sample of people applying for parole, versus only three for all the other measures.

Looking, as I did before, for the number of addicts I found 54.9%, which is lower than usual, comprising 25.2% with an addiction to alcohol, 21.9% with an addiction to drugs and 7.6% with an addiction to both.

D. Reasons behind the decisions

As with former developments, I looked for the causes of the application rejections in the very last two to three paragraphs which immediately preceded the decisions themselves. Reasons were very diverse.

There were first reasons pertaining to **the person's behaviour**. However this was never the sole cause of rejection. The fact that the offender was not present at his/her hearing was mentioned in 16.4% of the rulings. The fact that he/she was rude or aggressive during the hearing was mentioned in 3.2% of them. Lastly, bad behaviour in prison was mentioned in 2.1% of the decisions.

Legal reasons were even more prohibitive. In 12% of the rulings the legal conditions of the measure were not met; in 2.1% of them, the person eventually refused the measure.

A series of reasons rejected the measure because there was not enough or no documented proof in the file. 3.29% decisions noted that the person could not send or bring such documents due to no fault of his/her own. It nonetheless made the decision legally impossible. In 25.2% it was his/her fault or responsibility. No less than 2.1% of the decisions found that the documents were counterfeit. I have already mentioned that the demands that JAPs have of documented proof are logical and unavoidable but raise difficulties with probation services. In terms of offenders, they reveal an important gap between the Justice system and their own world, where the importance of written documents is seldom understood, to a great extent because they often have difficulties with reading and writing. Precisely, such difficulties contribute to their being dissocialised. On the other hand, in most cases, the application is denied as the offender has had several appointments (with the JAPs alone or also with the probation service) and has been repeatedly told that he/she has to provide a specific list of documents. A great number of JAPs hand in a list with specifically ticked boxes which indicate in simple words the documents he/she needs to bring in at the hearing or meeting. Moreover, a great number of inmates lie and state that they have employment, take vocational training classes, have seen or are about to see Doctor X when all this is untrue or Doctor X is actually a GP or even a physiotherapist when he/she was actually supposed to see an addiction specialist. JAPs must also be vigilant in view of the great number of counterfeit documents which are the object of organised trafficking in some regions.

Other decisions are justified, *inter alia*, by the fact that the person presents a **risk** which is too important. Thus 8.7% of the rulings referred to the person's numerous past offences; 17.5% referred to the fact that the person has committed a serious offence or has committed serious obligation violations in the course of a previous sentence such as a probation order; 3.2% mentioned that there is a high risk of reoffending; 4.3% mentioned that the person escaped from prison; 11.1% of the decisions mentioned that the person minimises the offence or is in full denial.

Judges also referred to classic **insertion efforts** criteria or rather, since they reject the application, to the lack thereof. As a reminder, the law demands for most measures, that the person make some form of insertion effort; They thus justified their decision in 38.4% of the cases because there were no such effort or no commitment to a release plan or to a project for the future. In 9.8% of them, they mentioned that the person – an addict or a mentally ill person – was not seeking treatment, or had no intention to get treatment. In 1% of the decisions, the person had applied for a measure which did not fit him/her; for instance it was too loose in his/her case. In 4.3% of the decisions, the project was not adapted to his/her issues and unrealistic.

A minority of decisions (5.4%) were justified, *inter alia*, by the fact that the **victim** is still scared or at risk of further victimisation. This however only concerned conditional release applications.

Conclusion

In this book we have seen that JAPs are '**good judges**' (: 'Good Courts', Berman & Feinblatt, 2005), and have, for the most part, an experience-based understanding of desistance and act accordingly. Nonetheless, when it generalised judicial participation in supervision in 1958, France inevitably reduced the quality of this judicial intervention, compared to today's PSC. At the same time, it is remarkable that such a system has been able to go to scale whereas PSC remain a parallel and minority system. It is very difficult to process all cases whilst offering them equal access to quality and judicial care.

However, there is now on the horizon a serious risk regarding this unique French ancestor of PSC, which has managed to survive in this otherwise rather old school loose supervision coupled with non-evidence based prisonised criminal justice system. Indeed, it could well disappear or become marginalised. JAPs could very well disappear if the current short-sighted and superficial logic prevails in the background of the prison services' conquests of probation and of its consequent instrumentalisation of sentences' implementation with its own interests in mind along with political blindness and their belief in the intrinsic value of sentences' management measures, regardless of the content and despite offenders' agency.

For now, in the field, probation services and JAPs still manage to get along and respect each other. It is to be hoped that this mature attitude, despite adversity, is equally present at top level. As I mentioned *supra*, it is still currently possible to restore the harmony which used to exist and even better, to develop a partnership culture. In a context of extremely poor political grasp of the important issues, I dream of someone who, at least in the domain of probation, would have Tony Blair's stature. Whilst his policy was contentious, from France's viewpoint, his two key messages, evidence-based practices and partnership are exactly what France needs.

French JAPs do interest overseas academics and practitioners because they tick most legitimacy of justice literature boxes and because it is likely that, as with PSC, they reinforce supervision efficacy. Still, France should cast a critical eye upon its probation. It needs to reassess the intensity and the compatibility of its practices with scientific evidence. At this point in time, there is no evaluation culture in this jurisdiction. The sad debate pertaining to criminology faculties which took place in 2012 has deprived this country of the armies of evaluators it needs (Cario et al., 2012). The prison services are generally fearful of outsiders' scrutiny, and this constitutes a strong limitation to researchers' access to the field. France must urgently undergo a revolution on these different points.

A conference of consensus was created at the end of 2012 and presented its results in February 2013, after it had heard international experts. Unfortunately its recommendations were rather timorous and the jury did not understand the institutional and criminological issues of French probations (Herzog-Evans, 2013 c).

It would be dangerous to eliminate or marginalise the only positive and original thing that the French probation system has to offer, i.e. JAPs' participation, which has attracted interest from foreign academics (Padfield et al., 2012), has been partly replicated in Belgium (Snacken et al., 2010) and has surprised American specialists (Wexler, 2013) who might have imagined they had invented the much copied PSC (Nolan, 2009; McIvor, 201)).

Moreover, JAPs and their fair trial are a barrier against arbitrary. English authors (Eliott, 2007; Creighton, 2007) and others (e.g. New-Zealander, Ellis, 2007) complain about their Parole Boards whilst Spanish academics complain about the penitentiary obstacles to their own JAPs' work (Cid and Tébar, 2012). Such was precisely the context of French probation prior to judicialisation (Herzog-Evans, 1998) and as I was typing these last lines, France is unfortunately on the verge of heading exactly back to this era [98].

It is to be hoped that France shall choose progress over decline.

---

98. See detailed legal analysis of what the current government has planned: http://herzog-evans.com/commentaire-du-projet-sur-la-peine-de-contrainte-penale-french-probation-order-bill-a-comment/.

References

Andrews D. and Bonta J. (2010), *The Psychology Of Criminal Conduct*, Lexis-Nexis.

Andrews D.A., Zinger I., Hoge R.D., Bonta J., Gendreau P., and Cullen F.T., (1990) 'Does correctional treatment work? A clinically relevant and psychologically informed meta-analysis', *Criminology*, 1990, n° 28: 369-404.

Ascensi L. (2005), *Du principe de la contradiction*, Thèse Paris I.

Baratta A., Morali A., and Halleguen O. (2012), 'La vérité sur l'expertise post-sentencielle : évaluation clinique contre échelle actuarielle', *Annales Médico-Psychologiques* 170 : 96-98.

Barnes G.C., Ahlman H., Gill C., Sharman L. W., Kurtz E., and Malvestuto R. (2010), 'Low-Intensity community supervision for low-risk offenders : a randomized, controlled trial', *Journal of Experimental Criminology*, n° 6 : 159-189.

Bauwens A. (2011), 'Organisational change, increasing managerialism and social work values in the Belgian Houses of Justice, Department of Offender Guidance', *European Journal of Probation*, n° 3(3): 15-30.

Beech A. R., Craig L.A. and Browne K.D. (eds.) (2009), *Assessment and Treatment of Sex Offenders. A Handbook,* Wiley-Blackwell.

Belenko S. (2011), *Research on Drug Courts: A Critical Review 2000 Update*, New York, National Center on Addiction and Substance Abuse at Columbia University.

Benjamin G.A. H., Darling E.J., and Sales B. (1990), 'The Prevalence of Depression, Alcohol Abuse, and Cocaine Abuse Mong United-States Lawyers', *International Journal of Law and Psychiatry,* n° 13: 233-246.

Berman G. (2000), 'What is a traditional judge anyway? Problem-solving in the State Courts', *Judicature*, n° 84: 78-85.

Berman G. and Feinblatt J. (2005), *Good Courts. The Case for Problem-Solving Justice*, New York, The New Press.

Beyens K., Françoise C. and Scheirs V. (2010), 'Les juges face à l'(in)exécution des peines', *Déviance et société,* n° 34(3) : 401-424.

Beyens K. and Kaminski D. (2013), 'Is the sky the limit? Eagerness for electronic monitoring in Belgium', in M. Nellis, K. Beyens et D. Kaminski (dir.), *Electronically Monitored Punishment. International and Critical Perspectives*, Abingdon, Routledge: 150-171.

Bianchi V. (2005), *L'avocat et l'activité « application des peines »,* mémoire de Master II droit pénal et sciences criminelles, Université de Nantes (Master Plus dissertation University of Nantes)

Bianchi V. (2006) 'La loi du 23 janvier 2006 ou l'extension à l'application des peines de la compétence nationale en matière de terrorisme , *Gazette du Palais.* 17-18 mai 2006 : 4-6.

Blackburn R. (1993), *The Psychology of Criminal Conduct*, Wiley.

Blumstein A., Cohen J., Martin S., and Tonry M. (eds.) (1983), *Research on Sentencing: The search for Reform,* 2 volumes, National Academy Press.

Blumstein A. and Beck J. (2005), 'Reentry as a Transient State between Liberty and Recommitment': in Travis J. and Visher C. (dir.), *Prisoner Reentry and Crime in America*, New York, Cambridge University Press: 50-79.

Boelens R. (2009), 'Remote Alcohol Monitoring', Conférence de la Conférence Européenne de la Probation du 7 au 9 mai 2009 sur la surveillance électronique, available at http://www.cepprobation.org/uploaded_files/Pres%20EM09%20Boe.pdf (accessed on January 5, 2013).

Boldt R. C. (2002), 'The adversary system and attorney role in the drug treatment court movement', in Nolan J. L. Jr, *Drug Courts*, Hawthorne, Aldyne de Gruyter: 115-143

Bonta J., Wallace-Captretta S. and Rooney R., (2000), 'A quasi-experimental evaluation of an intensive rehabilitation supervision program', *Criminal Justice and Behaviour*, n° 27: 312-332.

Bonta A., Rugge T., Scott T.-L., Bourgon G., and Yessine A.K. (2008), 'Exploring the Black Box of Community Supervision', *Journal of Offender Rehabilitation*, n° 47(3): 248-270.

Bottoms A. (2001), 'Compliance with community penalties', in A. Bottoms, L. Gelsthorpe and S. Rex, *Community Penalties: Change and Challenge,* Cullompton, Willan Publishing: 87-116.

Bouloc B. (1991), *Pénologie*, Paris, Dalloz, 1st ed. (also see more recent eds.: 1999, 2005 and 2011).

Brizais R. (2006), *Enquête sociale rapide*, Mission Evaluation mesures socio-Judiciaires, Citoyens et Justice.

Bruckmüller K. (2012), 'Recalling conditionally released prisoners in Austria', *Ejprob*, n° 4(1): 6-18.

Burke K. and Leben S. (2007) *Procedural Fairness: A Key Ingredient in Public Satisfaction: A White Paper of the American Judges Association* (available at http://aja.ncsc.dni.us/htdocs/AJAWhitePaper9-26-07.pdf, accessed September 5, 2013).

Burnett, R. (2004), 'To Reoffend or Not to Reoffend? The Ambivalence of Convicted Property Offenders', in S. Maruna and R. Immarigeon (eds), *After Crime and Punishment: Pathways to Offender Reintegration,* Cullompton, Willan Publishing: 152–80.

Canivet G. (1999), *Amélioration du contrôle extérieur des établissements pénitentiaires: rapport au garde des Sceaux*, ministre de la justice, publié in Documentation Française, Collection des rapports officiels, 2000.

Canton R. (2011), *Probation. Working with offenders*, Abingdon, Routledge.

Cario R., Herzog-Evans M. and Villerbu L. M. (eds.) (2012), *La criminologie à l'Université. Mythes et réalités,* Paris, L'Harmattan.

Carlsson C. (2013), 'Process of Intermittency in Criminal Careers: Notes From a Swedish Study on Life Course and Crime', *International Journal of Offender Therapy and Comparative Criminology*, n° 57(8): 913-938.

Casey P., Burke K., and Leben S. (2012), *Minding the Court. Enhancing the Decision-making Process. A White Paper*, American Judges Association, October 1.

Castel P. (2001), 'La diversité du placement à l'extérieur. Etude sur une mesure d'aménagement de peine', *Déviance et société*, n° 25 : 53-73.

Céré J.-P., *Le contentieux disciplinaire dans les établissements pénitentiaire français à l'aune du droit européen*, Thesis, University of Pau, 1998.

Chauvenet A., Orlic F. and Benguigui G. (1994) *Le monde des surveillants de prison,* Paris, P.U.F.

Chauvenet A., Orlic F. (2002), 'Sens de la peine et contraintes en milieu ouvert et en prison', *Déviance et Société*, n° 26(4) : 443-461.

Chelіotis L. K. (2006), 'Penal managerialism from within: Implications for theory and research', *International Journal of Law and Psychiatry*, n° 29: 397-404.

Cid J. and Tebar B. (2012), 'Revoking early conditional release measures in Spain', *Ejprob* n° 4(1): 112-124.

Cid J. and Tebar B. (2010), 'Spain', in Padfield N., van Zyl Smit D. and Dünkel F., *Release from Prison. European policy and practice*, Cullompton, Willan Publishing: 358-392.

Cluley A. (2010), 'Serious Further Offence; The case of Dano Sonnex', *Probation Journal*, n° 57(1): 83-88.

Collins H. (2007), 'A consideration of discretion, offender attributes and the process of recall', in N. Padfield (ed.), *Who to Release, Parole Fairness and Criminal Justice*, Cullompton. Willan Publishing: 159-172.

Crawford A. and Hucklesby A. (2012), *Legitimacy and compliance in criminal justice*, Abingdon, Routledge.

Crew B. K. (1991), 'Sex differences in criminal sentencing: Chivalry or patriarchy?', *Justice Quaterly*, n° 8(1): 59-83.

Combessie P. (1996), *Prison des villes et des campagnes. Etude d'écologie sociale*, Paris, La Découverte.

Commission « Canivet » (2000), *Rapport sur l'amélioration du contrôle externe sur les établissements pénitentiaires,* March, ronéo.

Commission Nationale Consultative des Droits de l'Homme (2002), *Réflexions sur le sens de la peine, Texte adopté par l'Assemblée plénière,* 24 janvier.

Conseil National des barreaux (2010), *Avocat et Psychologie*, Assemblée Générale des 7 et 8 mai 2010, Commission Prospective.

Couvrat P. (2001), 'Le difficile passage du gué. De la décision d'administration judiciaire à la décision juridictionnelle', *RSC* 2001, Chron., 425.

Couvrat P. (2004), 'Les dispositions relatives à l'application des peines de la loi Perben II', *Dr. pén.* Juin.

Cowe F. and Cherry S. (2010), 'Residential work with adult offenders: greenhouses or wharehouses ?', in Brayford J., Cowe F. et Deering J. (dir.), *What Else Works? Creative work with offenders,* Cullompton, Willan Publishing: 117-154.

Daicoff S. (2009), 'Collaborative law: a new tool for the lawyer's toolkit', *Florida Journal of law and Public policy*, n° 20: 113-140.

Daicoff S. (2006), *Lawyer Know thyself. A psychological analysis of personality strengths and weaknesses,* Washington, American Psychological Association.

Daicoff S. (2011a), *Comprehensive Law Practice. Law as a Healing Profession*, Durham, NC, Carolina Academic Press.

Daicoff S. (2011b), 'The future of the legal profession', *Monash University Law Review*, n° 37(1): 7-32.

Danet J. (2006), *Justice pénale, le tournant*, Folio-Le Monde.

Danet J. (2010), *La justice pénale entre rituel et management*, Rennes, Presses universitaires de Rennes.

Danet J. (ed.) (2013), *La réponse pénale. Dix ans de traitement des délits,* Rennes, Presses Universitaires de Rennes.

Deering J. (2011), *Probation Practice and the New Penology. Practitioner Reflections,* Farnham, Ashgate.

Digard L. (2010), 'When legitimacy is denied: Offender perceptions of the prison recall system', *Probation Journal,* n° 57(1): 43-61.

Dindo S. (2011), *Sursis avec mise à l'épreuve : la peine méconnue. Une analyse des pratiques de probation en France,* Etude pour la Direction de l'administration pénitentiaire, bureau PMJ1, mai.

Direction de l'administration pénitentiaire (2012), *Les chiffres clefs de l'administration pénitentiaire au 1er janvier 2012.*

Direction de l'administration pénitentiaire (2013), *Les chiffres clefs de l'administration pénitentiaire au 1er janvier 2013.*

Direction des affaires judiciaires et Direction des affaires criminelles et des grâces, (2012), *Synthèse Nationale des Rapports d'Activité Annuels des Services de l'Application des Peines*, Novembre.

Dodgson K., Goodwin P., Howard P., Llewellyn-Thomas S., Mortimer E., Russell N. and Weiner M. (2001), *Electronic monitoring of released prisoners: an evaluation of the Home Detention Curfew scheme*, Home Office Research, Development and Statistics Directorate, March.

Dréan-Rivette I. (2005), *De la personnalisation de la peine dans le code pénal,* Paris, L'Harmattan.

Duflot J. and Martin E. (2011), *Traité de l'application des peines*, Paris, berger-Levrault.

Dugin L. (2004), 'The Legal Profession's Hidden Secret: Substance Abuse', *Michigan Law Journal*, September: 44-45.

Eliott M. (2007), 'The Parole Board and the changing face of public law', in N. Padfield (ed.), *Who to Release? Parole, fairness and criminal justice*, Cullompton, Willan Publishing: 43-62.

Enkaoua C. (2012), 'Le barreau de Paris lève le tabou du stress des avocats', *Gazette du Palais,* 4-6 March: 9-11.

B.J. Ennis and T.R. Litwack (1974) 'Psychiatry and the presumption of expertise: Flipping coins in the courtroom', *California Law Re*view, n° 62: 694-753

Farrall S., Mawby R. C. and Worrall A. (2009), 'Prolific/persistent offenders and desistance', in L. Gelsthorpe et R. Morgan, *Handbook of Probation*, , Cullompton, Willan Publishing.

Faugeron C. (1999), 'Les origines du juge de l'application des peines', *Revue de l'application des peines*, Sept.-Dec., 3.

Feuvrel K.E., Mongin D., Bambot S., faupel M., Panangadan A., Talukder A., and Pidva R. (2008), 'Clinical Evaluation of a Novel Insertitial Fluid Sensor System for Remote Continuous Alcohol Monitoring', *Sensors Journal*, n° 8(1): 71-80.

Fitzgibbon W. (2011), *Probation and social work on trial. Violent offenders and child abusers*, Basingstoke, Palgrave Macmillan.

Frazer M.S. (2006), *The Impact of the Community Court Model on Defendant Perceptions of Fairness. A Case Study at the Red Hook Community Justice Center*, Center for Court Innovation.

Freiberg A. (2010), 'Post-adversarial and Post-inquisitorial justice: Transcending Traditional Penological Paradigms', Monash University, Faculty of Law, Research Paper n° 2010/17.

Froment J.-C. and Kaluszinski M. (dir.) (2011), *L'administration pénitentiaire face aux principes de la nouvelle gestion publique*, PU de Grenoble.

Fox A. and Berman G., (2002), 'Going to Scale: A Conversation about the Future of Drug Courts', *Court Review,* Fall: 4-14.

Freiberg A. (2011), 'Post-adversarial and post-inquisitorial justice: transcending traditional penological paradigms', *European J. of Criminology*, n° 7: 77-93.

Garapon A. (2001), *Et ce sera justice: Punir en démocratie,* Paris, Odile Jacob.

Garçon E. and Peltier V. (2010), *Droit de la peine*, Paris, Litec.

Garland D., (2001) *The Culture of Control: Crime and Social Order in Contemporary Society.* Oxford: Oxford University Press.

Garreau P. (2004), 'Les Spip et le volet application des peines de la loi du 9 mars 2004 : l'écueil de l'ambiguïté – impératif de crédibilité', *AJ pénal* : 397-401.

Gautron V. (2013), 'Quelle est la part des pratiques et de l'organisation dans les politiques pénales mises en œuvre par les parquet', Contribution à la conférence de consensus sur la prévention de la récidive, available at http://conference-consensus.justice.gouv.fr/wp-content/uploads/2013/01/contrib_gautron.pdf.

Geiran V. (2012), 'Managing change in Irish probation: prioritising resources through evidence-based principles, organisational development and collaboration', *Eurovista,* n° 2(3): 61-69.

Gelsthorpe L. and Padfield N. (2003), 'Introduction', in Gelsthorpe L. and Padfield N. (dir.) *Exercising discretion. Decision-making in the criminal justice system and beyond*, Cullompton, Willan Publishing.

Golberg S. (2005), *Judging for the 21st century: A Problem-solving Approach*, National Judicial Institute.

Gottfredson D. G., Najaka S.S., and Hearley B. (2006), 'Effectiveness Of Drug Treatment Courts: Evidence From A Randomized Trial', *Criminology and Public Policy*, n° 2(2): 171-196.

Greene J. (2002), 'Getting Tough on Crime: The history and Political Context of Sentencing Reform Developments Leading to the Passage of the 1994 Crime Act', in Tata C. and Hutton N. (eds.), *Sentencing and Society*, Aldershot, Ashgate: 43-64.

Hannah-Moffat K. (2002), 'Creating choices: reflecting on choices', in P. Carlen (ed.), *Women and Punishment*, Cullompton, Willan Publishing: 199-219.

Hanson R. K., R. Harris A. J., Scott T. L., and Helmus L. (2007), *Assessing the Risk of Sexual Offenders on Community Supervision: the Dynamic Supervision Project*, Ottawa, Public Survey, Canada.

Haslewood-Pocik I., Merine L. and Roberts C. (2004), *The Evaluation of the Employment Pathfinder: Lessons from Phase I, and a Survey for Phase II*, Home Office Online Report 22/04.

Hattery A. and Smith E. (2010), *Prisoner reentry and social capital. The long road to reintegration,* Lanham, Lexington Books.

Hearnden I. and Millie A., (2004), 'Does tougher enforcement lead to lower reconviction ?', *Probation Journal,* n° 51(1) : 48-58.

Herzog-Evans M. and Péchillon E. (2003), *Le droit de l'exécution des peines. Problèmes et enjeux d'une discipline juridique en formation*, rapport de recherche pour la Mission Droit et Justice.

Herzog-Evans, M. (1994), *La gestion du comportement du détenu. L'apparence légaliste du droit pénitentiaire,* PhD thesis, Poitiers (later published as: *La gestion du comportement du détenu. Essai de droit pénitentiaire*, Paris, L'Harmattan, 1998.

Herzog-Evans M. (1998), 'La vie et le droit: usages et « groupes sociaux cohérents »', *Revue de la recherche juridique*, n° 4: 1203-1222.

Herzog-Evans M. (1999 a), 'Le juge de l'application des peines, juridiction de premier degré', *Revue de sciences criminelles et de droit pénal comparé*, vol. 2: 289 301.

Herzog-Evans M. (1999 b), ' "Ter in idem"', Comment on Cass. Crim. 27 March 1997, *Bykowski*, *Revue pénitentiaire et de droit pénal* 1999-1: 71-90.

Herzog-Evans M. (2005 a), '*Quantum* du crédit de réduction de peine et "bug juridique" : après l'alinéa 1er de l'article 721… l'alinéa 2 ?', *AJ pénal :* 448-451.

Herzog-Evans M. (2005 b), 'Récidive: surveiller et punir plutôt que prévenir et guérir', *AJPénal*, sept. 2005: 305-314.

Herzog-Evans M. (2007), 'La loi relative à la prévention de la délinquance et l'exécution des peines', *Recueil Dalloz*, n° 31 : 2174-2179.

Herzog-Evans M. (2008), 'Les victimes et l'exécution des peines. En finir avec le déni et l'idéologie', *Ajpénal* 2008: 356-360.

Herzog-Evans, M. (2009 a), 'French post-custody law (2000-2009): from equitable trial to the religion of control', *European Journal of Probation*, n° 2: 97-109.

Herzog-Evans M. (2009 b), *L'évasion*, Paris: L'Harmattan.

Herzog-Evans M. (2011 a), "Judicial rehabilitation in France: Helping with the desisting process and acknowledging achieved desistance", *European Journal of Probation*, n° 3(1): 4-19.

Herzog-Evans M. (2011 b), 'Probation in France: Some things old, some things new, some things borrowed and often blue', *Probation Journal*, n° 58(4): 345-354.

Herzog-Evans, M. (2011 c), 'Desisting in France: What probation officers know and do. A first approach', *European Journal of Probation* n° 3(12): 29-46.

Herzog-Evans M. (2011 c), 'Nouveaux enjeux dans l'application des peines. Les leçons du droit et de la criminologie comparée', *Ajpénal* : 177-181

Herzog-Evans M. (2011 d), 'Révolutionner la pratique judiciaire. S'inspirer de l'inventivité américaine', *Recueil Dalloz,* n° 44 : 3016-3022.

Herzog-Evans M. (2012 a), «Intérêt et difficultés d'une approche « désistante » en France', in P. Mbanzoulou, M. Herzog-Evans and S. Courtine (eds.), *Insertion et désistance des personnes places sous main de justice. Savoirs et pratiques*, L'Harmattan, 2012: 87-107.

Herzog-Evans M. (2012 b), 'Who is afraid of criminology?', http://papers.ssrn.com/sol3/papers.cfm?abstract_id=2034867.

Herzog-Evans M. (2012 c), 'Non-compliance: a human approach and a hair splitting legal system', *European Journal of Probation*, n° 4(1): 45-61.

Herzog-Evans (2012 d), 'The six months limit to community measures "under prison registry": a study of professional perception', *European Journal of Probation*, n° 4(2): 23-45.

Herzog-Evans M. (2012 e), 'Exécution des peines, délinquance sexuelle et « positionnement quant aux faits » : enjeux juridiques et criminologiques', *Ajpénal* : 632-635.

Herzog-Evans (2012 f), 'Outils d'évaluation : sortir des fantasmes et de l'aveuglément idéologique', *Ajpénal* 2012 : 75-80.

Herzog-Evans M. (2012 g), 'La bataille des juges et du parquet dans l'exécution des peines', in Boudon J. (ed.), *Concurrence des contrôles et rivalité des juges*, Paris, Mare et Martin: 199-224.

Herzog-Evans M. (2012-2013 a), *Droit de l'exécution des peines*, Paris, Dalloz, 4th ed.

Herzog-Evans M. (2012-2013 b), *Droit pénitentiaire*, Paris, Dalloz, 2e ed.

Herzog-Evans M. (2013 a), 'All hands on deck: (re)mettre le travail en partenariat au centre de la probation', *Ajpénal* : 139-144.

Herzog-Evans M. (2013 b), 'What's in a name: Penological and institutional connotations of probation officers' labelling in Europe', *Eurovista,* n° 2(3): 121-133.

Herzog-Evans M. (2013 c), 'Conférence de consensus: trop de droit ; pas assez d'envergure institutionnelle et scientifique', *Recueil Dalloz* : 720-724.

Herzog-Evans M. (2013 d), 'La déjuridictionnalisation de l'application des peines', in S. Boussard (ed.), *Les droits des personnes détenues. Après la loi pénitentiaire du 24 novembre 2009*, Dalloz, Series 'Thèmes et commentaires': 259-279.

Herzog-Evans M. (2013 e), 'Récidive et surpopulation: pas de baguette magique juridique', *Ajpénal*, March: 136-139.

Herzog-Evans M. (forthcoming a), 'Explaining French Probation: Social Work in a Prison Administration', in Durnescu I. and McNeill F. (eds.), *Understanding penal practices*, Abingdon, Routledge.

Herzog-Evans, (forthcoming b), 'To robe or not to robe: discussion internationale informelle autour du port de la robe par les magistrats et les avocats', *Actualité Juridique pénal.*

Herzog-Evans M. (forthcoming c), 'Sanctions for non-compliance in France: the practice of sentences implementation courts', in P. Raynor and P. Ugwudige (ed.), *What Works in Offender Compliance: International Perspectives and Evidence-Based Practice*. Basingstoke: Palgrave Macmillan.

Herzog-Evans M. (forthcoming d), 'Is the French juge de l'application des peines a Problem-Solving Court?', in M. Herzog-Evans (ed.), *Offender Release and Supervision. The role of Courts and the use of discretion in sentences' implementation and reentry,* Nijmegen, Wolf Legal Publishers.

Herzog-Evans M. (forthcoming e), 'Apports de la criminologie aux politiques et aux pratiques pénales', presentation at the conference 'L'efficacité de l'exécution des peines', University of Rheims, Law faculty, laboratory CEJESCO, 11 December 2012, Paris, Mare et Martin.

Herzog-Evans M. (unpublished, 2013), *Audit qualitative des placements à l'extérieur de X*, Unpublished report for the Probation Services of the X, 89p., 2013.

Hogarth J. (1971), *Sentencing as a Human Process*, University of Toronto Press and Center of Criminology, University of Toronto.

Höing M. (2011), *European handbook. COSA,* Circles Europe.

Hope T., Worrall A., Dunkerton L., and Leacock C. (2001), *The Newcastle Prolific Offender Project Final Evaluation Report,* Keele University/Straffordshire Probation Area, unpublished.

Inspection des services pénitentiaires (2011), *Rapport relative aux conditions de prise en charge de M. Tony Meilhon par le SPIP de Loire-Atlantique*, 10 February.

Inspection judiciaire (2011), *Inspection de fonctionnement du service de l'application des peines du tribunal de grande instance de Nantes*, February, n° 13 /2011.

Izzo, V. Carpel (2011), *Second-Hand Shock: Surviving and Overcoming Vicarious Trauma*, High Conflict Institute Press.

Jacobs J. B. and Larrauri E. (2012), 'Are criminal convictions a public matter? The USA and Spain', *Punishment and Society*, n° 14(1): 3-28.

Jones, R. S., Ross, J. I., Richards, S. C., and Murphy, D. S. (2009), 'The first dime: A decade of Convict Criminology', *The Prison Journal*, n° 89(2): 151-171.

Jury de la Conférence de Consensus (2013), *Rapport du jury de consensus remis au Premier ministre*, Conférence de consensus. Pour une politique publique de prévention de la récidive, 20 February.

Kerchove van de M. (2008), 'Le sens de la peine dans la jurisprudence du Conseil constitutionnel français', *Rev. Sc. Crim.* : 805-824.

King S. (2013 a), 'Assisted desistance and experience of probation supervision', *Probation Journal*: DOI: 10.1177/0264550513478320.

King S. (2013 b), 'Early desistance narratives: A qualitative: A qualitative analysis of probationers' transitions towards desistance', *Punishment and Society*, n° 15(2): 147-165.

Klein D. and Mitchell G. (2010) (dir.), *The Psychology of Judicial Decision Making*, New York, Oxford University Press, American Psychology-Law Society Series.

Kneusé E. (2003), 'Sous le strass, le stress', *Le Bulletin du Barreau de Paris*, Ordre des avocats à la Cour de paris, 18 nov. n° 39.

Koskas G. (forthcoming), 'Grandeurs et misères de la justice. L'efficacité et la question des moyens', presentation at the conference 'L'efficacité de l'exécution des peines', University of Rheims, Law faculty, laboratory CEJESCO, 11 December 2012, Paris, Mare et Martin.

Kovler J. A. (2007*), 'L'application des peines à la lumière de l'article 6 de la Convention européenne des droits de l'homme', in Le droit de l'exécution des peines. Une jurisprudence en mouvement*, Acts of the XVIIIe Congress of the Association Française de Droit pénal, Pau; 24 and 25 Mai 2007, *Rev. pénit.*: 165-174.

Kuziemko I. (2007), *Going Off Parole: How the Elimination of Discretionary Prison Release Affects the Social Cost of Crime,* Ph D thesis, Harvard University, Jan.

Kuziemko I. (2012), 'How Should Inmates Be Released from Prison? An Assessment of Parole Versus Fixed-Sentence Regimes', *The Quarterly Journal of Economics,* n° 128 (1): 371-424.

LaFree G. and Miller E. (2008), 'Desistance from terrorism: What can we learn from criminology ?', *Dynamics of Asymetric Conflict*, , vol. 1(3): 203-230.

Larminat X. (2012), *La probation en quête d'approbation. L'exécution des peines en milieu ouvert entre gestion des risques et gestion des flux,* Thesis Cesdip-University of Versailles-Saint Quentin.

Lavielle B., Janas M., and Lameyre X. (2012-2013), *Le guide des peines*, Paris, Dalloz, 5th ed.

Lee W.J., Koenigsberg M.R., Davidson C. and Beto D.R. (2010), 'A Pilot Study Linking Personality, Leadership Style and Leadership Success among Probation Directors in the he U.S.', *Federal Probation*, n° 74 (3).

Lemaire P. and Camu J.-M. (2011), *Rapport sur la réorganisation des SPIP, 9 mai.*

Lewis S., Raynor P., Smith D. and Wardak A. (2006), *Race and probation*, Cullompton, Willan Publishing.

Liebling A. (2007), 'Why Fairness Matters in Criminal Justice', in N. Padfield (dir.), *Who to Release. Parole, Fairness and Criminal Justice*, Willan Publishing, Collumpton, 2007: 63-71.

Ligue des droits de l'homme de Toulouse (2012), *Comparution immédiates : quelle justice ? regards citoyens sur une justice du quotidien,* D. Welzer-Lang (ed.), Toulouse, Erès.

Lhuilier D. (2007), *Changements et construction des identités professionnelles : les travailleurs sociaux pénitentiaires*, Final Report, July.

Loader, I., and Sparks, R. (2002) 'Contemporary landscapes of crime, order, and control: governance, risk, and globalization', in Maguire M., Morgan R., and Reiner R. (eds.), *The Oxford handbook of criminology*, 3rd ed., Oxford, Oxford University Press:

Lockwood B. (2012), 'The Influence of Travel Distance on Treatment Non completion for Juvenile Offenders', *Journal of Research in Crime and Delinquency*, n° 49(4): 572-600

Lösel F., Bottoms A. and Farrington DP. (2012), *Young adult offenders. Lost in transition?*, London and New York, Routledge.

Maguire M. and Raynor P. (2006), 'How the resettlement of prisoners promotes desistance from crime. Or does it?', *Criminology and Criminal Justice February*, n° 6(1): 19-38.

Mair G. Lloyd C., Nee C. and Sibbitt R. (1994) *Intensive Probation in England and Wales: An Evaluation,* Home Office Research Study 1994, 133, London, Home Office.

Malaval C. (2010), *La poste au pied de la lettre*, Paris, Fayard.

Mansuy I. (2005), 'Principe de légalité et d'exécution des peines en France et Allemagne, Droit = droits ?', *Champ pénal/Penal field*, available at http://champpenal.revues.org/397

Mansuy I. (2007), *La protection des droits des détenus en France et en Allemagne*, Paris, L'Harmattan.

Marshall W.L., Thornton D., Marshall L.E., Fernandez Y.M. and Mann R. (2001), 'Treatment of sexual offenders who are in categorical denial: A pilot project', *Sexual Abuse : A Journal of Research and Treatment*, 2001, vol. 13: 205-215.

Maruna S. (2001), *Making Good. How Ex-Convicts Reform and Rebuild their Lives,* American Psychological Association

Maruna S. and Farrall S., 'Desistance from crime: A theoretical reformulation', *Kvlner Zeitschrift fur Sociologie und Sozialpsychologie*, n° 43: 171-194.

Maruna S., Immarigeon R. and LeBel T. P. (2004), 'Ex-Offender reintegration: Theory and practice', in Maruna S. and Immarigeon R. (eds.) *After Crime and Punishment. Pathways to Offender Reintegration,* Cullompton, Willan Publishing: 3-26.

Maruna S. and Immarigeon R. (2004), *After Crime and Punishment. Pathways to Offender Reintegration,* Cullompton, Willan publishing.

Maruna S. (2011 a), 'Judicial rehabilitation and the 'Clean Bill of Health' in Criminal Justice', *European Journal of Probation*, n° 3-1): 97-117.

Maruna S. (2011 b), 'Reentry as a rite of passage', *Punishment and Society*, n° 13(1): 1-27

Marwan M. (ed.) (2012), *Les sorties de délinquance: Théories, méthodes, enquêtes*, Paris, La Découverte.

Massood S.A., Dani S. S., Burns N.D. and Backhouse C.J. (2006), 'Transformational leadership and organizational culture: the situational strength perspective', *Journal of engineering manufacture*, n° 220: 941-949.

Mattessich P. W., Murray-Close M. et Monsey B.R. (2001), *Collaboration: What Makes it Work?,* Saint Paul, MN, Amherst H. Wilder Foundation, 2e ed.

Matthews R. (2005), 'The myth of punitiveness', *Theoretical Criminology*, n° 9(2): 175-201.

Mawby, R.C. and Worrall, A. (2004), 'Polibation Revisited: Policing, Probation and Prolific Offender Projects', *International Journal of Police Science and Management* **6** (2): 63-73.

Mawby R. C. and Worrall A. (2011), 'They were very threatening about "do-gooding bastards": Probation changing relationships with the police and prison services in England and Wales', n° 3(3): 78-94.

May D.C. and Wood P. B. (2010), *Ranking Correctional Punishments. Views from Offenders, Practitioners, and the Public,* Carolina Academic Press.

Mbanzoulou P., Herzog-Evans M. and Courtine S. (eds.) (2012), *Insertion et désistance des personnes places sous main de justice. Savoirs et pratiques*, Paris, L'Harmattan.

McColl W. D. (2002), 'Theory and Practice in the Baltimore City Drug Treatment Court', in Nolan J. *Drug Courts*, New York, Walter de Gruyter.

McDougall C., Pearson D.A., Willoughby H. and Bowles R.A. (2012), 'Evaluation of the ADViSOR project: Cross-situational monitoring of high-risk offenders un prison and the community', *Legal and Criminological Psychology*, DOI:10.1111/j.2044-8333.2012.02059.x.

McDougall C., Pearson D.A., Willoughby H. and Bowles R.A. (2013), 'Evaluation d'un projet d'évaluation du risque basé sur l'observation des détenus (ADViSOR)', *Ajpénal*, April, 204-207.

McNeill F., Burns N., Halliday S., Hutton N., and Tata C. (2009), 'Risk, responsibility and reconfiguration. Penal adaptation and misadaptation', *Punishment and Society*, n° 11(4): 419-442.

McNeill F. (2010), 'La désistance: What Works et les peines en milieu ouvert en Ecosse', *Ajpénal*, September: 376-380.

McNeill F. and Robinson G. (2013), 'Liquid Legitimacy and community sanctions', in Crawford A. and Hucklesby A. (eds.), *Legitimacy and compliance in criminal justice*, Routledge: 116-137.

McIvor (2010), 'Beyond supervision: judicial involvement in offender management', in F. Mcneill, P. Raynor, and C. Trotter (eds.), *Offender Supervision. New Directions in theory, research and practice,* Cullompton, Willan Publishing: 215-238.

Meehl P. (1954), *Clinical versus Statistical Prediction: A Theoretical Analysis and a Review of the Evidence*, Minneapolis University of Minnesota Press.

Milburn P. Benech-Leroux P., Besnier C., Cardoso M., Champetier B., and Lameyre X. (2007), *Les procureurs de la République: de la compétence personnelle à l'identité collective*, Research Report Mission Droit et Justice.

Milburn P. Benech-Leroux P., Besnier C., Cardoso M., Champetier B., and Lameyre X. (2010), *Les procureurs: entre vocation judiciaire et fonctions politiques,* Paris, PUF.

Miller E. (2007), 'The Therapeutic Effects of Managerial Reentry Courts', *Federal Sentencing Reporter*, n° 20(2): 127-135.

Millon T., Simonsen E., Birket-Smith M., and Davis R.D. (eds.) (2003), *Psychopathy. Antisocial, Criminal And Violent Behavior*, New York, The Guilford Press.

Mills A. and Codd H. (2008), 'Prisoners' families and offender management: Mobilizing social capital', *Probation Journal*, n° 55(1): 9-24.

Mitterrand F. (1964), *Le coup d'état permanent*, Paris, Plon –reedited in 2010 by: Les belles lettres with a foreword of de HJ.-M. Guieu and G. Saunier.

Moore R., Gray E., Roberts C. and Merrington S. (2006), *Managing Persistent and Serious Offenders in the Community : Intensive Community Programmes in Theory and Practice,* Cullompton, Willan Publishing.

Morali A., Baratta A., Halleguen O., and Lefevre H. (2011), 'Etude sur la prise en charge des auteurs de violence sexuelle auprès d'une cohorte de psychiatres hospitaliers en France en 2011', *Annales Médico-Psychologiques*, n° 169: 578-580.

Morgenstern C. (2009), 'European initiatives for harmonisation and minimum standards in the field of community sanctions and measures', *European Journal of Probation*, n° 1(2): 124-137.

Mouhanna C. (2011 a), *La coordination des politiques judiciaires et pénitentiaires. Une analyse des relations entre monde judiciaire et administration pénitentiaire*, Research Report, Mission Droit et Justice.

Mouhanna C. (2011 b), *La coordination des politiques judiciaires et pénitentiaires. Une analyse des relations entre monde judiciaire et administration pénitentiaire*, Research Synthesis, Mission Droit et Justice.

Moulds E. F. (1978), 'Chivalry and Paternalism: Disparities of Treatment in the Criminal Justice System', *The Western Political Quarterly*, n° 31(3) : 416-430.

Murray D. C. (2008), 'Practical Pain Management for Lawyers Exposed to Vicarious Trauma', communication at the COLAP conference, Halifax, 10 May 2008; Nunavut Branch in Iqualuit, Nuvanut, Nova Scotia.

Nafekh M., Didenko E., and Anastasopoulos V. (2009), *Community Residential Alternatives. Evaluation branch*, Policy Sector, Correctional Services, Canada.

Nellis M. (1999), 'Politics, probation and the English language', *Vista*, n° 4(3): 233-240

Nellis M., Beyens K., Kaminski D. (dir.) (2013), *Electronically Monitored Punishment. International and Critical Perspectives,* Routledge.

Neuilly M.-A. (2010), 'Theory and Practice of the Criminal Choice', in Herzog-Evans M. (ed.), *Transnational Criminology Manual*, Nijmegen, Wolf Legal Publishers, vol. I: 541-559.

Nolan J. L. (2009), *Legal Accents, Legal Borrowing. The International Problem-Solving Court Movement*, Princeton University Press

Nunes K. L., Hanson K.R., Firestone P., Moulden H.M., Greenberg D.M., and Bradford J.M. (2007), 'Denial predicts recidivism for some sexual offenders', *Sex Abuse*, n° 19: 91-105.

O'Malley P. (2000), 'Criminologies of Catastrophe? Understanding Criminal Justice on the Edge of the New Millennium', *Australian and New Zealand Journal of Criminology*, n° 33(2): 153-167.

Padfield N., Liebling A. and Arnold H. (2003), 'Discretion and the release of life sentence prisoners', in L. Gelsthorpe N. Padfield (eds.), *Exercising discretion. Decision-making in the criminal justice system and beyond,* Cullompton, Willan Publishing, 97-124.

Padfield N. and Maruna S. (2006), 'The revolving door at the prison gate. Exploring the dramatic increase in recalls to prison', *Criminology and Criminal Justice*, n° 6(3): 329-352.

Padfield N., van Zyl Smit D. and Dünkel F. (2010), *Release from Prison. European policy and practice*, Cullompton, Willan Publishing.

Padfield N. (2012), 'Recalling conditionally released prisoners in England and Wales', *Ejprob*, n° 4(1): 34-45.

Padfield N., Morgan R., and Maguire M. (2012), 'Out of court, out of sight? Criminal sanctions and non-judicial decision-making', in M. Maguire, R. Morgan and R. Reiner, *The Oxford Handbook of Criminology,* Oxford University Press: 955-985.

Patrick C. J. (dir.) (2006), *Handbook of Psychopathy*, New York, Guilford Press.

Pawson R. and Tilley N. (1997), *Realistic Evaluation*, London, Sage.

Pawson R. (2013), *The science of evaluation. A realist manifesto*, London, Sage

Pearson D.A.S., McDougall C., Kanaan M., Bowles A. and Torgerson D.J. (2010), 'Reducing criminal recidivism: evaluation of Citizenship, an evidence-based probation supervision process', *Journal of Experimental Criminology,* n° 7(1):73-102.

Péchillon É. (1998) *Sécurité et droit du service public pénitentiaire,* Paris, LGDJ

Perrier Y. (2013), *Probation 1885-2005*, Paris, Dalloz-Sirey.

Petersilia J. et Turner, S (1990), *Intensive Supervision for High Risk Probation*, Santa Monica, Rand Corporation.

Petersilia J. (2003), *When Prisoners Come Home: Parole and Prisoners Reentry,* Oxford University Press.

Petricci C. J. (2002), 'Respect as a Component in the Judge-Defendant Interaction in a Specialized Domestic Violence Court that Utilizes Therapeutic Jurisprudence', *Criminal Law Bulletin* n° 38(2): 263-295

Planiol A., (2002), 'Peine, douleur et dépression', *Annales médico-psychologiques*, n° 160(9):615-21.

Poncela P. (2001), *Droit de la peine*, Paris,Thémis, 2ne ed.

Poncela P. (2004), 'Étranger et droit des sanction pénales. Les modifications résultant de la loi du 26 novembre 2003', *Revue de sciences criminelles et de droit pénal comparé*, Chron., 434.

Phillips J. (2011), 'Target, audit and risk assessment cultures in the probation service', *European Journal of Probation*, n° 3(3): 108-122.

Poinsignon F., 'Retrait de crédits de réduction de peine par le JAP: mode(s) d'emploi', *Ajpénal* 2013 : 28-34.

Pratt J. (2002), *Punishment and Civilisation*, London, Sage.

Prochaska J. and Di Clemente C.C. (1982), 'Trans-theoretical therapy: Towards a more integrative model of change', *Psychotherapy, Theory, Research and Practice*, n° 19: 276-288

Pruin I. (2012), 'Recalling conditionally released prisoners in Germany', *European Journal of Probation*, n° 4(1): 63-72.

Pycroft A. et Gough D. (dir.) (2010), *Multi-Agency working in criminal justice .Control and care in contemporary correctional practice*, Bristol, The Policy Press.

Raynor P., Ugwudike P. and Vanstone M. (2010), 'Skills and strategies in probation supervision: the Jersey study', in MCNeill F., Raynor P., and Trotter C. (eds.), *Offender Supervision. New Directions in theory, Research and Practice,* Willan Publishing: 113-129.

Richards, S. C. (2009), 'A convict perspective on community punishment: Further lessons from the darkness of prison', in J. I. Ross (Ed.), *Cutting the edge: Current perspectives in radical/critical criminology and criminal justice,* 2nd Ed., Edison, NJ: Transaction: 122-144.

Raimbourg D. and Huygues S. (2013), *Rapport d'information sur les moyens de lutte contre la surpopulation carcérale*, Assemblée Nationale, Commission des Lois constitutionnelles, de la législation et de l'administration générale de la République.

Rintaud N. (2008) *Probation et travail social: quelles missions pour les professionnels ?*, master 2 dissertation, University of Nantes, Sept.

Robinson G. and McNeill F. (2008), 'Exploring the Dynamics of Compliance with Community Penalties', *Theoretical Criminology*, vol. 12: 431-449.

Robinson G. and McNeill F. (2010), 'The dynamics of compliance with offender supervision', in F. McNeill, P. Raynor and C. Trotter, *Offender Supervision. New Directions in theory, research and practice*, Cullompton, Willan Publishing: 367-383.

Rumgay J. (2004), 'The barking dog? Partnership and effective practice', in Mair G. (ed.), *What Matters in Probation*, Cullompton, Willan Publishing: 122-145.

Salas D. (2005), 'Présence de la victime dans le procès et sens de la peine', *Ajpénal* 2005: 430-431.

Salleilles R. (1898), *L'individualisation de la peine. Étude de criminalité sociale*, Paris, Germer Baillière et Cie, Félix Alcan (in English *The Individualization of Punishment*, Bibliobazaar, reed. 2009).

Sarkozy N. (2003), 'La loi Misefen du 26 novembre 2003 : présentation générale', *AJ pénal* : 93-96.

Scheirs V. (2013), *De strafuitvoeringsrechtbank aan het werk. Een etnografisch onderzoek naar haar interacties, beslissingsprocessen en –praktijken*, PhD thesis, Vrije Universiteit Brussel.

Serran G. et O'Brien M. (2007), 'Treatment of categorical denial in sexual offenders', Presentation at the Annual Conference of the Association for the Treatment of Sexual Abusers, San Diego, California.

Severson M. and Pettus-Davis C. (2013), 'Parole Offices' Experiences of the Symptoms of Secondary trauma in the Supervision of Sex Offenders', *Offender Therapy and Comparative Criminology*, n° 57(1): 5-24.

Silver M. A., Portnoy S., and Peters J. K. (2004), 'Stress, Burnout, Vicarious Trauma, and Other Emotional Realities in the Lawyer/Client Relationship (Symposium: Lawyering and Its Discontents: Reclaiming Meaning in the Practice of law)', *TOURO LAW*, n° 1(1): 847-875.

Sloper P. (2004), 'Facilitators and barriers for co-ordinated multi-agency services', *Child Care, Health and Development* n° 30(6): 571-580.

Snacken S., Beyens K. and Beernaert M.A. (2010), 'Belgium', in Padfield N., van Zyl Smit D. and Dünkel F. (eds.), *Release from Prison. European policy and practice*, Cullompton, Willan Publishing : 70-103.

Solomon A. L., Kachnowski V. and Bhati A., *Does parole work? Analyzing the Impact of Postprison Supervision on Rearrest Outcomes*, Urban institute, March.

Staechele F. (1995), *Pratique de l'application des peines*, Paris, Litec.

Stivers C. (2001), *Impact of Discretionary Parole Release on Length of Sentence Served, Percent of Imposed Sentence Served, and Recidivism*, Master's thesis, 2001, Univ. of California, Irvine.

Stobbs N. (2013), 'The nature of juristic paradigms: Exploring the theoretical and conceptual relationship between adversarialism and therapeutic jurisprudence', *Washington University Jurisprudence Review*, n° 4: 97-149.

Sullivan H. and Skelcher C. (2002), *Working Across Boundaries. Collaboration in Public Services*, Basingtoke, Palgrave MacMillan.

Tait D. (2002), 'Sentencing as Performance: Restoring Drama to the Courtroom', in Tata C. and Hutton N. (eds.), *Sentencing and Society*, Aldershot, Ashgate, 469-480.

Tata C., Burns N., Halliday S., and McNeill F. (2008), 'Assisting and Advising the Sentencing Process. The Pursuit of "Quality" in Pre-Sentence Reports', *British Journal of Criminology*, n° 48(6): 835-855.

Taxman F.S. and Sachwald J. (2010), 'Managing the chaos: implementing evidence-based practices in correctional agencies', in F. McNeill, P. Raynor and C. Trotter (dir.), *Offender Supervision. New directions in theory, research and practice,* Willan Publishing, Cullompton: 172-192.

Thomas D. (2003), 'Judicial discretion in sentencing', in Gelsthorpe L. and Padfield N. (eds.), 'Introduction', in Gelsthorpe L. and Padfield N. (dir.) *Exercising discretion. Decision-making in the criminal justice system and beyond*, Cullompton, Willan Publishing: 50-73.

Tonry M. (1996), *Sentencing Matters*, New York, Oxford University Press.

Tournier P. V. and Robert P. (1991), *Etrangers et délinquances*, Paris, l'Harmattan.

Tournier P. V. (2013 a), 'La contrainte pénale communautaire', *Ajpénal*, March: 127-132.

Tournier P. V. (2013 b), *OPALE. Tableau de bord au 1er janvier 2013*, Université Paris 1.

Travis J. and Visher C. (2005), *Prisoner Reentry and Crime in America*, Cambridge, Cambridge University Press.

Trotter C., (2006), *Working with involuntary clients,* Sage Publications, 2nd ed.

Tyler T.R. and Huo Y.T. (2002), *Trust in the Law: Encouraging Public Co-operation with the Police and Courts,* New York, Russell Sage Foundation.

Tyler T. R. (2006), *Why People Obey the Law, New Haven, CT, Yale University Press, 2nd* ed.

Tyler (ed.) (2007), *Legitimacy and Criminal Justice. International Perspectives,* Russel, Sage Foundation, New York.

Tyler T. (2013), 'Legitimacy and compliance: the virtues of self-regulation', in A. Crawford and A. Hucklesby, *Legitimacy and compliance in criminal justice*, Routledge: 8-28.

Ugwudike P. and Raynor P. (eds.) (2013), *What Works in Offender Compliance. International Prespectives and Evidence-Based Practice,* Palgrave MacMillan.

Vrklevski L. P. and Franklin J., 'Vicarious Trauma: The Impact on Solicitors of Exposure to Traumatic Material', *Traumatology*, 2008, n° 14(1): 106-118.

Worrall, A. and Mawby, R.C. (2004), 'Intensive Projects for Prolific/Persistent Offenders', in A. Bottoms and al. (eds.) *Alternatives to Prison: Options for an Insecure Society*, Cullompton, Willan Publishing: 268-289.

Worrall A., Mawby R.C. and Herzog-Evans M. (forthcoming), 'La probation intensive des condamnés adultes en Angleterre et au Pays-de-Galles : Leçons et comparaison avec la France', presentation at the conference 'L'efficacité de l'exécution des peines', University of Rheims, Law faculty, laboratory CEJESCO, 11 December 2012, Paris, Mare et Martin.

Wacquant L. (2009), *Punishing the Poor: The Neoliberal Government of Social Insecurity*, urham, NC, Duke University Press Book.

Wexler D. (1995), 'Reflections on the scope of therapeutic jurisprudence', *Psychology, Public Policy and* Law, n° 1(1): 220-236.

Winick B and Wexler D. (eds.) (2003), *Judging in a Therapeutic Key. Therapeutic Jurisprudence and the Courts,* Durham, Carolina, Carolina Academic Press.

Wexler D.B. (2011), 'From Theory to Practice and Back Again in Therapeutic Jurisprudence: Now Comes the Hard Part', *Arizona Legal Studies*, discussion papers n° 10-12.

Wheatley J. et McCauley C. (2008), 'Losing your audience: Desistance from terrorism in Egypt after Luxor', *Dynamics of Asymetric Conflict*, vol. 1(3): 250-268.

Wilson, R.J., McWhinnie, A.J., and Wilson, C. (2008), 'Circles of Support & Accountability: An international partnership in reducing sexual offender recidivism', *Prison Service Journal, vol. 138:* 26-36.

Wilson, R.J., McWhinnie, A.J., and Wilson, C. (2010), 'Circles of Support and Accountability: An innovative Approach to Community-Based Risk Management for High-Risk Sexual Offenders', in Herzog-Evans M. (ed.), *Transnational Criminology Manual*, Nijmegen, Wolf Legal Publishers, 2010, volume III: 241-260.

Wilson, R.J., and McWhinnie, A.J. (2012), 'Les cercles de soutien et de responsabilite. Un partenariat international pour le management du risque en milieu ouvert', *Ajpénal* : 636-639.

Wilson, R.J., Leaver, W., and Whealy, G. (2007), *Collaborative care: Pairing police supervision and community volunteers to manage risk. Poster presented at the 26th Annual Conference of the Association for the Treatment of Sexual Abusers,* San Diego, CA, November.

Winick B. J. and Wexler D. B. (2003), *Judging in a Therapeutic Key. Therapeutic Jurisprudence ad the Courts,* Carolina Academic Press, Durham NC.

Wright J. K. (2010), *Lawyers as Peacemakers. Practicing Holistic, Problem-Solving Law,* American Bar Association.

Yablon C.M. (1995), "'udicial drag: An essay on wig, robes and legal change', *University of Wisconsin Law Review.*, p. 1129-1132.

Yates P., (2009) 'Is sexual offender denial related to sex offence risk and recidivism: A review and treatment implications', *Psychology, Crime and Law*, n° 15(2): 183-199.

Table of contents

L'HARMATTAN ITALIA
Via Degli Artisti 15; 10124 Torino

L'HARMATTAN HONGRIE
Könyvesbolt ; Kossuth L. u. 14-16
1053 Budapest

L'HARMATTAN KINSHASA
185, avenue Nyangwe
Commune de Lingwala
Kinshasa, R.D. Congo
(00243) 998697603 ou (00243) 999229662

L'HARMATTAN CONGO
67, av. E. P. Lumumba
Bât. – Congo Pharmacie (Bib. Nat.)
BP2874 Brazzaville
harmattan.congo@yahoo.fr

L'HARMATTAN GUINÉE
Almamya Rue KA 028, en face du restaurant Le Cèdre
OKB agency BP 3470 Conakry
(00224) 60 20 85 08
harmattanguinee@yahoo.fr

L'HARMATTAN CAMEROUN
BP 11486
Face à la SNI, immeuble Don Bosco
Yaoundé
(00237) 99 76 61 66
harmattancam@yahoo.fr

L'HARMATTAN CÔTE D'IVOIRE
Résidence Karl / cité des arts
Abidjan-Cocody 03 BP 1588 Abidjan 03
(00225) 05 77 87 31
etien_nda@yahoo.fr

L'HARMATTAN MAURITANIE
Espace El Kettab du livre francophone
N° 472 avenue du Palais des Congrès
BP 316 Nouakchott
(00222) 63 25 980

L'HARMATTAN SÉNÉGAL
« Villa Rose », rue de Diourbel X G, Point E
BP 45034 Dakar FANN
(00221) 33 825 98 58 / 77 242 25 08
senharmattan@gmail.com

L'HARMATTAN TOGO
1771, Bd du 13 janvier
BP 414 Lomé
Tél : 00 228 2201792
gerry@taama.net

Achevé d'imprimer par Corlet Numérique - 14110 Condé-sur-Noireau
N° d'Imprimeur : 104522 - Dépôt légal : janvier 2014 - *Imprimé en France*